Between Design and Making

Between Design and Making

Architecture and craftsmanship, 1630–1760

Edited by Andrew Tierney and Melanie Hayes
With a Foreword by Christine Casey

First published in 2024 by
UCL Press
University College London
Gower Street
London WC1E 6BT

Available to download free: www.uclpress.co.uk

Text © Contributors, 2024
Collection © Editors, 2024
Images © copyright holders named in captions, 2024
Foreword © copyright Christine Casey, 2024

The authors have asserted their rights under the Copyright, Designs and Patents Act 1988 to be identified as the authors of this work.

A CIP catalogue record for this book is available from The British Library.

Any third-party material in this book is not covered by the book's Creative Commons licence. Details of the copyright ownership and permitted use of third-party material is given in the image (or extract) credit lines. If you would like to reuse any third-party material not covered by the book's Creative Commons licence, you will need to obtain permission directly from the copyright owner.

This book is published under a Creative Commons Attribution-Non-commercial Non-derivative 4.0 International licence (CC BY-NC-ND 4.0), https://creativecommons.org/licenses/by-nc-nd/4.0/. This licence allows you to share, copy, distribute and transmit the work for personal and non-commercial use provided author and publisher attribution is clearly stated. Attribution should include the following information:

Tierney, A. and Hayes, M. (eds). 2024. *Between Design and Making: Architecture and craftsmanship, 1630–1760*. London: UCL Press. https://doi.org/10.14324/111.9781800086937

Further details about Creative Commons licences are available at https://creativecommons.org/licenses/

ISBN: 978-1-80008-695-1 (Hbk)
ISBN: 978-1-80008-694-4 (Pbk)
ISBN: 978-1-80008-693-7 (PDF)
ISBN: 978-1-80008-696-8 (epub)
DOI: https://doi.org/10.14324/111.9781800086937

Contents

List of figures	vii
List of contributors	xvii
List of abbreviations	xxii
Foreword	xxiii
Christine Casey	
Acknowledgements	xxvii
Introduction: Between design and making: architecture and craftsmanship, 1630–1760	1
Andrew Tierney and Melanie Hayes	

Part 1: Practice

1	Architect and mason-architect: Inigo Jones, Nicholas Stone and the development of the open-well suspended stone stair in the 1630s	27
	Gordon Higgott and Adam White	
2	The Townesend family and the building of eighteenth-century Oxford	65
	Geoffrey Tyack	
3	Codes, conventions, circulations: drawings as an instrument of collaboration in the work of Nicolas Pineau	85
	Bénédicte Gady	
4	Architects and artificers: building management at Trinity College Dublin in the 1730s and 1740s	119
	Melanie Hayes	
5	Artisans and architecture in eighteenth-century Saxony	153
	Nele Lüttmann	
6	Between concept and construction: conservation insights into the building of Damer House	183
	Máirtín D'Alton and Flora O'Mahony	

Part 2: Representation

7 Architects and craftsmen: a theme with variations 207
Alistair Rowan

8 Classical profiles: the 'alphabet of architecture'? 241
Edward McParland

9 Allegorising the space between architecture and craft:
mural painting 1630–1730 263
Lydia Hamlett

10 Material, curiosity and performance: the reception of
workmanship in early modern Britain and Ireland 289
Andrew Tierney

Index 323

List of figures

1.1 Inigo Jones's annotated copy of Palladio's *I Quattro Libri dell'Architettura* (Venice, 1601), Book I, p. 63, showing section and plan of Palladio's oval stair. 29

1.2 Inigo Jones's annotated copy of Palladio's *I Quattro Libri dell'Architettura* (Venice, 1601), Book IV, p. 75. Sketch-plan of east stair at the Pantheon, with note dated 1614. 31

1.3 Palladio's oval stair at the Convento della Carità, Venice (now the Gallerie dell'Accademia), early 1560s. Windows and landing at second-floor level. 32

1.4 Inigo Jones's annotated copy of Palladio's *I Quattro Libri dell'Architettura* (Venice, 1601), Book II, p. 30. Notes, with sketches, of the oval stair at the Convento della Carità, 10 August 1614. 33

1.5 Inigo Jones. Plan of a long lodging, probably for the Queen's House, Greenwich, 1616. Pen and brown ink with brown wash, 200 × 404 mm. 34

1.6 John James. Plan of the ground floor of the Queen's House, Greenwich, including the first-floor loggia on the south side, circa 1718. 35

1.7 The South Stair at the Queen's House. Balustrade, circa 1760, installed in 1936. 38

1.8 (a) The South Stair at the Queen's House. Detail of the top steps and the timber landing. (b) The South Stair at the Queen's House. Central flight and half-landings, showing riser rebates and chamfered soffits. 39

1.9 The Tulip Stair at the Queen's House. Looking up to the first-floor landing, entrance to the gallery, and upper flight. 40

1.10 The Tulip Stair at the Queen's House. Detail of the first landing of the upper flight. 41

1.11 Part-plan of Kirby Hall, Northamptonshire, from J. Alfred Gotch, *Old Halls and Manor Houses of Northamptonshire* (London, 1936, p. 18), showing the south-east staircase at bottom right. 46

1.12 Kirby Hall, Northamptonshire. The north range of the courtyard. 47

1.13 Kirby Hall, Northamptonshire. The north range from the forecourt side, showing the central tower. 48

1.14 Kirby Hall, Northamptonshire. The south-east staircase tower, view from the south-west. 49

1.15 Kirby Hall, Northamptonshire. The second and third flights of the south-east staircase. 49

1.16 Kirby Hall, Northamptonshire. The south-east staircase tower, view of the basement vault. 50

1.17 Kirby Hall, Northamptonshire. The plaster ceiling of the south-east staircase tower before its collapse. 51

1.18 Kirby Hall, Northamptonshire. Brickwork on the interior of the north range. 52

1.19 (a) Kirby Hall, Northamptonshire. Window in the south-east staircase tower. (b) Kirby Hall, Northamptonshire. Window in the north range, on the courtyard side. 53

1.20 Kirby Hall, Northamptonshire. The first flight of the south-east staircase. Detail. 53

1.21 Kirby Hall, Northamptonshire. The second flight of the south-east staircase, showing holes made for panelling and the line of a wooden balustrade. 54

1.22 Kirby Hall, Northamptonshire. The south wall of the south-east staircase tower from outside, showing the treads of the staircase flush with the wall. 55

1.23 Kirby Hall, Northamptonshire. The south-east staircase tower, showing holes for supports for the collapsed landing on the first floor, south side, with the exit at the north-east corner through a doorway with a brick-lined arch. 56

2.1 John Townesend's monument in the churchyard of St Giles, Oxford. 67

2.2 A view of Carfax with the Butter Bench on the right. From Rudolph Ackermann, *A History of the University of Oxford, its Colleges, Halls, and Public Buildings* (1814). 69

2.3 The front door of the Principal's Lodgings at Jesus College. 70

2.4 The west range of the North Quadrangle at Queen's College. 71

2.5 The Fellows' Building at Corpus Christi College. 72

2.6 The Library at Christ Church. 73

2.7 The Front Quadrangle at Queen's College, looking towards the Hall and Chapel. 74

2.8 Proposal by William Townesend and George Clarke for a block of rooms on the site of the Library at All Souls College. 74

2.9	The south front of the Clarendon Building.	75
2.10	The gate tower of the Radcliffe Quadrangle at University College.	76
2.11	The Radcliffe Camera.	77
2.12	Compton Beauchamp House.	78
2.13	The Woodstock Gate to Blenheim Palace.	79
2.14	Townesend's Building in the garden of Rousham House.	79
3.1	Nicolas Pineau, *Project for the door of the tabernacle at the Monastery in Lugny*, 1742–4. Graphite, pen and brown ink, 50 × 33 cm.	89
3.2	Nicolas Pineau, *Project for a cartouche*. Graphite, red chalk, pen and brown ink, 26 × 42 cm.	90
3.3	Nicolas Pineau workshop or late copy, *Panelling with a mirror*. Pen and brown ink, brown wash, watercolour, 28 × 21 cm.	92
3.4	Nicolas Pineau, *Project for the panelling of a niche at a 'cabinet d'assemblée' at château de la Tuilerie in Auteuil*, 1737. Pen and brown ink, 22.5 × 40 cm.	93
3.5	Nicolas Pineau, *Project for a 'cabinet en bibliothèque'*. Graphite, pen and black ink, 23.5 × 35.5 cm.	94
3.6	Nicolas Pineau, *Project for two keystones for the hôtel Bonneau*, circa 1741. Graphite, pen and black ink, 24 × 35.5 cm.	95
3.7	Nicolas Pineau, *Project for a porte-cochère*, 1738. Graphite, 50 × 34.5 cm.	96
3.8	Nicolas Pineau, *Project for a pier glass for Monsieur Fournier*, 1745. Pen and brown ink, 21.4 × 16 cm.	97
3.9	Nicolas Pineau, *Plan for the bedroom of Madame de Voyer d'Argenson at Château d'Asnières*, circa 1750. Graphite, pen and black and brown ink, 49.5 × 35.8 cm.	98
3.10	Jacques Hardouin-Mansart de Sagonne and Nicolas Pineau, *Study for the arrangement of cartouches above windows on the ground and first floors of the façade of the Château d'Asnières*, circa 1750. Pen and brown and grey ink, 13.5 × 45 cm.	99
3.11	François Gilles, *Proposal for the restitution of the façade of the Château d'Asnières with a hypothesis for the distribution of the cartouches*, according to the CD 1576, 2023.	101
3.12	Nicolas Pineau, *Project for the cartouche of the porte-cochère of the hôtel de Feuquières*, circa 1736. Graphite and red chalk, 35 × 50 cm.	103
3.13	Nicolas Pineau, *Project for a 'cabinet en bibliothèque', with flap*. Graphite, pen and black ink, 23.5 × 35.5 cm.	105

3.14 Nicolas Pineau, *Project for a wrought iron banister for the hôtel Bonneau*, 1743. Graphite, 22 × 33.5 cm.   106

3.15 Nicolas Pineau, *Invitation card used to sketch a wrought iron banister for the hôtel Bonneau*, 1743. Graphite, 22 × 33.5 cm. 106

3.16 Nicolas Pineau, *Study for the steps leading up to the tabernacle at the Monastery in Lugny*, 1742–5. Graphite, pen and brown ink, 17 × 21.5 cm.   107

3.17 Jacques Hardouin-Mansart de Sagonne, *Plan for the dining room in the hôtel Boutin*, circa 1738. Graphite, pen and black ink, 43.5 × 33 cm.   109

3.18 Nicolas Pineau, *Study for the moulding for the mirror and door frames and low panelling for the drawing room in the hôtel of the marquise de Feuquières*, circa 1736. Black and red chalk, pen and black ink, 27 × 43.5 cm.   110

3.19 Nicolas Pineau, *Study for three mirrors over fireplaces for the house of the comte de Middelbourg in Suresnes*, circa 1747. Pen and brown ink, 25 × 42 cm.   111

4.1 Detail from Samuel Byron, *A bird's-eye perspective plan of Trinity College park and gardens*, 1780.   120

4.2 Thomas Rowlandson, *An Architectural Inspection*, circa 1810. 122

4.3 Bernard Scale, *A plan of Trinity College Dublin, park gardens &c.*, 1761.   123

4.4 Printing House, Trinity College Dublin.   125

4.5 'Proposals made by Joseph McCleery carpenter for building a Printing House in the College of Dublin'.   126

4.6 'Proposals by Moses Darley, Stone Cutter for building a Printing House at the College of Dublin'.   127

4.7 'An Estimate of the Expence of the Printing House Intended to be Built in Colledge'.   128

4.8 Plan and elevation of the New Hall, Trinity College, attributed to Richard Castle, circa 1740.   131

4.9 'Plan of the Principal Floor by Mr Castle'. Headfort Album, IAA 96/68/3/1/7.   135

4.10 Plan and elevation, with alternative treatments, possibly by John Ensor. Headfort Album, IAA 96/68/3/1/9.   136

4.11 *A Prospect of the Library of Trinity College, Dublin, Ireland*, Joseph Tudor, 1753.   138

4.12 Detail from Samuel Byron, *A bird's-eye perspective plan of Trinity College park and gardens*, 1780.   139

4.13 The Bell Tower, Trinity College Dublin. From John William Stubbs, *The History of the University of Dublin*, 1889.   140

4.14 Francis Wheatley, *The Dublin Volunteers on College Green, 4th November 1779*. 140

4.15 Henry Armstrong's bill for carriage, 1743, 'To carrying 4 Blocks of Portland Stone from Marlborough Street to the College'. 142

4.16 Detail from Samuel Byron, *A Plan of Dublin*, 1782. 143

5.1 Johann Philipp Steudner, *View of Dresden*, copper engraving, circa 1700. 155

5.2 Map of Europe circa 1740, from Alfred Baldamus et al., *F. W. Putzgers Historischer Schul-Atlas Zur Alten, Mittleren Und Neuen Geschichte*. Bielefeld: Velhagen & Klasing, 1918. 157

5.3 Louis de Silvestre the Younger, *August II the Strong, 1670–1733, Elector of Saxony, King of Poland*, oil on canvas, 145 × 111 cm. 158

5.4 After Louis de Silvestre the Younger, *Fredrik August II / August III (1696–1763), Elector of Saxony, King of Poland, g.m. Maria Josefa, ärkehertiginna av Österrike*, oil on canvas, 148 × 112 cm. 158

5.5 'The Elevation of Stainborough in Yorkshire' (Wentworth Castle), in Colen Campbell, *Vitruvius Britannicus, or The British Architect* (London: Printed by the author, 1715), 93–4. 159

5.6 Index of people working at the Saxon building department ('Bau-Ambt') in 1728. In *Königlich-Polnischer und Churfürstlich Sächsischer Hoff- und Staats-Calender auf das Jahr 1728*, 97–8. Leipzig: n.p., 1728. 160

5.7 Matthäus Daniel Pöppelmann, *Site plan for the construction of a new residential palace in the area of the Zwinger and the Marstall (so-called Große Schlossplanung)*, pen and ink with polychrome washes, circa 1716/18. 166

5.8 Richard Castle, 'An illustrated essay on artificial navigation', written in connection with the construction of the Newry Canal, Figure 15, circa 1733–6. 167

5.9 Matthäus Daniel Pöppelmann and an anonymous draughtsman, *Design for the rampart pavilion (Wallpavillon) of the Dresden Zwinger*, pen, graphite and brush with grey, blue and opaque white washes, circa 1713/14. 170

5.10 Johann Christoph Knöffel, *Design for the Belvedere in Brühlscher Garten, Dresden*, pen, brush, ink with grey and green washes, 1748–55. 171

LIST OF FIGURES   xi

5.11 Samuel Locke, *Grochwitz, Palace Design, Elevation of the Façade*, pencil, pen and ink with coloured washes on paper, 45.6 × 61.8 cm, 1736. 172

5.12 Canaletto (Bernardo Bellotto), *Dresden from the Right Bank of the Elbe, below the Augustus Bridge*, oil on canvas, 133 × 237 cm, 1748. 174

6.1 Damer House, Roscrea, County Tipperary. 184

6.2 Mount Ievers Court, County Clare. 184

6.3 North façade, Damer House. Structural failure to window 1, with sagging of random rubble stone masonry. 186

6.4 Window lintel profile, Damer House. 187

6.5 (a) Decayed joint between window jambs reinforced with stainless-steel helical bars, Damer House; (b) Erosion had produced significant gaps between the window jambs and the window sash boxes, Damer House. 188

6.6 Timber lintels above window boxes, Damer House. 189

6.7 Window sill, Damer House. 190

6.8 First-floor windows, Damer House. 191

6.9 Master mason Gunther Wolters displays construction wedges used to support a timber lintel from the first-floor windows. Damer House. 192

6.10 Entrance floor plan, Damer House. 193

6.11 Pine staircase, Damer House. 194

6.12 Doorcase, Damer House. 194

6.13 Old photo of doorcase, Damer House. 195

6.14 No. 10 Mill Street Dublin, built circa 1720. Photograph taken prior to 1891. 195

6.15 Sample cleaning portion of doorcase with decorated floral scroll, Damer House. 196

6.16 Repaired joint with lime repair mortar and simulated silica sand joint, Damer House. 196

6.17 Window 11, Damer House, prior to repair (a); following repair (b). This was one of the more badly decayed windows. 197

6.18 Gunther Wolters with removed keystone and clay model of acanthus keystone. 198

6.19 New carved keystones on display for 30 August 2021 Heritage Week event at Damer House. 198

6.20 Different stages of carved keystones on display for 30 August 2021 Heritage Week event at Damer House. 199

6.21	North façade, Damer House, following completion of repair work in April 2023.	200
7.1	'The Tuscann Order' in John Shute, *The First and Chief Groundes of Architecture*, London, 1563 (1912 reprint).	211
7.2	'The Diminishing of the Colomne', from *The Mirror of Architecture: Or the ground-rules of the art of building, exactly laid down by Vincent Scamozzi, master-builder of Venice*. London, 1721, 6th edition. Plate 32.	213
7.3	Details of the dressing of the stonework on the garden front of Castletown House, County Kildare, showing the base of the lugged architrave.	215
7.4	Details of the dressing of the stonework on the garden front of Castletown House, County Kildare, showing a window sill.	215
7.5	Entrance front of Florence Court, County Fermanagh, building from 1758. T. U. Sadleir and P. L. Dickinson. *Georgian Mansions in Ireland*.	217
7.6	One side of the entrance hall at Florence Court, County Fermanagh.	219
7.7	The staircase at Florence Court, County Fermanagh. T. U. Sadleir and P. L. Dickinson, *Georgian Mansions in Ireland*.	220
7.8	The nave of Fulda Cathedral, Hesse, Germany. Detail of the Artari workshop stucco decorations of about 1710.	222
7.9	The stair hall at Russborough, County Wicklow.	223
7.10	William Adam, entrance front of Mavisbank, Midlothian, Scotland, built from 1723 for Sir John Clerk of Penicuik. In William Adam, *Vitruvius Scoticus*, Plate 47.	224
7.11	William Adam, entrance front of Arniston House, Midlothian, Scotland, built from 1726 for Robert Dundas, Lord Advocate of Scotland. In William Adam, *Vitruvius Scoticus*, Plate 42.	225
7.12	William Adam, entrance front of Hopetoun House, West Lothian, Scotland, built from 1721 to 1731 for John Hope, 2nd Earl of Hopetoun. In William Adam, *Vitruvius Scoticus*, Plate 16.	226
7.13	William Adam, entrance front of Hopetoun House, showing the pavilions and colonnades. In William Adam, *Vitruvius Scoticus*, Plate 17.	228
7.14	William and John Adam, entrance front of Hopetoun House, as completed in 1754.	229

7.15 Masonry of the front steps of Hopetoun House, built in accordance with John Adam's specification of 27 August 1751. 229

7.16 The State Drawing Room at Hopetoun House. 230

7.17 The ceiling of the State Drawing Room at Hopetoun House. 231

7.18 The State Drawing Room at Hopetoun House. A detail of the chair-rail decoration and door panels. 232

8.1 William Chambers, Casino at Marino, Dublin, begun 1758, detail. 242

8.2 Francesco Borromini, San Giovanni in Laterano, Rome, 1646–9, bases in the nave. 243

8.3 Sebastien Le Clerc, modillion cornice from *Traité d'Architecture*, Paris, 1714. 244

8.4 Thomas Cooley, Royal Exchange, Dublin (now the City Hall), 1769–79, detail of cornice with merged modillions. 245

8.5 Carlo Rainaldi, Santa Maria in Campitelli, Rome, 1658–74, detail of entrance door. 246

8.6 James Gandon, Custom House, Dublin, 1781–91. 247

8.7 Pantheon, Rome, early second century. 248

8.8 Giacomo Quarenghi, Anichkov Palace, St Petersburg. A range of shops along the Fontanka, commissioned 1803. 249

8.9 Christopher Wren, Sheldonian Theatre, Oxford, 1664–9, detail. 249

8.10 Thomas Cooley, Public Library, Armagh (now Armagh Robinson Library), established in 1771, with alternative proposals for a window drawn in 1770. 250

8.11 Thomas Burgh, Old Library, Trinity College Dublin, 1712–32. Detail of architrave. 251

8.12 Gian Lorenzo Bernini, Santa Maria di Galloro, near Ariccia, 1624. Façade. 252

8.13 Michelangelo, Palazzo dei Conservatori, Rome, begun 1563. 253

8.14 Castletown House, County Kildare, entrance hall, detail. 254

8.15 Thomas Cooley, Royal Exchange, Dublin (now the City Hall), 1769–79, detail. 255

8.16 Louis Le Vau, Collège des Quatre-Nations, Paris (Institut de France), begun 1662. 256

8.17 Thomas Cooley, Royal Exchange, Dublin (now the City Hall), 1769–79. Detail of bases in the rotunda. 257

8.18	Thomas Burgh, Old Library, Trinity College Dublin, 1712–32. Detail of architrave.	258
8.19	Edward Lovett Pearce, Parliament House, Dublin (now the Bank of Ireland), begun 1729. Entablature.	259
9.1	The Great Chamber, Chatsworth House, detail showing painted ceiling by Antonio Verrio and limewood carving by Joel Lobb, William Davis and Samuel Watson.	265
9.2	The Grand Staircase, Chatsworth House, detail showing statues by Caius Gabriel Cibber.	265
9.3	The Grand Staircase, Chatsworth House, showing painted ceiling by Antonio Verrio.	267
9.4	The Chapel, Chatsworth House, detail showing mural by Louis Laguerre.	268
9.5	The King's Staircase, Hampton Court Palace, mural by Antonio Verrio depicting Julian the Apostate, detail.	270
9.6	The Queen's Drawing Room, Hampton Court Palace, showing mural by Antonio Verrio and gilding by Peter Cousin.	271
9.7	The Grand Staircase, Petworth House, showing ceiling painting of Pandora and the Gods by Louis Laguerre.	272
9.8	The Grand Staircase, Petworth House, showing mural by Louis Laguerre (with real and painted jars, lower centre).	274
9.9	The Heaven Room, Burghley House, paintings by Antonio Verrio.	276
9.10	The Double Cube Room, Wilton House. Painted ceiling by Emmanuel De Critz and Edward Pearce (detail) and stuccoed frames.	278
9.11	The Great Hall, Castle Howard. Dome interior with Fall of Phaeton, originally by Giovanni Antonio Pellegrini, repainted by Scott Medd in the 1960s, following a fire in 1940.	280
9.12	The Great Hall, Castle Howard, painting of Vulcan by Giovanni Antonio Pellegrini, overmantel by Giovanni Bagutti and 'Signor Plura'.	281
9.13	The Saloon, Blenheim Palace. Detail showing mural by Louis Laguerre.	283
9.14	The Painted Hall, Old Royal Naval College, Greenwich. West wall by James Thornhill.	284
10.1	Altar of Borghese Chapel.	292
10.2	The Beauchamp Chapel at the Collegiate Church of St Mary, Warwick.	297

10.3	The late medieval cross at Coventry, from William Dugdale's *The Antiquities of Warwickshire Illustrated*. London: Printed by Thomas Warren, 1656.	298
10.4	Plate VII from Robert Wood et al., *The Ruins of Palmyra, Otherwise Tedmor, in the Desart*. London: Robert Wood, 1753.	303
10.5	View of the Marble Hall at Holkham, Norfolk.	307
10.6	View of the interior of King's College Chapel, Cambridge, from David Loggan, *Cantabrigia Illustrata*, 1690.	311

List of contributors

Andrew Tierney is a post-doctoral research fellow of the European Research Council Advanced Grant project, STONE-WORK, and former research fellow of the Irish Research Council Advanced Laureate Project, CRAFTVALUE, at Trinity College Dublin. He has an MA in the history of art and a PhD in archaeology from University College Dublin, and has taught at University College Dublin, NUI Maynooth, and the Institute of Irish Studies at the University of Liverpool. His research and publications cover a broad chronology from medieval to Victorian architecture. His volume *Central Leinster* (Yale University Press, 2019) was shortlisted for the 2020 Colvin Prize by the Society of Architectural Historians of Great Britain.

Melanie Hayes is a postdoctoral research fellow of the European Research Council Advanced Grant project, STONE-WORK, and former research fellow of the Irish Research Council Advanced Laureate Project, CRAFTVALUE, at Trinity College Dublin. Her doctoral research focused largely on Anglo-Irish eighteenth-century architectural history, with a specific interest in the transnational development of architectural culture and practice in the early Georgian period. She has previously taught early-modern architectural history, at Trinity College Dublin, and has written and spoken widely on these topics. She is author of *The Best Address in Town: Henrietta Street Dublin and its first residents, 1720–80* (Four Courts Press, 2020) and co-editor of *Enriching Architecture: Craft and its conservation in Anglo-Irish building production, 1660–1760*, published by UCL Press in 2023.

Christine Casey is Professor of Architectural History and a fellow of Trinity College Dublin. She has published widely on architectural history and craftsmanship in Ireland, Britain and Europe. Her books include the definitive reference work on Dublin city, *Dublin* (Yale University Press, 2005), and *Making Magnificence* (Yale University Press, 2017), for which she received the Alice Davis Hitchcock Medallion of the Society of Architectural Historians of Great Britain. She is co-editor of *Enriching Architecture: Craft and its conservation in Anglo-Irish building production, 1660–1760*, published by UCL Press in 2023. From 2019–23 she held an Advanced Laureate award of the Irish Research Council and in 2023 was awarded a European Research Council Advanced Grant for research on collective achievement in architectural production.

Máirtín D'Alton, BArch Sc DIT School of Architecture (1998), is a member of the Royal Institute of Architects of Ireland. He completed an MLitt in the Trinity College Dublin Department of History of Art and Architecture in 2009 and was a lecturer in the Dublin School of Architecture from 2012 to 2021. He has been an architect with the Office of Public Works National Monuments Service since 2021.

Bénédicte Gady joined the Musée des Arts Décoratifs in Paris after eight years at the Musée du Louvre, working on seventeenth- and eighteenth-century French drawings. She is in charge of the Graphic Arts Department, which holds around 200,000 drawings ranging from the fifteenth to twenty-first centuries. A former fellow of the German Centre for Art History, Paris, and the Académie de France à Rome (Villa Medici), she dedicated her PhD to the rise of Charles Le Brun ('L'ascension de Charles Le Brun: Liens sociaux et production artistique', Maison des Sciences de l'Homme, 2010). She has curated or co-curated twelve exhibitions, among which are *Parisian Ceilings in the Seventeenth Century* (Paris, Louvre, 2014), *Drawing Versailles*, comprising studies and cartoons by Charles Le Brun (Barcelona and Madrid, 2015–16), *Charles Le Brun* (Louvre-Lens, 2016), and *Drawing without Reserve*, drawing on the collections of the Musée des Arts Décoratifs (Paris, MAD, 2020).

Lydia Hamlett is Academic Director in History of Art at the Institute of Continuing Education, University of Cambridge, and a fellow of Murray Edwards College. Her current research is on British visual culture of the long seventeenth century and, in particular, mural painting, gender and classical reception. Lydia was a Leverhulme Early Career Fellow in the Department of History of Art at Cambridge. She was Programme Curator for the University of Cambridge Museums, when she co-curated *Discoveries: Art, Science and Exploration* (2014), and a post-doctoral researcher on *Court, Country, City: British Art 1660–1735* (Arts and Humanities Research Council), based at the University of York and Tate, where she curated *Sketches for Spaces: History painting and architecture 1630–1730* (2013–14). Before this, she was on the research team for *The Art of the Sublime* at Tate (AHRC). Lydia was a curator at the National Trust from 2008–9 and at the Fitzwilliam Museum 2007–8.

Gordon Higgott is an independent architectural historian who specialises in architectural drawings and design practice in early modern Britain. He has published on Inigo Jones's architectural and stage designs, on his work at St Paul's Cathedral and the Queen's House, and on Sir Christopher Wren's work at St Paul's and Westminster Abbey. He has also published online catalogues of the English Baroque drawings at Sir John Soane's Museum and the Wren Office drawings for St Paul's Cathedral at London Metropolitan Archives. He is currently preparing a new critical edition of Inigo Jones's annotated copy of Andrea Palladio's *I Quattro Libri dell'Architettura* (Venice, 1601) at Worcester College, Oxford. From 1989 to 2010 he was a historic buildings inspector and a senior investigator at English Heritage (Historic England).

Nele Lüttmann completed a BA in art history at Martin Luther University, Halle-Wittenberg, and an MA in British Art at the University of York. After several years of employment in the arts and heritage sector, she was awarded the Irish Research Council Advanced Laureate project scholarship at Trinity College Dublin. Her PhD research project, 'German architects in Britain and Ireland 1700–1750', explores the work of James Gibbs's draughtsman Johann Gottlieb Borlach in Britain and of architect Richard Castle in Ireland. Nele is particularly interested in early eighteenth-century architectural drawing and the education of draughtsmen in Europe, as well as the international diplomatic and artistic networks which facilitated the migration of artists and building professionals from Germany to Britain in that century.

Edward McParland, Fellow Emeritus and former lecturer in architectural history at Trinity College Dublin, is an authority on eighteenth-century architecture. He has published widely, including *James Gandon: Vitruvius Hibernicus* (Zwemmer, 1985) and *Public Architecture in Ireland 1680–1760* (Yale University Press, 2001). He jointly founded the Irish Architectural Archive in 1976. Active in architectural conservation, he jointly founded the Irish Landmark Trust and has been a committee member of the Alfred Beit Foundation and the Irish Georgian Society. He is an honorary fellow of the Royal Institute of the Architects of Ireland and an honorary member of the Royal Society of Ulster Architects. His latest book is *The Language of Architectural Classicism* (Lund Humphries, 2024).

Flora O'Mahony is a Senior Architect with the Office of Public Works National Monuments Service. She obtained a BArch (1996) from the School of Architecture, University College Dublin, in 1996 and is a member of the Royal Institute of Architects of Ireland. She later completed a Masters in the Conservation of Historic Towns and Buildings, at the Raymond Lemaire International Centre for Conservation, KU Leuven, Belgium. She subsequently worked with the Council of Europe, Bruges, and Paul Arnold Architects, Dublin. In her current role (since 2006) she is responsible for the management, maintenance and conservation of 123 national monuments in the southeast of Ireland.

Alistair Rowan qualified as an architect at the Edinburgh College of Art in 1961, took a PhD at Cambridge in 1965 and held a scholarship at Padua University in 1965 and 1966. As an editor and Scottish correspondent for *Country Life* from 1966 to 1976 he contributed major research articles on some 31 great houses in Britain and Ireland. He was, successively, a Lecturer in Fine Art at the University of Edinburgh, Professor of the History of Art at UCD, Principal of the Edinburgh College of Art, and first Professor of the History of Art in UCC. He retired in 2003. He was Slade Professor of Fine Art at the University of Oxford for 1988 when he lectured on the architecture of Robert and James Adam. He is the founder and editor of *The Buildings of Ireland* (Pevsner Architectural Guides), and author of the first volume on *North West Ulster* (1979). His collection of European architectural pattern books was acquired by the National Library of Ireland in 2019 and is held at the Irish Architectural Archive in Dublin.

Geoffrey Tyack grew up in London and read history at Oxford University. He gained a PhD from the University of London, and is now an Emeritus Fellow of Kellogg College, University of Oxford. His publications include *Sir James Pennethorne and the Making of Victorian London* (Cambridge University Press, 1992), *Oxford: An architectural guide* (Oxford University Press, 1997), *John Nash: Architect of the picturesque* (English Heritage, 2013), *The Making of Our Urban Landscape* (Oxford University Press, 2021) and *The Historic Heart of Oxford* (Bodleian, 2022). He is editor of the *Georgian Group Journal*, a council member of the London Topographical Society, and President of the Oxfordshire Architectural and Historical Society.

Adam White is a retired museum curator, based in the UK, with a special interest in British sculpture and architecture of the early modern period.

His *Biographical Dictionary of London Tomb Sculptors c.1560–1660* was published by the Walpole Society in London in 1999, with a supplement ten years later. He is currently at work on a monograph on Nicholas Stone the Elder (c.1587–1647), the leading sculptor and master mason of the period, and his family.

List of abbreviations

BL	British Library
IAA	Irish Architectural Archive
NLI	National Library of Ireland
OPW	Office of Public Works (Ireland)
PHA	Petworth House Archive
RD	Registry of Deeds (Ireland)
RIBA	Royal Institute of British Architects
SächsStA-D	Sächsisches Staatsarchiv, Hauptstaatsarchiv Dresden
SLUB	Sächsische Landesbibliothek – Staats- und Universitätsbibliothek Dresden
TCD	Trinity College Dublin
TNA	The National Archives (UK)

Foreword
Christine Casey

Tangible evidence of the interface between design and making in architecture is rare, hard won and too often tantalisingly laconic. For instance, at the Royal Hospital for Seamen in Greenwich, in June 1707, 'a proposition by Mr Stone, the mason, for the Entablature of the two middle fronts of the West Building of King William's Court' was debated by the building committee, but adjourned in the absence of Sir Christopher Wren.[1] This recorded discussion about a specific element of the building, two emphatic and doubtless challenging entablatures of immense proportions, suggests active agency of the stonemason in the design and deliberation process, though precisely what was being proposed remains elusive. No wonder then that histories of design and making in architecture have taken divergent and circumscribed paths in modern scholarship. This volume sets itself the ambitious task of uniting these pathways by exploring the creative collaboration of architects and artisans in seventeenth- and eighteenth-century architecture and the professional structures and societal perception of architecture that underpinned contemporary building activity.

Distinctions between the conceptual and manual aspects of architectural production became pronounced in the modern period when increasing professionalisation stimulated 'separation between the *design* of architecture and the *making* of architecture'.[2] In the past such boundaries were by no means clear and countless architects emerged from artisanal and artistic backgrounds, Brunelleschi, Giuliano da Sangallo, Bramante, Palladio, Borromini and Inigo Jones to name but a few. Likewise, the transition to architecture from other walks of life necessitated dependence upon building professionals. Inigo Jones was firstly a joiner and then a set designer before turning to architecture, Sir Christopher Wren was an astronomer, Sir John Vanbrugh a playwright and Sir Edward Lovett Pearce an army officer. Wealthy amateur architects likewise required the services of building professionals. Conversely, these relationships aided upward mobility through the trades and the drawing office and produced many practitioner-architects such as Thomas Ripley, James Essex, Isaac Ware and Francis Johnston. While burgeoning research is beginning to illuminate the wider office practice of the period, there remains a great deal to discover about the vast 'no-man's land' of architectural labour that underpinned the building world in the seventeenth and eighteenth centuries, the clerks of works, building supervisors, *Baumeister*, surveyors, measurers and clerks, whose labour supported design and construction.[3] This book contributes to knowledge of this wider arena of architectural labour.

In this volume, quarry-owning building contractors, stonemasons, joiners, mural painters and on-site practitioners collaborate in the design and production of buildings. Inigo Jones is shown to have relied upon the master mason Nicholas Stone for innovative solutions to structural design, the Augustan city of Oxford and its radical modern facelift is seen to reflect the exigencies of contractor-led stone provision and the Saxon royal office of works is shown to have filled its architectural posts with professionals from the building world. Accounting and supervision procedures developed to support the chain of command and contributed to the increasing professionalisation of architecture. Multifarious agency is further explored in the actual processes of design and making, through the evidence of drawings and documents and the findings of architectural conservation. The richly annotated designs of the eighteenth-century French carver and designer Nicolas Pineau offer precise insight into the elusive relationship of direction and execution, while the economy-led decisions made by the masons of Damer House in County Tipperary demonstrate the role of pragmatism and contingency in the building process. Knowledge production was thus complex, multi-faceted and bound up with materials and making. Problems or errors in extant buildings are brilliantly illustrative of the quotidian challenges in architectural practice. Classical detailing is a case in point, the canonical rules of engagement necessarily modified by on-site exigencies. Here, awkwardly colliding modillions, in the cornice of the superlative Royal Exchange in Dublin, are shown to result from decisions made early in the design process, as the projection of the entablature was simply too shallow to accommodate the usual arrangement of modillions set at right angles to one another. Like the vast entablatures at Greenwich, such details exercised architects, building supervisors and craft practitioners. Whether the merchants of the Royal Exchange noticed their botched modillions is another matter entirely and we learn from this volume that the sensory effects of materials and workmanship had greater impact upon early modern travellers and observers than the niceties of design that would exercise aficionados and antiquarians in the later eighteenth century.

The exploration of collective agency in building production, exemplified in this volume, is part of a shift away from emphasis on individual achievement towards understanding architecture as a wider societal endeavour, enabled by interdependent agents and entities.[4] However, there remains a strong constituency for the seminal and transformative role of the individual designer and this argument is also clearly articulated here, contending that design alone is the progenitor of meaning in architecture and that *execution* is just that, however much the quality of buildings might depend upon excellence in craft practice. This book therefore prompts us to interrogate the relationship of design and making in architecture, to question old and new narratives about the interaction of architects and artisans and ultimately to learn more about how buildings are designed, made and understood.

Notes

1　Bolton and Hendry (eds), *The Royal Hospital for Seamen at Greenwich*, 56.
2　Lucey, *Building Reputations*, 12.
3　Nègre, 'Craft knowledge in the age of encyclopedism', 303–34; Nègre, 'Virtuosité technique et esthétique artisanale'; Deans, 'Architects' albums and architectural practices in England'; Hayes, 'Retrieving craft practice on the early eighteenth-century building site', 160–96.
4　McKellar, *The Birth of Modern London*; Campbell, *Building Saint Paul's*; Saint, 'The conundrum of '"by"'; Nègre, *L'art et la matière*; Casey, *Making Magnificence*; Lucey, *Building Reputations*; Martínez de Guereñu (ed.), 'Who designs architecture?'.

References

Bolton, Arthur T. and H. Duncan Hendry, eds. *The Wren Society: The Royal Hospital for Seamen at Greenwich 1694–1728*, vol. 6. Oxford: Wren Society at the University Press, 1929.
Campbell, James W. P. *Building Saint Paul's*. London: Thames and Hudson, 2007.
Casey, Christine. *Making Magnificence: Architects, stuccatori and the eighteenth-century interior*. New Haven, CT and London: Yale University Press, 2017.
Deans, Elizabeth. 'Architects' albums and architectural practices in England, c.1660–1720'. PhD thesis, University of York, 2022.
Hayes, Melanie. 'Retrieving craft practice on the early eighteenth-century building site'. In *Enriching Architecture: Craft and its conservation in Anglo-Irish building production, 1660–1760*, edited by Christine Casey and Melanie Hayes, 160–96. London: UCL Press, 2023.

Lucey, Conor. *Building Reputations: Architecture and the artisan, 1750–1830*. Manchester: Manchester University Press, 2018.

Martínez de Guereñu, Laura, ed. 'Who designs architecture?', special issue of *R.A.: Revista de Arquitectura*, 23 (2021). Accessed 12 December 2023. https://revistas.unav.edu/index.php/revista-de-arquitectura/issue/view/1444.

McKellar, Elizabeth. *The Birth of Modern London: The development and design of the city, 1660–1720*. Manchester: Manchester University Press, 2021.

Nègre, Valérie. *L'art et la matière: Les artisans, les architects et la technique 1770–1830*. Paris: Classiques Garnier, 2016.

Nègre, Valérie. 'Craft knowledge in the age of encyclopedism'. In *Crafting Enlightenment: Artisanal histories and transnational networks*, edited by Lauren R. Cannady and Jennifer Ferng, 303–34. Liverpool: Liverpool University Press, 2021.

Nègre, Valérie. 'Virtuosité technique et esthétique artisanale dans l'architecture aux XVIIe et XVIIIe siècles', *Images Re-Vues*, Hors-série 7 (2019). Accessed 2 January 2024. https://doi.org/10.4000/imagesrevues.6451.

Saint, Andrew. 'The conundrum of "by"'. In *Architectural History after Colvin: The Society of Architectural Historians of Great Britain Symposium 2011*, edited by Malcolm Airs and William Whyte, 58–70. Donington: Shaun Tyas, 2013.

Acknowledgements

This book is the outcome of an Advanced Laureate Award of the Irish Research Council based in the Department of History of Art and Architecture at Trinity College Dublin. The editors wish to acknowledge the generous support of the Office of Public Works of Ireland in the publication of this volume. We are grateful to the Armagh Robinson Library, Irish Architectural Archive, the Board of Trinity College Dublin, Dublin City Council, Historic Royal Palaces, the Lewis Walpole Library, Yale University, the National Library of Ireland, University Art Collections and Manuscripts and Archives, Trinity College Dublin.

Introduction
Between design and making: architecture and craftsmanship, 1630–1760

Andrew Tierney and Melanie Hayes

> ... the learning of our Architect without the diligence of our Workman, *umbram, non rem consecuta videtur*, may serve to rear a Tabernacle, not build a Temple, there being as much difference between speculation and practice in this Art, as there is between a Shadow and a Substance.[1]
>
> John Evelyn, 1664

Context

There is a mystery about the creative process that has done much to bolster our modern conception of the architect. How are great buildings conceived? Much can be attributed to the patron, the brief, the budget, the current mode of building, and the degree to which an architect sails with or against the prevailing winds of style. After that, we must turn to the more oblique question of 'creative vision'. But there is an equal, though less considered, generative mystery at the heart of architecture that concerns the productive process. How are a knowledge of materials, high quality execution, and mastery of detail achieved, and to what extent does architectural conception draw from or push towards such standards in practice? The answer, we contend in this volume, lies between design and making. It is not our intention to pursue the reductive question of credit or to polarise further the roles of architect and artisan, or the respective rank of design and making in architecture. Rather it is to problematise, as scholars such as Andrew Saint and Laura Martínez de Guereñu have done,[2] the question of 'by' in search of a more satisfactory understanding of the means by which buildings come to be built, and to reintegrate the discursive, hesitant, reflective, and unresolved moments that sit at the intersection between conception and execution. As Howard Colvin has commented, 'the history of British architecture is bound up in its own practice', and for many early practitioners, 'architecture was a craft rather than an art'.[3] For Colvin this truth was best expressed by the quarry-owning master builder families such as the Strongs of Taynton, the Grumbolds of Raunds, the Townesends of Oxford, the Platts of Rotherham. Long underrepresented in scholarly literature, the tacit artisanal knowledge and skills of such families made a major contribution to architectural achievement during this golden age of craftsmanship. While there is a long thread of such thinking swerving in and out of the mainstream of architectural historiography, there has been a notable attempt in the last ten years or more to think more inclusively about productive processes. The work of Alina Payne, Brian Hanson, James Campbell, Christine Casey and Conor Lucey, among others, has made valiant strides towards recognising the role and agency of a plethora of creative figures within the building industry.[4] As Saint has argued, many buildings are not really 'by' any one individual in the way that a painting might be. Rather, architecture 'is a highly organised collaborative business. The designer never stands alone'.[5] Likewise, Casey has observed 'the tendency of commentaries to overlook building professionals and attribute all buildings of pretension to known architects'.[6] While traditionally understood as operating within separate intellectual and manual spheres, these writers show that the continuous social, technical, and creative exchanges between architects and craftsmen, and the fluid assumption of those roles by a diverse range of actors, underpinned the building trade across the seventeenth and eighteenth centuries. This book intends to build on that work, across a range of media and geographic and socio-political contexts.

The process of enrichment, explored in detail in *Enriching Architecture: Craft and its conservation in Anglo-Irish building production 1660–1760,* the sister volume to this book, stands at the intersection of design and making; this series of chapters picks up on and elaborates on many adjacent themes but examines more closely and more explicitly the interplay between designer and maker. If the craftsman is too often silent in the archive, it is in ornament that his voice, with all its individual sonority and timbre, cries out to us – rising sometimes above the conceptual trappings of the architectural whole, at other times forming a rich and carefully controlled harmony with its setting. Since the period when classical principles began to inform British architecture, workmen have manipulated the planar surface, bending light and shade around its edges, sometimes riffing creatively on the established conventions of Antique mouldings, at other times breaking free in their own cadenzas. Inigo Jones had celebrated such work as something 'to delight, amase us sometimes moufe us to laughter, sumtimes to contemplation and horror'.[7] Where the craftsman was left to his own invention, this was praise indeed. As Laurence Turner and Henry Ward commented of St Paul's Cathedral, 'When we turn to the decorative crafts we know not which more to admire, the verve and accomplishment of the artists or the genius of the architect'.[8] Likewise, David Brett has discussed the paradox at the heart of Owen Jones's assessment of ornament as both an 'accessory' to architecture and 'the very soul of an architectural monument'. 'Architectural decoration', he remarked, 'was that which through its associations and vivid sensual characteristics was seen to bear the meaning of a building – yet it had, in nearly every case, an arbitrary relation to the building's plan and structure'.[9]

Christine Casey has noted William Chambers' homage to the craftsmen with whom he collaborated, when he wrote that architecture 'is indebted to sculpture of a great part of its magnificence'.[10] Yet this debt has been too rarely acknowledged. Alina Payne's complaint about the lack of scholarship on Renaissance architecture's dialogue with the other arts rings true for the seventeenth and eighteenth centuries, 'in particular with sculpture and the so-called minor arts'.[11] This problem is partly due to the outsized influence of the theoretical writings of Renaissance architects themselves, and, as Payne has commented, their failure to theorise the interface of the arts.[12] Two separate types of architect emerged quite early. Filippo Brunelleschi (1377–1446), the goldsmith and sculptor turned engineer-architect, who left no writings, and Leon Battista Alberti (1404–1472), the cleric and writer, whose approach was analytical rather than practical from the start, and whose treatise dominated architectural discourse for centuries. It is Alberti's seemingly rationalist approach that most shaped the enduring perception of the architect as a desk-bound conceptual creator.[13] Caroline van Eck, in her overview of British architectural writing, has charted the shift from a public understanding of architecture as an 'expedient, skilled practice ... transmitted orally and by example' to the Renaissance view of it as a primarily intellectual activity.[14] Inhibited by archival resources that remain all too silent about the reservoirs of tacit knowledge that informed building practice, this relationship does not reveal itself easily to the casual researcher. Christine Casey has thus referred to the craftsman as the 'silent partner'. 'To prise open the elusive space between design and making', she writes, 'we must cast the net wide and capture fugitive instances of interaction between material, technology, and design'.[15] But as this volume shows, the privileging of conception over making, and the polarised positioning of each, is hard to sustain.

As both Payne and Casey have noted, twentieth-century scholarship, the product of an era in which architectural production has been bound up with industrial processes, has marginalised workmanship by hand.[16] Of course there are many complex historical reasons for this. Djabarouti and O'Flaherty, in writing about modern conservation practice, have argued that 'the rise of the architectural profession (and subsequently other built heritage professions) led to a decline of the craftsperson – both socially and professionally'.[17] Juhani Pallasmaa, who notes the importance of craft skill to Renaissance architects such as Brunelleschi, sees the division between design and making as a post-war phenomenon, noting the decline in a traditional route into architecture through bricklaying, carpentry, and cabinet making, in countries such as Denmark.[18]

This division of labour into the intellectual and the manual has long been a cause of concern. Warnings against professional overreach by incompetent and 'vulgar' workmen can be found in every period, from John Evelyn (1620–1706) to Christopher Wren (1632–1723), Nicholas Hawksmoor (c.1661–1736) and James Gibbs (1682–1754) (the latter as discussed by Rowan in Chapter 7).[19] While this abuse was aimed at less skilled operatives working unsupervised, it certainly helped crystallise the division between architects and artisans in the public perception. Whereas Evelyn criticised 'Vulgar workmen, who for want of some more Solid Directions, Faithful and easy Rules in this Nature', filled the city with 'Rubbish and a thousand Infirmities', Robert Morris (1703–1754) blamed both the 'Badness of the Materials, and the Employment of illiterate Workmen', as 'the general Cause of the Decay' in building.[20] Isaac Ware, the son of a cordwainer, who served his apprenticeship under Thomas Ripley, who himself had trained as a carpenter before becoming an official of the Royal Works, was equally harsh in his criticism of 'workmen at the present time, who at best are too negligent, and often shamefully dishonest'.[21]

The Gothic revival, stimulated by the writings of Augustus W. N. Pugin (1812–1852), brought a reactionary regard for the agency of the craftsman; it became a core principle in the writings of John Ruskin (1819–1900) and William Morris (1834–1896), influencing craft-related studies in architecture into the early twentieth century, including the work of Walter Godfrey, H. Avray Tipping and Margaret Wood in Britain,

Walter Dyer in the United States, and the early volumes of the *Georgian Society Records* (1910–13) in Ireland.[22] Such interest in crafted elements (as opposed to the architectural whole) reflected the era's immersion in historicism of ever widening breadth, and a synthetic approach to style and detailing. The broad appeal of the Arts and Crafts Movement, that marked the last phase of Victorian and Edwardian historicism, had an unfortunate side-effect in the disassembly, sale, and reassembly of Stuart and Georgian British interiors in the nascent collections of American cities, as charted by John Harris.[23] Divorced from its outer envelope, plasterwork and joinery took centre stage, and it was in the work of the artisan rather than the architect that Walter Dyer sought to establish the origins of a 'national and indigenous school of architecture' for America.[24]

The manual worker, if frequently absent from the archive, was nevertheless present in the object – physically connected and personally distinct. The supremacy of the craftsman at this period was such that Latham and Tipping, in their richly illustrated three-volume *In English Homes* (1904), often dispensed with external views of buildings, in favour of highlighting their richly crafted interiors. For example, of the six photographs they published of Tythrop, Oxfordshire, five were of the staircase (at that time attributed to Grinling Gibbons); the sixth, a chimneypiece.[25] The attempt by *Country Life* (in six volumes by H. Avray Tipping) to reorganise early modern British architectural history in the 1920s along strictly chronological lines (following his earlier and much more diffused three-volume analysis of the country house, with photographer Charles Latham) paved the way for more rigorous academic analysis by Christopher Hussey, in the 1950s, that focused entirely on the achievements of the Georgian age.[26] This more linear narrative found its driving force in the architect. 'Classical architecture, in the infinite scope that it affords for the use of perfected forms and ratios, gives to the imagination of genius perhaps the most satisfying visual medium devised by man'. But he acknowledged the tension that existed between theory and practice. 'Yet the English temperament is seen to be happiest in the arts when its native empiricism, or faculty for finding a way, has succeeded in striking a compromise with logic alien to it'.[27] Citing Thomas Sharp's observation, that 'the aesthetic process tends in the English to take place below the level of full consciousness', he notes the difficulty such inarticulacy poses for the researcher.[28] It also implies something of the racial undercurrent that had earlier found its way into the work of Reginald Blomfield, whereby the craftsman working silently confers onto a building something of vernacular tradition, and a mystic and folkloric nationalism; the same collective unconscious, of course, might be equally attributed to the kind of 'romantic socialism' associated with Ruskin and Morris.[29]

Andrew Saint's recent contention, that 'In the end, "by" in architecture does not mean design. What it means is authority, decisiveness, and control', was a response to the obsessive 'train-spotting' for the authorial hand that has come to dominate architectural history of the early modern period.[30] Designer-focused and formalist monographs of English architects in the classical tradition, building on the seminal work of Fergusson (1862), became pervasive from the second quarter of the twentieth century, with Gotch's *Inigo Jones* (1928), Gunther's *The Architecture of Sir Roger Pratt* (1928), Summerson's *John Nash: Architect to King George IV* (1935), Marcus Whiffen's *Thomas Archer* (1950), Summerson's *Sir Christopher Wren* (1953) and Kerry Downes's *Hawksmoor* (1959). Indeed, that John Nash (1752–1835) and Wren, the designers most pilloried by A. W. N. Pugin a century earlier, should return to centre stage, was perhaps indicative of the 1930s pivot away from craft. Architectural production fell within a 'great man' framework that foregrounded the intellect of the individual genius over the cooperative and manual skills of the many, which paralleled attempts to rescue the 'architect as hero' ideal in an age of mass production and commercial design, as charted by Saint.[31] In addition, the work of Geoffrey Scott and Albert Richardson, under the influence of German art history, had propelled a shift towards spatial analysis that marginalised the enriched walls and ceilings that defined the great contribution of craftsmanship to the architecture of the seventeenth and eighteenth centuries.[32] As a result, much mid-twentieth-century research was concerned with authorial attribution, work that often depended as much on formal analysis as it did archival research. Summerson's *Architecture in Britain 1530–1830* (1953), the synthetic narrative which emerged among these monographs, sketched out a national framework dependent on illustrations of plan and elevation, harking back to Colen Campbell's *Vitruvius Britannicus*. Like Fergusson's seminal *History of the Modern Styles of Architecture* (1862), such an authorial approach had little room for workmanship – with the brief exception of St Paul's, acknowledged as 'something resembling a national school of building and decoration' and setting the high standard for workmanship for the next generation.[33]

The removal of craft from the survey of British architecture, and the nexus of collaboration on which it depended, can be best seen by comparing Alfred Gotch's illustrations in *The English Home, from Charles I to George IV* (1919), the first book to offer a synthesis of this period, with

Summerson's *Architecture in Britain 1530–1830* (1953). Gotch's broad appraisal captures everything from the architectural ground plan to the wall-enriching festoon (the latter presented as a full-page drawing from St Lawrence Jewry); but this suppleness of scale and variety of illustration types, also seen in Belcher's *Later Renaissance Architecture in England* (1901), was abandoned as analyses switched to an architect-centred narrative.[34] Unsurprisingly, the staircases of Edward Pearce and his circle, which feature so prominently in both Belcher and Gotch, as one of the great achievements of late seventeenth-century craftsmanship, did not make it into Summerson's survey. Though continental parallels existed, there was no easy way to explain such virtuoso artisan ingenuity and skill, at the intersection of design and making, within a purely conceptual narrative of architectural development. John Michael Rysbrack (1694–1770), whose relief carvings forms part of the outstanding surface enrichments of the Palladian movement (at Houghton and Clandon Park), likewise failed to feature, while Giovanni Batista Bagutti and Giuseppe Artari fared only slightly better.[35] Of course, Gotch was writing at the end of a tradition of practice-led 'sourcebook' literature that would soon after have no specialist audience. This is something that Summerson recognised himself in the closing paragraphs of his 1953 biography of Christopher Wren; when looking back at the enthusiasm that surrounded the Wren bicentenary of thirty years earlier, he noted that then 'the architecture of the past was still valued as a direct visual source of suggestion and inspiration for contemporary buildings'.[36] Indeed, his own assessment of workmanship at St Paul's must have drawn on the 1923 paper by Turner and Ward which highlighted its importance as a hub of high-quality craftsmanship and artisan-led design.[37] But the late Victorian rehabilitation of Wren, which reached its crescendo at the bicentenary, had irked Summerson for this reason:

> … the rehabilitation came in a curious way. If the Gothic revival did nothing else it gave architects a sense of the crafts, of the quality of materials and the handling of them; such things were thought to be of more real and lasting importance than the intellectual postulates of classical architecture. So as the architecture of Wren's period came to be rediscovered it was not the precise intellect of Wren himself which made its appeal, but the imprecise and unlearned, the hearty and vigorous works of his humbler contemporaries![38]

But since then, he noted, things had changed. The project of architectural history, as he saw it, 'is not with the idea of collecting nuggets of wisdom with which to enrich our own buildings', but something much loftier: 'the study of human-kind, and especially of those creatures of our kind who have been exceptional in sensibility or intellect'.[39] Thus raised to the humanist and intellectual sphere, classical architecture became somewhat stripped of its grain. It was this lost element, ever 'finding a way' that Hussey had recognised as unarticulated, residing 'below the level of full consciousness'. And yet, Summerson himself, in a rather contradictory way, acknowledged the essential contribution of the artisan. While St Paul's at once embodied 'the exertions of one outstandingly brilliant and self-reliant mind', he elsewhere posited the masons as 'next to the architect, the real makers of St Paul's – extremely able men, accustomed to build important buildings themselves to their own designs, and in some cases excellent sculptors into the bargain'.[40] Howard Colvin's similar observation (in his *A Biographical Dictionary of British Architects 1600–1840* (1954)) on the independence and ingenuity of the 'highly competent craftsmen' employed by Wren in the City churches, wasn't taken up until James Campbell's *Building St Paul's* (2008), one of the first monographs to focus on a major British building from the perspective of its construction rather than design.[41]

Behind such irreconcilable appraisals is the confused and often contradictory historiographical positioning of the craftsman. Lack of clear terminology has not helped; put simply, there is no easy distinction between craftsman, artist, and architect. As Summerson acknowledged: 'Among the craftsmen of London there were, as there had always been, masons and carpenters of high quality as artists, whether as sculptors or architects', while acknowledging that in the Restoration period one has to turn to 'the craftsman class ... to discover the designers of the majority of buildings of the period'.[42] Likewise, Christopher Hussey commented:

> Responsibility for the completion of the decoration of Blenheim by James Moore, a cabinet-maker, was not thought unusual at a time when many master-carpenters (e.g. T. Ripley) graduated into architecture. When, in the succeeding Palladian phase, the language of ornament could be largely learnt from pattern books, it was often a short step from the design of rooms to that of a house.[43]

The less architect-centred work of Hussey, and later Oliver Hill and John Cornforth, drawing on the rich photographic archives of *Country Life*, was better placed to reassert the contribution of individual craftsmen working within architectural contexts, a debt to long out-of-fashion connoisseurial analysis, now increasingly acknowledged.[44]

Much information on the relationship between craftsmanship, the building trade and architects is hidden in plain sight in existing reference texts. Rupert Gunnis's *Dictionary of British Sculptors* (1953)[45] was followed by Howard Colvin's *A Biographical Dictionary of British Architects 1600–1840* (1954) now in its 4th edition; the latter contains extensive information on the artisanal background of many architects. Colvin's astute observations on the independence and ingenuity of the 'highly competent craftsmen' employed by Wren in the City churches has never been fully evaluated:

> Wren's City churches, in particular, were the result of cooperation between Surveyor-General and the highly competent craftsmen whom he employed – men who were quite capable of designing and building a church without the supervision of a member of the Royal Society. And to a great extent they actually did so: the ceilings, altarpieces, pulpits and other furnishings were usually designed by those who executed them. Sometimes they submitted a drawing or a model to Wren or one of his colleagues: but more often they did not, and it is a tribute to the high standard of contemporary craftsmanship that the resultant interiors were so rarely disharmonious.[46]

Similar work is more dispersed in an Irish context, most notably Rolf Loeber's useful but now outdated *Biographical Dictionary of Architects in Ireland 1600–1720* (1981), which includes entries on many artisan builder/architects, and for the later period Ann Martha Rowan's online *Dictionary of Irish Architects*. Nevertheless, the biographical approach, focused on authorial attribution, has largely privileged design over making. Attempts to chart the identities of master craftsmen who worked alongside architects has helped create a more broadly textured understanding of the creative processes in architecture. Geoffrey Beard's 1966 study of Georgian craftsmanship, revised and expanded in 1981, provided a cohesive dictionary of the major craftsmen working in stone, timber and plaster, with biographical and career details,[47] while Andor Gomme's work on Francis Smith of Warwick has given detailed insights into the artisans operating in his circle.[48] Since then, Claire Gapper and Jenny Saunt have expanded the study of craftsmanship in plasterwork extensively in Britain,[49] while in Ireland Con Curran's work on Dublin-based craftsmen, in particular plaster workers operating in the late seventeenth and eighteenth century, paved the way for more recent investigations by McDonnell, Casey and Lucey.[50] While parallel histories of interior design and decoration, by Peter Thornton and Charles Saumarez Smith, celebrate the design and craft achievement of craftsmen, separate to mainstream architectural history,[51] studies of woodwork have provided insight on architectural craftsmen who moved fluidly between furnishing and interior fittings. J. C. Rogers and Margaret Jourdain's pioneering research was developed in the later work of Adam Bowett on British furniture, while in Ireland The Knight of Glin and James Peill's *Irish Furniture: Woodworking and carving in Ireland from the earliest times to the Act of Union* (2007) was the first major contribution to the study of craftsmanship in wood; again, it contains a dictionary of craftsmen with biographical details but addresses itself primarily to a furniture-history audience.[52] While Maurice Craig's important and pioneering surveys of Irish architecture, most notably *Dublin 1660–1860* (1952) and his *The Architecture of Ireland: From the earliest times to 1880* (1982), offered necessarily limited insights into collaborative building practice, the more detailed studies of Edward McParland (for whom, see Chapter 8 of this volume) have highlighted the contribution of stonemasons and carvers, such as the Tabary brothers, Simon Vierpyl, and Edward Smyth in the success of several of Dublin's most famous buildings.[53] The appearance so far of six Pevsner volumes for Ireland, begun by Alistair Rowan (for whom, see Chapter 7 of this volume) has shone a light on the reach of skilled craftsmanship throughout regional parts of the country.[54] Likewise, Arthur Gibney's *The Building Site in Eighteenth-Century Ireland* (2017) has refocused attention towards a broader range of actors within architectural practice and emphasised the role of materials in shaping that practice. Recently granular archival research on the construction and enrichment of buildings such as Ham House and Powerscourt, County Wicklow, has been bringing to light the individual contributions of skilled craftsmen across a range of media in single buildings,[55] while detailed research on individual artisan families, and the drawings they produced, has shown the value of a dynastic approach.[56]

Despite the availability of reference works, returning the craftsman to the larger narrative of mainstream British and Irish architectural history has proved challenging. This is largely because architectural historians have been preoccupied elsewhere. The conceptual turn of the 1990s and early 2000s, seen in the work of Alice Friedman and Dana Arnold, Kari Boyd McBride and others, saw progressive forays into gender, spatiality, representation and meaning derived from literary theory.[57] Likewise, histories produced in the wake of Mark Girouard's groundbreaking *Life in the English Country House* (1978) considered buildings in largely socio-economic terms that, groundbreaking as it was, could not simultaneously take account of the active agency of complex networks of craftsmen. That would have been an insurmountable task. While the material turn in the humanities has focused largely on consumption rather than production in the Stuart and Georgian eras,[58] a wider literature in the social sciences and anthropology engages with matters of materiality and conditions of making, seeking to challenge the supremacy of form over material, to deconstruct oppositional design–craft binaries, and considering craft activity as knowledge production.[59] James Ayres's *Building the Georgian City*, refocused attention on processes rather than results. As he noted at the start of his book: 'As a word "architecture" remains determinedly static or passive in contrast to more active "building"'.[60] Like Colvin, he saw craftsmen as 'men for whom making and designing were simultaneous activities'.[61] The process whereby making and designing came to be separated has surfaced in studies of urban development. Elizabeth McKellar's *The Birth of Modern London: The development and design of the city, 1660–1720* saw this as a more critical point than the traditional view of the craftsman as subservient to the architect. She notes, in response to Adrian Forty's *Objects of Desire*, that such separation is complicated in building practice where a multitude of skills and working practices made collaborative work a necessity.[62] As McKellar argues, 'One result of the measure and value system was it required a worker who was sufficiently literate and numerate to understand and administer the sophisticated techniques of quantity surveying'.[63] David Yeomans, in his paper 'Managing eighteenth-century building', describes the emergence of the professional architect within the well-documented Queen Anne churches in London. 'Architects were finding a niche for themselves between the design skills of the craftsmen and the management skills of the surveyors, providing a wider range of design skills than the former but a more limited range of services than those of the latter'.[64] The result of this transition, he notes, was an unclear division of responsibilities, inadequate cost control, and difficulties ensuring quality of workmanship. The social complexities and political context of the urban building trade have also come under scrutiny in Christine Stevenson's *The City and the King: Architecture and politics in Restoration London* (2013).

Ultimately, the successful architect had to become a successful orchestrator, as Christine Casey has argued, drawing on Gottfried

Semper's description of the 'choragus' in Antiquity 'chosen from among the artists … for his special gift of assessing the situation, allocating the resources, and for having a sharp eye for disposition and economy of means' and, critically, 'not yet enfeebled by theoretical matters'.[65] Central to this discussion are changing perspectives on artisanal identity and knowledge production, which seek to challenge the deep-rooted oppositional binaries of 'mind' and 'hand'. While Jasmine Kilburn-Toppin argues that 'knowledge of the "mind" and skills of the "hand" were perceived to be mutually reinforcing',[66] Conor Lucey's work has stressed the rising professional and social status of the artisan builder in the context of urban development during the period 1750–1830.[67] He writes that: 'Although historically disparaged as members of the "lower orders", the labourer and the craftsman were elevated within the social pecking order by eighteenth century Enlightenment thinking'.[68] Similarly, in discussing the humble background of artists, Lawrence Klein has written of the polite comportments of those 'who served up culture' to the elite and who were 'caught between the demands of the market and the ideals of art'.[69] Johnathan Djabarouti and Christopher O'Flaherty have pointed to the long term impact of these divisions between these spheres: 'the impact of their fragmentation has led not only to a disintegration of building culture but also to the repression and erosion of the craftsperson and their role'.[70] Modern conservation has to some degree mitigated these elisions, and deference to the insights and tacit knowledge of craftspeople is a feature of collaboration in heritage practice where traditional skills continue to be required and nurtured (see O'Mahony and D'Alton, Chapter 6 in this volume).

As notions of architectural agency are gradually being expanded, a burgeoning scholarship on artisanal culture and labour has demonstrated the multifaceted and collaborative nature of building practice in the early modern period.[71] Christine Casey's *Making Magnificence: Architects, stuccatori and the eighteenth-century interior* was a departure in its insistence on exploring the fuller stratigraphy of skilled labour that lay under the achievements of the eighteenth-century architect. Expanding beyond plasterwork, Casey and Hayes's edited collection, *Enriching Architecture: Craft and its conservation in Anglo-Irish building production, 1660–1760* is the most recent volume to insist on the agency of a broader spectrum of actors, breaking down old boundaries between design and construction history in seeing architecture as a practice-led phenomenon. Looking at a broader terrain, *Between Design and Making* brings together scholars from several European countries to propose this medial zone as necessarily discursive, exploratory, and multifaceted, and as such integral to architectural achievement. It also digs deeper into archival sources, the chapters here focused more on processes than finishes, illuminating 'making' through pedagogy, social networks, visual communications, on-site management, and language. This wider framework brings a much-needed comparative dimension to studies of Anglo-Irish architectural production, which often restricts itself to a narrow political and geographical jurisdiction. As becomes apparent from the following chapters, continental Europe is a constant point of reference, from the sourcing of ideas, materials and craft skills to the establishment of qualitative standards in workmanship; it is also a key context for the public reception of early modern architecture in Britain and Ireland.

Content

The papers in this volume form a collective argument for the processual nature of design and making, further developing the shift towards a collaborative and qualitative analysis of architectural production pursued at Trinity College Dublin.[72] Combining the scholarship of established architectural historians and fresh perspectives from emerging voices, it argues for a re-evaluation of the traditional framework for architectural appraisal, considering a network of material resources and skills that extended far beyond the architect. Bringing together scholars from Britain, Ireland, France and Germany, this thematically cohesive series of chapters pushes us to reassess our understanding of practice in design, training and building management, as fundamentally collaborative. Arranged in a loosely chronological sequence, the chapters take the reader from the earliest phase of early modern British architectural development, which emerged from the heart of the building establishment in early Stuart London, to the inner workings of building practices across Britain and Ireland, demonstrating both regional variance and more widespread continental influence during an important period of cultural exchange in Western Europe. The chapters by Gady and Lüttmann more explicitly widen the lens to a European perspective in Paris, St Petersburg, and Dresden. Hamlett builds on this wider view by looking at European craftsmen collaborating with architects on allegorical interiors in England, where craft itself was a well-established topos of allegorical painting.

Whatever the individualistic aspirations of specific artisans within the building trade, several chapters in this volume emphasise architectural production as a networked activity. In a wide-ranging and connoisseurial analysis, the book's opening chapter (Higgott and White) examines the working relationship between two key figures of early modern architectural endeavour: Inigo Jones and Nicholas Stone. The chapter proposes Stone as the major technical innovator of the suspended stone stair, one of the most spectacular architectonic features of the seventeenth- and eighteenth-century interior. In this collaboration, we find a compelling synthesis of theoretical and empirical knowledge. Perhaps more than anything else, the staircase is the subject of relentless technical and aesthetic innovation during the seventeenth century – so much so that much of what followed in the eighteenth century was merely the refinement of ideas first generated there. It is a reminder that many material and technical innovations on which eighteenth-century architecture depended, such as the use of Portland stone, the structural carpentry for coved ceilings and domes, all emerged during the seventeenth century, a period when craftsmanship and architectural design were more intimately aligned. Crucially, this chapter connects the early Stuart innovations of Inigo Jones and his circle with architectural developments of the post-Restoration period.

New archival research is a key component of this volume, developing this collaborative theme across a range of European contexts. Several contributions mine important state and institutional repositories in Oxford, Paris, Dresden, Utrecht, London and Dublin, to pry open the working processes between designers and artisans on the building site (Tyack, Gady, Hayes) and the institutional training of architects (Lüttmann). Confronting the grey area between design and making, Geoffrey Tyack offers a dynastic view of the stone trade in Oxford at the end of the seventeenth century, through the lens of an archive of papers relating to the Townesend family. As Tyack notes, 'William Townesend's papers, [are] probably the best surviving archive of any English mason-architect of the eighteenth century' (Chapter 2, p. 68). The family blended a mastery of materials, commercial acumen, and an associated range of craft skills that often merged seamlessly into design.

Analysis of the formal vocabulary of classicism (McParland, Rowan and Hamlett) shows the conceptual, practical and at times allegorical nexus around which architects and craftsmen had to work, from conception and design to execution. We see evidence of collaborative design and the authoritative refinement of mouldings on the part of an architect working with joiner and carver Nicholas Pineau, but as McParland rightly points out: 'independence of expertise on the part of artisans is suggested by Daviler's list of workmen's own terms for profiles, different to those of architects – *baguette* for *astragal, boudin* for *petit tore*' (Chapter 8, p. 253).

By the late-seventeenth century, architecture assumes a more knowing and self-referential guise. Hamlett's exploration of *techne* and *poesis* in the allegorical representations of patron and craftsman reveals mural painting as an intermedial and discursive junction between patron, architect and artisan. As several of the chapters demonstrate, the final expression of canonical classical forms rested on layered and intergenerational knowledge of building techniques that blur the traditional abstractions of architect and builder/artisan. Gady argues for the discursive quality of drawings within the workshop practice of Pineau, drawing the input of a range of decision-makers into the design process, with complex interplays of functionality, regularity, proportion and representation. In a more institutional context, Lüttmann shows that craft apprenticeships, as well as knowledge of draughtsman-ship in a range of drawing types, was an integral part of the formal training of the Saxon *Conducteur*, a rigorous system that produced such distinguished architects as Matthäus Daniel Pöppelmann and Johann Christoph Knöffel. As Lüttmann establishes, such rigorous training may well have informed the work of Richard Castle in Ireland. Castle's workshop practices are dissected by Hayes in her analysis of building accounts in Trinity College Dublin, which reveal the degree of coordination and monitoring the workforce required, 'not just master craftsmen and major building contractors, but smaller scale operators and labour on sundry works' (Chapter 4, p. 122). Castle introduced the competitive tendering system that Wren had used at St Paul's. As Hayes notes: 'This not only ensured the best price for the client, it promoted higher quality work and increased control for the architect or overseer' (p. 125). He also brought about a more formalised use of the 'measured contract', a key form of risk management and quality control. A chapter from practising conservation architects (D'Alton and O'Mahony, Chapter 6) demonstrates what happens when such safeguards do not appear to have been employed, leaving a gap between conception and execution at Damer House, County Tipperary: window openings and their architraves were of differing dimensions, requiring last-minute improvisation and contributing to later structural defects. Further lack of cohesion between the rubble wall construction, soft sandstone dressings, and unexecuted render finish added to its long-term problems.

This theme is also picked up by Alistair Rowan in his analysis of the undocumented building of Florence Court, County Fermanagh

(Chapter 7), where he argues that craftsmen 'technically competent in their craft, worked independently with little concept of the building as a whole, so that the final appearance of the house, lacking the input of an architect or other 'person of judgement', such as Gibbs advised, is much less satisfactory than it might otherwise have been' (Chapter 7, p. 218). Rowan fights a valiant rearguard action on behalf of the enduring authority of the architect and their right to be 'credited as the agents of their own designs', warning against a levelling out of individual contributions in the name of a contemporary concern with equity (p. 208). The inclusion of this chapter raises a broader question about the direction of architectural history, should it pivot too much toward the granularity of making. While it is important not to pitch designer and maker against each other, or indeed polarise architect- and artisan-centred approaches, there is also room to acknowledge the space between design and making as potentially stressful and contested.

In the final chapter, Tierney engages with this overarching theme in relation to the reception of workmanship and the popular understanding of the respective roles of materials, designer and maker as they emerged in a range of sixteenth-, seventeenth- and eighteenth-century texts. This analysis points to a long-standing interest in the crafted nature of construction, picking up on issues of knowledge, materiality and performativity in architectural writing. It also shows that the way buildings were consumed by the eye was not always in sync with the way they were conceived. As shown here, for much of the seventeenth and eighteenth centuries, craftsmanship was the most readily consumed element of architectural production, reflecting a fragmented consumption, focused on skills and materials – stylistic analysis and cohesive architectural appraisal coming very late. This was micro rather than macro consumption, the latter depending for its reception on abstracted representations of elevation and plan – in engravings such as *Vitruvius Britannicus*, or those in Gibbs's *A Book of Architecture*, which reduced buildings to their ideal, conceptual form.

Top-down narratives, which depend heavily on such abstracted representation of buildings, are pleasingly succinct and teleologically efficient. But in moving away from this, how are we to manage an ensemble cast within a cogent narrative of national and international architectural development? If Summerson's elevated treatment of the architect now seems too much to stomach, it did at least introduce structure and momentum into a potentially chaotic research environment. There is at present no easy answer to the challenge of writing a synthetic account of early modern architecture that manages to find a happy middle ground between disparate formal, social and economic approaches. Clear storytelling demands that we keep our distance and don't get lost among the footnotes (to which craftsmen have long been exiled). Is there room for everyone to crowd into the main plot, or do we simply abandon the grand narrative entirely? In many cases the footnotes provide enough yarn to spin their own tale. But if we are to trace our fingers along these tangled, knotted threads, it must be from curiosity rather than moral imperative; otherwise it becomes a mere task, leaden and perfunctory. It is easy to forget that architectural history, which on the one hand aspires to objective record and analysis, is at the same time a visceral, embodied response – however muted we might strive to make it appear. The dichotomy of mind and body must also be traversed by the historian and critic. While there is no doubt that the good architect brings creativity, control, quality and cohesion to a building, it is only done in concert with responsive craftsmen, sympathetic to that vision, and nuanced in their performance. The space between design and making may be filled with conflict and compromise: competing visions, squandered resources, spiralling costs, mechanical failure. At other times all elements align in concert, the right patron, the right location, the right builder, the best craftsmen. But more often, good buildings emerge from well-established working practices, solid, dependable relationships built up over time, and a mutual respect for hard-won skill sets and experience. Such was the case in the successful careers of Wren, Gibbs and Castle. And it is this in-between space of practice that we must increasingly search to re-establish the various processes behind architectural achievement.

Editorial note

In quoting from texts written during the seventeenth and eighteenth centuries, we have preserved the source material's variations in spelling and avoided the overuse of [sic].

Notes

1 *umbram, non rem consecuta* – 'obtained a shadow not a thing'; Evelyn, 'An account of architects and architecture', 121.
2 Saint, 'The conundrum of "by"'; Saint, *Architect and Engineer*; Martínez de Guereñu, 'Who designs architecture?'.
3 Colvin, *A Biographical Dictionary of British Architects*, 21.

4 See Campbell, 'The finances of the carpenter in England, 1660–1710', 'Building a fortune', *Building Saint Paul's*; Casey, 'Silent partner', 'Surface value: Ways of seeing decoration in architecture', *Making Magnificence*; Casey and Hayes (eds), *Enriching Architecture*; Hanson, *Architects and the 'Building World'*; Lucey, *Building Reputations*, 'Classicism or commerce?'; Payne, 'Materiality, crafting, and scale in Renaissance architecture'; Saint, 'The conundrum of '"by"'. See also Nègre, 'Craft knowledge in the age of encyclopedism'; Pallasmaa, *The Thinking Hand*'; Scott, *The Rococo Interior*.

5 Saint, 'The conundrum of "by"'.

6 Casey, 'Silent partner', 134.

7 Van Eck, *British Architectural Theory*, 25.

8 Turner and Ward, 'The crafts at St Paul's', 96.

9 Brett, *Mackintosh: The poetics of workmanship*, 46.

10 Casey, 'Silent partner', 134.

11 Payne, 'Materiality, crafting and scale in Renaissance architecture', 367.

12 Payne, 'Materiality, ornament, and media overlaps', 138.

13 Alberti's complicated relationship with craft knowledge, and the way it has been represented in the historiography, is discussed by Hanson, *Architects and the 'Building World' from Chambers to Ruskin*, 1–3.

14 Van Eck, *British Architectural Theory*, 8.

15 Casey, 'Silent partner', 134.

16 For Payne's discussion of Jacob Burkhardt's more inclusive view of architecture, see 'Materiality, crafting and scale in Renaissance architecture', 369. For Casey's views on the influence of modernism on perceptions of craftsmanship, see Casey, 'Surface value'. On this point, see also Hanson, *Architects and the 'Building World' from Chambers to Ruskin*, 21; and, Lucey, *Building Reputations*, 2.

17 Djabarouti and O'Flaherty, 'Architect and craftsperson', 434–5.

18 Pallasmaa, *The Thinking Hand*, 65.

19 Evelyn, 'An account of architects and architecture', 5; for Hawksmoor's comments on good and bad masons, see Webb, 'The letters and drawings of Nicholas Hawksmoor', 141; see also McKellar, *The Birth of Modern London*, 30.

20 Evelyn, *A Parallel of the Antient Architecture with the Modern*, 5; Morris, *Defence of Ancient Architecture*, 102.

21 Colvin, *A Biographical Dictionary of British Architects*, 1020; Ware, *A Complete Body of Architecture*, 111.

22 Godfrey, *The English Staircase*; Tipping, *Grinling Gibbons*; Dyer, *Creators of Decorative Styles*.

23 Tierney, 'Reviving the artisan sculptor'; Harris, *Moving Rooms*.

24 Dyer, *Early American Craftsmen*, 19. A counterpoint to this communitarian tradition came from the writings of Herbert Spencer and J. A. Symonds, see Ricci, 'Who is the Renaissance? Where did he come from?'.

25 Latham and Tipping, *In English Homes*.

26 Tipping, *English Homes*; Hussey, *English Country Houses: Early Georgian 1715–1760*; Hussey, *English Country Houses: Mid Georgian 1760–1800*; Hussey, *English Country Houses: Late Georgian 1800–1840*.

27 Hussey, *Early Georgian*, 9.

28 Hussey, *Early Georgian*, 9.

29 See Watkin, *The Rise of Architectural History*, 97–8; see also Watkins comments on the work of E. S. Prior, 105–7.

30 Saint, 'The conundrum of "by"', 69.

31 See 'The architect as hero and genius' in Saint, *The Image of the Architect*, 1–18.

32 Scott, *The Architecture of Humanism*; Richardson, *Monumental Classic Architecture in Great Britain and Ireland*. For an analysis of this shift towards the spatial in architecture, see Watkin, *The Rise of Architectural History*, 115–16.

33 Summerson, 'The craftsmen of St Paul's' in Summerson, *Architecture in Britain*, 143–5.

34 Similar attention to architectural detail can also be observed in Blomfield's *A History of Renaissance Architecture in England* and Jackson's *The Renaissance of Roman Architecture*.

35 For Rysbrack's role in the design of the relief sculpture he executed in architectural interiors, see Baker, 'Sculpture for Palladian interiors: Rysbrack's reliefs and their setting'.

36 On this point see William Whyte 'The success of Sir Howard Colvin', 9, and Watkin, *Rise of Architectural History*, ix.
37 Turner and Ward, 'The crafts at St Paul's'.
38 Summerson, *Sir Christopher Wren*, 155.
39 Summerson, *Sir Christopher Wren*, 157–8.
40 Summerson, *Sir Christopher Wren*, 122 and 128.
41 In addition, Paul Jeffery's *The City Churches of Sir Christopher Wren* (1996), though principally concerned with design and attribution, includes a useful gazetteer with the names of the craftsmen for each building.
42 Summerson, *Architecture in Britain*, 159–60.
43 Hussey, *Early Georgian*, 15.
44 Hill and Cornforth, *English Country Houses: Caroline, 1625–1685:* Casey and Hayes, *Enriching Architecture*, 3.
45 Now in its 3rd edition, edited by Roscoe, Hardy and Sullivan under the title *A Biographical Dictionary of Sculptors in Britain 1660–1851*.
46 Colvin, *A Biographical Dictionary of British Architects*.
47 Beard, *Georgian Craftsmen and their Work;* Beard, *Craftsmen and Interior Decoration in England 1660–1820*; Beard, *Decorative Plasterwork in Great Britain*.
48 Gomme, *Francis Smith of Warwick*; Gomme, 'An eighteenth-century builder's notebook'.
49 See, for example, Gapper, 'The impact of Inigo Jones on London decorative plasterwork'; Gapper, 'Caroline plasterwork at Ham House'. See also Gapper's online gazetteer of British Renaissance plasterers. Accessed 14 December 2023. https://clairegapper.info/. Saunt, 'Drawing out a surface in lime and hair'.
50 Curran, 'Dublin plaster work', 'The Parliament House 1728–1800', *Dublin Decorative Plasterwork of the Seventeenth and Eighteenth Centuries*. See McDonnell, *Irish Eighteenth-Century Stuccowork*; Lucey, *The Stapleton Collection*; Casey and Lucey, *Decorative Plasterwork in Ireland and Europe*; Casey, *Making Magnificence*.
51 Saumarez Smith, *Eighteenth-Century Decoration*; Thornton, *Form and Decoration*.
52 See McKellar, 'Representing the Georgian', for discussion of the construction and representation of eighteenth-century interiors in journals and books of the late nineteenth and early twentieth century, in particular the pioneering work of Jourdain.
53 McParland, *Public Architecture*, 53–69; McParland, *James Gandon*, 38, 70, 163–4. For Vierpyl's work, see also Helen Byrne, 'Simon Vierpyl (c.1725–1810), sculptor and stonemason'.
54 *North West Ulster*; *North Leinster*; *Dublin*; *South Ulster*; *Central Leinster*; *Cork*.
55 Rowell, *Ham House: Four hundred years of collecting and patronage*; Rowell, 'Seventeenth century and later floors at Ham House'; Hayes, 'Retrieving craft practice on the early eighteenth-century building site'.
56 Casey, *Making Magnificence*; Hayes, 'Retrieving craft practice on the early eighteenth-century building site'; Saunt, 'The Abbotts and their book'.
57 See Friedman, 'Architecture, authority, and the female gaze'; Arnold, *Reading Architectural History*; McBride, *Country House Discourse in Early Modern England*.
58 Wilson and Mackley, *Creating Paradise*, explores issues of material and cost.
59 Pye, *The Nature and Art of Workmanship*; Sennet, *The Craftsman*; Frayling, *On Craftsmanship*; Adamson, *The Invention of Craft*; Ingold, *Making*; Smith et al., *Ways of Making and Knowing*; Adamson, *Craft: An American history*.
60 Ayres, *Building the Georgian City*, 1. See also Gibney, *The Building Site in Eighteenth-Century Ireland*.
61 Ayres, *Building the Georgian City*, 1.
62 McKellar, *The Birth of Modern London*, 94–5.
63 McKellar, *The Birth of Modern London*, 105.
64 Yeomans, 'Managing eighteenth-century building', 4.
65 Casey, 'Silent Partner', 134.
66 Kilburn-Topping, *Crafting Identities*, 3.
67 Lucey, *Building Reputations*.
68 Lucey, *Building Reputations*, 29.
69 Klein, 'Politeness and the interpretation of the British eighteenth century', 880–1.
70 Djabarouti and O'Flaherty, 'Architect and craftsperson: Project perceptions, relationships and craft', 425.

71 Campbell, 'Building a fortune'; Bertucci, *Artisanal Enlightenment*; Campbell, 'The finances of the carpenter in England'; Nègre, 'Craft knowledge in the age of encyclopedism'; Stephenson, *Contracts and Pay*; Kilburn-Toppin, *Crafting Identities*.

72 Casey, *Making Magnificence*; Lucey, *Building Reputations*; Casey and Hayes, *Enriching Architecture*.

References

Adamson, Glenn. *The Invention of Craft*. London: Bloomsbury, 2013.

Adamson, Glenn. *Craft: An American history*. London: Bloomsbury, 2021.

Arnold, Dana. *Reading Architectural History*. London: Routledge, 2002.

Ayres, James. *Building the Georgian City*. New Haven, CT and London: Yale University Press for the Paul Mellon Centre for Studies in British Art, 1998.

Baker, Malcolm. 'Sculpture for Palladian interiors: Rysbrack's reliefs and their setting'. In *Michael Rysbrack: Sculptor 1694–1770*, edited by Katherine Eustace, 35–41. Bristol: City of Bristol Museum and Art Gallery, 1982.

Beard, Geoffrey. *Georgian Craftsmen and Their Work*. London: Country Life, 1966.

Beard, Geoffrey. *Craftsmen and Interior Decoration in England 1660–1820*. London: John Bartholomew & Son, 1981.

Beard, Geoffrey. *Decorative Plasterwork in Great Britain*. London: Phaidon, 1975.

Belcher, John. *Later Renaissance Architecture in England: A series of examples of the domestic buildings erected subsequent to the Elizabethan period*. 2 vols. London: Batsford, 1901.

Bertucci, Paola. *Artisanal Enlightenment: Science and the mechanical arts in old regime France*. New Haven, CT: Yale University Press, 2017.

Blomfield, Reginald. *A History of Renaissance Architecture in England*. London: George Bell and Sons, 1897.

Bowett, Adam. *Woods in British Furniture-Making 1400–1900: An illustrated historical dictionary*. Wetherby: Oblong Creative and Royal Botanic Gardens, Kew, 2012.

Brett, David. *C. R. Mackintosh: The poetics of workmanship*. Boston: Harvard University Press, 1992.

Byrne, Helen. 'Simon Vierpyl (c.1725–1810), sculptor and stonemason'. In *Lord Charlemont and His Circle*, edited by Michael McCarthy, 177–94. Dublin: Four Courts Press, 2001.

Campbell, Colen. *Vitruvius Britannicus*. 3 vols. London: Printed for the author, 1715–25.

Campbell, James W. P. *Building Saint Paul's*. London: Thames and Hudson, 2007.

Campbell, James W. P. 'Building a fortune: The finances of the stonemasons working on the rebuilding of St Paul's Cathedral 1675–1720'. In *Proceedings of the Third International Congress on Construction History*, vol. 1: 297–304. Cottbus: Brandenburg University of Technology, 2009.

Campbell, James W. P. 'The finances of the carpenter in England, 1660–1710: A case study on the implications of the change from craft to designer-based construction'. In *L'Histoire de la construction / Construction History. Tome II. Relevé d'un Chantier Européen / Survey of a European Building Site*, vol. 2, edited by A. Becchi, R. Carvais and J. Sakarovitch, 697–736. Paris: Classiques Garnier, 2018. Accessed 14 December 2023. https://doi:10.15122/isbn.978-2-406-08245-3.

Casey, Christine. *Making Magnificence: Architects, stuccatori and the eighteenth-century interior*. New Haven, CT and London: Yale University Press, 2017.

Casey, Christine. 'Silent partner: Design and making in the early modern architecture of Britain', *R.A.: Revista de Arquitectura*, 23 (2021): 132–45. Accessed 14 December 2023. https://doi.org/10.15581/014.23.132-145.

Casey, Christine. 'Surface value: Ways of seeing decoration in architecture', *Architectural Histories*, 9:1 (2021): 1–17.

Casey, Christine and Melanie Hayes, eds. *Enriching Architecture: Craft and its conservation in Anglo-Irish building production, 1660–1760*. London: UCL Press, 2023. Accessed 14 December 2023. https://www.uclpress.co.uk/EnrichingArchitecture.

Casey, Christine and Conor Lucey, eds. *Decorative Plasterwork in Ireland and Europe: Ornament and the early modern interior*. Dublin: Four Courts Press, 2012.

Colvin, Howard. *A Biographical Dictionary of British Architects*, 1600–1840. 4th edition. New Haven, CT and London: Yale University Press, 2008.

Craig, Maurice. *Dublin 1660–1860: The shaping of a city*. London: Cresset Press, 1952.

Craig, Maurice. *The Architecture of Ireland: From the earliest times to 1880*. London: Batsford, 1982.

Curran, Constantine Peters. 'Dublin plaster work', *Journal of the Royal Society of Antiquaries of Ireland*, 10:1 (31 March 1940): 1–56.

Curran, Constantine Peters. 'The Parliament House 1728–1800'. In *The Bank of Ireland 1783–1946*, by F. G Hall, 425–54. Dublin: Hodges Figgis, 1949.

Curran, Constantine Peters. *Dublin Decorative Plasterwork of the Seventeenth and Eighteenth Centuries*. London: Alec Tiranti, 1967.

Djabarouti, J. and C. O'Flaherty. 'Architect and craftsperson: Project perceptions, relationships and craft', *Archnet-IJAR*, 14:3 (2020): 423–38. Accessed 14 December 2023. https://doi-org.elib.tcd.ie/10.1108/ARCH-01-2020-0010.

Downes, Kerry. *Hawksmoor*. London: Zwemmer, 1959.

Dyer, Walter. *Early American Craftsmen*. New York and London: The Century Company, 1915.

Dyer, Walter. *Creators of Decorative Styles: Being a survey of the decorative periods in England from 1600 to 1800, with special reference to the masters of applied art who developed the dominant styles*. New York: Doubleday, Page & Company, 1917.

Evelyn, John. 'An account of architects and architecture'. In *A Parallel of the Antient Architecture with the Modern*, by Roland Fréart de Chambray, translated by John Evelyn, 115–42. London: Thomas Roycroft for John Place, 1664.

Fergusson, James. *History of the Modern Styles of Architecture*. London: J. Murray, 1862.

Forty, Adrian. *Objects of Desire: Design and society since 1750*. London: Thames and Hudson, 1986.

Frayling, Christopher. *On Craftsmanship: Towards a new Bauhaus*. London: Oberon Books, 2011.

Friedman, Alice T. 'Architecture, authority, and the female gaze: Planning and representation in the early modern country house', *Assemblage* 18 (1992): 41–61. Accessed 14 December 2023. https://doi.org/10.2307/3171205.

Friedman, Alice T. 'Inside/Out: Women, domesticity, and the pleasures of the city'. In *Material London ca. 1600*, edited by Lena Cowen Orlin, 232–50. Philadelphia: University of Pennsylvania Press, 2000.

Gapper, Claire. 'The impact of Inigo Jones on London decorative plasterwork', *Architectural History*, 44 (2001): 82–7.

Gapper, Claire. 'The Caroline plasterwork at Ham House'. In *Ham House: Four hundred years of collecting and patronage*, edited by Christopher Rowell, 49–66. New Haven, CT and London: Yale University Press, 2013.

Georgian Society. *The Georgian Society Records of Eighteenth-Century Domestic Architecture and Decoration in Dublin*. 5 vols. Shannon: Irish University Press, 1909–13.

Gibbs, James. *A Book of Architecture*. London: n.p., 1728.

Gibney, Arthur. *The Building Site in Eighteenth-Century Ireland*, edited by L. Hurley and E. McParland. Dublin: Four Courts Press, 2017.

Girouard, Mark. *Life in the English Country House: A social and architectural history*. New Haven, CT and London: Yale University Press, 1978.

Glin, The Knight of and James Peil. *Irish Furniture: Woodwork and carving in Ireland from the earliest times to the Act of Union*. New Haven, CT and London: Yale University Press, 2007.

Godfrey, Walter. *The English Staircase*. London: Batsford, 1911.

Gomme, Andor. *Francis Smith of Warwick: Architect and master builder*. Stamford: Shaun Tyas, 2000.

Gomme, Andor. 'An eighteenth-century builder's notebook', *The Volume of the Walpole Society*, 67 (2005): 193–236. Accessed 24 January 2024. http://www.jstor.org/stable/41827683.

Gotch, Alfred. *The English Home, from Charles I to George IV*. New York: C. Scribner's Sons, 1918.

Gotch, Alfred. *Inigo Jones*. London: Methuen, 1928.

Gunnis, Rupert. *Dictionary of British Sculptors*. London: Odhams Press, 1953.

Gunther, R. T. *The Architecture of Sir Roger Pratt*. Oxford: Oxford University Press, 1928.

Hanson, Brian. *Architects and the 'Building World' from Chambers to Ruskin: Constructing authority*. Cambridge: Cambridge University Press, 2003.

Hardy, Emma, Ingrid Roscoe and M. G. Sullivan. *A Biographical Dictionary of Sculptors in Britain 1660–1851*. New Haven, CT and London: Yale University Press, 2009.

Harris, John. *Moving Rooms: The trade in architectural salvage*. New Haven, CT and London: Yale University Press, 2007.

Hayes, Melanie. 'Retrieving craft practice on the early eighteenth-century building site'. In *Enriching Architecture: Craft and its conservation in Anglo-Irish building production, 1660–1760,* edited by Christine Casey and Melanie Hayes, 160–96. London: UCL Press, 2023.

Hill, Oliver and John Cornforth. *English Country Houses: Caroline, 1625–1685*. London: Country Life, 1966.

Hussey, Christopher. *English Country Houses: Early Georgian, 1715–1760*. London: Country Life, 1955.

Hussey, Christopher. *English Country Houses: Mid Georgian, 1760–1800*. London: Country Life, 1956.

Hussey, Christopher. *English Country Houses: Late Georgian, 1800–1840*. London: Country Life, 1958.

Ingold, Tim. *Making: Anthropology, archaeology, art and architecture*. London: Routledge, 2013.

Jackson, Sir Thomas Graham. *The Renaissance of Roman Architecture*, Part 2: *England*. Cambridge: Cambridge University Press, 1922.

Jeffery, Paul. *The City Churches of Sir Christopher Wren*. London and Rio Grande: The Hambledon Press, 1996.

Jourdain, Margaret. *Furniture in England from 1660–1770*. London: Batsford, 1914.

Kilburn-Toppin, Jasmine. *Crafting Identities: Artisan culture in London, c.1550–1640*. Manchester: Manchester University Press, 2021.

Klein, Lawrence. 'Politeness and the interpretation of the British eighteenth century', *The Historical Journal*, 45:4 (2002): 880–1.

Latham, Charles and Henry Avray Tipping, eds. *In English Homes*. London: Country Life and George Newnes. New York: C. Scribner's Sons, 1904.

Likos Ricci, Patricia. 'Who is this Renaissance? Where did he come from?': Englishness and the search for an American national style, 1850–1900', *Architectural History*, 64 (2021): 45–68.

Loeber, Rolf. *Biographical Dictionary of Architects in Ireland 1600–1720*. London: J. Murray, 1981.

Lucey, Conor. *The Stapleton Collection: Designs for the Irish neoclassical interior*. Tralee: Churchill House Press, 2007.

Lucey, Conor. 'Classicism or commerce? The townhouse interior as commodity'. In *The Eighteenth-Century Dublin Town House*, edited by Christine Casey, 236–48. Dublin: Four Courts Press, 2010.

Lucey, Conor. 'British agents of the Irish Adamesque', *Architectural History*, 53 (2013):135–70.

Lucey, Conor. *Building Reputations: Architecture and the artisan, 1750–1830*. Manchester: Manchester University Press, 2018.

Martínez de Guereñu, Laura. 'Who designs architecture? On silenced and superimposed authorship', *R.A.: Revista de Arquitectura*, 23 (2021): 7–17. Accessed 14 December 2023. https://doi.org/10.15581/014.23.7-17.

McBride, Kari Boyd. *Country House Discourse in Early Modern England: A cultural study of landscape and legitimacy*. London: Routledge, 2001.

McDonnell, Joseph. *Irish Eighteenth-Century Stuccowork and its European Sources*. Dublin: The National Gallery of Ireland, 1991.

McKellar, Elizabeth. 'Representing the Georgian: Constructing interiors in early twentieth-century publications, 1890–1930', *Journal of Design History*, 20:4 (2007): 325–44. Accessed 14 December 2023. https://www.jstor.org/stable/25228552.

McKellar, Elizabeth. *The Birth of Modern London: The development and design of the city, 1660–1720*. Manchester: Manchester University Press, 2021.

McParland, Edward. *James Gandon: Vitruvius Hibernicus*. London: Zwemmer, 1985.

McParland, Edward. *Public Architecture in Ireland 1680–1760*. New Haven, CT and London: Yale University Press, 2001.

Morris, Robert. *An Essay in Defence of Ancient Architecture*. London: D. Browne, 1728.

Nègre, Valérie. 'Craft knowledge in the age of encyclopedism'. In *Crafting Enlightenment: Artisanal histories and transnational networks*, edited by Lauren R. Cannady and Jennifer Ferng, 303–34. Liverpool: Liverpool University Press, 2021.

Pallasmaa, Juhani. *The Thinking Hand: Existential and embodied wisdom in architecture*. Chichester: Wiley, 2009.

Payne, Alina. 'Materiality, crafting, and scale in Renaissance architecture', *Oxford Art Journal*, 32:3 (2009): 365–86. Accessed 14 December 2023. https://www.jstor.org/stable/25650875.

Payne, Alina. 'Materiality, ornament, and media overlaps'. In *Renaissance and Baroque Architecture*, edited by Alina Payne, 136–59. Chichester: Wiley & Sons, 2017.

Pye, David. *The Nature and Art of Workmanship*. Cambridge: Cambridge University Press, 1968.

Richardson, Albert E. *Monumental Classic Architecture in Great Britain and Ireland*. London: Batsford, 1914.

Rogers, John C. *English Furniture: Its essentials and characteristics simply and clearly explained for the student and small collector*. London: Country Life, 1923.

Rowan, Ann Martha. *Dictionary of Irish Architects*. Accessed 14 December 2023. https://www.dia.ie/.

Rowell, Christopher. 'Seventeenth century and later floors at Ham House'. In *Historic Floors: Their care and conservation*, edited by Jane Fawcett, 172–9. London: Routledge, 1998.

Rowell, Christopher, ed. *Ham House: Four hundred years of collecting and patronage*. New Haven, CT and London: Yale University Press, 2013.

Saint, Andrew. *The Image of the Architect*. New Haven, CT and London: Yale University Press, 1983.

Saint, Andrew. 'The conundrum of "by"'. In *Architectural History after Colvin: The Society of Architectural Historians of Great Britain Symposium 2011*, edited by Malcolm Airs and William Whyte, 58–70. Donington: Shaun Tyas, 2013.

Saumarez Smith, Charles. *Eighteenth-Century Decoration: Design and the domestic interior in England*. London: Weidenfeld & Nicholson, 1993.

Saunt, Jenny. 'The Abbotts and their book: A dynasty of decorative plasterers and their work in Devon, c.1580–1727', *Architectural History*, 64 (2021): 285–320.

Saunt, Jenny. 'Drawing out a surface in lime and hair'. In *Enriching Architecture: Craft and its conservation in Anglo-Irish building production 1660–1760*, edited by Christine Casey and Melanie Hayes, 262–88. London: UCL Press, 2023.

Scott, Geoffrey. *The Architecture of Humanism: A study in the history of taste*. New York: W. W. Norton & Company, 1974.

Scott, Katie. *The Rococo Interior: Decoration and social spaces in early eighteenth-century Paris*. New Haven, CT and London: Yale University Press, 1995.

Sennet, Richard. *The Craftsman*. New Haven, CT and London: Yale University Press, 2008.

Smith, Pamela H., Amy R. W. Meyers and Harold J. Cook, eds. *Ways of Making and Knowing: The material culture of empirical knowledge*. Ann Arbor: University of Michigan Press, 2014.

Stephenson, Judy. *Contracts and Pay: Work in London construction 1660–1785*. Cham: Palgrave Macmillan, 2020. Accessed 14 December 2023. https://doi.org/10.1007/978-3-319-57508-7.

Stevenson, Christine. *The City and the King: Architecture and politics in Restoration London*. New Haven, CT and London: Yale University Press, 2013.

Summerson, John. *John Nash: Architect to King George IV*. London: Allen & Unwin, 1935.

Summerson, John. *Architecture in Britain 1530–1830*. London: Penguin, 1953.

Summerson, John. *Sir Christopher Wren*. London: Collins, 1953.

Thornton, Peter. *Form and Decoration: Innovation in the decorative arts 1470–1870*. London: Weidenfeld & Nicolson, 1998.

Tierney, Andrew. 'Reviving the artisan sculptor: The role of Ruskin, science and art education'. In *The Museum Building of Trinity College Dublin: A model of Victorian craftsmanship*, edited by Christine Casey and Patrick Wyse Jackson, 189–216. Dublin: Four Courts Press, 2019.

Tipping, Henry Avray. *Grinling Gibbons and the Woodwork of His Age (1648–1720)*. London: Country Life, 1914.

Tipping, Henry Avray. *English Homes*. 6 vols. London: Country Life, 1920–26.

Turner, Laurence A. and W. Henry Ward. 'The crafts at St Paul's'. In *Sir Christopher Wren, A.D. 1632–1723: Bicentenary memorial volume*, 83–114. London: Hodder & Stoughton, 1923.

Van Eck, Caroline, ed. *British Architectural Theory 1540–1750: An anthology of texts*. Aldershot: Ashgate Publishing, 2003.

Ware, Isaac. *A Complete Body of Architecture*. London: T. Osborne and J. Shipton, 1756.

Watkin, David. *The Rise of Architectural History*. London: Architectural Press, 1980.

Webb, G. 'The letters and drawings of Nicholas Hawksmoor relating to the building of the mausoleum at Castle Howard 1726–1742', *The Volume of the Walpole Society*, 19 (1930): 111–64.

Whiffen, Marcus. *Thomas Archer*. London: Art and Technics, 1950.

Whyte, William. 'The success of Sir Howard Colvin'. In *Architectural History after Colvin*: *The Society of Architectural Historians of Great Britain Symposium 2011*, edited by Malcolm Airs and William Whyte, 1–17. Donington: Shaun Tyas, 2013.

Wilson, R. and A. Mackley. *Creating Paradise: The building of the English country house, 1660–1880*. London: Hambledon Continuum, 2000.

Yeomans, David. 'Managing eighteenth-century building', *Construction History*, 4 (1988): 3–19.

Part 1
Practice

1

Architect and mason-architect: Inigo Jones, Nicholas Stone and the development of the open-well suspended stone stair in the 1630s

Gordon Higgott and Adam White

The open-well suspended stone stair owes its origins in Britain to the royal architect and stage designer Inigo Jones (1573–1652), who studied Palladio's famous oval stair at the Convento della Carità in Venice during a visit in August 1614, and became Surveyor of the King's Works in October the following year. It is well known that Palladio's stair was the source for Jones's celebrated round stair, or 'Tulip Stair', at the Queen's House, Greenwich Palace. But though Jones planned this stair when work started on the basement and ground floor of the villa in 1616–18, for Queen Anne of Denmark (who died in 1619), it was not built until the second phase of work, when the architectural shell was completed, from 1632 to 1635, for Queen Henrietta Maria. It was then that almost all the features in Portland stone in the villa were put in hand.

To this second phase belongs the less familiar South Stair at the Queen's House. This large rectangular open-well suspended stone stair has been mistaken for an eighteenth- or early nineteenth-century reconstruction, but the stonework is in fact original. The stair was intended to provide access to the first floor of the villa through the entrance range on the south side, within the royal park. A room bridging a public road between the park and the garden of the palace led to the gallery around the great hall in the north range and to the queen's apartments. The Tulip Stair in the north range connected the hall with these apartments, and to a roof platform above the queen's Cabinet Room on the east side.

Both suspended stone stairs at the Queen's House – so essential to the functioning of Jones's unusual bridge-villa, flanking both sides of a public road – were unprecedented structures in Britain at that time. They could not have been built without the close involvement of Jones's colleague in the Office of Works, the mason, sculptor and architect, Nicholas Stone (c.1587–1647). Stone had served as Jones's master-mason at the Banqueting House, Whitehall in 1619–22, and he became royal master mason in October 1632, shortly after work resumed at the Queen's House. That he contributed to the *design* of both these stairs is now apparent from a large, suspended stone stair that he built himself at Kirby Hall in Northamptonshire in 1638–40. Previously thought to date from the 1670s, this daring structure is strikingly similar in construction and carved ornament to the two stairs at the Queen's House. It indicates Stone's vital role in the development of a distinctive type of stair – known in France as *'l'escalier à l'anglaise'*[1] – that was to become prevalent in classical-revival buildings in Britain and Ireland in the eighteenth and early nineteenth centuries.[2]

Several characteristics of the open-well suspended stair in Britain and Ireland stand out. One is its naked structural form. The treads of the stair are not carried on vaults, as in many contemporary French and Italian examples, but form a self-supporting structure.[3] Each tread interlocks with the one below while being held in place by the staircase wall, which resists the rotation of the treads from the downward pressure of the cumulative weight above. The ends of the treads are 'open string', or exposed to view, and the soffits are usually moulded or cut back in sunken panels in such a way as to reduce the weight of the stonework and add visual interest.[4] The balustrade is typically in wrought iron, consisting of posts, scrollwork balusters, or a combination of the two. Such stairs allowed light to pass down the central well, illuminating the moulded soffits of the treads. These stairs positively invite ascent and require no further embellishment to achieve a striking visual effect.

Inigo Jones and the open-well suspended stone stair in Italy

When, in about 1608, Inigo Jones first turned to architecture, while working as a stage designer at the court of King James I in London, he studied Palladio's chapter 'On stairs and their various types' in Book I, Chapter 28 of *I Quattro Libri dell'Architettura* (Fig. 1.1).[5] Jones had trained as a painter and joiner and had travelled in Italy sometime between 1597

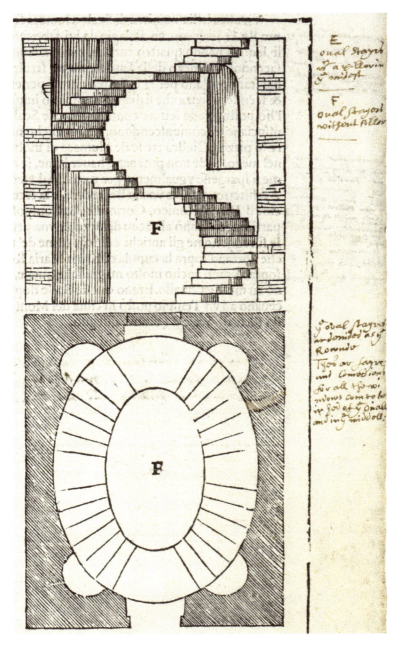

Figure 1.1: Inigo Jones's annotated copy of Palladio's *I Quattro Libri dell'Architettura* (Venice, 1601), Book I, p. 63, showing section and plan of Palladio's oval stair.

Reproduced by permission of the Provost and Fellows of Worcester College, Oxford.

and 1603, but though he was keenly interested in Renaissance design and its sources in Antiquity he knew little about masonry construction when he began his architectural studies.[6] In his chapter, Palladio describes the positioning, proportioning and lighting of stone-built stairs and especially commends the circular and oval stair with a central void rather than a solid core, 'because they can be lit from above and those who are at the top of the stair can see everyone coming up, or about to ascend, and can likewise be seen by them'. He adds that his oval stair at the Convento della Carità in Venice 'succeeds admirably'.[7] However, Palladio, who had worked as a stonemason, neither explains nor illustrates how such stairs are built. He does not indicate how far the steps are inserted into the wall and leaves out balustrades from all his diagrams, presumably to show the stone structure more clearly. In Fig. 1.1 his section through an oval open-well stair omits the window and does not show how the staircase is lit from above.[8] Only by seeing a built example in Italy, and by reading more widely, was Jones able to understand the design and construction of this type of stair.

Jones knew from Palladio that there were two open-well triangular stairs at the Pantheon in Rome.[9] He travelled around Italy with Lord Arundel between July 1613 and September the following year and was in Rome by 2 January 1614. He went with Arundel to Naples in late February and returned in May. On the last day of that month he inspected the Pantheon for a second or third time.[10] Jones was impressed by the structural ingenuity of the Pantheon stairs, which rise behind the north-facing portico, through six levels, to the base of the dome. He sketched a plan of the east stair (the better preserved of the two), in a space on the plate next to the west stair (Fig. 1.2).[11] Jones's sketch corrects Palladio's plan by adding a small straight flight at the sharp end of the triangle. In the margin he observes how each flight is carried on an arch which supports the arch under the next flight to maintain the same headroom: 'Rome 1614. This staire is as that of Capua but Trianglle and on[e] Arch beares up another butting against yt so that yf you begin the first to have head roome all the rest ryse equally on[e] over the other'. He was recalling the stairs he had recently seen at the Roman amphitheatre at Capua, on the route to Naples, where the barrel-vaulted flights rise around a solid wall in parallel flights, rather than in four suspended flights around a triangular void, with the vault of each flight giving support to the one above.[12]

However, it was a suspended stone staircase built around an oval void that caught Jones's imagination when, on his return to Venice in August 1614, he paid a second visit to the Convento della Carità (now

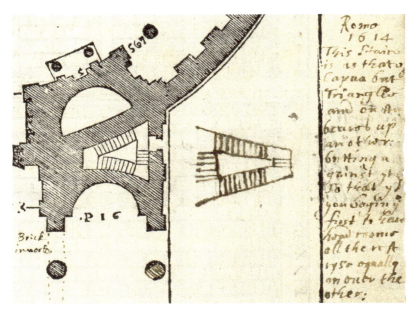

Figure 1.2: Inigo Jones's annotated copy of Palladio's *I Quattro Libri dell'Architettura* (Venice, 1601), Book IV, p. 75. Sketch-plan of east stair at the Pantheon, with note dated 1614.

Reproduced by permission of the Provost and Fellows of Worcester College, Oxford.

the Gallerie dell'Accademia). Here he made notes and sketches about Palladio's most celebrated stair, built in the early 1560s (Figs 1.3 and 1.4).[13] It rises through three storeys and originally gave access to a roof terrace around a giant Corinthian atrium. This internal court was part of Palladio's unfinished project to reconstruct the monastery on the pattern of an ancient Roman house. The atrium was destroyed by fire in 1630 and its loss has obscured the significance of the stair as a primary route up to a roof terrace, carried on the giant columns. After walking around the roof terrace and commenting on its poor wooden construction Jones wrote enthusiastically, 'the Ovall staire vacuo is exellent and ther goeth an apogio [balustrade] of Iorne up to the tope'.[14] He noted that the iron posts of the balustrade were fastened on the outside of the steps and he was struck by the upward-sloping soffits of the treads, adding 'Sloping of the staires' above his sketch.[15] This also shows an upward curve beneath a lip at the ends of the treads. These features reduced the bulk of the masonry, and they anticipated the more refined methods of cutting back the soffits that Jones was to develop with Nicholas Stone at the Queen's House (see Figs 1.8 and 1.9).

ARCHITECT AND MASON-ARCHITECT 31

Figure 1.3: Palladio's oval stair at the Convento della Carità, Venice (now the Gallerie dell'Accademia), early 1560s. Windows and landing at second-floor level.

Photograph © Gordon Higgott, 2015.

Jones admired the lighting of Palladio's oval stair, sketching a plan marked 'Lume'. He observed how some windows had been cut into niches, and that one of the landings had been built across a window to maintain uniformity in the openings on the outside.[16] Significantly, Jones returned to this page in the 1630s to rewrite his note on this subject in ink: 'the third half pace of the staire breakes the window to be uniforme without'.[17] In the same period he noted in his copy of Vincenzo Scamozzi's *L'Idea della Architettura Universale* (Venice, 1615) the Venetian architect's advice on lighting open-well stairs from above. In Scamozzi's chapter on his Villa Corner ('*il Cornaron*'), at Poisolo, Castelfranco (1588) Jones transferred to the margin of the plan the architect's comment on the staircase in this building: 'F oval Staires with a lanterne or fano on the topp wch gives sufficient light'.[18] Scamozzi does not show the lantern in his elevation of the villa, and Jones did not see the building, but this example probably encouraged him to set a large octagonal roof lantern above his round staircase at the Queen's

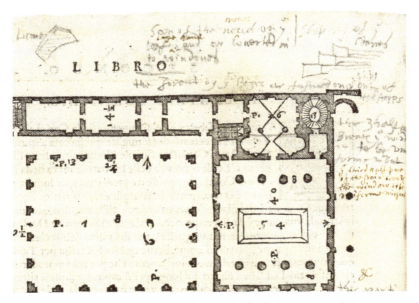

Figure 1.4: Inigo Jones's annotated copy of Palladio's *I Quattro Libri dell'Architettura* (Venice, 1601), Book II, p. 30. Notes, with sketches, of the oval stair at the Convento della Carità, 10 August 1614.

Reproduced by permission of the Provost and Fellows of Worcester College, Oxford.

House, since Palladio also recommended lighting such stairs from above. The Queen's House lantern was reduced to a low octagonal base in the nineteenth century, but originally it rose higher than the chimney stacks, and had windows on all sides with an opening for access to a roof platform on the east side of the north range. This feature first appears in a drawing of the north elevation of the building in about 1635 and in a topographical view by Wenceslaus Hollar in 1637.[19]

Jones's two suspended stone stairs at the Queen's House, Greenwich, 1632–5

Jones became Surveyor of the King's Works on 1 October 1615 and a year later began the villa now known as the Queen's House, for Queen Anne of Denmark, at her palace at Greenwich.[20] A plan for a long lodging with a central square hall, 40 feet wide, with an adjoining circular suspended stone stair, can be associated with the first phase of its design (Fig. 1.5).[21] This initial plan anticipates the north range of the completed villa (Fig. 1.6), in the garden of the palace, although its central hall

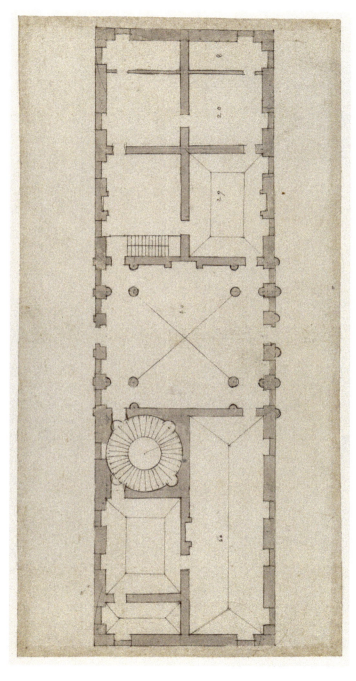

Figure 1.5: Inigo Jones. Plan of a long lodging, probably for the Queen's House, Greenwich, 1616. Pen and brown ink with brown wash, 200 × 404 mm.

RIBA Drawings and Archives Collection; Jones & Webb, 18.

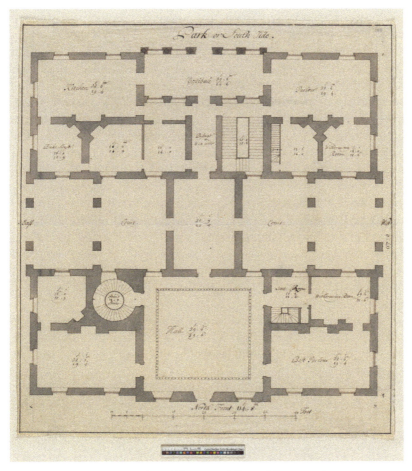

Figure 1.6: John James. Plan of the ground floor of the Queen's House, Greenwich, including the first-floor loggia on the south side, circa 1718.

Reproduced by permission of the Provost and Fellows of Worcester College, Oxford; Colvin catalogue no. 209.

is a single-storey space, with four columns supporting an upper floor, rather than the two-storey 'Cube Hall' of the finished building. The open-well round staircase adjoining the hall in this plan is 20 feet in diameter (6.1 m). This is half the width of the hall, and far larger than the completed stair (14 feet 6 inches (4.4 m) in diameter); but it is similar in size to the Carità stair (20 feet 4 inches (6.2 m) on its longer axis), which suggests that Jones recalled the impressive dimensions of this structure. It would have been the principal stair of the lodging, leading up to the first-floor apartments, and probably also to a roof platform, but it is drawn schematically, without landings at the openings and with two niches oddly positioned in relation to the doors.

At this early stage in his career as Surveyor of the King's Works, Jones was enamoured with the idea of a round suspended stone staircase, but not yet able to master its detailed design. He was still learning his trade as an architect, and did not gain access to Scamozzi's comprehensive, two-volume architectural treatise, *L'Idea della Architettura Universale*, until he acquired a copy on 25 March 1617, more than six months after work had begun at the Queen's House. In notes of c. 1618–20 in the two chapters dealing with staircases in Parts I and II of the treatise, Jones summarised Scamozzi's main observations on their planning and construction.[22] In the chapter on construction in Part II he noted that the treads of those rising in straight flights around solid newels should be embedded in the walls; but he passed over without comment Scamozzi's advice that the treads of suspended stairs carried on vaults should be recessed into the full depth of the wall, or by one-and-a-half or two blocks of stone, writing simply: 'how the waales of the Stares must be maad / the endes of the Staires Putt into the waall / others layd on voltes'. Jones probably knew, by the late 1610s, that he could rely on masons in the Office of Works to solve such problems for him. Indeed, this proved to be the case, when Nicholas Stone began working with him at the Queen's House in the 1630s.

When work stopped at the villa, in April 1618, Jones had finished the brick structure in an H-plan, in two parallel ranges linked by a bridge over the public road that separated the garden of the palace from its hunting park.[23] King Charles I granted Greenwich Palace and its hunting park to Queen Henrietta Maria in 1628–9.[24] Within a year the queen had appointed Jones as her personal surveyor at Greenwich, paying him a pension of £20 a year.[25] Work resumed in the summer of 1632 and in October that year Nicholas Stone became the royal master mason.[26] He was well acquainted with Portland stone, a strong, dense white limestone from the Isle of Portland which was ideally suited for the steps and landings of suspended stone stairs (see below).[27]

Stone must have collaborated closely with Jones on the design and construction of the architectural shell of the Queen's House, finished in 1635 (the date on a plaque on the north range), but no records exist of his activities or those of other artisans at the building, save for minor additional works in 1638–9. This is because there are no accounts for the completion and fitting out of the villa, which was paid for privately by the queen and not audited by the king's Office of Works. All we have is a series of warrants issued by the queen's paymaster, Henry Wickes, between

36   BETWEEN DESIGN AND MAKING

June 1632 and March 1638, totalling £7,500, and three 'bounties', each of £100, paid to Jones in 1634, 1637–8 and 1639–40.[28] Nevertheless, the design and construction of the two open-well stone suspended stairs at the Queen's House – the principal stair in the south range and the Tulip Stair in the north range – must belong to the second phase, beginning in 1632, since little was spent on masonry in the first phase.[29]

The Tulip Stair has long been regarded as the principal staircase at the Queen's House, but the arrangement of flights and half-landings suggests that, when work resumed at the house in 1632, Jones planned this as a secondary staircase. It is relatively small in diameter and there are no half-landings in the lower flight between ground- and first-floor levels. This implies a route *down* to the ground floor from the first-floor gallery around the hall, rather than up, as there are two half-landings in the upper flight, which gives access to a roof platform (see Fig. 1.9). The reason for this is that Jones planned the south range as the main entrance to the villa. The loggia above the entrance hall gave views of the park during the hunt, as did the roof platform on the north range.[30] After the hunt, the royal party would have entered through the south range. Only when the terrace and front steps were added to the north side in 1635–6 did the Great Hall become the principal point of entry to the villa.

The South Stair rises in straight flights, with quarter turns, in a large rectangular hall behind the entrance vestibule and loggia and is plainly the principal stair of the building (Fig. 1.7). The queen's apartments in the north range of the villa were reached from here through the room bridging the road and around the gallery of the two-storey hall on the north side. In the five years until the cessation of work in 1641, Henrietta Maria restricted her use of the villa to the more private north range and concerned herself almost exclusively with the decoration of the central hall and her apartments at first-floor level on that side.[31] Apart from the plaster barrel-vault over the South Stair, no equivalent decorative work was undertaken in the apartments on the opposite side.[32] The semi-abandoned state of the south range in the later 1630s appears to have had consequences for the decorative treatment of this staircase.

The principal stair in the south range of the Queen's House is, in fact, a hybrid of the stone and carpentry open-well types. The upper flight has a moulded wooden top step which forms part of a deep timber landing, faced with an architrave (Fig. 1.8a). In 1937 George Chettle noted the 'awkward junction of the upper flight with the first-floor landing' and concluded that the staircase had been reconstructed at a later period.[33] But there is no evidence in the eighteenth- or nineteenth-century works

ARCHITECT AND MASON-ARCHITECT

Figure 1.7: The South Stair at the Queen's House. Balustrade, circa 1760, installed in 1936.

Photograph © Gordon Higgott, 2023.

accounts for such an intervention.[34] Moreover, the treads of the stair display heavy wear and tear consistent with nearly four centuries of use. It would seem that Jones and Stone, lacking any built precedent in England for an open-well suspended stone stair on a rectangular plan, looked to contemporary carpentry stairs for a method of treating the soffits of the treads and half-landings. An unusual feature of the South Stair, not found in later stone-built examples, is the dressing of the soffits of the treads with plain chamfers (Fig. 1.8b). This chamfering was probably intended both as a means of reducing the bulk of the stonework, as in Palladio's oval stair, and to create continuous sloping surfaces rendered in plaster, with painted or relief ornaments on the soffits, as on contemporary open-well carpentry staircases.[35] Jones's background in joinery and carpentry may explain what appears to be an attempt to combine stone and timber features in the design of this stair. Alongside these unresolved features is an innovation of consequence for later stairs of this type: the continuation of the nosing profile around the sides of the treads to create a full 'open string'. This treatment was made

Figure 1.8a: The South Stair at the Queen's House. Detail of the top steps and the timber landing.

Photograph © Gordon Higgott, 2023.

Figure 1.8b: The South Stair at the Queen's House. Central flight and half-landings, showing riser rebates and chamfered soffits.

Photograph © Gordon Higgott, 2023.

possible by fixing the iron balustrade on the tops of the treads, a method common on stone stairs of all types in Italy at this time.

The South Stair has also lost its original iron balustrade. It was replaced in the nineteenth century by another of the same type, with two posts on each tread, probably using the original fixing holes.[36] This balustrade was replaced in 1936 by an ornate wrought-iron example of c.1760, taken from Pembroke House, Whitehall, shortly before its demolition.[37] The Pembroke House balustrade has single, S-shaped scrolls on each tread and a mahogany handrail which ramps up smoothly to the half-landings and top landing of the stair. Jones's handrail, if made of wood, could not have run continuously, as techniques for moulding and jointing such handrails in smooth curves were not widely available until the 1680s.[38] Inadequacies in the detailing of the original balustrade, which may have had an iron handrail, like that of the Tulip Stair (Fig. 1.9), could explain its loss in the nineteenth century.

Both stone stairs at the Queen's House have a method of joining the steps in rebates at the bottoms of the risers, which is not found in suspended stone stairs by Palladio and Scamozzi (see Figs 1.8b and 1.10). This important innovation can be attributed with confidence to Nicholas Stone.[39] In Palladio's oval stair each step is recessed deeply into the wall and rests on the back of the one below, transferring the load downwards in a continuous action (see Fig. 1.3).[40] Joining the steps in rebates while recessing them into the wall prevents clockwise and anticlockwise rotation along the full length of each step. Moreover, flights with jointed treads tend to function as single units and are therefore stronger at the junctions with quarter-landings in rectangular stairs. Indeed, it may have been the structural challenge of building a suspended stair in straight flights with quarter turns that prompted Jones and Stone to introduce

Figure 1.9: The Tulip Stair at the Queen's House. Looking up to the first-floor landing, entrance to the gallery, and upper flight.

Photography © Gordon Higgott, 2016.

Figure 1.10: The Tulip Stair at the Queen's House. Detail of the first landing of the upper flight.

Photography © Gordon Higgott, 2016.

this detail. The riser rebate, known as the 'pencheck' in Scotland, was widely adopted in a variety of forms in later stone suspended stairs in Britain.[41]

The Tulip Stair is celebrated for its wrought-iron balustrade, in which decorative panels, formed as scrolled lily flowers (later described as tulips), are joined to slender iron posts, which are placed centrally on each tread (see Fig. 1.9). The posts are fixed to the sides of the treads, as on Palladio's oval stair in Venice, but with the addition of leaf-shaped flanges. The scrolled lily flowers curl down across the sides of the treads, which are cut flush, so that the baluster panels can run across the nosings. They rise in elegant S-shapes and are connected to the handrails by undulating iron bars that are fixed with bolts to the lily flowers. The panels at the landings are doubled scrolled lilies with a single central lily flower and two undulating bars. The staircase today has 75 single lily-flower panels and five double panels at the landings.

Remarkable though this decorative treatment is, there is no record of the design or execution of the balustrade in the 1630s. It is first mentioned in an account by the ironsmith Richard Ashworth in June 1665 for repairs and additions to 'the round stair case in the Queens new buildings' (meaning the Queen's House).[42] These works were substantial. They involved 30 new 'branches', or scrolled lily flowers, and seven new 'half Double branches', or doubled scrolled lilies for the landings. In addition, Ashworth fixed 49 new 'half Branches', which cost half as much as the full branches (3s. 6d. compared with 7s.). These half branches are probably the undulating bars that join the lilies to the handrail. He also installed 18 new square bars and was paid a small sum for 'fastening the old barrs to the Rails being flown out from them'. The works were done when Henrietta Maria was resident again at Greenwich Palace as the dowager Queen Mother, having returned to England soon after the Restoration of Charles II in May that year. She left England for France for the last time at the end of June 1665, after undertaking large-scale works at her palaces of Somerset House and Greenwich, those at the latter including the addition of outer bridge-rooms linking the ends of the two ranges of the Queen's House and much internal decoration.[43] At the very least, we can surmise that Henrietta Maria judged her round staircase inadequate when she returned to her villa in the early 1660s, and ordered the repair and completion of its wrought-iron balustrade, including the replacement of all the double-scrolled lilies on the landings. The shortcomings of Jones's wrought-iron balustrade were probably the result of his attempt to enrich Palladio's simple form of iron-post balustrade with decorative panels fixed between them, an innovation that may have been connected with a change in the status of this staircase in the late 1630s, when it became the de facto principal stair of the building.

Inigo Jones and Nicholas Stone

Nicholas Stone had worked intermittently in the Office of the King's Works (the royal building department) since 1616, when he was summoned to help with the fitting out of the Chapel Royal and chapel closet at Holyrood Palace in Edinburgh, because no-one could be found locally to do the work.[44] At the time he was a young man in his late twenties or early thirties and had only recently finished his training under Hendrick de Keyser in Amsterdam. The work he did at Holyrood was mainly, if not entirely, in wood, a material with which thereafter he had little to do, except when it was needed for the buildings he erected. Primarily he worked as De Keyser did, as a sculptor, master mason and architect.[45]

In England at the time there was no separate profession of sculptor: training was governed by materials, so that apprentices who learned to work in stone and marble could learn their use in buildings as well as in statues and ornament. The master mason and the carver of statues were often the same person and Stone developed this combination of skills to a very high degree. In London the full range of this work was regulated by the Masons' Company. Stone held office in the company from 1626 onwards, serving as Master in 1632–4.

Stone's work at Holyrood brought him into contact with Inigo Jones, who was almost certainly instrumental in gaining him the commission, although his writ as Surveyor, the head of the department, did not run north of the English border. Thereafter the two men were close colleagues for the rest of their working lives. It was very fortunate for Stone that the master mason in the King's Works, William Cure the Younger (d. 1632) was not well regarded, for this caused Jones to put work his way, even though he held no official position. It was he, and not Cure, who undertook the most important royal building commission of the Jacobean period, the erection of the Banqueting House, Whitehall, after Cure absented himself when work began in 1619.[46] As soon as a suitable post fell vacant in the King's Works, Stone was appointed to it. In 1626 he succeeded William Suthes as master mason at Windsor Castle. On his appointment, the title of the post was changed to master mason and Architect, the first time that the word 'architect' had been so used in England, implying that, at Windsor, Stone had a role in building design which was not allowed to him elsewhere. This was a measure of Jones's confidence in him, and it is no surprise to find that when the office of master mason finally became free, on Cure's death in August 1632, Stone was appointed. The queen had ordered the completion of her villa at Greenwich in June of that year, and her Surveyor, Inigo Jones, now turned to his trusted colleague to put his designs into execution.

We know what Stone did, mainly from two documents: a notebook which covered the years 1614–41, almost his entire working life as an independent mason-sculptor in England, and an account book which was kept in his workshop for the last twelve years of his career, 1631–42.[47] They provide far more information than we have for any of his professional contemporaries, yet the record of his work which they give is known to be incomplete, even for the years covered by both of them. Other account books would have been kept in his workshop: one for the Whitehall Banqueting House is recorded,[48] but is now lost, and others no doubt existed. The two surviving manuscripts thus serve as an invaluable resource for a reconstruction of Stone's *oeuvre* but they do not

ARCHITECT AND MASON-ARCHITECT

in themselves provide it. The Queen's House at Greenwich is not even mentioned in the notebook, and the account book only records a few minor tasks there, mainly paving work,[49] but the circumstantial evidence that Stone was in charge of the completion of the building is extremely strong. When it came to the two staircases, Stone had expertise which Jones lacked. Jones knew how to design a building and by this date he knew a great deal about the theory of architecture but he had no hands-on experience of making a stone staircase of this kind stand up. The two staircases were highly adventurous in this regard. Their success depended on the stone – and the individual stones – of which they were made. They had to be dense and strong and to have no cracks or flaws, and to be very precisely fitted together, otherwise the whole structure could collapse.

Stone's surname was probably occupational, like Taylor or Smith. He is said, on reasonable authority, to have been the son of a 'quarry man', that is a stonemason who owned his own quarry. The 'quarry man' in question can probably be identified with one 'John Stone, freemason', who was buried at Sidbury, Devon, near the south coast of the county[50] and some way west of the famous limestone quarries at Beer. Generations of stonemasons may have preceded him, hence the family name. Trading in stone and marble was the bread and butter of the family business. Stone went to law over these valuable commodities[51] which were imported and exported over the North Sea, sometimes in transactions with the De Keyser family,[52] long after Stone had returned to England. Commerce in stone and marble continued to support the family during the English Civil War when commissions for sculpture and buildings were thin on the ground. Stone's intimate knowledge of his materials was developed in the carving of effigies in marble and alabaster, on the tombs he made. For a full-length effigy, which was normally recumbent on a tomb chest, it mattered greatly that the main part of the figure should be made of a single, unblemished piece of material, particularly when white marble came into vogue in the early years of the seventeenth century. The ability to select blocks of material suitable for their purpose was an important element of the sculptor's skill.

Nicholas Stone's open-well suspended stone stair at Kirby Hall, Northamptonshire, 1638–40

Stone was retained in the King's Works on the understanding that the king's business had first claim on his time. He was paid by the task for the work he did; beyond this, he was free to do as he chose and he also ran a flourishing business as a sculptor and master mason for private clients, on occasion acting as the designer of the buildings which he erected. Prominent among these clients was Sir Christopher Hatton (1605–1670), later Lord Hatton of Kirby. Hatton was the squire of Kirby Hall, near Corby in Northamptonshire. He had inherited the house from his father in 1619 and proceeded to remodel it. The core of the building, south of the forecourt, or 'Green Court', was an Elizabethan mansion which had been built by Sir Humphrey Stafford from 1570 onwards, probably around an existing house, and was left incomplete at his death five years later (Fig. 1.11).[53] By 1578 it had been sold to Sir Christopher's ancestor, Sir Christopher Hatton, sometime Lord Chancellor to Queen Elizabeth I. From him it passed down the family, the third Sir Christopher being the fourth Hatton owner. From the late eighteenth century onwards, the house was not fully lived in and in the early nineteenth century it was largely abandoned. In its present ruined state it is sad to behold, but also a source of much fascination, since features have survived which would almost certainly have been replaced if later generations of the Hatton family and their successors, the Finch-Hattons, had continued to maintain it.

This lack of maintenance makes it possible to see some aspects of Stone's work more clearly than would otherwise be possible. His account book reveals three consignments of goods that were supplied to the third Sir Christopher in 1638–40, from Stone's workshop in London, some of them being specifically mentioned as being destined for Kirby Hall.[54] The goods in question range from '4 cartoses' (cartouches) and a 'sheald of portland ston', the latter despatched in July 1639, to 'the Iron work of on[e] window' for which transport had been paid in the previous May. Then there was a Portland bust of Apollo, twice life-size, which was sent in July or August 1640. Most significantly for the present discussion, on 27 May 1639 Stone paid one Peter Walker the sum of £1 10s. 'for the modell of the starecase' which was intended for the house.

It has long been recognised that Stone did far more work at Kirby than the account book records. The fragmentary character of the written evidence is apparent from two of the payments, those for the cartouches and the window ironwork. These were made to a carrier, one Sparow Smeth or Smith, for transport to the site rather than for the objects themselves and if it were not for this passing reference to the transport we would know nothing about them. The only transaction recorded with Hatton himself is a part payment which was 'receved of Ser Christopher Hatton's man' in July 1638, for a marble chimneypiece 'to be spedely don'. It may have been destined for Kirby, but may not.

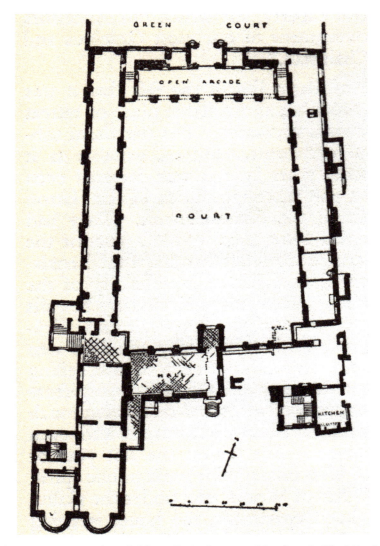

Figure 1.11: Part-plan of Kirby Hall, Northamptonshire, from J. Alfred Gotch, *Old Halls and Manor Houses of Northamptonshire* (London, 1936, p. 18), showing the south-east staircase at bottom right.

Because the accounts are so incomplete, stylistic and typological evidence becomes all the more important. The north range of the courtyard has pedimented window architraves on the first and second floors which are characteristic of the 1630s (Fig. 1.12). The late Mark Girouard discovered that some of the details are derived from plates in a treatise published in 1590 by Domenico Fontana, a copy of which was

Figure 1.12: Kirby Hall, Northamptonshire. The north range of the courtyard.
Photograph by Cameron Newham.

bought in Rome in 1639 by Stone's son, Nicholas Stone the Younger, at his father's request.[55] The same north range is adorned by no fewer than six of the newly-fashionable 'pergolas', balconies with ironwork. Each of them is approached through a door framed by an architrave and surmounted by an open segmental pediment with a pair of small scrolls in the opening. Pediments of this type were a favourite device of Stone's. On the courtyard side of the north range, the opening in the pediment is filled by the bust of Apollo which Stone sent to Kirby in 1640. There was probably a complementary bust, in the equivalent position, in the pedimented frame of the doorway behind the pergola, above the door to the Great Hall on the opposite side of the courtyard, this being another feature which Stone had added to the building.[56] His hand can be recognised elsewhere at Kirby, in the two-storey tower which Sir Christopher added to the north range, for example (Fig. 1.13) and in the refenestration of the forecourt side and in two garden gateways, one of which was later moved to the forecourt of the house.[57] He was also probably responsible for decorating – or redecorating – Sir Christopher's long gallery, on the west side of the courtyard, with a ribbed plaster ceiling, of which only fragments now survive.

Sir Christopher's work at Kirby appears to have been interrupted by the English Civil War (1642–51). After that he seems to have lost interest in the house, or perhaps ran out of money, leaving it to his son, Christopher Hatton (1632–1706), 2nd Baron and 1st Viscount Hatton, to

Figure 1.13: Kirby Hall, Northamptonshire. The north range from the forecourt side, showing the central tower.

Photograph by Cameron Newham.

develop it and bring it up to date. The abortive character of the building in the third Sir Christopher's day can still be seen at the south-east corner, adjacent to the kitchen quarters, where there is a large open-well suspended stone stair, enclosed within a tower which is almost square in form (Fig. 1.14).

A similar staircase in roughly the same position is shown in the ground-floor plan of the house, dated 1570, which is among the Thorpe drawings in the Soane Museum, London. The plan shows the stairs adjoining a south-east wing which differs substantially from what was eventually built.[58] As executed, the staircase tower is set on a basement and is formed of two stages. Three different materials have been used in its construction. The basement is of limestone rubble which is also used for most of the north wall, where the building once adjoined an existing structure and now descends into ruin. The lower stage, which contains the staircase, is of brick, while the top stage is of limestone ashlar, on the west, south and east sides. Inside, the staircase rises in three flights around an open well and is suspended from the walls (Fig. 1.15). The whole edifice was clearly designed to impress, with two pairs of niches in the walls between the first and second flights and the second and third flights, all possibly intended for sculpture, or candles to light the stairs. Almost certainly, it was left incomplete. It has no rail and no fixings for

Figure 1.14: Kirby Hall, Northamptonshire. The south-east staircase tower, view from the south-west.

Photograph by Cameron Newham.

Figure 1.15: Kirby Hall, Northamptonshire. The second and third flights of the south-east staircase.

Photograph by Cameron Newham.

one, beyond a pair of dowel holes on the first step. At first floor level it peters out in a landing which has now partly collapsed.

The three materials of which the staircase tower is made mark three distinct phases of construction. The basement and the rubble parts of the north wall match the internal walls of the Elizabethan kitchen range, which stands to the north of it. The evidence of the plan and the matching materials strongly suggests that the basement dates from the period of Sir Humphrey Stafford and that it marks an attempt to build a staircase which was not proceeded with. It is unclear how this staircase would have been constructed: probably it would have been of wood, the basement being very likely used for kitchen storage. Into it, a handsome barrel vault has been inserted, composed of ashlar blocks, to brace the existing structure and provide a more solid foundation when it was eventually decided to build in stone (Fig. 1.16). The staircase as executed is the most ambitious at Kirby and the only one in the house which can securely be dated to the seventeenth century. It would therefore seem logical that Peter Walker's model related to it. Historians have been prevented from drawing this conclusion by the tower's ceiling, which survived into the era of photography and had plasterwork of late seventeenth-century character, with heraldry which can be dated to the

Figure 1.16: Kirby Hall, Northamptonshire. The south-east staircase tower, view of the basement vault.

Photograph by Cameron Newham.

Figure 1.17: Kirby Hall, Northamptonshire. The plaster ceiling of the south-east staircase tower before its collapse.

Northamptonshire Archives Service TBF/364/269.

time of the 1st Viscount (Fig. 1.17). From this it has been inferred that the staircase itself is of this period.

The tower's top storey relates convincingly to the 1st Viscount's ceiling but the two storeys below it can firmly be attributed to Stone, together with the staircase itself and the vault below. There are three points of comparison here. Two of them relate to Kirby itself. The first is the brickwork, which matches that of the wall linings on the first floor of the north range of the courtyard, where Stone made significant alterations, dividing, or perhaps further dividing, the existing rooms. The bricks are bright red, laid in English bond with alternating courses

Figure 1.18: Kirby Hall, Northamptonshire. Brickwork on the interior of the north range. Compare the brickwork in Fig. 1.22.

Photograph by Cameron Newham.

of headers and stretchers (Fig. 1.18). The second point of comparison is the iron window frames, a remarkable survival of which there are several examples in both the north range and the staircase tower, all incomplete but substantially intact. They are of a uniform pattern, with an opening casement occupying the lower two thirds and, above this, an oval glazing bar held in place by two smaller vertical bars and two horizontal bars, the oval being subdivided by two more verticals (Figs 1.19a and b). One of these windows may very well be the item, referred to above, which was despatched to Kirby for Sir Christopher in 1639 as part of the second consignment of goods which Stone records: 'the Iron work of on[e] window … the cas[e]ments waying 84 pond and the Bares … 13 the pond'. This looks at first sight like a bigger window with more than one casement, but 'casement' could mean 'frame' in the modern sense.

The third point of comparison is with the two staircases at Greenwich which are of the same construction as that at Kirby. The Kirby staircase is built of a fine-grained, very white limestone. This is probably Portland, which is specifically mentioned as having been used for the bust of Apollo and for a shield, almost certainly an armorial shield which was despatched by Stone to Kirby in 1639. Each tread overlaps the one below by means of a rebate at the bottom of the riser (Fig. 1.20). Their nosings have similar torus profiles, with fillets below them that curve into the faces of the risers. Importantly, the soffits of the treads are cut back in concave mouldings, very like

Figure 1.19a: Kirby Hall, Northamptonshire. Window in the south-east staircase tower.

Photograph by Cameron Newham.

Figure 1.19b: Kirby Hall, Northamptonshire. Window in the north range, on the courtyard side.

Photograph by Cameron Newham.

Figure 1.20: Kirby Hall, Northamptonshire. The first flight of the south-east staircase. Detail.

Photograph by Cameron Newham.

those on the Tulip Stair (see Fig. 1.10). The sides of the staircase are cut flush. This may have been done with the intention of fixing an iron balustrade on the sides of the treads, as on the Tulip Stair. If so, it was never carried out.

It has been claimed that the stone staircase replaced a more conventional wooden construction.[59] This, as already noted, may well be what was intended when the staircase tower was first conceived but there is no evidence that it was actually put into effect. The idea that it once existed is suggested by the two parallel lines of holes in the east wall of the staircase tower, above the second flight of stairs (Fig. 1.21). These, however, are probably fixings for a later panelled dado, the top of which is marked by a slight depression in the brickwork, indicating its profile. At the top end, the dado ramps up in a sweeping curve that is characteristic of timber staircase dados and handrails of the 1670s–90s.[60] The dado and rail must belong to the post-Restoration period when the tower was completed. Throughout there is good evidence that the staircase is part of the original construction. It is securely bonded into the brickwork with no sign of the disturbance that would have been caused by a later insertion. Outside, on the south wall the ends of six of the staircase treads can be seen, flush with the wall surface where they have been fully built into the wall for maximum strength, a type of construction recommended by Scamozzi in his treatise (Fig. 1.22).[61]

Figure 1.21: Kirby Hall, Northamptonshire. The second flight of the south-east staircase, showing holes made for panelling and the line of a wooden balustrade.

Photograph by Cameron Newham.

Figure 1.22: Kirby Hall, Northamptonshire. The south wall of the south-east staircase tower from outside, showing the treads of the staircase flush with the wall.

Photograph by Cameron Newham.

The purpose of the staircase is uncertain, but Stone's account book provides one significant clue. Among the final consignment of goods, despatched to Kirby Hall in the summer of 1640, were '6 Emperours heads, with there Pedestalles cast in Plaister, molded from the Antiques' which were supplied at a cost of £7 10s. Sir Christopher Hatton was a cultivated and learned man. He collected books and antiquities, patronised the poet Thomas Randolph and, after the Restoration, became a founder member of the Royal Society. A new library would certainly have suited his tastes, with a prestigious staircase providing access and indicating its importance, while the busts of Roman emperors would have been suitable furnishing items. There is even a clue as to where the room was to be. On the north side of the staircase well, at first-floor level, where the landing comes to an end, there is an arched doorway, with the archway lined in brick, that stands out from the stone rubble used elsewhere on this side (Fig. 1.23). This doorway may have been the intended entrance. The room beyond it would probably have been refurbished from space in the existing structure, east of the hall.

A stone staircase at Hatton House, London, 1634–5

Stone's account book reveals that in November 1634 he had delivered the components of a stone staircase to Lady Elizabeth Hatton, for

Figure 1.23: Kirby Hall, Northamptonshire. The south-east staircase tower, showing holes for supports for the collapsed landing on the first floor, south side, with the exit at the north-east corner through a doorway with a brick-lined arch.

Photograph by Cameron Newham.

Hatton House, her London residence.[62] Lady Elizabeth Hatton was the wife of Sir William Newport, the nephew and heir of Sir Christopher Hatton, Queen Elizabeth's Lord Chancellor. On Sir Christopher's death in 1591 he changed his name to Hatton as a condition of accepting the inheritance and was the squire of Kirby for six years, until his death in 1597. Elizabeth long outlived her husband and later married Sir Edward Coke, the famous lawyer with whom she was on famously bad terms.[63] She refused to take his name and it was as Lady Hatton that she was known to the Stone workshop.

Stone's account for the Hatton House staircase is fortunately quite detailed. It reveals that there were thirty-two steps and four 'hath paces'. A 'hath pace' is a half-pace, or perhaps a hearth-piece, a term which Stone used mainly to denote the hearth at the foot of a chimneypiece which was fitted with stones.[64] Here it is used to indicate the large stone slabs at the foot and the top of the staircase, and on the landings. This implies that it rose in three flights, like the staircase at Kirby. Alternatively, it could have been circular or oval in plan, like the Tulip Stair (see Fig. 1.10) or

56 BETWEEN DESIGN AND MAKING

Palladio's example in Fig. 1.1, with small landings every six or seven steps. The Hatton House steps were each 'wrought with a bothell moulding'. This suggest that the treads had nosings in a torus or 'boutell' profile, the latter being the word Jones frequently used in his annotations to denote a torus moulding of half a circle in diameter,[65] as in the nosing mouldings of the two stairs at the Queen's House.

Hatton House is long gone and there appears to be no record of its internal appearance.[66] It is tempting to suppose, however, that the staircase could have been suspended like those at Greenwich and Kirby, in which case it would have given Stone valuable experience in this form of construction. His account book suggests that it was completed very late in 1634 or early in 1635, the year in which Jones and Stone were completing the architectural shell of the Queen's House. It is interesting to speculate as to whether Inigo Jones had a hand in it, or indeed at Kirby. For Goldsmiths' Hall in the City of London, Stone's greatest independent commission of the 1630s, Jones 'did advise and direct before the perfecting and finishinge of each [of Stone's designs]'[67] and he may have done the same in these two cases.

Conclusion

The Kirby and Greenwich staircases show Stone's skill and expertise to have been essential to Jones's achievement, not just in this type of structure but in the construction and detailing of stonework more generally. For without his master mason's knowledge of the sourcing, jointing and profiling of limestone blocks – and especially those in Portland stone – it is hard to imagine how Jones could have produced elevations as accomplished as those of the Banqueting House, Whitehall, less than five years after his return from Italy. Jones's masterful handling of classical details in Portland stone at the Queen's Chapel at St James's Palace (1623–6) and the Queen's House itself – to name the two most important surviving buildings from the second half of his career[68] – suggests that Stone's early involvement alongside the Surveyor was critical to the latter's success at court and his subsequent reputation as an architect. For his part, Stone's innovation in the jointing of the treads, by overlapping them in rebates at the bottoms of the risers, significantly enhanced the structural capabilities of the suspended stone stair, making it possible for architects and masons in Britain and Ireland to design and build such staircases on a larger scale and with increasingly dramatic effect.

Acknowledgements

The authors wish to acknowledge Pieter van der Merwe for much valuable advice and assistance at the Queen's House, Greenwich; Mark Wilson Jones for advice on the stairs at the Pantheon in Rome; the late Mark Girouard for his advice on the history of Kirby Hall; Paola Modesti, Andrew Tierney and Melanie Hayes for many helpful comments and editorial suggestions; and Jeremy Ashbee, Head Properties Curator for English Heritage, and Kate North, Senior Properties Curator (Curatorial Department), English Heritage for access to the south-east staircase which is currently closed to the public.

Notes

1   Pérouse de Montclos, 'La vis de Saint-Gilles et l'escalier suspendu dans l'architecture française du XVIe siècle', 86.
2   For the development of suspended stone stairs in Ireland in the earlier eighteenth century, alongside carpentry open-well stairs, see Tierney, 'A glorious ascent', 338–48.
3   Pérouse de Montclos, *L'architecture à la Française*, 167–78; Price and Rogers, 'Stone cantilevered staircases' (for a full technical analysis of historic examples); and Taylor, 'Stone cantilevered stairs'.
4   See, for example, the geometrical stair by Thomas Ripley at the west end of the south range of Queen Mary Building, Greenwich Hospital, 1736–40, in Bold, *Greenwich*, Fig. 211.
5   Jones's annotated copy of Palladio's *I Quattro Libri* (Venice, 1601) is at Worcester College, Oxford; see Allsopp, *Inigo Jones on Palladio*, for a facsimile and transcription (although this has many inaccuracies). Jones's notes cited below are Gordon Higgott's transcriptions from the original volume. For the dating of Jones's earliest annotations, including his notes on stairs, see Newman, 'Inigo Jones's architectural education before 1614', 18–20 and 25–7.
6   For Jones's early career, see Newman, 'Jones, Inigo', *ODNB*. See also the entries on Jones in Colvin, *Biographical Dictionary*, 584–92, and Girouard, *Biographical Dictionary*, 175–87.
7   Book I, 61.
8   Jones notes in the margin, 'Thes ar fayre and Comodious for all the windows com to be in hed [the top] of the Ovall and in the midell'. As Newman observes in 'Jones's architectural education', 26, his peculiar wording suggests that the idea of a top-lit staircase was new to him at this stage.
9   Note in Book I, 64, c.1608, 'Triangular stares that Convay [go] up to the Cupolo of the Rotonda'.
10 Note in Book IV, Chapter XX, 74, 'This Tempell I Ocerved exactly the last of maye 1614 [*added later*:] and have noated what I found more then is in palladio'.
11 For the history of this part of the fabric and a survey of the east stair in 2005–6, see Marder and Wilson Jones, *The Pantheon*, 204–9. For a plan and perspective drawing of the east stair by an anonymous sixteenth-century French draughtsman (Berlin Kunstbibliothek, HDZ 4151, Codex Destailleur D. folio 38 recto), see Yerkes, *Drawing after Architecture*, 94–7 and Fig. 52.
12 An Elizabethan example, perhaps known to Jones, is the 'Roman Stair' at Burghley House, built 1561–4, which has stone barrel vaults rising in parallel flights. See Newman, 'The development of the staircase in Elizabethan and Jacobean England', 175.
13 For Palladio's incomplete project at the Convento della Carità and his oval stair, see: Bassi, *Il Convento della Carità*, 32–121, and Plates xc–xciv; Modesti, *Il Convento della Carità e Andrea Palladio*, 195–200, 248–52; and Beltramini and Burns, *Palladio*, 156–63. Jones visited on Sunday 10 August 1614, when he wrote in ink in the top margin of p. 30, Book II, that he had 'obsearved' the building again.
14 Last line of note in Book II, 29.

15 Book II, 30, top margin, 'the Iorens [irons] of the Pogio ar fastned on the outside of the stepps'. The lip gave the treads extra depth beneath the iron fixings. However, most of these lips have since been trimmed away, leaving the soffits flat, without the distinctive curved profile noted by Jones.

16 'Som of the neces on the Leaft hand ar Co[n]verted in to windoues [...] the third half pace of the staire breakes the window to be uniforme without'. The oval stair has niches on all four diagonals, as in Palladio's plan of this type of stair in Book I (see Fig. 1.1). Palladio does not show them in his small-scale plan of the monastery (see Fig. 1.4) but Jones added them in black chalk in his copy.

17 For a summary of the main phases of Jones's handwriting, of which this is the penultimate one, see Higgott, 'Inigo Jones and the architects of antiquity', note 7.

18 Jones's copy of Scamozzi's *L'Idea* is at Worcester College, Oxford. The plan in question is in Part I, Book III, 296–7, with Jones's note on p. 296. He was responding to Scamozzi's description on p. 294, '& à sinistra sono le Scale principali F ovate, e comode, lequali ascendono fino in cima, e prendono abbondante lume da un Fanò' – and on the left are the main stairs, oval, and convenient, which ascend to the top and take abundant light from a lantern. For the Villa Corner and a photograph of the oval stair looking up, see Barbieri and Beltramini, *Vincenzo Scamozzi*, 266–8 (contribution by Ilaria Abbondandolo). For an English translation of Scamozzi's Book III in *L'Idea*, Part I, see Vroom, *Vincenzo Scamozzi*.

19 See Harris and Higgott, *Inigo Jones*, Fig. 67; Higgott, 'Design and setting of Inigo Jones's Queen's House', Figs 4A, 5A, 6B; Higgott, 'Roof walks and roof platforms', 189 and Fig. 5.

20 For the history of the design and construction of the Queen's House from 1616 to c.1640, see Chettle, *The Queen's House*, 25–105; Colvin, *History of the King's Works*, 4, ii, 114–23; Bold, *Greenwich*, 35–93; Higgott, 'Design and setting of Inigo Jones's Queen's House'; Higgott, 'Jones's designs for the Queen's House in 1616'; and Van der Merwe, *The Queen's House*, 6–75.

21 RIBA Drawings Collection, London: Jones & Webb, cat. no. 18; see Harris and Higgott, *Inigo Jones*, cat. no. 13.

22 Scamozzi, *L'Idea*, Part I, Book III, Chapter XX, 'De'siti, e forme convenevoli a varie maniere di Scale private ad uso de tempi nostri, & alcune introdotte dall'Autore' – of the sites and forms suitable for different types of stairs in private houses, for use in our times, and some introduced by the author, 312–17, with plates on pp. 313 and 317, all annotated by Jones with identifying remarks; and Part II, Book VIII, Chapter XII, 'In que'modi si possino costruer bene diverse maniere di Scale, e le Porte, e Fenestre de gli edifici, e tutte le loro parti' – on the ways one can construct well the various types of stairs, doors and windows in buildings, and all their parts 311–15. See p. 312: 'Mà le Scale à rami sospese ... deono haver i loro gradi; in modo che piglino tutta la grossezza delle mura, ò siano d'una pietra, e meza, overo di due' – but the stairs with suspended flights ... these must have steps that are recessed the entire thickness of the wall, or a stone-and-a-half, or two stones.

23 For the building accounts, 8 October 1616 to 30 April 1618 (The National Archives, TNA/ AO1/356/2487), see Chettle, *The Queen's House*, 97–103.

24 Thurley, *Palaces of Revolution*, 164.

25 Jones's pension is first recorded in the Declared Accounts for 1629–30: TNA SC6/CHASI/1696.

26 A note by Jones about a balcony detail on Palladio's Palazzo Porto, written at Greenwich on 2 June 1632 on p. 9 in Book II of his *I Quattro Libri*, indicates a start on design work for the upper floor of the Queen's House; see Higgott, 'Jones's designs for the Queen's House in 1616', 154–6. Stone's architectural career is summarised in Colvin, *Biographical Dictionary*, 2008, 990–2.

27 See Williamson, 'Hendrick de Keyser, Nicholas Stone, Inigo Jones and the founding of the modern Portland Stone industry'; Williamson, *Inigo's Stones*, 109–207; and Clifton-Taylor, *Pattern of English Building*, 49, 68–70. In the south staircase the two half-landings are 4 ft 9 inches (1.45 m) square, and the upper of the two was cut from a single block of stone.

28 See Higgott, 'Mutual fruitfulness', 296–8, where the activities of decorative painters at the Queen's House are considered.

29 The Portland stone cost £150 in 1616–18, but only £5 15s. 10d. was spent on masonry work; see Chettle, *The Queen's House*, 98 and 100.

30 See Higgott, 'Design and setting of Inigo Jones's Queen's House', 143–7.

31 Higgott, 'Design and setting of Inigo Jones's Queen's House', 143–6. The building is currently entered from the north side, and the significance of the south front as the original entrance is lost to most visitors.

32 The plaster ceiling of the south staircase, illustrated in Bold, *Greenwich*, Fig. 124, is configured like the main timber ceiling over the hall in the north range, in nine compartments with a deeper, circular central field, and appears to date from the 1630s.

33 See Bold, *Greenwich*, 90, which follows Chettle, *The Queen's House*, 69, in describing the stair as a 'later reconstruction'.

34 No evidence exists for such work in the three most likely periods. These are: (1) during repairs under John James (1718–23; TNA ADM 66/28); (2) in 1745–7, when £4,700 was spent (TNA WORK 5/60); and (3) in 1807–13, when the house became the central component of three linked buildings forming the Royal Naval Asylum schools, to designs by Daniel Alexander (TNA ADM 67/254). See Bold, *Greenwich*, 85–9 and 230–4. That the stair was indeed of stone construction at the outset, and not carpentry, is clear from a payment to the Sergeant Painter, Robert Streeter, in June 1695, for '60 foot run of iron worke painted in the great Staircase with fine Smalte with the trouble of making the Scaffelling [£5 2s.]' (TNA WORK 5/47; see Chettle, *The Queen's House*, 112).

35 Notable examples are the great staircases at Knole House, Kent (1605–8), Hatfield House, Hertfordshire (c.1612), and Ham House, Richmond (1638–9). See Girouard, *Elizabethan Architecture*, 368–76, and Figs 494–6; Adshead and Rowell, *Ham House*, 72–3, and Figs 61–2; and Newman, 'The development of the staircase in Elizabethan and Jacobean England', 175–6.

36 Illustrated in a long section of 1935 in Chettle, *The Queen's House*, Plate 30. On p. 69 Chettle describes it as having 'the cast-iron balusters and heavy handrail of the nineteenth century'.

37 Cox and Norman, *Survey of London*, vol. 14, 171–2, Plate 73. See also Brindle, *Pembroke House*, 102–4. An outward curve was added to the bottom step of the South Stair to accommodate the turning newel of the balustrade.

38 See Ayres, *Building the Georgian City*, 148–56, and Fig. 220; Joseph Moxon's *Mechanick Exercises: or, The Doctrine of Handy-Works* (1677–1703).

39 Taylor, 'Stone cantilevered stairs'. See also Price and Rogers, 'Stone cantilevered staircases', 29–32, on which Taylor's study depends. Taylor first proposed Stone as the inventor of the riser rebate. He notes that the rebates on the Tulip Stair are 50 mm high by 38 mm wide.

40 The landings are probably recessed about 0.45 m into the wall. See the large-scale plan in Bassi, *Il Convento della Carità*, relievo VIII and X; and Nicodemus Tessin's plan and section drawn in 1677 (Stockholm Nationalmuseum H THC 2198) in Modesti, *Il Convento della Carità e Andrea Palladio*, Fig. 105.

41 Noted by Taylor in 'Stone cantilevered stairs'.

42 See Chettle, *The Queen's House*, 111, in a version of the account dated August 1665 (TNA WORK, 5/7, fol. 180r.): 'To Richard Ashworth smith for 18 new square barrs for the round stair case in the Queens new buildings, weight 126 pounds at 10d. a pound – £5 5s. For two new balls for the Rails there – 2d. For fastening the old barrs to the Rails being flown out from them – 10d. For making 30 new branches to the same staircase each branch weight 5 pounds – £10 10s. For 48 half branches – £8 11s. 6d. For making of 7 new half Double branches – 49s. [£2 9s.]'. This account gives the number of 'half branches' incorrectly as 48. The correct figure is 49. This is consistent with the stated costs of 3s. 6d. for a half branch and 7s. for a full branch. It is given twice in two other versions of the account at TNA Works, 5/8, folios 201v. and 254v. The latter is part of a larger bill submitted in June 1665. The first reference to the flowers as 'tulips' (and hence 'Tulip Stair') is in a bill for the repair of the ironwork of the stair by William Beach Smith in June 1694; see Chettle, *The Queen's House*, 112 (TNA WORK 5/46). We are most grateful to Pieter van der Merwe of Royal Museums Greenwich for his advice on this topic.

43 Bold, *Greenwich*, 76–80; Colvin, *History of the King's Works*, vol. 5: 140–7.

44 Spiers, 'Note-book and account book', 43.

45 For an account of Stone's career as a master mason and architect, see Colvin, *Biographical Dictionary*, 990–2 and Girouard, *Biographical Dictionary*, 281–9. For his career as a sculptor, particularly a tomb sculptor, see White, *Biographical Dictionary*, 118–38.

46 White, *Biographical Dictionary*, 44.

47 Published in Spiers, 'Note-book and account book'.

48 Vertue, *Notebooks*, vol. 4: 9. Vertue notes that the notebook was 'writ by H. Stone ye Mason', that is, by Stone's eldest son Henry Stone (1616–1653). Whether this is a mistake is not clear, but in either case it would not have detracted from the notebook's authenticity as the elder Stone sometimes delegated bookkeeping tasks to his children. There are several entries in

the surviving account book in the hands of Henry's brothers, Nicholas Stone junior and John Stone.

49 Spiers, 'Note-book and account book', 113–14, 118, 119, 121. The most interesting of these tasks was the making of a chimneypiece in the closet adjoining the Queen's Bedchamber. However, it only cost £3 14s so it must have been small and simple. It does not survive. In 1637–8 Stone was paid for setting up five pedestals of Purbeck Marble, apparently for sculpture in the Great Hall (Colvin, *History of the King's Works*, vol. 4: *ii*, 121). In the following year he was paid 'for altering and new carving the thighs legs and feet of a marble statue of a young man' for a display of statuary in the same room (Bold, *Greenwich*, 65).

50 He is commemorated by a wall tablet in the chancel of Sidbury parish church which records his burial there in January 1617/18.

51 He twice sued the estate of Mrs Elizabeth Van de Steen (variously spelt Van de Stene, Van de Steene, etc). She was a stone and marble merchant with whom he had dealings. The lawsuits were for money which he claimed he was owed. Judgement was awarded in his favour in one of the cases in 1642; the outcome of the other case is unknown (TNA, KB 27/1677; C8/37/56; C8/84/63; Spiers, 'Note-book and account book', 81, 104).

52 Spiers, 'Note-book and account book', 93–4. Stone's son, Nicholas Stone the Younger was also much involved in the stone trading business which seems to have sustained the family after the outbreak of the English Civil War when commissions for sculpture and building were hard to come by. See White, *Biographical Dictionary*, 138–9.

53 For the history of Kirby Hall, see Heward and Taylor, *Country Houses of Northamptonshire*, 245–56 and Thurley, *Kirby Hall*. Earlier accounts are less reliable.

54 Spiers, 'Note-book and account book', 119, 125, 128–9.

55 *Della Trasportatione dell'Obelisco Vaticano, e delle Fabriche di Nostro Signore Papa Sisto V*, Rome, 1590. The discovery is reported and illustrated in Thurley, *Kirby Hall*, 12–13. The book was bought for Stone's colleague Edmond Kinsman, as recorded in the younger Stone's travel diary (Spiers, 'Note-book and account book', 193). The fact that Stone did not ask his son to buy a copy for him as well suggests that he already owned one (Girouard, *Biographical Dictionary*, 289).

56 For illustrations of this feature, see Thurley, *Kirby Hall*, 16, 47.

57 For illustrations of the gateways, see Thurley, *Kirby Hall*, 2, 28.

58 Sir John Soane's Museum, London, Thorpe drawings collection, T139–40; Summerson, 'Architecture of John Thorpe', 81–2 and Fig. 63. A plan of the upper floor of the house by Thorpe also survives (T 137–8; 'Architecture of John Thorpe', 81–2 and Fig. 62). As Summerson points out, this probably predates the ground-floor plan. The latter appears to show a scheme for the building which is more fully developed.

59 Heward and Taylor, *Country Houses of Northamptonshire*, 254–6.

60 For examples of this type of handrail profile, which only became prevalent in the 1670s–80s, with the introduction of specialist joining planes, see Ayres, *Building the Georgian City*, 148–56, and Fig. 220, and editions of Joseph Moxon's *Mechanick Exercises: or, The Doctrine of Handy-Works* (1677–1703), where such planes are illustrated. They facilitated the joining of curved pieces of wood. A fine example of such a handrail is on the great stair at Belton House, 1685–90. See Gomme and Maguire, *Design and Plan in the Country House*, 278, Fig. 284.

61 Scamozzi, *L'Idea*, Part II, p. 312: 'Mà le Scale à rami sospese ... deono haver i loro gradi; in modo che piglino tutta la grossezza della mura, ò siano d'una pietra, e meza, overo di due' (but the stairs with suspended flights ... these must have steps that are recessed the entire thickness of the wall, or a stone-and-a-half, or two stones). See note 22.

62 Spiers, 'Note-book and account book', 101–2.

63 For Lady Hatton, see Kate Aughterson, 'Elizabeth, Lady Hatton', *ODNB*.

64 He fitted 'hath paces' in this way at the Queen's House, Greenwich in 1639 (Spiers, 'Note-book and account book', 118–19).

65 See Newman, 'Inigo Jones's architectural education', 48, and Jones's *I Quattro Libri* in many places, for example, Book I, p. 20, where he translates Palladio's description of the Tuscan base with its single torus moulding measuring three parts high, 'the other 3 goeth too the Boultell'.

66 It stood in Ely Place, Holborn, named after Ely Palace, the London residence of the Bishops of Ely before the Reformation. During the Elizabethan period the palace had been granted to Lord Chancellor Hatton, and Lady Hatton inherited it.

67 Newman, 'Goldsmiths' Hall', 33.
68 See commentary and illustrations in Summerson (ed. Colvin), *Inigo Jones*; and Worsley, *Inigo Jones and the European Classicist Tradition*, 95–9, and Figs 127, 143 and 182.

References

Adshead, David and Christopher Rowell, eds. *Ham House: 400 years of collecting and patronage*. New Haven, CT and London: Yale University Press, 2013.

Allsopp, Bruce. *Inigo Jones on Palladio: Being the notes by Inigo Jones in the copy of I Quattro Libri dell'Architettura di Andrea Palladio 1601, in the library of Worcester College, Oxford*. 2 vols. Newcastle upon Tyne: Oriel Press, 1970.

Aughterson, Kate. 'Elizabeth, Lady Hatton (née Lady Elizabeth Cecil; also known as Elizabeth Coke, Lady Coke)' in *Oxford Dictionary of National Biography*, 2016. Accessed 15 December 2023. https://doi.org/10.1093/ref:odnb/68059.

Ayres, James. *Building the Georgian City*. New Haven, CT and London: Yale University Press, 1998.

Barbieri, Franco and Guido Beltramini. *Vincenzo Scamozzi, 1548–1616*. Venice: Marsilio, 2003.

Bassi, Elena. *Il Convento della Carità, Corpus Palladianum,* vol. 6. Vicenza: Centro Internazionale di Studi di Architettura 'Andrea Palladio', 1971.

Beltramini, Guido and Howard Burns. *Palladio*. London: Royal Academy of Arts, 2008.

Bold, John. *Greenwich: An architectural history of the Royal Hospital for Seamen and the Queen's House*. New Haven, CT and London: Yale University Press, 2000.

Brindle, Steven. 'Pembroke House, Whitehall', *The Georgian Group Journal*, 8 (1998): 88–113.

Chettle, George. *The Queen's House, Greenwich: Being the fourteenth monograph of the London Survey Committee*. London: National Maritime Museum, 1937.

Clifton-Taylor, Alec. *The Pattern of English Building*. 4th edition. London: Faber & Faber, 1987.

Colvin, Howard, ed. *The History of the King's Works*: vol. 5: *1660–1782*. London: HMSO, 1976.

Colvin, Howard, ed. *The History of the King's Works*: vol. 4: *1485–1660 (Part II)*. London: HMSO, 1982.

Colvin, Howard. *A Biographical Dictionary of British Architects, 1600–1840*. 4th edition. New Haven, CT and London: Yale University Press, 2008.

Cox, Montagu H. and Philip Norman, eds. *Survey of London*, vol. 14: *The Parish of St. Margaret, Westminster – Part III: Whitehall II*. London: Batsford, 1931.

Girouard, Mark. *Elizabethan Architecture: Its rise and fall*. New Haven, CT and London: Yale University Press, 2009.

Girouard, Mark. *A Biographical Dictionary of English Architecture 1540–1640*. London: Paul Mellon Centre for Studies in British Art, 2021.

Gomme, Andor and Alison Maguire. *Design and Plan in the Country House: From castles and donjons to Palladian boxes*. New Haven, CT and London: Yale University Press, 2008.

Harris, John and Gordon Higgott. *Inigo Jones: Complete architectural drawings*. London and New York: Philip Wilson Publishers, 1989.

Heward, John and Robert Taylor. *The Country Houses of Northamptonshire*. London: Royal Commission on the Historical Monuments of England, 1996.

Higgott, Gordon. 'The design and setting of Inigo Jones's Queen's House, 1616–40', *The Court Historian*, 11:2 (2006): 135–48.

Higgott, Gordon. 'Inigo Jones's designs for the Queen's House in 1616'. In *The Renaissance Villa in Britain, 1500–1700*, edited by Malcolm Airs and Geoffrey Tyack, 140–66. Reading: Spire Books, 2007.

Higgott, Gordon. 'Roof walks and roof platforms on English country houses, c.1550 to c.1700'. In *Toits d'Europe: Formes, structures, décors et usages du toit à l'époque moderne (XVe – XVIIe siècle)*, edited by Monique Chatenet and Alexandre Gady, 185–98. Paris: Picard, 2016.

Higgott, Gordon. 'Inigo Jones and the architects of antiquity', *Annali di Architttura*, 31 (2019):127–34.

Higgott, Gordon. '"Mutual fruitfulness": A nuptial allegory on Queen Henrietta Maria's bedchamber ceiling at the Queen's House, Greenwich'. In *The Wedding of Charles I and Henrietta Maria, 1625*, edited by Marie-Claude Canova and Sara J. Wolfson, 295–320. Turnhout: Brepols, 2020.

Marder, Tod A. and Mark Wilson Jones, eds. *The Pantheon: From antiquity to the present.* Cambridge: Cambridge University Press, 2015.

Modesti, Paola. *Il convento della Carità e Andrea Palladio: Storie, progetti, immagini.* Verona: Cierre Edizioni, 2005.

Moxon, Joseph. *Mechanick Exercises: or, The Doctrine of Handy-Works.* London: n.p., 1677–1703.

Newman, John. 'Nicholas Stone's Goldsmiths' Hall: Design and practice in the 1630s', *Architectural History*, 14 (1971): 30–9.

Newman, John. 'The development of the staircase in Elizabethan and Jacobean England'. In *L'Escalier dans l'Architecture de la Renaissance*, edited by André Chastel and Jean Guillaume, 175–7. Paris: Picard, 1985.

Newman, John. 'Inigo Jones's architectural education before 1614', *Architectural History,* 35 (1992): 18–50.

Newman, John. 'Jones, Inigo (1573–1652)', in *Oxford Dictionary of National Biography*, 2010. Accessed 15 December 2023. https://doi.org/10.1093/ref:odnb/15017.

Pérouse de Montclos, Jean. 'La vis de Saint-Gilles et l'escalier suspendu dans l'architecture française du XVIe siècle'. In *L'Escalier dans l'Architecture de la Renaissance*, edited by André Chastel and Jean Guillaume, 83–9. Paris: Picard, 1985.

Pérouse de Montclos, Jean. *L'Architecture à la Française du Milieu du XVe à la Fin du XVIIIe Siècle.* Paris: Picard, 2001.

Price, Sam and Helen Rogers. 'Stone cantilevered stairs', *The Structural Engineer*, 83:2 (2005): 29–36.

Scamozzi, Vincenzo. *L'Idea della Architettura Universale* (Venice, 1615). 2 vols. Upper Saddle River, NJ: Gregg Press, 1964.

Spiers, Walter Lewis, ed. 'The note-book and account book of Nicholas Stone', special issue, *The Volume of the Walpole Society*, 7 (1919).

Summerson, John. 'The Book of Architecture of John Thorpe in Sir John Soane's Museum', special issue, *The Volume of the Walpole Society*, 40 (1966).

Summerson, John. *Inigo Jones.* 2nd edition (with a Foreword and notes by Sir Howard Colvin). New Haven, CT and London: Yale University Press, 2000.

Taylor, Russell. 'Stone cantilevered stairs', in *Building Conservation Directory*, 2006. Accessed 15 December 2023. http://www.buildingconservation.com/articles/stonecantstairs/stonecant stairs.htm.

Thurley, Simon. *Kirby Hall.* Guidebook to the house. Swindon: English Heritage, 2020.

Thurley, Simon. *Palaces of Revolution: Life, death and art at the Stuart court.* London: William Collins, 2021.

Tierney, Andrew. 'A glorious ascent: Staircase design, construction and craft in the circle of Richard Castle'. In *Enriching Architecture: Craft and its conservation in Anglo-Irish building production, 1660–1760*, edited by Christine Casey and Melanie Hayes, 316–53. London: UCL Press, 2023.

Van der Merwe, Peter. *The Queen's House, Greenwich.* London: Royal Museums Greenwich, 2017.

Vertue, George. 'The notebooks of George Vertue IV', special issue, *The Volume of the Walpole Society*, 24 (1936).

Vroom, Wolbert, ed. *Vincenzo Scamozzi, The Idea of a Universal Architect: Villas and country houses.* Amsterdam: Architectura & Natura Press, 2003.

White, Adam. 'A biographical dictionary of London tomb sculptors c.1560–c.1660', *The Volume of the Walpole Society*, 61 (1999): 1–162.

Williamson, Tom. 'Hendrick de Keyser, Nicholas Stone, Inigo Jones and the founding of the modern Portland Stone industry', *Proceedings of the Dorset Natural History and Archaeological Society*, 133 (2012): 33–6.

Williamson, Tom. *Inigo's Stones: Inigo Jones, royal marbles and imperial power.* Beauchamp: Matador, 2012.

Worsley, Giles. *Inigo Jones and the European Classicist Tradition.* New Haven, CT and London: Yale University Press, 2007.

Yerkes, Carolyn. *Drawing after Architecture: Renaissance architectural drawings and their reception.* Milan: Marsilio, 2017.

Further reading

Hill, Oliver and John Cornforth. *English Country Houses: Caroline, 1625–1685*. London: Country Life Books, 1985.

Lees-Milne, James. *English Country Houses: Baroque, 1685–1715*. London: Country Life Books, 1970.

2

The Townesend family and the building of eighteenth-century Oxford

Geoffrey Tyack

> A most skilled Master of Architecture, who carried out many buildings both for the advancement of knowledge and the adornment of this University[1].

The architecture of eighteenth-century Oxford cannot be understood without reference to the stone employed in its most handsome buildings, or to the men who quarried and worked it. In his poem 'Duns Scotus's Oxford', Gerard Manley Hopkins (1844–1889) bemoaned indeed the 'base and bricky skirt' that had already begun to engulf the ancient university city during his own short lifetime, souring 'that neighbour-nature [its] grey beauty is grounded best in'.[2] That 'grey beauty' – really, at least in the sunshine, a rich honey colour – derived from the use of locally quarried stone. The city stands at the edge of a belt of easily workable limestone, running north-east from Dorset to Lincolnshire. Although most of the houses in the city were timber-framed, and continued to be, well into the nineteenth century, stone had been used for its larger buildings – churches, university buildings and some public buildings, since at least the eleventh century. These were designed and built by stonemasons, most of whom also owned or leased quarries on the rising ground to the north-east of the city. They included William Orchard, the master mason who was the builder, and almost certainly the designer, of Magdalen College (1474–c.1490) and also of the University's Divinity School – now part of the Bodleian Library complex – with its spectacular lierne vault (1478–82), one of the triumphs of English late Gothic architecture and craftsmanship.[3] Masons brought in from elsewhere were employed for some of the most important college and university commissions in the late sixteenth and early seventeenth centuries, such as the Fellows' Quadrangle at Merton College, the main quadrangle of the Bodleian Library, and the newly-founded Wadham College (1610–12), but that practice had largely ceased by the end of the seventeenth century.[4] Local masons and quarry-owners continued meanwhile to dominate the building trades, as they had done for most of the previous three hundred years. The Townesends, who were heirs to the tradition of stonemasonry that Orchard and his successors had represented, became Oxford's most famous dynasty of master masons in the eighteenth century. Through their quarrying interests they gained a foothold in the city's building industry, winning major contracts for the construction, and in the design, of many of the city's most prestigious buildings. This chapter will chart the varied activities of this family and consider how they negotiated their place as quarrymen, contractors, craftsmen and designers.

The Townesends of Oxford

John Townesend (1648–1728), the founder of the family dynasty, was the son of a labourer and was apprenticed to Bartholomew Peisley (1620–1692), builder of the Senior Common Room at St John's College in 1673–6, and from 1687 to 1694 one of the suppliers of stone to Sir Christopher Wren's St Paul's Cathedral, as it rose from the ashes of the Great Fire of London.[5] Townesend became a freeman of Oxford and was mayor of the city in 1720–1 . The inscription, quoted above, on his impressive tomb in the churchyard of St Giles (Fig. 2.1), which was no doubt designed and built by his son William, described him as 'a most skilled master in architecture', 'a faithful friend to all, a consistent and merciful colleague in the administration of justice', and in domestic matters 'an indulgent and far-sighted father'.[6] The local antiquary Thomas Hearne wrote about him in less flattering terms, recording that he was 'commonly called Old Pincher, from his pinching his workmen':[7] charging the clients more than he paid the men who worked for him on a daily basis and pocketing the surplus, a practice that was not uncommon at the time.[8] Like his Cambridge contemporary Robert Grumbold (1639–1720),[9] he ran what was in effect a family business, and he and his descendants were involved as designers or contractors in most of the buildings that together transformed central Oxford in the first half of the eighteenth century, and which still play a major part in shaping the city's architectural character.

Figure 2.1: John Townesend's monument in the churchyard of St Giles, Oxford.

Photograph by Geoffrey Tyack.

Four generations of Townesends worked in Oxford: John; his son William (1676–1739), who went to France as a young man in 1699, presumably with a view to receiving an architectural education, and succeeded his father in the business; William's son John II (1709–46); and another John, who died in 1784.[10] Nothing is known about the older William's visit to France apart from the fact that he bought a picture there, the subject and artist of which have not been recorded. But the fact that he went abroad, presumably at his father's expense, suggests that he was aiming to follow the precedent of earlier gentleman architects such as Sir Christopher Wren, for whom foreign travel was an essential component of an architectural education. Hearne recorded that William, whom he called 'a proud, conceited fellow', had 'a hand in all the buildings in Oxford, & gets a vast deal of money that way'.[11] Much of the family's success rested on their leasing of quarries, remnants of which can still be seen in the bumpy landscape of the suburb now known as Headington Quarry to the north-east of the city. According to Nicholas Hawksmoor, William had 'all the best quarrys of stone in his own hands'.[12] Covering some ninety acres in all, they supplied two types of stone: a durable 'hardstone' and a more easily carvable freestone, which could be dressed to give a smooth ashlar facing. As Robert Plot noted in his *Natural History of Oxfordshire* (1677): 'In the quarry it [the stone] cuts very soft and easy and is worked accordingly for all sorts of building; very porous, and fit to imbibe lime and sand, but hardening continually as it lies to the weather'.[13] But it did not weather well, 'blistering' and crumbling as later generations discovered to their cost: a problem subsequently accentuated by smoke-blackening from coal fires. By the end of the eighteenth century, the inferior weathering quality of the stone was beginning to be realised. From the mid eighteenth century its use had begun to decline, and where Headington Stone continued to be specified, as at Oriel College (1778), it tended to be used in less conspicuous areas. Headington was not the only freestone to fail in Oxford; Burford stone and other stones of the Taynton group also suffered from blistering, albeit on a smaller scale than Headington. Various alternative building stones were brought in from other parts of England to carry out repairs in the nineteenth century, notably Bath stone, which was increasingly used as a facing material following the opening of the Kennet and Avon Canal in 1810.[14]

Contracts and college commissions

William Townesend's papers, probably the best surviving archive of any English mason-architect of the eighteenth century, were acquired, together with those of other members of the family, by Oxford University's Bodleian Library in 2012. They include copious accounts, measurements and records of stone deliveries and payments to workmen. The papers show that the workmen employed by William and other members of the family were sometimes paid by the day, sometimes through contracts for prices ('measure and value'), and sometimes out of lump-sum payments made to the main contractor ('by the great').[15] They give a detailed insight into the construction of some of the most notable buildings in the city, including numerous college and university commissions, among them James Gibbs's Radcliffe Library (Radcliffe Camera) of 1737–48, for which William contracted in 1737, together with another successful mason-architect, Francis Smith of Warwick.

Despite the prestige of its university, eighteenth-century Oxford was a moderately sized provincial town, with a population of just under 12,000 in 1801. By then it had not spread very far outside its medieval boundaries,[16] and most of its domestic buildings were timber-framed, though many had recently been given stuccoed façades to impart a veneer of classical propriety. Wealthier citizens began to build stone houses in the seventeenth century; St Giles House, built in 1702 for Thomas Rowney, a lawyer and Member of Parliament for the city, was probably designed and built by Bartholomew Peisley the younger, whose own stone-fronted house in St Michael's Street still survives. The centre of Oxford was, and still is, at Carfax, the crossroads formed by the intersection of the main north–south and east–west roads through the city. A series of improvements took place here in the eighteenth century, designed to give the city a more impressive market place; they included the Doric-columned Butter Bench (c.1710), probably designed by John Townesend, founder of the family dynasty, as part of a wider redevelopment scheme (Fig. 2.2).[17] But the main factor that enabled Oxford to punch above its weight architecturally was the concentration of university and college buildings in the eastern part of the city. The building work here was not caused by pressure of population: student numbers declined significantly after the early seventeenth century and

Figure 2.2: A view of Carfax with the Butter Bench on the right. From Rudolph Ackermann, *A History of the University of Oxford, its Colleges, Halls, and Public Buildings* (1814).

© The Board of Trinity College Dublin.

grew relatively little over the century following the Civil War.[18] There was, however, a growing demand for accommodation for wealthy commoners: fee-paying students, many of whom saw a period of study at the university as a rite of passage rather than as part of a professional training. Many of the new buildings that resulted from their presence were funded by former commoners who, like their modern equivalents, were energetically canvassed for money by their colleges after they graduated. Their generosity helped transform the face of the city.

While much of the Townesends' business was made up of routine maintenance work, the family also became involved in more ambitious schemes for rebuilding and extending colleges and university buildings. John Townesend designed and built the gate tower and Master's lodgings at Pembroke College in 1691–5;[19] he also carved the ornate stone hood (demonstrating his skill as a stone carver and mason) over the door of the Principal's Lodgings at Jesus College in 1698 (Fig. 2.3), and he built a summerhouse in the Warden's garden at New College in 1722.[20] His most important collegiate commission was at Queen's College, where he was described as *lapicida* or stonemason.[21] An illustration of 1675 by David Loggan shows the mainly medieval buildings, which were entered from Queen's Lane, leading north from the High Street. Townesend

Figure 2.3: The front door of the Principal's Lodgings at Jesus College.
Photograph by Geoffrey Tyack.

was paid in 1691 for a ground plan and a design for the college 'if new modelled', but his design – which has not survived – seems to have been modified by someone else, probably on the initiative of the Provost (head of the college), Timothy Halton. The Library, of 1692–5, was built, like most college libraries in the early eighteenth century, in order to house collections of books given by old members, most of whom were clergymen; the books were placed in a handsome room on the first floor of the new building, lit by large round-headed windows and standing over an open loggia (Fig. 2.4).[22] Henry Aldrich (1648–1710), the polymath Dean of Christ Church, may have been responsible for the final design; an accomplished amateur architect, he certainly designed the nearby All Saints church (now Lincoln College library) in the High Street, built in 1701–10,[23] and he was also involved, together with John Townesend's son William, in the design and construction of the handsome pedimented Fellows' Building at Corpus Christi College, that followed soon afterwards in 1706–12, close to the southern city wall and overlooking Christ Church Meadow (Fig. 2.5).[24]

In 1701–3 William Townesend had constructed the impressive saucer-domed vault under the gate tower of Exeter College in Turl Street, built to his father's design. Between 1707 and 1714 he built the first

Figure 2.4: The west range of the North Quadrangle at Queen's College.
Photograph by Geoffrey Tyack.

Figure 2.5: The Fellows' Building at Corpus Christi College.
Photograph by Andrew Tierney.

three ranges of Peckwater Quadrangle at Christ Church, Corpus Christi's much larger neighbour.[25] Here too the noble, if somewhat monotonous, design was supplied by Aldrich, who died before work could begin on the massive Library which faces it from the south side of the quadrangle. Built in 1717–38, but not finished internally for another twenty years, the façade of this majestic structure, of Headington (replaced by Portland in 1960–2) and Burford (replaced in 1960–2 by Clipsham) ashlar, has an engaged giant order of Corinthian columns, and a lesser Doric pilaster order at ground-floor level. The distinct contrast of colours became more apparent when the stonework was refaced in the 1960s, raising the question of whether in their choice of stone the Townesends put their own commercial interests ahead of the client's. The Library was designed by another amateur architect, George Clarke (1661–1736), a Fellow of All Souls College, though with the invaluable help of Townesend, who seems to have acted as his amanuensis (Fig. 2.6).[26]

From 'mechanick' to *'architectus'*?

William Townesend inherited his father's stonemasonry skills, demonstrated in the older man's Baroque-inspired tomb (see Fig. 2.1), and he

Figure 2.6: The Library at Christ Church.
Photograph by Andrew Tierney.

stepped into his father's shoes at Queen's College, where the medieval buildings were gradually swept away over a period of some forty years to make way for the present Front Quadrangle, entered from the High Street. Hawksmoor had already prepared designs for this ambitious project, but they were shelved, and when work began on the west range in 1710 it was to a different design conceived by Clarke and Townesend, who supplied the stone from his quarries at Headington.[27] Townesend was, significantly, described in the accounts as architect ('*architectus*') for the building: not, as John Evelyn had put it, 'the commonly illiterate Mechanick … but the Person who Superintends, and Presides over him with so many Advantages'.[28] And it is Townesend, together with Clarke, who should also be given the credit for the design of the noble Hall and Chapel in the north range of 1714–19, with its pedimented Doric frontispiece that crowns the composition (Fig. 2.7).[29]

Meanwhile, in 1709, William – 'Young Mr Townesend', as he was described – had made a draft design for a new building containing sets of rooms for the fellows of All Souls College. Nineteen bays wide and three storeys high, with a central portico of the Tuscan-Doric order, it was intended to stand on an open site, formerly occupied by a cloister, to the north of the fifteenth-century quadrangle (Fig. 2.8).[30]

Figure 2.7: The Front Quadrangle at Queen's College, looking towards the Hall and Chapel.

Photograph by Geoffrey Tyack.

Figure 2.8: Proposal by William Townesend and George Clarke for a block of rooms on the site of the Library at All Souls College.

By permission of the Provost and Fellows of Worcester College, Oxford. © Worcester College, Oxford.

This project was shelved following a gift of funds from the West Indies plantation owner Christopher Codrington. It allowed the college to build a spacious new library on the same site as part of a west-facing courtyard, externally Gothic in style, designed by Hawksmoor and built in 1716–22. The fellows' rooms were now placed in the east range, with its twin towers, and a new hall was built in the south range, next to the surviving medieval chapel. Townesend was the mason-contractor here, and he acted in the same capacity for the university's new printing house (the Clarendon Building), also built to Hawksmoor's designs in 1712–14 (Fig. 2.9).[31] Here too there is a preliminary plan and elevation in Townesend's hand.[32] But it is Hawksmoor's handsome building that still serves as a ceremonial northern entrance to Oxford's 'Forum Universitatis', as he called it himself,[33] with the seventeenth-century Bodleian Library complex at its heart. The Hawksmoor-Townesend team, together with Clarke, was also responsible for the building of the hall, chapel and library block at Worcester College, a new collegiate foundation on the north-western edge of the city. Work began here in 1720, but, as was often the case with such ambitious schemes, it dragged on for many years and was not finally completed until the end of the century.[34]

Alongside these large projects, William Townesend continued to prepare and to carry out designs of his own for other, less ambitious, college buildings. They included the Radcliffe Quadrangle (1716–19) at University College, funded by a gift from the immensely wealthy physician John Radcliffe, an alumnus of the college. He insisted that the new buildings should be 'answerable' to those of the existing

Figure 2.9: The south front of the Clarendon Building.
Photograph by Andrew Tierney.

seventeenth-century Front Quadrangle, from which they are indeed all but indistinguishable (Fig. 2.10). Townesend also made two alternative, but unexecuted, neo-Palladian designs for a new Master's house at the same college, 'intended', as the handwritten inscription states, 'to stand in the garden, over against Dr Radcliffe's statue'.[35] He also built, and probably designed, the Bristol Buildings at Balliol College (1716–20), the Robinson Building at Oriel College (1719–20), the chapel at Pembroke College in 1728–32 and the south side of the open-ended Garden Quadrangle at Trinity College (1728).[36] And he was consulted, along with others, including James Gibbs, about the design of the New Building at Magdalen College, built to the designs of Edward Holdsworth, a fellow of the college, in 1733–9.[37] The Townesends took on smaller commissions too. The chimneypiece in the Hall (1731) at St John's College was built, and presumably designed, by William Townesend, and the screen at the 'lower' end, designed by James Gibbs, was built in 1743 by William's son John (1709–1746),[38] who took over the family business when his father died in 1739.

It was the same John Townesend who, following his father's death, was the main contractor for what is arguably Oxford's finest classical building, the Radcliffe Library, known since 1860 as the

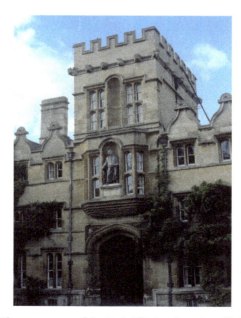

Figure 2.10: The gate tower of the Radcliffe Quadrangle at University College. Photograph by Geoffrey Tyack.

Radcliffe Camera (Fig. 2.11). Work began here in 1739 to a design by Gibbs, following the death of Hawksmoor, who had prepared the first design three years earlier.[39] Radcliffe had died in 1714 and was buried in the University Church of St Mary, where his grave, under a simple slab, was constructed by the first John Townesend.[40] Radcliffe envisaged the domed, centrally planned library as his own virtual memorial; it was even dubbed 'Ratcliff's mausoleum' by contemporaries.[41] Occupying an open site between the Bodleian Library and the University Church, the rusticated ground floor was faced with blocks of Headington hardstone, which weathered reasonably well, but the Burford (Taynton) ashlar facing of the *piano nobile*, as in so many Oxford buildings of its date, decayed irreparably, initially as a result of pollution from coal fires, and was refaced, together with the capitals and cornice, in 1965–8.[42] Yet, despite these vicissitudes, it is this building, first conceived by Hawksmoor, redesigned by Gibbs, and built under the supervision of John Townesend's grandson, that, more

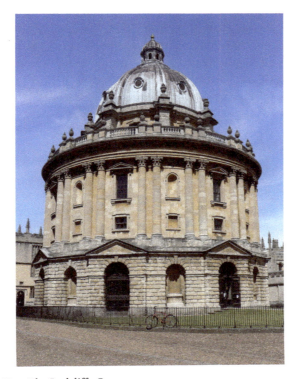

Figure 2.11: The Radcliffe Camera.
Photograph by Geoffrey Tyack.

than any other, defines and symbolises the University of Oxford in the twenty-first century.[43]

The Townesends also carried out a number of country-house commissions in the Oxford area: at Compton Beauchamp House in Berkshire (now Oxfordshire) in 1707–9, where John Townesend built, and may have designed, the impressive entrance range with its three-bay centre, Doric pilaster order and balustrade roof-line (Fig. 2.12);[44] at Rycote Park, Oxfordshire, and Wytham Abbey, Berkshire (now Oxfordshire);[45] at Cirencester Park, Gloucestershire, built for first Earl Bathurst (1725–7);[46] and at Blenheim Palace, where William contracted to build both Nicholas Hawksmoor's noble Woodstock Gate in 1722–3 (Fig. 2.13) and the Column of Victory commemorating the Duke of Marlborough's military campaigns (1727–31).[47] The family's name is also immortalised in the diminutive, octagonal Temple of Echo, also known as Townesend's Building (1738–9) in the arcadian landscape first conceived by William Kent at another Oxfordshire country house, Rousham (Fig. 2.14).

The Townesend firm continued to carry out maintenance work in Oxford in the second half of the eighteenth century, and another John Townesend (d. 1784), possibly William's nephew, was responsible for constructing the handsome stone fan vault over the seventeenth-century Convocation House, next to the Divinity School, in 1758–9, probably imitating the plaster vault that it replaced.[48] He also built the bridge

Figure 2.12: Compton Beauchamp House.
Photograph by Geoffrey Tyack.

Figure 2.13: The Woodstock Gate to Blenheim Palace.
Photograph by Geoffrey Tyack.

Figure 2.14: Townesend's Building in the garden of Rousham House.
Photograph by Geoffrey Tyack.

over the River Thames at Maidenhead (1772–7), designed by Sir Robert Taylor, and that at Henley, begun to the designs of William Hayward in 1782. John Townesend lived in a house at the corner of High Street and Longwall Street, which still survives, but the family firm, or what remained of it, was sold by John's son Stephen in 1796 to Thomas Knowles, in the hands of whose descendants it still survives.[49]

'Towesending is all Out'

As early as 1736, Sir Nathaniel Lloyd, a fellow of All Souls College, and one of the main sponsors of the North Quadrangle there, remarked that 'Hawksmooring and Townesending, is all Out for this century'.[50] With the completion of the Radcliffe Camera in 1748 the heroic period of Oxford's architectural transformation by master masons and gifted amateurs came to an end. The future, at least with regard to public architecture, lay with professional architects. But architecture still is, as it always has been, a collaborative process, and recent research has underlined the fact that, even now, buildings are rarely, if ever, designed 'by' a single architect, however illustrious he or she might be. The tacit skills of the artisan, the managerial skills of the contractor, and the creative agency of the designer naturally coalesced in enterprising families keen to get ahead in the building trade. That was certainly true in the first part of the eighteenth century, when the architectural profession as we understand it now had yet to emerge. Knowledge and expertise was transmitted through books, but it was also handed down by word of mouth, often within family dynasties, and if we understand these dynasties we are better able to understand the buildings on which they were employed. Nowhere is that more the case than in Oxford.

Notes

1 Translated inscription from John Townesend's (1648–1728) tomb at St Giles's Church, Oxford. See Tyack, 'The restored tomb of John Townesend at St Giles's church, Oxford'.
2 Gardner, *Poems and Prose of Gerard Manley Hopkins*, 40.
3 Gee, 'Oxford masons 1370–1530', 75. For the precise dating of buildings, here and elsewhere in this chapter, I am grateful to Simon Bradley for allowing me to see the drafts of his revised Pevsner *Buildings of England* volume on the city of Oxford and south Oxfordshire (2023).
4 See Tyack, *Oxford: An architectural guide*; *Historic Heart of Oxford University*, 88–114.
5 Bodleian Library, Oxford, MS Don. b. 41, ff. 8–15; Colvin, *Biographical Dictionary of British Architects*, 795–6; Sturdy, *A History of Knowles & Son*, 1–9. See also Roscoe, *Dictionary of Sculptors in Britain*, 1278–80.
6 Tyack, 'The restored tomb of John Townesend at St Giles's church, Oxford', 198–9.

80   BETWEEN DESIGN AND MAKING

7   Hearne, *Remarks and Collections of Thomas Hearne*, 171.
8   Stephenson, *Contracts and Pay*, 100; Stephenson '"Real" wages?', 106–32. For rejoinder, see Allen, 'Real wages once more', 738–54.
9   Webb, 'Robert Grumbold and the architecture of the Renaissance', 315–19; Colvin, *Biographical Dictionary of British Architects*, 454–5.
10 Colvin, *Biographical Dictionary of British Architects*, 1045–51; Roscoe, *Biographical Dictionary of Sculptors in Britain*, 1278–80. The Townesend archive does not record which buildings were seen by William in France.
11 Hearne, *Remarks and Collections of Thomas Hearne*, 171.
12 Bodleian Library, MS All Souls c. 255, 8b, No. 9, quoted in Colvin, 'The Townesends of Oxford', 50.
13 Plot, *Natural History of Oxfordshire*, 75.
14 Arkell, *Oxford Stone*, 23–6, 43–5, 152–3.
15 Bodleian Library, MS Don. b. 41–2 and c. 208–11 (ledgers of works undertaken by John Townesend, 1687–1725); MS Don. d. 211 and e. 221–37 (account books, ledgers, bills and quarry books from his son William, 1719–44). For more detail, see htpps://archives.bodleian. ox.ac.uk/repositories/2/archival_objects/49493 (Accessed 4 January 2024); see also Colvin, 'The Townesends of Oxford', 54–5.
16 Faden, *Plan of the City of Oxford*.
17 Crossley, *History of the County of Oxford*, 333.
18 Stone, *The University in Society*, 6.
19 Bodleian, MS Don. b.41, ff. 58–63, etc.
20 Colvin, 'The Townesends of Oxford', 45–6; Bodleian, MS Don. e. 11, f. 34 v.
21 Magrath, *The Queen's College*, 68–70; Hodgkin, *Six Centuries of an Oxford College*, 127–31.
22 Bodleian, MS Don. b. 41, ff. 64–83; MS Don. 4, ff. 14. The loggia was filled in by C. R. Cockerell in 1843–5.
23 Colvin, 'The architects of All Saints Church, Oxford', 112–16. The west tower was added in 1718.
24 Bodleian, MS Don. e. 222, ff. 1–69. The Gentleman-Commoners' building in its own diminutive quadrangle, also by William Townesend, was built in 1737.
25 Bodleian, MS Don. e. 223.
26 Bodleian, MS Don. e. 225–7; Hiscock, *A Christ Church Miscellany*, 49–52; Hiscock, 'William Townesend, mason and architect of Oxford'; Curthoys, *The Stones of Christ Church*, 122–32. For Clarke, see Colvin, *Biographical Dictionary of British Architects*, 253–5.
27 Bodleian, MS Don. e. 224.
28 Evelyn, *An Account of Architects and Architecture*, 3.
29 Bodleian, MS Don. e. 225. The cupola over the entrance lodge (1733–4), was designed by Hawksmoor but was modified in execution.
30 Colvin, *Catalogue of Architectural Drawings*, 4 and Plate 51.
31 Bodleian, MS Don. e. 211, ff. 21–3; Tyack, *The Historic Heart of Oxford University*, 118–32.
32 Colvin, *Unbuilt Oxford*, 60–1.
33 See White, *Nicholas Hawksmoor and the Replanning of Oxford*, 86–8.
34 Bodleian, MS. Don, e. 231; White, *Nicholas Hawksmoor and the Replanning of Oxford*, 71–8.
35 Colvin, *Architectural Drawings,* 10 and pls. 99–102; Darwall-Smith, *A History of University College*.
36 Colvin, 'Architecture', in Sutherland and Mitchell, *The History of the University of Oxford*, 855–6; Colvin, *Biographical Dictionary of British Architects*, 1049–50. The north side of the Garden Quadrangle at Trinity College was begun by Wren as a freestanding building in 1668, and was later joined to the west range, which went up in 1682. The south range, of 1728, is by Townesend.
37 Ferdinand, *An Accidental Masterpiece*.
38 Colvin, *Biographical Dictionary of British Architects*, 1047, 1050.
39 Guest, *John Radcliffe and his Trust*; Hebron, *Dr Radcliffe's Library*; Gillam, *The Building Accounts of the Radcliffe Camera*; Tyack, *Historic Heart of Oxford University*, 136–57; Sturdy, *Knowles & Son*, 6.
40 Bodleian, MS Don. c. 209, f. 3.
41 Salmon, *The Present State of the Universities*, 43.
42 See Oakeshott, *Oxford Stone Restored*, 36–40; H. Viles, 'Unswept stone, besmeer'd by sluttish time', 359–72.

43 Bodleian, MS Don. e. 211, f. 88.
44 Bodleian, MS Don. b. 42, f. 97. He made more than fifty visits to the site in 1707–8: Colvin, 'Townesends of Oxford', 48. See also Tyack, Bradley and Pevsner, *The Buildings of England: Berkshire*, 251.
45 Bodleian, MS Don. e. 211, f. 88.
46 Bodleian, MS Don. e. 233, ff. 36–6; Verey and Brooks, *Gloucestershire,* 279–80.
47 Bodleian, MS Don. e. 231, f. 20, 26; e. 232, ff. 3–5, 11–14, 17–18, 26–9; e. 233, ff. 2–4, etc. See Brooks and Sherwood, *Oxfordshire: North and West*, 166, 168. John Townesend supplied building materials for the Kitchen Court: see Brooks and Sherwood, *Oxfordshire: North and West*, 155.
48 Roscoe, *Biographical Dictionary of Sculptors in Britain*, 1280.
49 Sturdy, *Knowles & Son*, 15 *et seq.*
50 https://www.asc.ox.ac.uk/eighteenth-century. Accessed 3 January 2024.

References

Ackermann, R. *A History of the University of Oxford, its Colleges, Halls, and Public Buildings*, Volume 1. London: R. Ackermann, 1814.
Allen, Robert C. 'Real wages once more: A response to Judy Stephenson', *Economic History Review,* 72:2 (2019): 738–54.
Arkell, W. J. *Oxford Stone*. London: Faber and Faber, 1947.
Bradley, S., N. Pevsner and J. Sherwood. *The Buildings of England: Oxfordshire: Oxford and the South-East*. New Haven, CT and London: Yale University Press, 2023.
Brooks, A. and J. Sherwood. *The Buildings of England: Oxfordshire North and West*. New Haven, CT and London: Yale University Press, 2017.
Colvin, H. M. 'The architects of All Saints Church, Oxford', *Oxoniensia* 19 (1954): 112–16.
Colvin, H. M. *Catalogue of Architectural Drawings of the 18th and 19th Centuries in the Library of Worcester College, Oxford*. Oxford: Clarendon Press, 1964.
Colvin, H. M. *Unbuilt Oxford*. New Haven, CT and London: Yale University Press, 1983.
Colvin, H. M. 'The Townesends of Oxford: A firm of Georgian master-masons and its accounts', *The Georgian Group Journal*, 10 (2000): 43–60.
Colvin, H. M. *Biographical Dictionary of British Architects 1600–1840*. 4th edition. London: Paul Mellon Centre for Studies in British Art, 2008.
Crossley, A., ed. *A History of the County of Oxford*, vol. 4: *The city of Oxford*. London: Victoria County History, 1979.
Curthoys, J. *The Stones of Christ Church: The story of the buildings of Christ Church, Oxford*. London: Profile Books, 2017.
Darwall-Smith, Robin. *A History of University College, Oxford*. Oxford: Oxford University Press, 2008.
Evelyn, John. *An Account of Architects and Architecture*. London: n.p., 1706.
Faden, William. *Plan of the City of Oxford*. London: Wm. Faden, 1789.
Ferdinand, C. *An Accidental Masterpiece: Magdalen College's new building*. Oxford: Magdalen College, 2010.
Gardner, W. H., ed. *Poems and Prose of Gerard Manley Hopkins*. Harmondsworth: Penguin Books, 1953.
Gee, E. A. 'Oxford masons 1370–1530', *Archaeological Journal*, 109:1 (2024): 54–131. Accessed 4 January 2024. https://doi.org/10.1080/00665983.1952.10854051.
Gillam, S., ed. *The Building Accounts of the Radcliffe Camera*. Oxford: Clarendon Press, 1958.
Guest, I. *John Radcliffe and his Trust*. Oxford: Radcliffe Trust, 1991.
Hearne, Thomas. *Remarks and Collections of Thomas Hearne*, vol. 7: *9 May 1719–22 September 1722*. Oxford: Oxford Historical Society at the Clarendon Press, 1906.
Hebron, S. *Dr Radcliffe's Library*. Oxford: Bodleian Library, 2014.
Hiscock, W. G. 'William Townesend, mason and architect of Oxford', *Architectural Review*, 98 (October 1945): 99–107.
Hiscock, W. G. *A Christ Church Miscellany*. Oxford: Oxford University Press, 1946.
Hodgkin, R. H. *Six Centuries of an Oxford College*. Oxford: Basil Blackwell, 1949.

Magrath, J. T. *The Queen's College*, vol. 2: *(1646–1877)*. Oxford: Clarendon Press, 1921.

Oakeshott, W. F., ed. *Oxford Stone Restored*. Oxford: Oxford University Press, 1975.

Plot, Robert. *Natural History of Oxfordshire*. Oxford: Printed by Leon Lichfield, 1677.

Roscoe, I. *Biographical Dictionary of Sculptors in Britain 1660–1851*. New Haven, CT and London: Yale University Press, 2009.

Salmon, T. *The Present State of the Universities*. London: J. Roberts, 1744.

Stephenson, J. '"Real" wages? Contractors, workers, and pay in London building trades, 1650–1800', *Economic History Review*, 71:1 (2018): 106–32.

Stephenson, J. *Contracts and Pay: Work in London construction 1660–1785*. Palgrave Studies in Economic History. London: Palgrave Macmillan, 2020.

Stone, L., ed. *The University in Society*, vol. 1: *Oxford and Cambridge from the 14th to the early 19th century*. Princeton, NJ: Princeton University Press, 1974.

Sturdy, D. *A History of Knowles & Son*. Oxford: Archaeopress, 1997.

Sutherland, L. S. and L. G. Mitchell. *The History of the University of Oxford*, vol. 5: *The eighteenth century*. Oxford: Clarendon Press, 1986.

Tyack, G. *Oxford: An architectural guide*. Oxford: Oxford University Press, 1998.

Tyack, G. 'The restored tomb of John Townesend at St Giles's church, Oxford', *Oxoniensia*, 73 (2008): 198–9.

Tyack, G. *The Historic Heart of Oxford University*. Oxford: Bodleian Library Publishing, 2022.

Tyack, G., S. Bradley and N. Pevsner. *The Buildings of England: Berkshire*. New Haven, CT and London: Yale University Press, 2010.

Verey, D. and A. Brooks. *The Buildings of England. Gloucestershire 1: The Cotswolds*. New Haven, CT and London: Yale University Press, 1999.

Viles, H. '"Upswept stone, besmeer'd by sluttish time": Air pollution and building stone decay in Oxford, 1790–1960', *Environment and History*, 2/3 (October 1996): 359–72.

Webb, Geoffrey. 'Robert Grumbold and the architecture of the Renaissance in Cambridge – I', *The Burlington Magazine for Connoisseurs*, 47:273 (1925): 315–19. Accessed 3 January 2024. https://www.jstor.org/stable/862710.

White, R. *Nicholas Hawksmoor and the Replanning of Oxford*. London and Oxford: British Architectural Library Drawings Collection and Ashmolean Museum, 1997.

3
Codes, conventions, circulations: drawings as an instrument of collaboration in the work of Nicolas Pineau

Bénédicte Gady

The rare collections of drawings that have passed from the workshop of an artist to the portfolios of a museum, if not in their entirety, at least in a consistent manner, are exceptional sources for deepening our knowledge of artistic and artisanal practices in the early modern period.[1] This type of collection contains material that is particularly interesting because it has not suffered – or has suffered less than others – the selective effects of time, which generally leads to the conservation of only those works considered to be of great value. It is often in the secondary sheets, which some might consider purely documentary, that the most information can be found on the stages of a creative process and the real circumstances of artistic production. This chapter will focus on a unique collection of drawings in the Musée des Arts Décoratifs in Paris, made up of over 450 works by Nicolas Pineau (1684–1754), members of his studio and his descendants. Pineau was an important French sculptor of wood and stone in the first half of the eighteenth century, who worked in St Petersburg, having been invited by Peter the Great in 1716. Upon his return to Paris in 1728, he played a major role in the development of the new manner, commonly called the Rococo style. His place in the vibrant artistic scene in Paris in the second quarter of the eighteenth century has been highlighted many times, notably by Fiske Kimball, Bruno Pons, Katie Scott and Peter Fuhring.[2] The object of this specific chapter is not to study this collection in its entirety, but rather to focus on the drawings that allow us to better understand or to raise new questions regarding the collaborative nature of artistic creation, including oral communication, which is often difficult to pin down. Focusing on drawings as a means of communication, or of dialogue between various participants, it will examine the different graphic signs used to transmit information to the parties involved, whether they be patrons, architects, collaborators or engravers. It will assess how typical Pineau's use of graphic signs was, beyond the standard graphic convention of plan, section and elevation, in use since the Renaissance, and suggest that the variety of signs employed reflects the incomplete codification in workshop practice.[3] This chapter will also show how many of these drawings, far from characterising a state of the artist's thought at a given moment or transmitting a fixed piece of information to an addressee, often serve as a support to a collective elaboration that extends in space and time.

The Pineau collection: acquisition and overview

The majority of the collection of Pineau drawings in the Musée des Arts Décoratifs in Paris were passed down through his family and acquired from them by Émile Biais, a curator and historian from Angoulême, during the second half of the nineteenth century. Several drawings by Pineau were bought by the museum at auctions starting in the 1880s, but the majority were given by a group of patrons who had acquired the collection for the museum directly from Biais in 1908.[4] A second substantial group of about 130 drawings, also originating from Émile Biais's collection via Alfred Beurdeley, is now held by the Hermitage Museum in St Petersburg. In 2021 a major restoration and study project of the drawings was launched at the Musée des Arts Décoratifs. The systematic restoration of the drawings was entrusted to Marion Dupuy, the archival and documentary research and coordination to Turner Edwards. The findings of a series of workshops that brought together a group of international researchers to discuss the drawings will be published in a forthcoming collective monograph.

The Musée des Arts Décoratifs' collection contains more than 450 drawings, ranging in size and subject matter, from depictions of sculpture in stone, in timber, furniture, silverware, and editorial projects. At first glance, this collection includes all types of drawings that historians customarily organise into well-distinguished categories corresponding to successive steps in the process of creation: exploratory drawings, presentation drawings and working drawings, mainly reduced scale but in some exceptional cases full scale, and finally, drawings for prints.[5] Traditionally, this classification of drawings is considered to be overlaid by a description of the intervening parties: the artist alone, the artist and his patron, the artist and his collaborators, and finally, the artist and those translating his art. Anthony Geraghty's study of Christopher Wren's drawings in All Souls, Oxford and his correspondence supports this classification.[6] A detailed analysis of Pineau's drawings shows, however, that the determination of the status of each sheet and its addressee is not always as simple as these categories might suggest: his drawings may serve several of these functions and be addressed successively to different parties in the course of the long process of creating the work.

Changing and unevenly understood graphic signs

While drawing allows for the searching and realisation of a form, the notation and transformation of an artist's idea at any given moment, it is far from limited to this seminal function. In the field of decoration, which implies the participation of a number of different people, drawing also aspires to the transmission of a clear visual discourse, be it to those called upon to make decisions, to incorporate the project into a wider scheme, to scale up the drawing or to translate it into a different material. In the language of art, as in language itself, the signifier's reference to the signified is never one of exact identity. The draughtsman and the person looking at the drawing often forget about this implicit link, either because the sign is intuitive, or because it has gained, because of its frequency and consistency, the status of a *convention*, which implies a general consensus.[7] Some semantic precision is necessary here, as the terms 'code' and 'convention' are ambivalent when used to describe modes of representation. 'Code' refers, in the legal and sociological domains, to a set of laws, rules or customs, which implies a diffusion of these norms, but, in semiology, it refers to a system of symbols representing information in a technical domain, whether this system is secret or explicit. Here, I will use the term 'code' in its semiotic sense and reserve the words 'codification' and 'codified' to refer to the standardisation of practices. The common use of the term 'convention' is also variable: it is frequently used to highlight the arbitrary nature of a sign or mode of representation (positing that the mimetic is not arbitrary), but its exact meaning refers to an agreement, be it explicit or tacit. In this text, I will stick to the latter definition and use it only when a consensus seems to be reached.

Certain graphic codes are so widespread that they can be called conventions: they are used quite naturally by the draftsman and spontaneously understood by the recipient. Other codes are the artist's own, or even internal to a specific drawing. Although it is difficult to know to what extent these codes were understood, and whether they were understood by everyone, handwritten notes prove that it was sometimes necessary to make them explicit. One of the most common conventions in architectural and ornamental design is the orthogonal articulation of plans, elevations and sections, the origins of which Ackerman traces back to Alberti's prescriptions in the fifteenth century, and their implementation in the designs of Antonio da Sangallo the Younger and Andrea Palladio in the first half of the sixteenth century.[8] This architectural drawing practice, which provided a standardised mode of representation and, in turn, a legible and accurate means of communication, became widespread on the continent as well as in Great Britain, as shown for example by the drawings of Christopher Wren and his collaborators.[9] It was later adopted in the field of decorative arts, and it is no surprise that many examples are present in Pineau's drawings.[10] From this is also derived the superimposition of elevations and sections, visible already in the middle of the seventeenth century in a ceiling-design print by Jean Marot.[11] This convention is found in the drawing for the door of the tabernacle at the Monastery in Lugny, for which Pineau worked between 1742 and 1744. The drawing combines a representation of the *Supper at Emmaus* with a horizontal section of the wood carving and part of the adjacent marble step (Fig. 3.1).[12] The combination or superimposition of views allows the joiner to determine the required thickness of wood more accurately, and to anticipate its fitting together with the carved marble surround. The objective is to render three dimensions, not by using the traditional means of mimetic representation, but rather through an analytical process allowing the person looking at the drawings to accurately project the contours and volumes and to understand the way in which they all hold together. This layering responds to a need for efficient communication and coordination between participants. Rarer indeed, but just as efficient, is this articulation between a section and the projection of an element situated on a different plane, such as a cornice or ceiling decoration.[13]

In ornament drawing, colours frequently convey specific information. Basile Baudez has brilliantly studied the shift from mimetic to taxonomic colours in architectural design, in France at the end of the seventeenth century, under the influence of engineers and cartographers.[14] This development had little effect in England, where, although Christopher Wren tended to favour imitative colour, the tradition of monochrome architectural design predominated in the first half of the eighteenth century.[15] However, colour is sometimes used for taxonomic

Figure 3.1: Nicolas Pineau, *Project for the door of the tabernacle at the Monastery in Lugny*, 1742–4. Graphite, pen and brown ink, 50 × 33 cm.

© Musée des Arts Décoratifs, Paris (CD 1624). Photograph by Marion Dupuy.

purposes, as in a plan of Westminster Abbey by William Dickinson.[16] In Pineau's drawings, colour is rarely mimetic, but its use can vary. The diverse colours may reflect a difference in status between the elements represented. For a sculpted cartouche flanked by a crosier and a mitre and topped by a ducal crown, Pineau carefully sketched his motif in red chalk, before quickly hatching a graphite background to evoke the support on which the ornament will stand (Fig. 3.2).[17] He then added indications of measurements, first in graphite and then in pen and brown ink. A sharper graphite stick, used more flexibly in the upper corners of the drawing, is used to search for a form that does not create any confusion with the sanguine motif. The differences in mediums, colours and firmness of execution, are immediately perceptible and accompany the transmission of numerical information to the craftsmen responsible for translating it into the full-scale working drawing, before its execution in stone. Like most of his contemporaries, Pineau makes pragmatic, even spontaneous, use of colours for distinction, in this case graphite and red chalk at his disposal in order to distinguish different stages of work and different status of the motif.[18]

In the Pineau collection at the Musée des Arts Décoratifs, few of the drawings show distinctions based on the colour of the watercolours. All of them are similar to presentation drawings, and one of them was also used to mark measurements and note, for the record, the work to be done

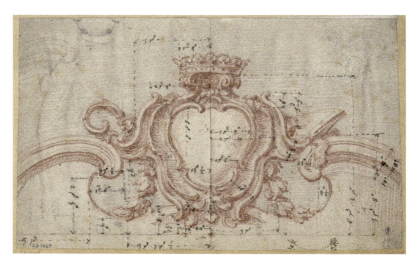

Figure 3.2:   Nicolas Pineau, *Project for a cartouche*. Graphite, red chalk, pen and brown ink, 26 × 42 cm.

© Musée des Arts Décoratifs, Paris (CD 1469). Photograph by Marion Dupuy.

and the checks to be made.[19] All of them pose problems of attribution. One is a project with an alternative for a wall on the side of the fireplace, which shows similarities with the large salon of Michel Tannevot's house in Paris, 26 rue Cambon, executed by Pineau around 1742, but also, for its upper part, with a print published in the re-edition of d'Aviler's *Cours d'Architecture* in 1738.[20] Above a mantelpiece, the background of which is washed with grey ink and the marble heightened with different watercolour washes to imitate the material – an exceptional case of mimetic colour in this corpus – two panels are superimposed, one in green watercolour, the other pink. Basile Baudez has noted that a convention in architectural drawing, probably dating back to the Italian Renaissance and widespread in continental Europe, attributes the colour green to window panes.[21] At the beginning of the eighteenth century, for interior design, mirrors were sometimes coloured green, as an extension of this use, and sometimes coloured blue, to distinguish them from window panes.[22] The usage is not completely fixed: for in one of the drawings in the Pineau collection now attributed to the architect Contant d'Ivry, a simple shade distinguishes the windows, in light green, from the glass, in green made even lighter by diluting the watercolour.[23] Nevertheless, in extant panelling designs in France in the first half of the eighteenth century, green is most commonly assigned to mirrors and pink to pictures.

Four of these drawings are interior elevations linked to prints, bought at the sale of the decorator Alexandre-Eugène Prignot under Pineau's name.[24] They use pen and grey ink heightened with grey wash and green watercolour to indicate the presence of a mirror or a picture (Fig. 3.3). By transcribing this type of drawing into prints, an engraver, who can only play with blacks and whites, transforms the chromatic code into a geometric one: he renders the surface of the mirror by a succession of parallel horizontal lines, and the surface of a picture by vertical ones, trading one code for another. The opposite may also be true if we consider that these drawings are later copies made after the prints, as suggested by Aurora Laurenti.[25] Aside from the limpness of the drawing, the rarity of this colour coding in Pineau's corpus supports this hypothesis. It also invites us to look carefully at the function of the drawing of a wall on the side of the chimney mentioned above: is it a presentation drawing for a specific setting or a model for the engraving, the colours simply indicating to the engraver the materials for which he will have to find black and white equivalents? Did the drawing fulfil both functions successively, and in what order? Regardless of attribution and function, once more, colour is not mimetic but rather serves a distinction or taxonomy of materials.

Figure 3.3: Nicolas Pineau workshop or late copy, *Panelling with a mirror*. Pen and brown ink, brown wash, watercolour, 28 × 21 cm.

© Musée des Arts Décoratifs, Paris (inv. 3398).

In the same way, and as the example of the print starts to reveal, the lines, by their size or their orientation, often carry a codified discourse. In a study for panels for the Château de la Tuilerie in Auteuil, dated 1737 (Fig. 3.4), three different types of hatching are visible: horizontal, to show mirrors, i.e. a difference in materials; left-handed hatching, which renders shadows and a difference of levels (on the right part, the hatched panel is shown as further away than the side panel of the niche); and short right-handed hatching showing the thickness of walls on cross-sections.[26] Pineau rarely uses wash to signify shadows in his projects for wood panelling. He also does not use watercolour to indicate masonry – the convention of using pink wash became widespread for civil architectural design, in representing buildings in section, in the second quarter of the eighteenth century, first in France, then in Sweden and Russia, and only in the second part of the century in England, as Basile Baudez demonstrated.[27] Thus, in this drawing, Pineau has chosen to vary the orientation of hatching in order to visually distinguish different materials, depths and heights. No convention or codification, however,

Figure 3.4: Nicolas Pineau, *Project for the panelling of a niche at a 'cabinet d'assemblée' at Château de la Tuilerie in Auteuil*, 1737. Pen and brown ink, 22.5 × 40 cm.

© Musée des Arts Décoratifs, Paris (inv. 29131A). Photograph by Marion Dupuy.

lends a certain meaning to a particular kind of hatching. Here, the code is specific to the drawing.

Another study for panelling shows similar principles deployed in a different combination (Fig. 3.5).[28] It is preparatory for a *cabinet en bibliothèque*. The shadows sketched out with right-handed hatching indicate a depth to these panels; the annotation *'armoire pour les livres'* (cabinets for books) gives the reason for the depth and confirms our intuitive understanding of this widespread graphic code, which is not specific to ornament drawing. The shadowing of the niche is somewhat different, being represented by vertical lines. The niche is not shown by a perspective drawing (there is a slight inclination in the horizontal lines of the left-hand panels, but not on the right). Perspective drawing is unsuitable to show off Rococo ornament which is the object of this drawing. To understand this drawing, the viewer – initially, the one whose agreement was required, being the owner of the house or the architect acting for him – has to look at both the shadowing of certain panels and the profile of the cornice above. The variations in how these signs are used demonstrate that, while they may be widespread, their function is not strictly codified. One graphic sign, however, extremely discreet in appearance, is perfectly comprehensible to architects, sculptors and joiners, but its meaning escapes general understanding. In designs for panelling, these professionals are able to

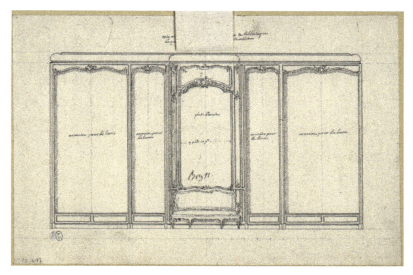

Figure 3.5: Nicolas Pineau, *Project for a 'cabinet en bibliothèque'*. Graphite, pen and black ink, 23.5 × 35.5 cm.

© Musée des Arts Décoratifs, Paris (CD 1497).

interpret that two parallel lines are indicative of moulding, whereas a single line is the code for the edge of a panel meant to be joined into a frame of moulding.[29] In all these cases, the differentiated use of colours and lines is pragmatic, without any systematism. It can vary from one design to another. Its purpose is to distinguish – materials, functions – no matter how this distinction is made.

The overriding importance of communication over the search for intrinsic beauty in a drawing is equally visible in ellipses. The practice of the ellipsis was common from the sixteenth century onwards in architectural and decorative drawings.[30] It takes advantage of the repetitive or symmetrical nature of the projected or copied work to reduce the workload of the draftsman and supposes that the viewer will be able to mentally complete the sketched motif by duplicating it in an intuitive and spontaneous manner. Pineau made extensive use of this convention, as shown by drawings for halves or two-thirds of a cartouche. The part left blank sometimes reveals a first motif in graphite different from the one finally chosen (Fig. 3.6).[31] If the practice of ellipsis satisfies the principle of economy, it offers – voluntarily or not – an invitation to let the imagination run in infinite variations.

Drawings with alternatives, where each half-pattern constitutes a proposition that the viewer must mentally duplicate in symmetry, are

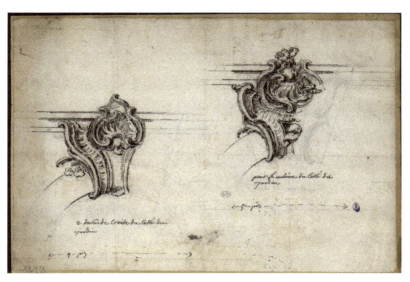

Figure 3.6: Nicolas Pineau, *Project for two keystones for the hôtel Bonneau*, circa 1741. Graphite, pen and black ink, 24 × 35.5 cm.

© Musée des Arts Décoratifs, Paris (CD 1472). Photograph by Marion Dupuy.

less intuitive, because the absence of a void, of a reserve, slows down the activation of cerebral automatisms. The mind understands the presence of a visual ellipse only when it notices the non-symmetrical character of the motif, or more precisely, in the case of the Rococo ornament which subtly plays with measured asymmetries, the unsightly connection of the two parts of the motif. The presence of a central axis can also serve as a visual clue to alert the viewer. The process of mental restitution is then more complex: to complete the pattern on the left, the mind must disregard the pattern the eye sees on the right, and vice versa. Here again, Pineau, like his seventeenth-century predecessors and contemporaries, makes extensive use of drawings with alternatives. He uses them to offer two options on the same sheet for *porte-cochères* (Fig. 3.7), cartouches, doors, panelling, fireplaces and furniture.[32] The need to represent a central ornament in its entirety sometimes leads to modifications to traditional codes, introducing a gap between the two options.[33] In all these cases, only the understanding of the draftsman's process and familiarity with these elliptical conventions can allow the viewer to reconstruct the definitive project, which is far different from what the eye sees.

This very common convention seems to pose no difficulty within a given professional community: it is easy to understand for artists and

Figure 3.7: Nicolas Pineau, *Project for a porte-cochère*, 1738. Graphite, 50 × 34.5 cm.

© Musée des Arts Décoratifs, Paris (CD 1475). Photograph by Marion Dupuy.

craftsmen in the modern period, as it is for art historians. However, there are clues that even this code was not universally understood. In one of the earliest known examples, a design for an altarpiece in Krakow by the German painter Georg Pencz, around 1530–40, the artist proposes a choice between ivy-covered columns and simple fluted columns, as well as, on either side of the altar, a sculpted scroll or an angel holding a votive candle. Fearing these alternatives may not be perfectly understood, the artist took care to spell it out in a written note: 'this sketch is for two different designs'.[34] In the same way, on a drawing for a pier glass which shows a high mirror ('glace de hauteur') to the left of a central axis drawn in dotted lines, and a lower mirror to the right ('moindre glace') topped by a painting ('Tableau') Pineau thought it necessary to explain that these were 'deux ydées différentes' ('two different ideas') (Fig. 3.8).[35] This specification was obviously intended for a patron unfamiliar with artistic practices. A long letter confirms this. The progress of the project is documented through the exchange of drawings and bills between Pineau and his patron, potentially via the architect. Nonetheless, the final bill of works received by Pineau is ambiguous: 'It is difficult to tell if this article confirms the side of the drawing with a painting, or the side with a mirror above. This article confirming only a panel mounted in two parts, does it mean a high mirror in two parts or a painting with a mirror underneath?'.[36] Written instructions thus

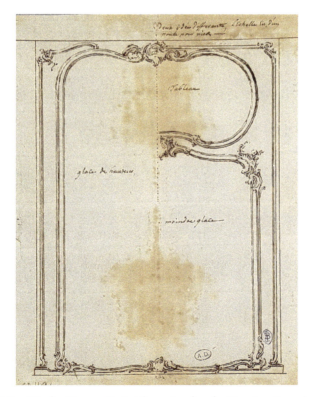

Figure 3.8: Nicolas Pineau, *Project for a pier glass for Monsieur Fournier*, 1745. Pen and brown ink, 21.4 × 16 cm.

© Musée des Arts Décoratifs, Paris (CD 1491A). Photograph by Marion Dupuy.

appear essential to avoid any miscommunication and highlight the shortcomings of graphic codes.

But even within a professional group, some information to be conveyed may not be translated by a conventional graphic sign, either because it is too rare to give rise to such a convention, or because it is faster to give the information through a written indication. In the absence of a specific convention to represent different materials without risk of misunderstanding, Pineau specifies in the above-mentioned drawing for the Lugny tabernacle (see Fig. 3.1) the distribution of wood and marble, writing 'planche de bois' and 'marbre' inside of their respective limits.[37] Short hatchings are used to clarify the boundary between the two materials, which is intuitively understandable, but they do not suffice to reveal their nature. In a drawing for the bedroom of Madame de Voyer d'Argenson at Château d'Asnières (Fig. 3.9), Pineau indicates that 'toutes les parties marqué A seront tendue en étoffes' ('all the parts marked A will be hung with fabric').[38]

A drawing for the arrangement of cartouches above windows on the ground and first floors of a façade, that Turner Edwards identifies with the Château d'Asnières, poses a more complex problem (Fig. 3.10).[39]

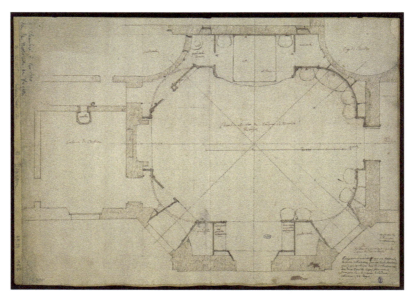

Figure 3.9: Nicolas Pineau, *Plan for the bedroom of Madame de Voyer d'Argenson at Château d'Asnières*, circa 1750. Graphite, pen and black and brown ink, 49.5 × 35.8 cm.

© Musée des Arts Décoratifs, Paris (CD 1655).

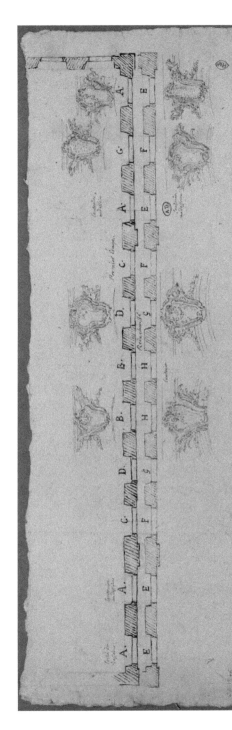

Figure 3.10: Jacques Hardouin-Mansart de Sagonne and Nicolas Pineau, *Study for the arrangement of cartouches above windows on the ground and first floors of the façade of the Château d'Asnières*, circa 1750. Pen and brown and grey ink, 13.5 × 45 cm.

© Musée des Arts Décoratifs, Paris (CD 1576). Photograph by Marion Dupuy.

This one drawing shows two plans that are clearly marked 'Rédechaussé' (ground floor) and 'Premier Etage' (first floor), with letters above each opening (figured by two lines between hatchings representing masonry) and eight drawings of cartouches that are accompanied by annotations: 'costé du dessein' once; 'contraire au dessein' four times and once 'contraire'. The plans and their legends, as well as some of the letters, are written in brown ink. The cartouches and 'costé' / 'contraire' annotations and the other letters are in grey ink. The arrangement and accompanying annotations are initially perplexing. The art historian is able to recognise that a code exists because of the ordering of letters: A – A – C – D – B – B – D – C – A – C – A for the first floor, E – E – F – G – H – H – F – E – F – E for the ground floor, but is incapable of going any further. One is suddenly struck with sympathy for the person to whom Pineau had had to explain that a drawing with alternatives represented 'deux ydées différentes', two different ideas. Once the code is made explicit – François Gilles found the first indication to crack it – it seems evident, and one is tempted to redescribe this drawing in a more ordered fashion. Each of the eight cartouches is placed above a letter, the repetition of which above a bay implies the repetition of the cartouche. The specification 'contraire au dessein' (and its shorthand 'contraire') means that it's the cartouche's mirror image that is meant to be reproduced in this spot. 'Costé du dessein' marks the spots where the cartouche is to be reproduced as it is drawn.

The use of this code has the double benefit of limiting the number of cartouches needing to be drawn and setting up a subtle game of symmetry and asymmetry. The architecture of the building is itself slightly irregular: four bump outs in the masonry reveal the presence of four pilasters, surrounding six central bays, flanked by two bays on the left and three on the right. The rhythm of letters has the same scansion on both levels. For the six central bays, the rhythm is chiastic: C – D – B – B – D – C and F – G – H – H – G – F. Then, instead of repeating the first two bays (A – A and E – E) in 9th and 10th position (implying the creation of a new cartouche for the 11th bay), Pineau chose to repeat the first cartouche in bays 9 and 11, reusing for bay 10 the cartouche of bay 8 (A – C – A and E – F – E). To sum up, within an ornamental scheme thought out as a poem in chiastic rhythm, Pineau has chosen to introduce an 'error', thereby creating a pair of crossed rhymes, thus taking advantage of the architecture's irregularity in order to loosen the hold of symmetry. Some cartouches, very static, are almost perfectly symmetrical (B, D, G) and are never inverted. Others (A and E) play on the type of asymmetry with which Pineau made a name for himself ('le contraste dans les ornements'). They lend themselves well to being mirrored, thus creating a symmetrical effect across a number of bays by balancing asymmetrical cartouches with their mirror images.

Faced with so many variations, one wonders how to interpret and make up for the ellipses symbolised by these letters. When unspecified, should one simply reproduce the cartouche without inversion? This seems logical, or at least intuitive. But then, the sole annotation '*costé du dessein*' seems redundant. When the bay of one level bears an annotation, should one not just imagine it applies to both the ground and first floor? What is implicit? Does the lack of annotation imply an unchanged design? Or does it imply the repetition of an annotation on both levels (this is the choice made for the proposal for the restitution drawn by François Gilles, Fig. 3.11)? When complexified, combining both drawings and text, a code becomes increasingly ambiguous.

What is the place of this drawing in the creative process and for whom was it made? The use of two inks suggests an execution in two stages. The letters in brown on a freely drawn plan correspond to the search for a logic for the rhythm of the sculptures of the façade: this part of the drawing is thus either an exploratory drawing or the recording of the result of other exploratory sheets. The freehand sketched designs of the cartouches in grey ink translate a second stage in the exploration, illustrative this time. The result of the two stages on the same sheet may have served as a support for the presentation of the project to the client, either the owner, probably with oral explanations,

Figure 3.11: François Gilles, *Proposal for the restitution of the façade of the Château d'Asnières with a hypothesis for the distribution of the cartouches*, according to the CD 1576, 2023.

© François Gilles.

or the architect, doubtless more familiar with this key-letter code. This sheet was then used as a starting point for the execution of eight working drawings, now preserved in the Hermitage in St Petersburg, which specify the shape of each cartouche and its articulation with the stones of the façade.[40] The drawings here are more descriptive and the handling of the black chalk is particularly heavy: they may have been executed by a member of the workshop. Above each one, a letter refers to the illustrated plan described above, which serves then as a legend: it was written by the same hand, as evidenced by the characteristic form of the letter G. Such an example proves that the same drawing can fulfil several functions at different stages of the preparation of a project, a plurality that our categories as art historians do not convey well.

Drawing as a support for collective multiphase work

An ornamental design destined to be realised is thus drawn not only as an illustration of the artist's idea but also as a set of signs to be understood by the audience of such drawings. Its execution is not an independent step in the process of creation. On the contrary, it is open-ended, both temporally and spatially. As a means of communication, ornamental drawings are the basis for dialogue between various participants during a single, but evolving, creative process. As Katie Scott pointed out in the case of a fireplace design initially meant for the small cabinet of the Hôtel de Mazarin, a single drawing can provide evidence for at least four different stages of a design's existence: its creation, its validation, its instrumentalisation and its dissemination.[41]

Ornamental designs sometimes seem to function as a *livre-journal* (a sort of logbook). It can serve to register decisions made by participants after presentation or discussion. These decisions are communicated through annotations on the drawings, and their position on the sheet or drawing is almost as important as the information contained in them. Such annotations can give information about pricing, decisions between alternatives, requests for modifications, or any other remarks. For example, on a cartouche drawn by Pineau in red chalk for the topping of the *porte-cochère* for the 'house of Madame la marquise de Feuquière rue [de] Varenne', a simple annotation in the middle of the cartouche gives the price of projected work: 250 *livres tournois* (Fig. 3.12).[42] In the case of a double project, the position of the approval indicates the option to be executed. This was a longstanding practice.

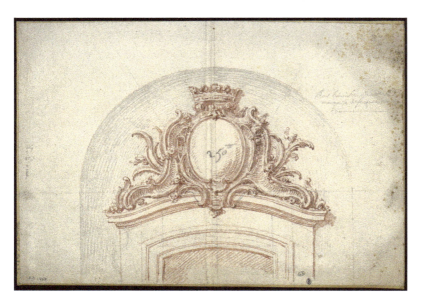

Figure 3.12: Nicolas Pineau, *Project for the cartouche of the porte-cochère of the hôtel de Feuquières*, circa 1736. Graphite and red chalk, 35 × 50 cm.

© Musée des Arts Décoratifs, Paris (CD 1468). Photograph by Marion Dupuy.

In the 1660s, the Surintendance des Bâtiments du Roi made ample use of it. Thus, Jean-Baptiste Colbert chose the designs for the ceilings of the King's Apartments in the Tuileries by signing half of the drawings to be executed.[43] On many drawings by Pineau, a simple '*bon*' has been written on part of the drawing to signify either the patron's or the architect's approval.[44] The arrangement of approvals on the drawing lends a certain degree of inventiveness to the decision maker.[45] Less frequent, on the right-hand panel of a door, the annotation includes the date and signature of the patron, lending it a contractual status (see Fig. 3.7).[46] Written contracts – whether notarised or privately signed – often included attached drawings in continental Europe and in Britain. Historians have called these sheets 'contract drawings', the use of which dates back to at least the end of the fifteenth century in Venice.[47] This drawing does not fit neatly into such a category: if it had been attached to a contract, the sheet would also bear the signature of the second contracting party (the architect or the sculptor). In my opinion, this drawing should be understood as an exceptionally formalised stage within a wider commission. It is worth noting that Pineau, working as a designer and sculptor, can seek approval both directly from the patron or from the architect, depending on the commission.

CODES, CONVENTIONS, CIRCULATIONS **103**

The project for the wall of a library, previously mentioned, contains one proposed modification. The main sheet of paper shows the initial proposal, traced in graphite then retraced with pen and black ink (see Fig. 3.5).[48] The flap – that is, a second piece of paper glued on one side to the initial sheet, allowing it to be raised and lowered – proposes a modification for the top of the panel at the back of the niche. The change in paper (the flap is thinner than the main sheet) and the graphic technique (graphite instead of ink) suggests that this modification was proposed at a later date (Fig. 3.13). This may have been done at either the patron's or the architect's request, or on the basis of a discussion between Pineau and them. Evidently, this new proposal was favourably received. The 'bon' is given twice: at the bottom of the panel in the main design and on the flap for the top of the panel. This makes clear that either the patron or the architect preferred a larger upper panel in which a mirror or a painting could be placed (I deduce that from the diagonal hatching). This solution may have been chosen precisely for this purpose. Beyond the simple question of the codification of information, this example begs the question of the temporality and collective nature of creation, with one informing the other. While we do not know what was being said between Pineau and decision-makers, the fact that two proposals were made at two different times, and one ultimately given the seal of approval, proves that discussions were indeed taking place. This process, spread out in time, implies the involvement of various participants and the circulation of the drawings themselves.

The recent conservation of a drawing for a wrought iron banister shed a surprising light on the relation between artist and patron at the very moment of the first formulation of the creative idea (Fig. 3.14).[49] When this drawing was unglued from the acidic paper it had been mounted on, the verso became visible (Fig. 3.15): it is an invitation to the *fête du Bon Pasteur* addressed to Madame Bonneau in 1743. This reveals not only the identity of Pineau's patron but also gives a clear date for the drawing. Above all though, it gives valuable information as to how the drawing itself was made. It is difficult to imagine that Pineau was working on a letter sent to his patron in his own atelier. The most evident hypothesis is that Pineau was at Madame Bonneau's house, and since 'a picture is worth a thousand words', decided to trace out his idea for her banister on a spare piece of paper at hand. This situation also explains the quick and approximative handling of the drawing. Here again, we get a glimpse of the collective and both oral and written nature of the process.

Figure 3.13: Nicolas Pineau, detail of *Project for a 'cabinet en bibliothèque'*, *with flap*. Graphite, pen and black ink, 23.5 × 35.5 cm.

© Musée des Arts Décoratifs, Paris (CD 1497, and detail).

In this case, Pineau drew his first idea in front of his patron and then took it home with him to rework. In other cases, the dialogue between Pineau and his patrons took place in the form of letters and drawings sent back and forth. This is the case for a study for the 'steps leading up to the tabernacle' at the Monastery in Lugny (1742–5) (Fig. 3.16).[50] This floorplan is drawn on a piece of paper addressed

Figure 3.14: Nicolas Pineau, *Project for a wrought iron banister for the hôtel Bonneau*, 1743. Graphite, 22 × 33.5 cm.

© Musée des Arts Décoratifs, Paris (CD 1704 recto).

Figure 3.15: Nicolas Pineau, *Invitation card used to sketch a wrought iron banister for the hôtel Bonneau*, 1743. Graphite, 22 × 33.5 cm.

© Musée des Arts Décoratifs, Paris (CD 1704 verso).

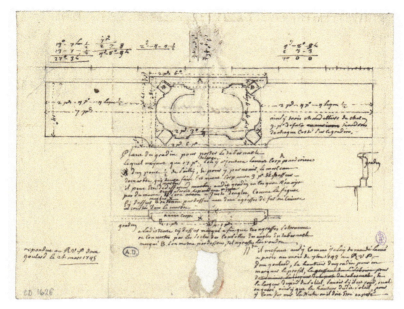

Figure 3.16: Nicolas Pineau, *Study for the steps leading up to the tabernacle at the Monastery in Lugny*, 1742–5. Graphite, pen and brown ink, 17 × 21.5 cm.

© Musée des Arts Décoratifs, Paris (CD 1626).

to Pineau: this leads me to believe that he, having been sent the plan, then annotated it himself. The annotations mention certain difficulties (the width of the tabernacle) and his suggestions for overcoming them (adding an *avant-corps* that juts out one-and-a-half *pouces*, around 3.6 cm), the consequences of these solutions (the required thickness of the marble to achieve this, the positioning of ties to secure the *avant-corps* so that they can 'be covered by the bases of the consoles at the corners of the tabernacle'),[51] alternatives (the possibility of using different marbles in case there isn't enough of that used for the platform) and Pineau's preferences (that the marbles should all match), as well as some uncertainties:

> NB: I also need, as I asked Father Goulard in Paris in October 1743, the height of the step up in order to draw its profile ([crossed out:] the width of the *ciborium* will determine the width of the door to the tabernacle), and the width of the *ostensorium*, whether it is round, oval or square, as well as its height, so as to draw up the niche in which it will be housed.

This note shows that certain doubts remained for long periods of time: here, Pineau references a conversation in September 1743, while an annotation on the drawing indicates that he responded to Father Goulard on 26 March 1745 (18 months later).[52] How can we interpret these doubts? Is it down to the fact that the *ostensorium* was being ordered or made at the same time? Or, if the *ostensorium* was already made, are these questions the result of poor planning or inefficient communication? The written proof of this is only available because Pineau was working from Paris and not on site at Lugny. What is generally done during a site visit or oral discussions becomes written. This process of back and forth must have been frequent in the cases of 'mail orders': one early example is visible in the field of painting with a drawing by Antoine Bouzonnet-Stella, dated 1680, for an altarpiece representing *The Martyrdom of Saint Peter of Verona*, which also bears an annotation on its verso containing questions for a far-removed patron.[53]

The circulation of information is not always so clear. The Musée des Arts Décoratifs holds two very different floorplans for the dining room in the Hôtel Boutin.[54] These were undoubtedly done by the agency of the *hôtel*'s architect, Jacques Mansart de Sagonne, and given to Pineau so that he could plan the panelling of the room. The fact that these drawings ended up in Pineau's studio proves that work by the architect and sculptor was not done in parallel but intertwined in time, and that there was much discussion and back and forth between the two. The second floorplan (Fig. 3.17, CD 1642) is itself the result of just such a process. It includes a flap with a correction and its basis: 'All things considered, here is what is best, both for its usefulness and the regularity of decoration' – 'Tout bien considéré voycy le mieux pour l'exécution, tant pour son utilité que par la décoration qui sera régulière'. On the other side of this flap is the address of Pineau, sculptor, rue Neuve Saint-Martin, written by Mansart de Sagonne. The paper is quite fine in contrast with the thick paper on which the floorplan has been drawn. The text of the flap is not in Pineau's writing as it appears on other drawings. The handwriting is not Mansart de Sagonne's either.[55] Should we then imagine that it was Pineau who proposed this correction, using a piece of paper he had at hand? Or, more plausibly in terms of each participant's role, was the correction thought up and sent by the architect. This implies that architect and sculptor were working on plans of the same scale (which is not the same as the previous floorplan, CD1645), that the architect sent the correction to the sculptor, who then fixed it to his version of the floorplan. This is quite complex but remains the most plausible explanation.

BETWEEN DESIGN AND MAKING

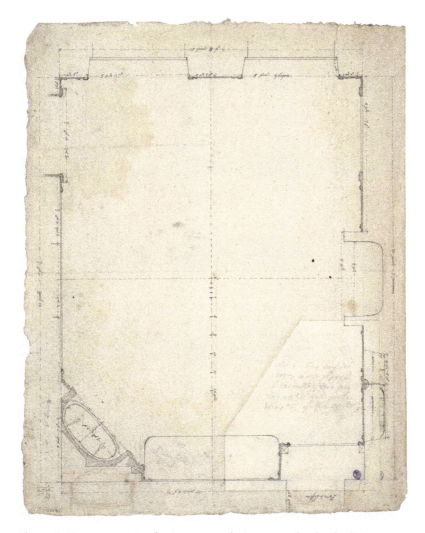

Figure 3.17: Jacques Hardouin-Mansart de Sagonne, *Plan for the dining room in the Hôtel Boutin*, circa 1738. Graphite, pen and black ink, 43.5 × 33 cm.

© Musée des Arts Décoratifs, Paris (CD 1642).

The trial and error visible on these drawings can be connected to ongoing formal discussions. But they are also linked to a necessity to better accommodate certain limitations or to adapt to new ones. The floorplan of the bedroom of the marquise de Voyer, previously mentioned (see Fig. 3.9), has a second piece of paper that has been glued down on the right.[56] As it has been glued down completely, it is not a flap, it does not designate an alternative proposal but a correction. Viewed on a lightbox, the modification appears to be above all of the seating arrangement. The text at the bottom right reveals that the number of seats in this bedroom was a serious preoccupation for the owners: 'one can have only 12 seats and 2 armchairs next to the fireplace'.[57]

One of the most fascinating drawings in the collection has already been published by Katie Scott in *The Rococo Interior*.[58] It is a technical drawing of the moulding for the mirror and door frames and low panelling for the drawing room in the hôtel of the marquise de Feuquières (Fig. 3.18). It is a masterful demonstration of Pineau's desire to coordinate all of these individual elements. It also displays a process of successive approximations and progressive adaptations throughout the elaboration of the design. The long inscription on this drawing contains questions for the architect, whose answers will affect the progress of the project:

> Since we need the width to be able to trace our pieces, I have sketched the moulding that I hope you will have the kindness to take to Monsieur Boscrit [Pierre Boscry, the architect] so that he can correct them if needed, or so that he can do others, and please also take him the drawings, so that he can better judge the mouldings.

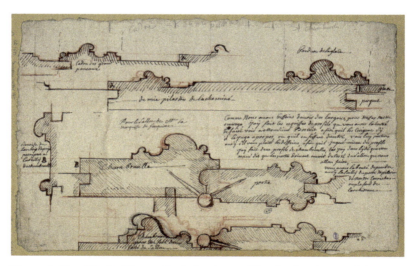

Figure 3.18: Nicolas Pineau, *Study for the moulding for the mirror and door frames and low panelling for the drawing room in the hôtel of the marquise de Feuquières*, circa 1736. Black and red chalk, pen and black ink, 27 × 43.5 cm.

© Musée des Arts Décoratifs, Paris (CD 1651). Photograph by Marion Dupuy.

I have made up two options for the door frames, because I seem to remember you said that the doors need to open into the drawing room we are doing. And please also take the measurement of the tapestry from the cornice to the ceiling architrave.[59]

These questions are aimed at the architect, but whose questions are they and who is passing them along? One could imagine that it is one of Pineau's subcontractors asking questions that he has for the architect, but Turner Edwards recognises Pineau's own handwriting in these annotations. Who then is the intermediary between Pineau and Boscry? Why does the drawing bear questions and not answers given that it remained in the possession of or was returned to Pineau? Was a copy made that was sent or were larger models done? Whatever the case may be, this long inscription is evidence of oral instructions and the circulation of drawings.

A study for three mirrors over fireplaces for the house of the comte de Middelbourg in Suresnes gives an example of trial and error on a project that is already well advanced (Fig. 3.19).[60] Again, the conjoined study of panelling for three different rooms is proof of a quest for general harmony in the interior decoration of a residence. Initial numbers attributed to the three projects and written in red chalk have been modified in ink and the final destination of each has been

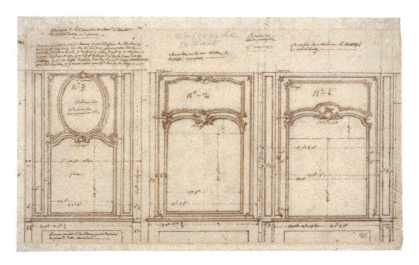

Figure 3.19: Nicolas Pineau, *Study for three mirrors over fireplaces for the house of the comte de Middelbourg in Suresnes*, circa 1747. Pen and brown ink, 25 × 42 cm.
© Musée des Arts Décoratifs, Paris (inv. 29131 B).

clearly written out. Traces of initial graphite sketching are visible on the righthand project, though they have not been kept in the final version. With individual or collective decisions having been made, the designs have been traced over in ink. The same drawing then serves for the delegation of its execution, with dimensions being given to each element and the names of specific workmen next to each part: Mr Laforest; Mr Baltazard; Mr Germain; Mr Bergé. Even more fascinating are the annotations above and bottom left which show that there was a certain amount of adjustment necessary because of uncertainty regarding the dimensions of an over-mirror painting, with a margin of error of three *pouces* (8.1 cm). Below: 'we need to have the painting to be able to draw this fireplace in full scale'.[61] It was evidently the arrival of the painting and its measurement that led Pineau to bring up the error in calculations and to propose, above the drawing, a whole chain of adaptions – the dimensions of the mirror, the way it should be assembled – so as not to modify the height of the lower panels. From this drawing with measurements to full-scale drawings for the carvers, the proportions must then be adjusted. In a period long described as being that of the victory of panelling over painting, this example suggests the latter may have had its revenge on the former.

Conclusion

While Rococo décor is often seen as a light-hearted medium in which its contemporaries lauded the 'pleasures of imagination', behind it is hidden a painstaking process aimed at perfect execution, far from imagined spontaneity. Close examination of the drawings in the Pineau collection has shown that, although they bring up an illusion of unity of time, space and action, in reality they often are proof of processes that take place over the course of days, months and even years; of discussions with various participants, in the same place or separated by time and space, of individual and collective trial and error, and of progressive decision-making processes. These interactions, marked on the drawings, require a nuanced reading of the traditional classification of drawings according to the supposed successive steps in the process of creation (sketches, presentation drawings, working drawings, copies for engravings). They also reveal certain expectations and hierarchies within the project: its utility, its compatibility with specific functions of representation and reception, the regularity of the whole and the possible importance of paintings in determining the proportions of wood panels.

A number of questions persist though, in relation to specific projects, regarding annotations, back and forth in the process, and final decisions. But also, in a more general sense, parts of the process, that vary from commission to commission, escape our understanding: for furniture, the role of models, large and small, in wax, wood or plaster; [62] like the oral aspects, the drawings executed directly on wood planks and even directly onto walls.[63] In a letter to the architect Mansart de Sagonne, Pineau regrets that the two were not able to work out the outline of the Doric entablature on the façade of Saint-Louis de Versailles together. On the basis of this study, I would argue that part of the excellence of these interior designs is thanks to the lively, evolving and discursive nature of their creation. It would follow then that the mix of the numerous rules, the strict delegation of specific tasks to a number of collaborators and the rigid control of each and every step, before, during and after, would bear the risk of reducing creativity which, by its very nature, necessitates flexibility and allowances.

Acknowledgements

My thanks go to Turner Edwards for his translation and numerous suggestions, to Marion Dupuy and François Gilles for their insights, and to Christine Casey, Andrew Tierney and Melanie Hayes for having included me in the exciting debates during the conference, 'Architects and Artisans', at Trinity College Dublin in April 2022. This article also owes much to the workshops that brought together a group of international researchers to discuss the Pineau drawings at Musée des Arts Décoratifs in Paris in 2021.

Notes

1 The collection of drawings by Charles Le Brun, which was seized at his death for the benefit of the Crown and is now kept at the Musée du Louvre, provides a particularly rich example. For its complete publication, see Beauvais, *Musée du Louvre*. For an example of the quantitative and qualitative exploitation that can be made of it, see Gady, 'Los cartones'. See Moulinier, 'Traces de collaboration', for a recent study of the collection of drawings from the studio of Claude III Audran, an artist situated chronologically between Le Brun and Pineau. This collection was acquired during his lifetime by Carl Johan Cronstedt and is now in the collection of the Nationalmuseum in Stockholm, see Moselius and Weigert, *Dessins du Nationalmuseum*.

2 See Kimball, 'Nicolas Pineau' and *The Creation of the Rococo*; Pons, *De Paris à Versailles*; Scott, *The Rococo Interior* and 'Persuasion'; Fuhring, 'Le fonds de Nicolas Pineau', 170.

3 See Ackerman, 'The conventions and rhetoric'.

4 Closely linked to the institution, the donors were Félix Doisteau, Jacques Doucet, Maurice Fenaille, Raymond Koechlin, Jules Maciet and André Peytel. See Biais, *Les Pineau*; Deshairs, *Les Dessins du Musée et de la Bibliothèque*.

5   Full-sized drawings have very rarely been preserved, even though they were frequently used, perhaps because of this utilitarian function. The Christopher Wren collection at St Paul's, for example, contains only one (Higgott, *The Wren Office Drawings*, online). For the counter-example of the 350 Charles Le Brun cartoons for painted decorations, see Gady, 'Los cartones'. In Pineau's collection, see Inv. 8545.1 and Inv. CD 1735 (both reproduced in Fuhring, 'Le fonds de Nicolas Pineau'), CD 1710. Some are pounced for transfer: 8545.77, CD 1709, CD 1711. Even more exceptional, some have large holes on the axis to maintain the cartoon on the support to be sculpted: CD 1711 (Nicolas Pineau), CD 1713 (Dominique Pineau).

6   Geraghty, *The Architectural Drawings*. Studying exploratory drawings, presentation drawings and construction drawings, Geraghty notes: 'In each case the function of the drawing determined the method of architectural representation'.

7   In *The Languages of Art*, Goodman shows how even mimetic representation makes a choice in the reality it chooses to represent or in the procedural conditions of such representation.

8   Ackerman, 'Origins, imitation, conventions', 28–9.

9   Deans, 'Rethinking drawing', 9 and note 46.

10 See, for example, Musée des Arts Décoratifs CD 1685, Inv. 29085A, analysed by Katie Scott, 'Persuasion', paragraph 8. Unless otherwise stated, all drawings mentioned are held at the Musée des Arts Décoratifs in Paris. On this point see also Casey, 'Agreeable to live in', 304–5.

11 Fuhring, 'La circulation des modèles de plafonds', 117 and Fig. 63.

12 Musée des Arts Décoratifs CD 1624.

13 For this, see François Gilles's forthcoming paper in Edwards and Gady (eds), *Nicolas Pineau (1684–1754): Un sculpteur rocaille entre Paris et Saint-Pétersbourg*.

14 Baudez, 'La couleur dans le dessin d'architecture', and *Inessential Colors*.

15 Baudez, *Inessential Colors*, 26–9 ; Geraghty, *The Architectural Drawings*, for example AS I.100 and AS II.6.

16 Deans, 'Rethinking drawing', 11–13, where houses next to the Abbey are heightened with red wash.

17 Musée des Arts Décoratifs CD 1469.

18 On non-codified uses of colour for working drawings, see Baudez, *Inessential Colors*, 116–18.

19 Musée des Arts Décoratifs CD 1674.

20 Musée des Arts Décoratifs Inv. 29096.

21 Baudez, *Inessential Colors*, 112.

22 For France, see for example the project for the decoration of the Hôtel de Bourvalais by Jean-Baptiste Bullet de Chamblain, in Paris, c. 1709–20, in Baudez, *Inessential Colors*, 117, Fig. 86.

23 Musée des Arts Décoratifs CD 1674. Green watercolour for windowpanes and mirrors is still used c. 1770–80 in France, as shown by a *Design for the window wall of a reception room*, preserved in Amsterdam (Rijksmuseum, RP-T-2016-26; Paris, 2023, 105, cat. 48).

24 Musée des Arts Décoratifs Inv. 3396–9. These drawings show similarities with the fireplace engravings published by Mariette in his *Architecture Françoise* in 1727 (t. I and II) and 1738 (t. III); see Laurenti, *Disegni e modelli d'ornati*, 169–70, cat. 13.N.

25 Laurenti, *Disegni e Modelli d'Ornati*, 29, proposes an attribution of these drawings to the decorator Alexandre-Eugène Prignot, at whose sale the museum acquired them. She backs up her hypothesis on the basis of a comparison between these drawings and two drawings signed by Prignot at the Cooper Hewitt, Smithsonian Design Museum (1987–86–1 and 1987–86–2).

26 Musée des Arts Décoratifs Inv. 29131 A.

27 Baudez, *Inessential Colors*, ch. 2.

28 Musée des Arts Décoratifs CD 1497.

29 Over the course of study days devoted to Pineau, François Gilles brought this code to the team's attention. Further analysis will be in the collection's forthcoming publication: Edwards and Gady (eds), *Nicolas Pineau (1684–1754): Un sculpteur rocaille entre Paris et Saint-Pétersbourg*.

30 See for example, Fuhring, *Design into Art*, 19.

31 For example, Musée des Arts Décoratifs CD 1472.

32 Musée des Arts Décoratifs CD 1475 and CD 1600; CD 1577, CD 1579, CD 1598 and CD 1599; CD 1734; CD 1686; Inv. 29123 B.

33 Musée des Arts Décoratifs Inv. 29115.

34 Ader Sale, 20 March 2023, lot 8 (attributed to Peter Flötner; new attribution to Georg Pencz by Benjamin Peronnet).

35 Musée des Arts Décoratifs CD 1491A.

36 'Il n'est pas aysé sur cette article quy ne décident point sy sur le dessein on a choisie le costé où est marqué un tableau, ou le costé quy marque la glace jusqu'en haut. Cette article disant seulement un trumeau monté en deux pièce, savoir sy par les deux pièces l'on entend la grande glace en deux morceaux, ou sy par les deux pièces l'on doit entendre le costé où est un tableau et une glace au-dessous'. Musée des Arts Décoratifs CD 1491B.

37 Musée des Arts Décoratifs CD 1624.

38 Musée des Arts Décoratifs CD 1655.

39 Musée des Arts Décoratifs CD 1576. See the forthcoming volume by Edwards and Gady (eds), *Nicolas Pineau (1684–1754): Un sculpteur rocaille entre Paris et Saint-Pétersbourg*.

40 Hermitage OP-30546 to OP-30553.

41 Musée des Arts Décoratifs CD 1685; Scott, 'Persuasion', paragraph 7.

42 Musée des Arts Décoratifs CD 1468.

43 Sainte Fare Garnot, *Le Décor des Tuileries*.

44 Musée des Arts Décoratifs CD 1685, among many examples.

45 Musée des Arts Décoratifs CD 1494. Katie Scott has pointed out that Pineau, for simpler projects, sometimes sought to influence decisions by taking greater care to finish the right-hand section of a drawing in order to seduce the eye (Scott, 'Persuasion', paragraph 15). This difference in degrees of finish may also be partly explained by the fact that Pineau was himself right-handed.

46 Musée des Arts Décoratifs CD 1475.

47 Ekserdjian, *The Italian Renaissance Altarpiece*, 71–6; Paris, 2023, 174, cat. 92.

48 Musée des Arts Décoratifs CD 1497.

49 Musée des Arts Décoratifs CD 1704.

50 Musée des Arts Décoratifs CD 1626. 'Plant du gradin pour porter le tabernacle'.

51 'Afin que les agraffes se trouvent recouvertes par les socles des consoles des angles du tabernacle'.

52 The verso bears also a later annotation, proof of this back and forth: 'au très reverend Père'.

53 Paris, musée du Louvre, Inv. 25034; Gady, *Dessiner pour Prier*. Following a well-established convention, Bouzonnet-Stella placed the light source in the upper left corner of his painting, but, in a second phase, inquired as to the natural lighting of the spot where his painting would be exhibited so as to make it coincide with the light represented.

54 Musée des Arts Décoratifs CD 1645 and CD 1642.

55 The handwriting differs from Mansart de Sagonne's, as we see it on a letter to Pineau (Musée des Arts Décoratifs CD 1730). My thanks to Turner Edwards for his help in this graphological matter.

56 Musée des Arts Décoratifs CD 1655.

57 'L'on peut n'avoir que 12 fauteuils et mettre 2 bergères proche de la cheminée ...'.

58 Musée des Arts Décoratifs CD 1651. Scott, *The Rococo Interior*, 16, Fig. 17.

59 'Comme nous avons bessoins d'avoir des largeurs, pour trasser nostre ouvrage, j'ay fait les esquisses de profils que vous aurés la bonté de faire voir à Monsieur Boscrit [sic pour Charles Boscry, l'architecte], afin qu'il les corigent sy il le juge à propos, ou qu'il en fassent d'autre, vous luy portez ausy s'il vous plaits les desseins, afin qu'il jugent mieux des profils. J'ay fait deux profils de chambralles, car j'ay dans l'ydé que vous m'avé dit que les portes doivent ouvrir du costé du sallon que nous allons faire, vous aurés la bonté de prendre ausy la sailly du porte tapicerie de nostre corniche au plafond de l'architrave'.

60 Musée des Arts Décoratifs Inv. 29131 B.

61 'Il faut avoir le tableau pour dessiner en grand cette cheminée'.

62 Pradère, 'L'âge d'or', 49.

63 Exceptional images of the walls of the Great Drawing Room of the hôtel d'Orrouer after the dismantling of the panelling in the 1930s are preserved in the Médiathèque du Patrimoine and Carlhian Archive at the Getty Research Institute, discovered by Turner Edwards and François Gilles (see forthcoming volume by Edwards and Gady (eds), *Nicolas Pineau (1684–1754): Un sculpteur rocaille entre Paris et Saint-Pétersbourg*). On this dismantling, see Verdier, 'Les boiseries de l'hôtel de Bauffremont', 180–3.

References

Ackerman, James S. 'The conventions and rhetoric of architectural drawing'. In *Conventions of Architectural Drawing: Representation and misrepresentation*, edited by James S. Ackerman and Wolfgang Jung, 9–36. Cambridge, MA: Harvard University Graduate School of Design, 2000.

Ackerman, James S. *Origins, Imitation, Conventions: Representation in the visual arts*. Cambridge, MA: MIT Press, 2002.

Baudez, Basile. 'La couleur dans le dessin d'architecture au XVIIe siècle: Une histoire de peintres, d'ingénieurs et d'architectes'. In *Architectes du Grand Siècle: Du dessinateur au maître d'œuvre*, edited by Alexandre Cojannot and Alexandre Gady, 162–87. Paris: Le Passage, 2020.

Baudez, Basile. *Inessential Colors: Architecture on paper in early modern Europe*. Princeton, NJ: Princeton University Press, 2021.

Beauvais, Lydia. *Charles Le Brun (1619–1690): Inventaire général des dessins*. Paris: Réunion des musées nationaux, 2000.

Biais, Émile. *Les Pineau, sculpteurs, dessinateurs des bâtiments du Roy, graveurs, architectes (1652–1886): D'après les documents inédits, contenant des renseignements sur J. Hardouin-Mansard, les Prault, imprimeurs-libraires*. Paris: Société des Bibliophiles François, 1892.

Casey, Christine. '"Agreeable to live in": The wainscoted interior in eighteenth-century Britain and Ireland'. In *Enriching Architecture: Craft and its conservation in Anglo-Irish building production*, edited by Christine Casey and Melanie Hayes, 289–315. London: UCL Press, 2023.

Deans, Elizabeth. 'Rethinking drawing and office practices in early eighteenth-century England: A study of William Dickinson's pocketbook', *The Georgian Group Journal*, 29 (2021): 1–22.

Deshairs, Léon. *Les Dessins du Musée et de la Bibliothèque des Arts Décoratifs: XVIIIe siècle, Nicolas et Dominique Pineau*. Paris: D. A. Longuet, 1911.

Edwards, Turner and Bénédicte Gady (eds), *Nicolas Pineau (1684–1754): Un sculpteur rocaille entre Paris et Saint-Pétersbourg*. Paris: Le Passage, forthcoming 2024.

Ekserdjian, David. *The Italian Renaissance Altarpiece*. New Haven: Yale University Press, 2021.

Fuhring, Peter. *Design into Art: Drawings for architecture and ornament. The Lodewijk Houthakker collection*. London: Philip Wilson Publishers, 1989.

Fuhring, Peter. 'La circulation des modèles de plafonds à travers l'estampe'. In *Peupler les Cieux: Les plafonds parisiens au XVIIe siècle*, exhibition catalogue edited by Bénédicte Gady, 112–27. Paris: Passage, 2014.

Fuhring, Peter. 'Le fonds de Nicolas Pineau et de son atelier'. In *Le Dessin sans Réserve: Collections du Musée des Arts décoratifs*, exhibition catalogue edited by Bénédicte Gady, 170–1. Paris: Musée des Arts Décoratifs, 2020.

Gady, Bénédicte. *Dessiner pour Prier: Projets pour les églises de Paris au XVIIe siècle*, exhibition pamphlet. Paris: Musée du Louvre, 2013.

Gady, Bénédicte. 'Los cartones de Charles Le Brun: Un testimonio único de la fabricación de las grandes decoraciones'. In *Dibujar Versalles: Bocetos y cartones de Charles Le Brun (1619–1690) para la Escalera de los Embajadores y la Galería de los Espejos*, exhibition catalogue edited by Bénédicte Gady, 23–37. Madrid: CaixaForum, 2016.

Geraghty, Anthony. *The Architectural Drawings of Sir Christopher Wren at All Souls College, Oxford: A complete catalogue*. Aldershot: Lund Humphries, 2007. Accessed 5 January 2024. https://library.asc.ox.ac.uk/wren/.

Goodman, Nelson. *Languages of Art: An approach to a theory of symbols*. Indianapolis, IN: Hackett, 1976.

Higgott, Gordon. 'Wren and his draughtsmen'. In *St Paul's Cathedral Wren Office Drawings catalogue*, 2013. Accessed 5 January 2024. https://web.archive.org/web/20140530135211/http://www.stpauls.co.uk/Cathedral-History/The-Collections/Architectural-Archive/Wren-and-his-draughtsmen.

Kimball, Fiske. 'Nicolas Pineau and the cabinet of Peter the Great', *Art in America*, 30:4 (1942): 232–7.

Kimball, Fiske. *The Creation of the Rococo*. Philadelphia: Philadelphia Museum of Art, 1943.

Laurenti, Aurora. *Disegni e Modelli d'Ornato per la Decorazione Intagliata Rococò: Da Parigi a Torino, 1730–1750*. Torino: Fondazione 1563, 2019.

Mariette, Jean. *L'architecture Françoise, ou, Recueil des plans, elevations, coupes et profils*. Paris: Jean Mariette, 1727.

Moselius, Carl David and Roger-Armand Weigert. *Dessins du Nationalmuseum de Stockholm: Collections Tessin & Cronstedt*, exhibition catalogue. Paris: Bibliothèque nationale de France, 1950.

Moulinier, Axel. 'Traces de collaboration entre Claude III Audran et Claude Gillot: Les plafonds pour le château de Petit-Bourg et la "Chaise du Roy"'. *Les Cahiers d'Histoire de l'Art,* 18 (2020): 57–67.

Pons, Bruno. *De Paris à Versailles, 1699–1736: Les sculpteurs ornemanistes parisiens et l'art décoratif des bâtiments du roi*. Strasbourg: Association les publications près les Universités de Strasbourg, 1986.

Pons, Bruno. *Grands Décors Français 1650–1800: Reconstitués en Angleterre, aux États-Unis, en Amérique du Sud et en France*. Dijon: Faton, 1995.

Pradère, Alexandre. 'L'âge d'or du mobilier français'. In *18e Aux Sources du Design: Chefs-d'œuvre du mobilier 1650–1790*, exhibition catalogue, 36–52. Versailles: Château de Versailles, 2014.

Sainte Fare Garnot, Nicolas. *Le Décor des Tuileries sous le Règne de Louis XIV*. Paris: Editions de la Réunion des Musées Nationaux, 1988.

Scott, Katie. *The Rococo Interior: Decoration and social spaces in early eighteenth-century Paris*. New Haven, CT and London: Yale University Press, 1995.

Scott, Katie. 'Persuasion: Nicolas Pineau's designs on the social', *RIHA Journal*, 86 (2014): 1–23.

Verdier, Paul. 'Les boiseries de l'hôtel de Bauffremont à Paris: L'heureuse issue d'un long procès', *Monuments historiques*, 5 (1938): 180–3.

4
Architects and artificers: building management at Trinity College Dublin in the 1730s and 1740s

Melanie Hayes

> Mr Castles was remarkably ready at drawing, and so clear in his directions to workmen, that the most ignorant could not err … When the effect of his works was not such as he liked he frequently pulled them down, and whenever he came to inspect them, he required the attendance of all the artificers who followed him in a long train.[1]

Between 1734 and his death in 1751 Richard Castle (c.1691–1751) acted as the chief architect for Trinity College Dublin, overseeing a wide range of building works during this period. In addition to surveying the repair of older structures and overseeing more ad hoc works like the Tennis Court or the canal in College Park, Castle – who had only arrived in Ireland five years earlier, by way of continental Europe and Britain – designed the Printing House (1734–7), a new Dining Hall (c.1740–4, repaired 1748, rebuilt 1760s) and the Bell Tower or 'Steeple' (c.1740–6, demolished 1792) as it was known, as well as unexecuted designs for a new entrance front to the college (Fig. 4.1). Of these only the Printing House survives, the others either collapsed or were demolished within decades of building and Castle has come under criticism for his engineering 'embarrassments' at the college; but whether one comes down on the side of 'laudably daring' or 'merely cavalier', Castle's real legacy can be found in the introduction of new efficiencies in the management of these large and diverse works.[2] According to Arthur Gibney – who has done much to rehabilitate Castle's reputation both as a structural engineer and in building management – he introduced a new level of professionalism into the college in the 1730s. In contrast to his predecessor Thomas Burgh's (1670–1730) 'casual management

Figure 4.1: Detail from Samuel Byron, *A bird's-eye perspective plan of Trinity College park and gardens*, 1780.

TCD MUN-MC-9. © The Board of Trinity College Dublin.

style', which according to Gibney involved minimal 'written instructions or certificates', Richard Castle appears to have been 'highly formalised and carefully regulated'.[3] Drawing on the rich and valuable evidence of the financial records in the college muniments, this chapter explores the mechanisms employed by Castle in the 1730s and 1740s, to establish more professional forms of trade relations and competitive contractual systems, which would transform building practice in the college for the century to come. Through close analysis of these discrete agreements and financial operations, combined with comparative material from Britain and Ireland, it seeks to recreate a clearer picture of the collaborative nature of building process during this period, and the interconnected networks of actors involved in Richard Castle's workshop practice at Trinity College Dublin.

Surveying, supervision and set up on site

Following the Restoration and the Great Fire of London, England saw an exponential rise in building activity, with increased demand for skilled personnel and access to materials. Major public and church building schemes called for a new organisational structure in which the 'architect' emerged as new professional entity, and by the early 1700s, David Yeomans notes: 'architects were finding a niche for themselves between the design skills of the craftsmen and the management skills of the surveyors'.[4] A new breed of practically-minded, craft-trained architects came up through the Office of Works – men like Nicholas Hawksmoor (c.1661–1736) or Thomas Ripley (1683–1758), whose role was often as much about the coordination and management of the building project, as it was the design of the building, or the drafting of plans.[5] Sir Christopher Wren (1632–1723), architect of St Paul's Cathedral, London, and Surveyor of the King's Works, has been characterised a 'coordinator of an army of craftsmen and artisans by means of an efficiently run office'.[6] The executant architect was frequently as much an orchestrator as initiator, tendering separate building contracts for each aspect of the work, coordinating and sometimes supervising a range of building contractors, each with their own responsibilities, workforce and materials, not to mention general labour and site management. Indeed, as Robert Morris (1703–1754) remarked, the architect or surveyor must 'take care that every part, both general and particular, be perform'd with sound Materials, neatly and ingenious wrought, and united artfully by the Hands of the Artists'.[7] This shift in practice, which spread outwards from London, across the British Isles, reflects a move away from artisanal autonomy, towards increased intervention and control of the building process by the overseeing architect, as illustrated in scenes such as that by Thomas Rowlandson (Fig. 4.2). The successful negotiation of the complex and sometimes overlapping trade divisions within the building crafts, and the practicalities of such hands-on management, required a new form of interaction between artisan and architect.[8]

At Trinity College, Richard Castle was responsible for coordinating a diverse range of building tasks, both 'ordinary', or maintenance of existing works, and 'extraordinary', work on new buildings.[9] As well as payments for his own time preparing designs and overseeing building on the major new works, Castle submitted numerous bills for surveying and supervising repairs, and certified over 80 bills for maintenance to existing works between 1737 and 1746.[10] This compares to only 15 recorded instances in the college muniments where Thomas Burgh certified or signed off on bills for works (new or maintenance) at Trinity.[11] For example, Castle regularly signed off on repairs to carpentry and joinery including 'seats and wainscot in the college chapel', or 'work done att the [old] Provost's house', 'making a press' and mending floors.[12] Glazing and slating repairs were also frequently required and

Figure 4.2: Thomas Rowlandson, *An Architectural Inspection*, circa 1810.
Courtesy of the Lewis Walpole Library, Yale University.

the college had ongoing agreements with a number of contractors, who were overseen by Castle with a degree of efficiency not hitherto apparent: on 9 October 1742 Agnes Heatly submitted a bill 'for keeping ye Roofs of ye College in repair', four days later Castle signed off on these costs, noting: 'I have examined the above bill and find it to be just, Rich. Castle Oct 13 1742'.[13] This stands in contrast to previous practice at the college, where tradesmen often waited several months, if not years to be paid. One notable example was a bill for joiners' work carried out by John Sisson in 1704, but not paid until July 1708.[14] The need for efficient oversight is clear from the college muniments, which show increasingly large amounts of repair work compared to new builds during the period in question. A bill for painting and plastering repairs to several staircases in the residential quarters in 1736 shows the extent of maintenance work required. Therein William Wall noted the staircases had been 'repaired as to lath and Plaster stoping whitewashing sizeing and blacking the bottoms of said Stairs, they having not been done these seven years past and best be done Every three years'.[15]

The muniments also show the degree of coordination and monitoring the workforce required, not just master craftsmen and major building contractors, but smaller scale operators and labour on sundry works. In 1740, when building at the New Hall and Bell Tower was underway, Castle was employed overseeing works on the Tennis or

Ball Court, which was built near the northern boundary of the college (Fig. 4.3).[16] In addition to coordinating the supply of materials Castle was also responsible for contracting general labour.[17] 'An account of the labourers working at the Ball court by order of Rich.d Castle Esq. under the Care [of] John Kane', which is broken down by day of the week and labourers required, not only provides insights into the day rates charged for labour, it also demonstrates the level of oversight required on the part of the surveyor. Over the course of one week, working Monday to Saturday inclusive, 71 labourers were employed, 'cutting the ground and filling the Ball Court floor'; another week 66 men were employed, 'filling the Ball Court floor and Levelling the Ditches'.[18] This same year Castle was also occupied with works on the canal in College Park, which was constructed between 1740–3 on part of the site on which New Square was built the following century, east of a well-planted lawn next to the tree-lined avenue which ran between the Anatomy House (1710–11) and Printing House (1734–7).[19] Here, Gilbert Plummer's account of 'work Diging out ye Canall in the Park' shows the extent of the labour involved: '2406 yards of Earth Dug out of ye Canall' as well as 'Five nights Eight men & One night nine men Scooping out ye water'.[20] A similar degree of oversight was evident in site preparation. The Bell Tower which was built at the corner of the Old Quadrangle in front of the Old

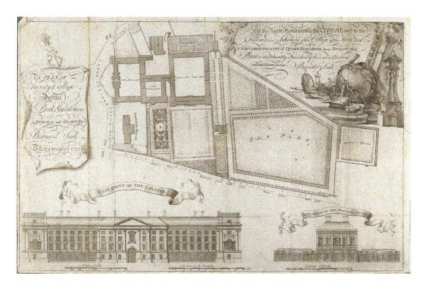

Figure 4.3: Bernard Scale, *A plan of Trinity College Dublin, park gardens &c.*, 1761.

© The Board of Trinity College Dublin.

Hall, proved particularly problematic. The water table was high at this point and required considerable investment of time and labour digging out and driving wooden stakes into the foundations and fitting a pump in a timber trough 'to drane ye foundation' in the spring of 1740.[21] James Thompson, pump borer, who fitted 'a new pump for the use of ye stiple' in May 1740 returned a further four times that month 'to mend ye steeple pump' including 'going at 12 a clock a Sunday night to mend it'.[22] This begs the question as to whether the site had been adequately tested in advance of construction. At St John the Evangelist, Westminster, where there had been similar issues with the water table, Nicholas Hawksmoor, along with two bricklayers, visited the site prior to construction in 1711 to ascertain if the ground would provide adequate foundations for building.[23] Castle, like Hawksmoor, had a reputation for such practical professionalism and close supervision of workmen.[24] He certainly took a hands-on role in the setting out of the site. In May 1740 John Connell, carpenter, submitted a bill for work on the College Steeple which included costs for '5 men 1 day fixing the Running Scaffold, making stakes & attending Mr Castles when he was setting out for ye foundation walls'.[25]

While time consuming, there was a benefit of such close supervision for the overseeing architect. Unlike his predecessors at the college, Castle did not hold the salaried post of Surveyor General, and so relied solely on professional fees from clients. On top of his design fees and other ad hoc payments, Castle was paid 5 per cent of building costs for 'surveying sundry works' at Trinity College in 1738.[26] This was the same rate as was charged by surveyors in the Office of Works in England, who received a percentage of contracting artisans fees for such superintendence, and Arthur Jones Neville (Surveyor General, 1743–52) later claimed that this was also customary practice in Ireland.[27] Another benefit, it has been suggested, of such close supervision and oversight, was that it negated, to an extent, the need to produce large volumes of working drawings.[28]

Cost control: competitive tenders

Another key responsibility of the overseeing architect was the financial management of the building project. At the Printing House (Fig. 4.4) Richard Castle instigated a more rigorous management structure than had previously been in place at the college, and introduced a system of competitive contracting, whereby different trades or contractors tendered costed estimates, vying against each other to win the building

Figure 4.4: Printing House, Trinity College Dublin.
© The Board of Trinity College Dublin.

contract.[29] For instance, in 1733–4 both Isaac Wills and Joseph McCleery submitted estimates for carpentry and joiners work. McCleery, in fact, submitted two separate estimates, one for workmanship alone and the other including materials (Fig. 4.5); these were mainly for structural carpentry but also included costs for joinery such as 'Bead raised pannell wainscott', decorative mouldings and a 'ramp'd and kneed' stair.[30] James Morris and John Plummer submitted proposals for brick and stone walling, or rough masonry, while Moses Darley, the principal stonecutter at the College Library (1712–32) bid for the stone cutting contract at the Printing House, submitting estimates for 'superficial mouldings', 'Ashlar and Rustik' work and materials (Fig. 4.6).[31] This competitive process, which had been utilised on a larger scale by Wren at St Paul's Cathedral, and later by the Office of Works, involved individual trades, who submitted their tenders or 'proposals' for work, which was then let to the lowest bidder.[32] This not only ensured the best price for the client, it promoted higher quality work and increased control for the architect or overseer. Yet, although cost was likely the deciding factor, other considerations may also have come in to play at Trinity, which suggest the limitations of Castle's jurisdiction when it came to appointing

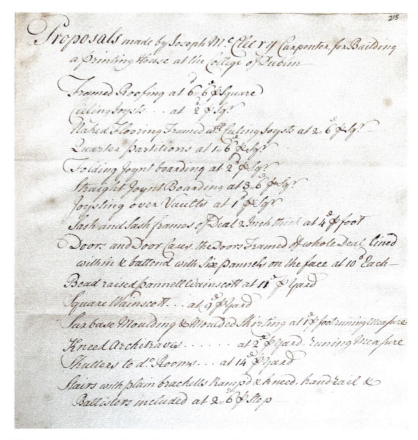

Figure 4.5: 'Proposals made by Joseph McCleery carpenter for building a Printing House in the College of Dublin'.

TCD MS MUN/P/2/65/3. © The Board of Trinity College Dublin.

contractors. For example, despite having established links with Richard Castle at Powerscourt, County Wicklow, where he oversaw much of the carpentry and joinery work between 1732 and 1740, Joseph McCleery was unsuccessful in his bid at the Printing House.[33] And although he retained some form of professional relationship with Castle, for whom he later witnessed a lease for property at Proud Lane in Dublin in 1743, McCleery does not appear to have bid for, or been awarded any other contract at the college.[34] Instead, the carpentry contract was awarded to John Connell, who, we shall see, seems to have had prior connections at the college.[35]

'An estimate of the expense of the Printing House intended to be built' (Fig. 4.7) submitted by Castle's office, highlights the discrete

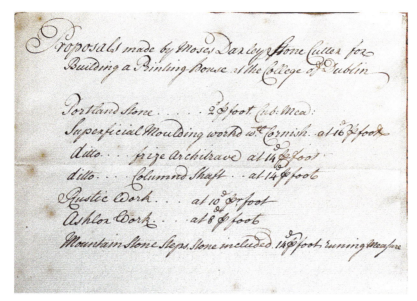

Figure 4.6: 'Proposals by Moses Darley, Stone Cutter for building a Printing House at the College of Dublin'.

TCD MS MUN/P/2/65/1. © The Board of Trinity College Dublin.

nature of eighteenth-century building contracts or tenders. The project was broken down into a sequence of separate tasks, each with their own quantified unit costs: from the digging out and laying of the 'shore', the building of rough masonry and brick walling, to the provision of ironmongery, window fittings and roof coverings, which here included '1 ½ Tun of lead' and expensive Dutch pan tiles, as well as decorative enrichments in stone, timber and plaster.[36] This estimate also included costs for 'scaffolding Poles, Boards, Ropes etc.', while the later estimate for the Bell Tower included those for 'Diging & Carrying Away the Rubish out of the Foundations' indicating that, unlike Burgh, Castle took on the management of the overall building process, coordinating the supply of supporting materials and general labour.[37]

Risk management: the measured contract

At the same time Castle's use of the measured contract not only gave the architect more control over the project, it also served, according to the economic historian Judy Stephenson, as an 'advanced management tool to minimise risk and assure quality, with a minimum of monitoring'.[38]

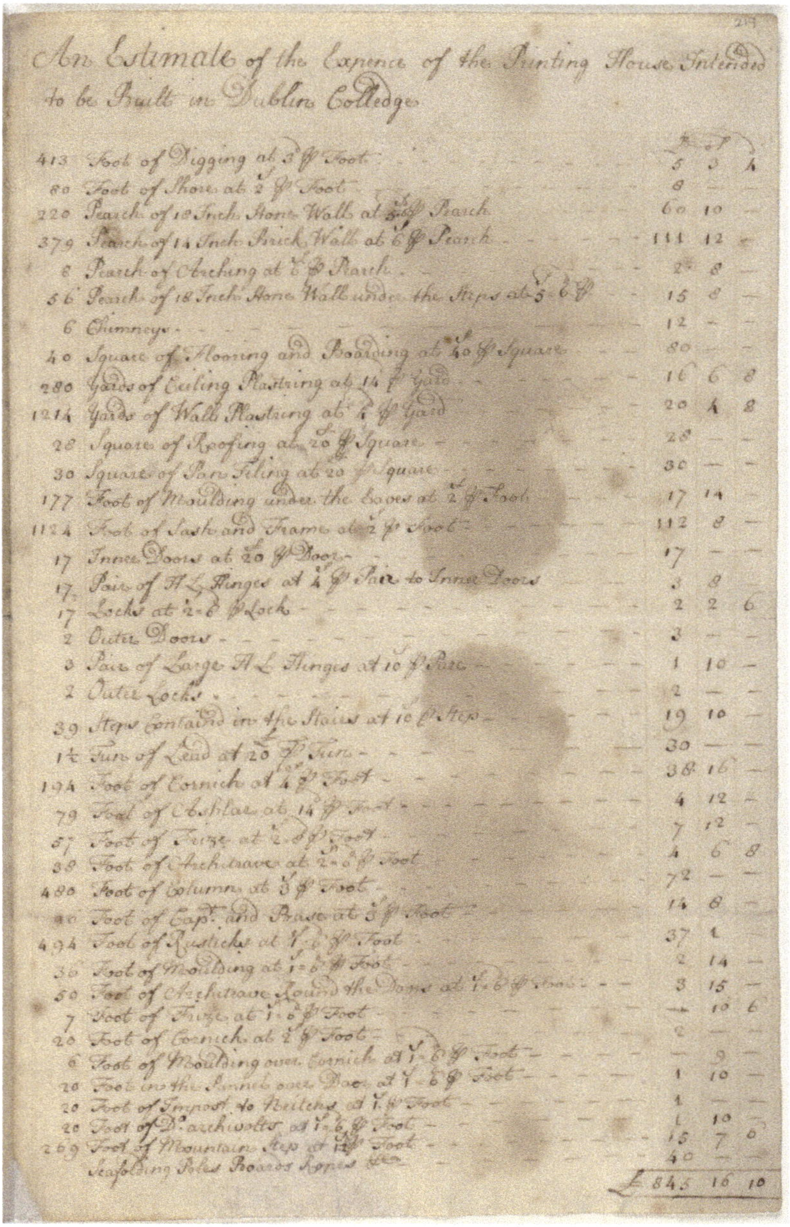

Figure 4.7: 'An Estimate of the Expence of the Printing House Intended to be Built in Colledge'.

TCD MS MUN/P/2/65/5. © The Board of Trinity College Dublin.

This form of contract, or way of working – which Castle also employed at Powerscourt, County Wicklow, in this period – was essentially a separate agreement, made with each trade, which specified set unit or piece-rates for individual tasks, and sometimes the supply of materials. The inspection and certification of each element, which usually took place before the bill was drawn up and certainly before it was passed for payment, ensured the work was completed to a satisfactory standard, at pre-agreed rates, regardless of the time taken or inflated costs incurred by the contractor. At Petworth House in Sussex, for example, the joiner's agreement of 1686 stated that work was to 'be measured when it shall be finished and the accompt made up according to the measurements thereon'. Payments were to be made 'as the worke shall goo on reserving the sum of fifty pounds for security of the ... better performance of the sd. joiners work until the sd. work is finished'.[39] Writing to the Bishop of Oxford in 1681 about the respective benefits of the three different ways of working or types of building contract, Sir Christopher Wren clearly favoured working by the measure:

> If by day it tells me when they are Lazy. If by measure it gives me light on every particular, and tells me what I am to provide. If by the Great I can make a sure bargain, neither to be overreached, nor to hurt the undertaker ... I think the best way in this business is to worke by measure: according to the prices in the estimate, or lower if you can, and measure the work in 3 or 4 measurements as it rises. But you must have a trusty measurer ...[40]

The first instance of a form of measured contract used at Trinity College dates to 1640, and although there were a small number of in-gross (essentially a fixed lump sum for completing the entire project or specific body of work) contracts issued in the 1720s, the college largely employed measured contracts throughout the eighteenth century. These agreements seem to have been based on costed estimates, sometimes with annexed plans or drawings, though no warranted building contracts survive in the college muniments for the eighteenth century.[41] These agreements and the subsequent bills sometimes included day work, for labour and ad hoc tasks, and occasionally the supply of materials. Although contracts in-gross or work by 'the great' were intended to save the client money, Gibney notes that they 'had a bad reputation among architects because of the opportunities it offered to contractors to skimp on materials and workmanship to ensure profit margins'. As Robert Morris noted, the 'Badness of the Materials, and the Employment

ARCHITECTS AND ARTIFICERS 129

of illiterate Workmen, all conducingly unite to the general Cause of the Decay of the whole Fabrick'.[42]

Another benefit to working by the measure was its incremental nature. Measurement of work undertaken often took place on a phased basis throughout the build, while occasional deductions or negotiations over costs as the job progressed ensured accuracy in billing. This allowed, according to Stephenson, for 'the transference of information ... about performance' as well as 'enforcement of costs'.[43] This is evident at the New Hall at Trinity College, which was designed by Castle about 1740, to the south of the Old Quadrangle.[44] David Sheehan's bill for 'Stonecutters work Done in the New Hall' offers considerable detail on the form and finishing of this now lost building, as well as the materials employed. At the same time it speaks to the incremental and cumulative processes involved in carrying out such measured contracts. We get a sense of the labour involved in 'Cutting 268 Dentils in the Great Mountain Stone Ionick Cornice' or the '91 feet and 1 inches of the Mountain Stone Sweld Frieze', and the skill required in 'Masoning & Carving 4 Ionick pilaster Capitals' or fashioning 'the Portland Stone Crowns to ye neaches'.[45] The first phase of works, which made up the bulk of the bill, was measured in September 1744, while the remaining elements – minor finishing details to the steps and floors – were not measured until the following October, 1745. At this point a deduction of £146 was made to the total costs, for 'Scotch flagging not finished'. Only then was the revised total of just over £518 certified for payment.

While there is some divergence between the formal arrangement of the New Hall in surviving plans (Fig. 4.8) and estimates, and what we can glean of the Hall as built – even down to the order used to articulate the external façade – the level of technical specification evident in the general estimates submitted by Castle's office suggests a thorough-going understanding of the requirements of each trade, and a practical knowledge of building process. At the same time, the level of correspondence between these estimates and the subsequent bills, may point to the ongoing collaboration between architect and craftsmen, in drawing up such building tenders and carrying out the costed works. For example, 'sashes and frames' cost 12d. per foot in both estimate and bill, whereas the costs of plastering the vaults in the cellar differed by only one pence per foot.[46] Detailed specifications notwithstanding, changes often occurred as the works progressed. This is evident with the timber eaves cornice to the Hall, which according to the estimate was to comprise of 360 feet of 'wood Cornice round ye Eves' at 18d. per foot, and was to be carried, as the drawing shows, across the principal

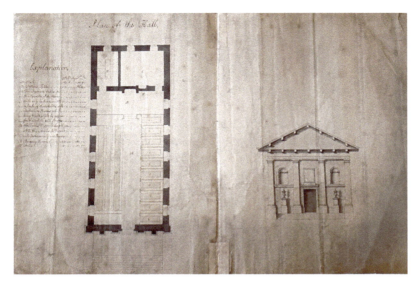

Figure 4.8: Plan and elevation of the New Hall, Trinity College, attributed to Richard Castle, circa 1740.

© The Board of Trinity College Dublin.

façade. In the Hall as built, John Connell executed 169 feet and one third of an inch 'Running of Mondilions Cornice on ye 2 Side fronts, the Mondillions being of Oak at 3*s*. 6*d*.' per foot. Indeed, as Yeomans notes: 'Designs generally were not complete at the time contracts were let, but were modified and refined during construction'.[47] Such refinement, or changes in direction, could have considerable cost implications and the disputes over contracted prices regularly arose due to the increased cost of materials or unforeseen issues with the build.[48] At Trinity College, Richard Castle rather unashamedly revised his own estimate upwards over the course of construction of both the Hall and 'Steeple' roofs, citing changes to the technical design specification and increased costs or rather miscalculations in the costed estimates of timber.[49] Such estimates could also be subjective. A memorandum by the carpenter-turned-architect Michael Wills was highly critical of the estimate for wainscotting in the New Hall, noting that: 'The person who makes the estimate mentions neither the thickness, nor the sort; of which you must be particularly careful'. Having given, in his opinion, the correct computation of costs, Wills notes: 'Upon which you may observe that oak work, which is properly Wainscot, is double in expence to Fir which is properly but lining. Had it been done of hewn stone the same with the front, it would not have exceeded £145.16'.[50] Whether it was due to the materials used, the workmanship, or more likely the conditions on site, Castle's ill-fated Hall lasted less than 20 years. In 1744 part of the building was brought down by a storm; three years later there was a partial collapse in the vaults and the cost of repair was borne by Castle.[51] A more catastrophic collapse occurred in 1758 during work on the foundations of a new kitchen adjoining the Hall, and the entire building had to be removed by John Semple, George Darley and George Stewart in 1759. The timber work, which had been stored in a specially constructed shed in the Physic Garden was reused, as was some of the original hewn stonework.[52]

Measurement and inspection

As Wren noted above, the measurer was a key figure in the management of eighteenth-century building process. Their job was to examine and measure the work of individual craftsmen or contractors, and from these measurements (often in conjunction with published rates of pay) extrapolate the measured costs, from which bills were drawn up and certified for payment.[53] While measurers could have a grounding in any of the building trades, they tended to come from the higher ranks or master craftsmen, capable, according to Gibney, of acting in a supervisory role.[54] At Petworth House the contract for carpentry in 1688 stated that all work 'shall be exactly measured by [a] knownd expert man according to the common way or practice'.[55] Yet, as was the case with architects at this time, there was no formal training or established route to achieving such expertise. Much like the modern quantity surveyor a degree of mathematical skill would have been required, as well as an understanding of the various processes used to measure different types of work. From the late seventeenth century a range of measuring guides were published with increasing regularity to assist tradesmen in this regard.[56] These were largely concerned with arithmetic and geometry, though works like William Hawney's *The Compleat Measurer* (London, 1717), which ran to multiple editions, also included some practical advice, such as the 'commodious' use of 'little Brass Centre-Pins' in calculating measurements for brickwork, or the use of string to measure the 'girt over all the mouldings' in wainscot.[57] Others, like *The Carpenter's Plain and Exact Rule* (Dublin imprint, 1738) included standard costs for set pieces of work, and sometimes wages for workmen. Casey, however, notes a lack of precision in many of these guides, which to some extent was 'symptomatic of measuring practice in Ireland at midcentury', and points to the fallibility of a system wherein 'Architects and builders with no special experience in the field were employed to assess the work of their professional rivals'.[58] The measurer Brian Bolger, writing later in the eighteenth century corroborates this picture, remarking that at this time 'there was some men who had assumed the practice of measuring without any knowledge or instruction in the profession to recommend them.'[59] A more formalised version of the measured contract or basis of calculating costs evolved towards the end of the eighteenth century, known as the measure and value system. This required two measurers (one for the building, one for the client) to take measurements during and after the building work and calculate costs on a 'cost plus basis' – based on current market rates for materials and labour at the 'rates of wages men are paid', plus 15 per cent profit – though this too was ultimately found to lack financial rigour.[60]

Perhaps for these reasons, contracts for large institutional works in England tended to be measured by the superintending architect or surveyor. Yet while Castle is known to have measured works himself at Powerscourt in County Wicklow, at Trinity College this task was largely carried out by his assistant and Clerk of Works, John Ensor (c.1715–1787). The Ensor family had come over to Dublin from Coventry in the mid 1720s, where Job, John Ensor's father, was employed as a carpenter at the Parliament House in 1729.[61] Little is known about John Ensor's formal training, he was not much more than 10 years of age when the family moved to Dublin, and only 14 when works began at the Parliament House, though it is believed that he first came under Castle's notice here, while assisting his father on the project. By the late 1730s he was certainly in Castle's employ (though no record of payments to Ensor can be found in the college accounts, suggesting he was paid by Castle directly) and from the subsequent quantity of bills measured by Ensor (though the final certification of costs was given by Castle), the extent of his role in supervising college works is clear.[62] In fact, one must wonder, given the sheer volume of commissions Castle is credited with during this period, how frequently he was actually present on site. Castle had lodgings in nearby Suffolk Street, while a number of documents in the muniments attest to his having a dedicated office at the college in the 1740s, which does not seem to have been the case for Thomas Burgh.[63] William Wall's bill for painting in 1741 included '5 yards 6 feet Painting on ye Finishing in Mr Castles Office', as well as painting four 'Winser Chairs in ditto a Green colour'.[64] While this would seem to suggest a sizeable operation, and regular presence on site, we cannot be certain how often one of these chairs was left vacant. Susannah Este's complaints over 'Mr Castles' tardiness in attending the building site at the Bishop's Palace at Waterford, points to Ensor's deputation:

> Mr Castles's Clerk (Mr Ensor) was here yesterday to let me know y.t his going to Waterford is Again put of till some time next Week y.s is ye way he has served me constantly for these 2 months past putting me off from week to week & I really fear it is so.t He intends to do for ever … of late I have depended on His Clerk but tho He is very inclineable to go yet Castles still finds out some new employment to delay his going down …[65]

Ensor, who succeeded to Castle's practice after the latter's death in 1751, also appears to have acted as a middleman between Richard Castle and his client Sir Thomas Taylour in the proposed design for Headfort, County Meath. The Irish Architectural Archive holds two sets of drawings for a seemingly unexecuted scheme for Headfort, one in Richard Castle's hand, in a folio marked 'Mr Castles Plan', and another folio marked 'Mr Ensors Plans'. The latter contains a set of three alternative plans, which also appear to be in Castle's hand, though one of these is inscribed – clearly by someone other than Castle – 'Plan of the Principal Floor by Mr Castle' (Fig. 4.9). Another, slightly nuanced version of the plan and elevation (Fig. 4.10) contained within this folio is in a different hand, perhaps John Ensor's.[66] Although these plans are undated, a series of substantial payments made to Richard Castle between 1737 and 1740, recently discovered within the Headfort papers at the National Library of Ireland, suggest that Castle, in the capacity of principal contractor, and therefore Ensor as his clerk, carried out works for Sir Thomas Taylour, prior to George Semple in the 1760s.[67] In 1748 Ensor, who at this time was engaged in several speculative developments in the vicinity of Trinity College,[68] once again stepped into the breach at the Hon. Hayes St Leger's house on Kildare Street (Doneraile House), when Castle was preoccupied with works at nearby Kildare House (later Leinster House). Two alternative plans for Doneraile House, one by Castle and the other seemingly by Ensor, attest to the latter's deputising role, taking over works which Castle was too busy or simply disinclined to execute. These plans and the executed works show a clear debt to Castle, but at the same time point to Ensor's growing independent practice and the connections he built up at Trinity College.[69] For although Ensor was paid for 'Directing & Drawing Different Designs for finishing the New House in Kildare Street' and oversaw works here between 1748–53, he employed many of the same craftsmen as Richard Castle had, at Trinity

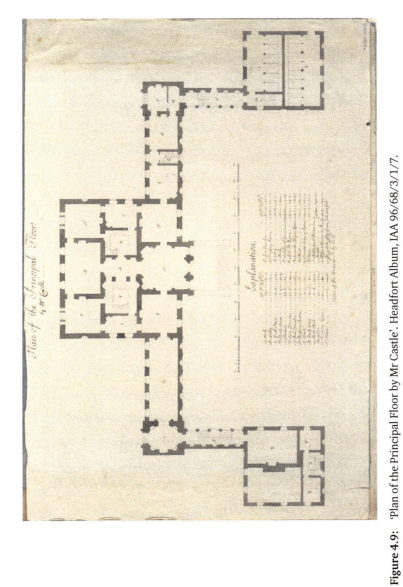

Figure 4.9: 'Plan of the Principal Floor by Mr Castle'. Headfort Album, IAA 96/68/3/1/7.

Courtesy of the Irish Architectural Archive.

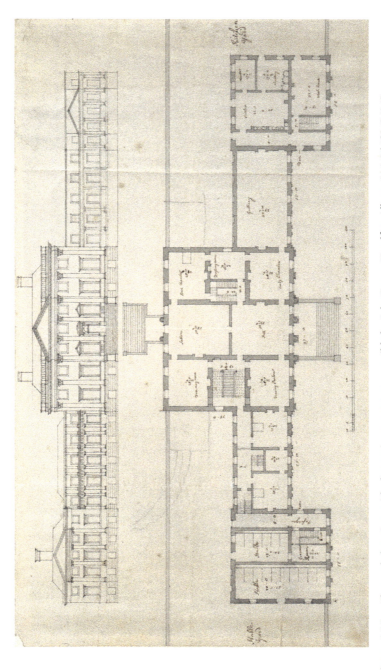

Figure 4.10: Plan and elevation, with alternative treatments, possibly by John Ensor. Headfort Album, IAA 96/68/3/1/9. Courtesy of the Irish Architectural Archive.

College, including the stonecutter David Sheehan, carver John Kelly and measurer Simon Ribton.[70]

Relational capital

As well as a more competitive contracting system Richard Castle also drew on established relational capital, to ensure quality and reduce the financial risk of transacting.[71] Like Wren or Hawksmoor in London, or indeed, Thomas Burgh in Dublin, Castle showed a preference for building contractors and suppliers who were known to him, those who had been employed at the Parliament House and on his early domestic works.[72] This seems an obvious choice. Stephenson, pointing to the difficulty of monitoring the quality of building works, and the risk involved in appointing contractors, notes the importance of prior performance.[73] At Carton, County Kildare, one disgruntled craftsman who had been disappointed in his bid for work remarked on Castle's tendency to bring in his own contractors, noting that 'for any thing that is material to be done. Mr Cassels put in his own acquaintance'.[74] Interestingly, however, Castle did not make a complete break with the past at Trinity College; alongside these 'new men' Castle awarded contracts to established craftsmen, who had previously worked at the college under Thomas Burgh.

One such appointment was Moses Darley, the head of a fraternity of stonecutters and quarry owners, who had settled in Newtownards, County Down in the seventeenth century and gained a foothold at the college and in Dublin's wider building industry under the auspices of Thomas Burgh. Moses and his father Henry had worked as the principal stonecutters at the Library (Fig. 4.11) and Moses continued to carry out maintenance works in the college throughout the 1720s and early 1730s. In 1734 Moses Darley was awarded the stonecutter's contract for the Printing House, perhaps due to price – his was the only estimate for stonecutters work to survive – or maybe in an effort on Castle's part to retain an element of continuity in his first commission at the college. There were certainly longstanding connections between particular tradesmen and the college administration.[75] Edward McParland, who has raised valid questions over the proficiency of Moses Darley's prior performance at the college – in particular the rusticated stonework on the Library arcades – points to the involvement of one of the 'Parliament House men' at the Printing House, brought in, perhaps, as means of mitigating this risk.[76] The stonecutter and quarrying agent Thomas Gilbert, who was one of the four principal stonecutters involved at the Parliament

Figure 4.11: *A Prospect of the Library of Trinity College, Dublin, Ireland,* Joseph Tudor, 1753.

© National Library of Ireland.

House in the early 1730s, provided Portland stone for the Printing House portico, and although this is not evident in the written record, it has been suggested that Gilbert was brought in to keep 'Darley up to scratch' with the skills necessary to execute the complex rusticated stone work on the Printing House portico.[77] Castle certainly had an ongoing working relationship with Gilbert, from whom he sourced 18 tons of Portland Stone for Powerscourt, County Wicklow in 1734.[78] It is somewhat surprising then, that Castle once again appointed Moses Darley to carry out stonecutters work at Bell Tower, or Steeple, in 1740, this time alongside David Sheehan.

David Sheehan was certainly Castle's man. A Dublin-based stonecutter and carver, he was employed extensively at the college during the 1740s, having previously proven himself – albeit on a smaller scale – on Castle's works at Powerscourt and at Carton in the late 1730s.[79] Construction on the Bell Tower, as noted above, had proven problematic from the outset, and Castle is said to have made many drawings for it but 'regretted that the worst was adopted'.[80] The complexity of the site aside, the scale of the structure, which stood over 160 feet tall, and the degree of formal elaboration to the Doric frontispiece, octagonal clock tower and domed cupola, called for new levels of competency in executing its stonework. The finished work, which dominated the Old Quadrangle for almost half a century, had, according to McParland 'a good deal of swagger'.[81] By 1791, however, the Bell Tower had become unstable and was deemed too insecure for the bell to be tolled.[82]

The upper part was removed in October 1791, and sold for salvage, while the remaining structure was pulled down the following year.[83] Few accurate images survive (see Figs 4.12–14), and once again David Sheehan's bill for stonecutter's work provides illuminating detail on the extent of the structure, the decorative finishes and materials employed. The first part of the bill details work done in granite or 'Mountain stone', which included 'ashlers and quines from the top of the Dorick Cornice to … the Pedestal Under ye Ionick Columns'; the Ionic column shafts, as well as their entablature; the 'Circular Mountain Stone Stairs', and the 'Octagon Part of the Steeple'.[84] Beneath this list Sheehan noted: 'NB The Stone Cutter finished the Stone for all the above work', suggesting both the complexity of the work, and that the master craftsman responsible did not, in fact, always carry out the work themselves. Then follows the 'Work Done in Portland Stone', which included: 'Masoning & Carving 4 Ionick capitals 2 feet 1 inch diameter' and '8 columns with Antike Corinthian Capitals in the cupola', as well as 'Carving the eight sides of

Figure 4.12: Detail from Samuel Byron, *A bird's-eye perspective plan of Trinity College park and gardens*, 1780.

TCD MUN-MC-9. © The Board of Trinity College Dublin.

The Bell Tower, 1746.

Figure 4.13: The Bell Tower, Trinity College Dublin. From John William Stubbs, *The History of the University of Dublin*, 1889.

Public Domain via Google Books.

Figure 4.14: Francis Wheatley, *The Dublin Volunteers on College Green, 4th November 1779*.

Public domain via Wikimedia Commons.

the 4 Great Consoles'. While this work would have required considerable skill to execute, the bill also included more routine tasks, presumably carried out by less experienced members of Sheehan's team, such as 'Letting in 174 Cramp Holes into ye Curb Stones of ye Cone' and 'twice Cutting ye inside of [the dial plates], to make them wider after the first time they were Done'. Costs, which were measured by John Ensor and certified by Richard Castle were for 'Workmanship only & finding Morter', though the bill did include £31 17s. for '17 Tun 1 foot [of] Sollid of Portland Stone furnished by David Sheehan for the Cupilow'.

The procurement and supply of materials was another highly involved aspect of managing a building project. In earlier works, or more ad hoc schemes, the college administration, usually the Head Porter, was responsible for procuring materials.[85] Although the college continued to pay suppliers directly for materials during Richard Castle's time at the helm (thereby retaining control of costs and mitigating against potential mark ups – the 'fatal mischief' of undertaking)[86] and remained responsible for ensuring the security of the materials once on site (as evident in a bill for 78 nights 'watching the Tyles for the Hall'), Castle seems to have taken a more involved approach to procurement than his predecessors.[87] He regularly signed off on the supply of building materials, from bricks and nails and timber baulks for the Printing House to 24-foot lengths of 'Irish Oak' required for the Steeple, or 'stones drawn from the quarry' for use on the 'Ha Walk' in College Park, as well as regular deliveries of an unspecified variety of stone by the quarryman William Lovely, which was used in the walling of the Steeple and elsewhere in the college.[88] For the supply of Portland stone, Castle once again drew on established connections. Both Sheehan and Darley seem to have been actively involved in the procurement process, by way of middlemen, or women. In 1743 four blocks or six and three-quarter tons of Portland stone was brought from Henry Darley's premises at Marlborough Street for 'the use of the Steeple' (Fig. 4.15).[89] Two years earlier Moses Darley received eight blocks of Portland stone from a Mr Clark, whose wife or widow Catherine received payment.[90] A larger consignment was also received from the Fleet Street based stone merchants James and Isaac Simon, who supplied over £292 worth of Portland stone for the Steeple in 1741.[91] Originally from France, possibly Bordeaux, where Isaac was also involved in the wine trade, and possibly of Huguenot origins, the brothers Simon became deeply enmeshed in Dublin's mercantile community and established far-reaching commercial networks throughout Ireland and Britain, and beyond.[92] Correspondence in the Bodleian between David Sheehan and John Tucker, supervisor of

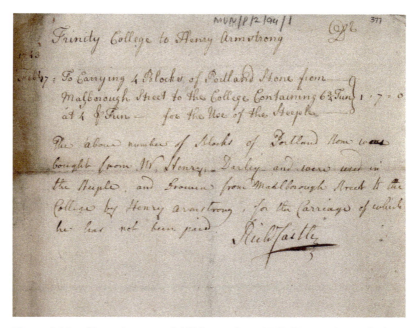

Figure 4.15: Henry Armstrong's bill for carriage, 1743, 'To carrying 4 Blocks of Portland Stone from Marlborough Street to the College'.

TCD MS MUN/P/2/94/1. Courtesy of the Board of Trinity College Dublin.

his majesty's quarries on the Isle of Portland, offers fascinating insights into the often fraught process of procurement and supply of Portland stone for the college, and establishes James and Isaac's involvement in a larger trade network involving Sheehan, Catherine Clark and the aforementioned Thomas Gilbert.[93] Procurement aside, there were other factors to consider in getting the stone on site: in a brief entry for general labour in July 1740, John Kane, foreman, noted costs for: '6 men Graveling and making way for the Portland Stone'.[94]

Alongside members of the stone trade, timber craftsmen also played a key supporting role in the building process. Carpenters worked on site throughout the build, assisting with excavation works and site preparation, including the construction of ancillary structures like sheds for the masons or sawyers; erecting the scaffolding and centring for the walling trades and slaters, and making tools such as ladders and handbarrows, 'Beaters & Floats & Rules for ye Plasterers & Moulds for Ye Masons'.[95] John Connell, a carpenter, joiner and timber merchant, who was admitted as a freeman of Dublin in 1726, by service, was regularly employed at the college during the 1730s and 1740s, carrying out such support work, as well as carpentry and joinery work on the Printing House, New Hall and Bell Tower. In March 1740, for example, Connell submitted a bill for 'pulling Down the Wainscott in the Hall: 3 men attending ye setting out ye foundations of ye steeple' and '1 dram of deal' for 'making a trough for ye pump to Draw ye foundation'.[96] As well as attending labourers Connell employed a team of skilled carpenters, who he charged out at two shillings per day.[97] Interestingly, this was the same rate he charged for his own labour, on at least one occasion. In fact, the degree of homogeneity between the rates of pay charged across a range of skill sets and trades (slaters, carpenters, brick layers and so on) at Trinity over a thirty-year period – one shilling per day for a labourer, two shillings for a skilled workman – supports the argument that the contractor charged their men out at a higher rate than they paid the workmen.[98] Connell also operated a timber yard at Lazers Hill and supplied fir and oak scantlings for the Printing House, as well as 'Boards Poles and Puttlocks' for the rough mason's scaffolding at the New Hall.[99] He must have enjoyed some success in these endeavours, as Connell was involved in a number of speculative building projects, at Earle Street on the Gardiner estate – in some form of collaboration with Henry Volquartz, timber merchant, who also had premises at Lazers Hill – and on the east side of Merrion Square in the 1750s (Fig. 4.16).[100] He also

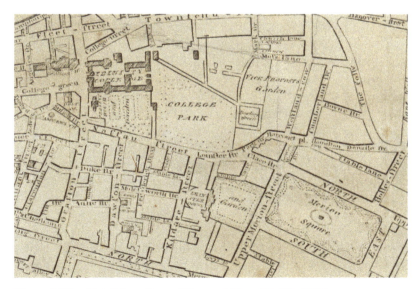

Figure 4.16: Detail from Samuel Byron, *A Plan of Dublin*, 1782.
© The Board of Trinity College Dublin.

had an interest in a large block of ground on 'ye south side of College Street ... being called the College Quarry' which he leased from 'the Provost Fellows and scholars of the College' in the 1740s.[101]

The close nature of Connell's working relationship with Richard Castle, as well as Castle's hands on supervision of works at the Steeple, is borne out by his attending 'Mr Castles' while setting out the foundation walls in 1740. That same year Richard Castle signed an order of payment to John Connell 'For Surveying the works in Trinity College'.[102] And yet, as the muniments suggest, John Connell's association with the college, or at least that of his family, began under Thomas Burgh. Between 1717 and 1723 another John Connell – perhaps his father – worked as a measurer, inspecting the work of several trades, from carpenters to slaters and bricklayers.[103] Later generations of the Connell family continued in this occupation, including Richard Connell, measurer of King Street, who trained as a carpenter under John Connell.[104] Does this then suggest (as with the repeated appointment of Moses Darley) the limitations of Castle's professional jurisdiction at the college, at least in the appointment of contractors? Or rather, as noted above, his pragmatism in appointing established craftsmen to ensure the smooth running of the project?

Over the course of a ten-year period, Richard Castle ingratiated himself at the college, moving from unproven outsider to the chief architect and surveyor of works. His strategy appears two-fold: on the one hand he drew on new and highly-skilled artisanal connections established at the Parliament House and his early domestic works, while at the same time he retained an element of continuity within the organisational structure of the college, maintaining existing multiple-generational trade relations. Like the new generation of practically-minded architects and surveyors who had emerged from Wren's reorganised Office of Works in London, Castle established new levels of professionalism and oversight in the management of building works, from maintenance and repairs, ad hoc works, to major new building projects. Although this can be seen as a move away from self-regulation by the artisanal trade federations or guilds and increased levels of control on the part of the architect, there is a degree of collaboration evident between architect and artisan to ensure the smooth running and financial viability of these works at Trinity College. While the majority of his works did not survive to see the close of the century, the ongoing impact of many of the practices introduced by Richard Castle can be seen in the works of later architects and overseers, such as Hugh and George Darley, and Christopher and Graham Myers.

BETWEEN DESIGN AND MAKING

Notes

1   Anon., 'History of the Fine Arts in Ireland', 242–3.
2   McParland, *Public Architecture*, 159.
3   Gibney, *The Building Site*, 34, refers to accounts for building work by Burgh at Trinity College Dublin and Steevens's Hospital, Dublin in the 1720s, noting the 'scarcity of certificates signed by Burgh' among the 'fairly full documentation' for the Hospital and Library. McParland, *Public Architecture*, 84 corroborates this picture, see note 11.
4   Yeomans, 'Managing eighteenth-century building', 4.
5   For more on Thomas Ripley's training and practice see Klausmeier, 'Houghton, Raynham and Wolterton Halls', 626–7; for Hawksmoor see Campbell, 'Nicholas Hawksmoor's building notebook'; Downes, *Hawksmoor*; Stephenson, *Contracts and Pay*, 54–5; Webb, 'The letters and drawings of Nicholas Hawksmoor'; Yeomans, 'Managing eighteenth-century building'.
6   Wilton-Ely, 'The rise of the professional architect in England', in Spiro Kostof, *The Architect: Chapter in the history of the profession* (New York, Oxford University Press, 1977), 183, cited in Hanson, *Architects and the Building World*, 11.
7   Morris, *Defence of Ancient Architecture*, 101.
8   Gibney, *The Building Site in Eighteenth-Century Ireland,* 23.
9   See Stephenson, *Contracts and Pay*, 37, for the contemporary distinction between ordinary and extraordinary works.
10 Somerville, *Early Residential Buildings*, 95.
11 See Trinity College Dublin, TCD MS MUN P/2; records for building works at the college are more limited prior to the 1710s. Purchase of materials and orders for payment were executed by college administrators such as the bursar and porters. McParland, *Public Architecture*, 84, notes how Burgh had 'distanced himself from the day to day contracting for the building' at Steevens's Hospital, appointing Michael Wills as overseer in his stead.
12 Trinity College Dublin, TCD MS MUN P/2/74/7, 'Carpenter's work done for Trinity College', John Connell, 4 June 1740; 21 December 1740; 26 December 1740.
13 TCD MS MUN P/2/83/18–19, Bills signed by Agnes Heatly 'for keeping ye Roofs of ye College in repair'.
14 TCD MS MUN P/2/17/25, Bill for 'Joyners work and materials done and used in Trinity College' in 1704 by John Sisson, payment received from Claud Gilbert, Bursar in July 1708.
15 TCD MS MUN P/2/70/22, Account of painting and plastering, William Wall, 1736.
16 Somerville, *Early Residential Buildings*, 315 ft. 3.
17 TCD MS MUN P/2/74/1, Bill for Lime delivered at the College and Tennis Court, John Arthur, 1740; TCD MUN/P/2/82/2, 'Account of work done at ye Tennis court examined July ye 29 1741 by Rich.d Castle', refers to 'Stone's Quarry'd for ye tennis courts', William Lovely.
18 TCD MS MUN P/2/74/28, 'An Actt of the labourers working at the Ball court by order of Rich.d Castle Esq. under the Care John Kane', 1740.
19 McParland, 'Trinity College, Dublin II', 1243; TCD MS MUN P/2/85/15, 'An Actt of Labourers Sinking the canal', 1743.
20 TCD MS MUN P/2/85/22, 'An Actt of the work digging out ye canal in the Park in Trinity College', Gilbert Plummer, 1742.
21 TCD MS MUN P/2/74/6, 'Carpenter's work done for Trinity College, Dublin', John Connell, April 1740; TCD MS MUN P/2/94/22–23, Orders of payment, from Richard Castle to John Kane, 'for the labourers emploi'd digging out the foundation for a Steeple', May 1740; TCD MS MUN P/2/94/25, Account of 'Diging work done at Trinity College sinking the Foundation for the Steeple under the care of John Cane overseer'.
22 TCD MS MUN P/2/94/54, 'Work Done for the Use of ye Colidge by order of Mr Castles By James Thompson turner and pump borer', 22 March 1739.
23 Yeomans, 'Managing eighteenth-century building', 5.
24 Klausmeier, 'Houghton, Raynham and Wolterton Halls', 612, 627–9.
25 TCD MS MUN P/2/94/11, 'Carpenters work … Done att the Steeple', John Connell, 19 May 1740.
26 TCD MS MUN P/2/68/4, 'Trinity College to Rich.d Castle…To surveying sundry works amounting to the sum of 300 pond att 5 per cent'; Gibney, *The Building Site*, 35.
27 McParland, 'The office of the Surveyor General in Ireland', 98; Nisbet, *A Proper Price*, 34–5 notes the practice among architects or surveyors at the Office of Works of deducting a

ARCHITECTS AND ARTIFICERS **145**

percentage of fees from tradesmen's accounts, citing the plasterer Charles Clarke's complaint against William Chambers for deducting 2.5 per cent of money 'advanced on account of work done at Somerset House' in the 1780s. Port, 'The Office of Works and building contracts', 103 notes that the 5 per cent fee charged by the architect often included costs for measurement.

28 Gibney, *The Building Site*, 45. See also Port, 'Office of Works and building contracts', 100–1 for complaints over a lack of design specifications and working drawings from the outset of works.

29 See Gibney, *The Building Site*, 38; Port, 'Office of Works and building contracts', 97. The proposals contained in TCD MS MUN P/2/65 is the first surviving example of such tenders or estimates at Trinity; this non- exhaustive series contains estimates for bricklaying, stonework, carpentry, joinery, and a general estimate for work to be carried out at the Printing House.

30 TCD MS MUN P/2/65/1, 'Proposals made by Joseph McCleery Carpenter, for Building a Print House', n.d., c.1733–4; TCD MUN P/2/65/3, 'Proposals made by Joseph McCleery Carpenter, for Building a Print House … Materials and Workmanship included'; TCD MUN P/2/65/8, Proposal for carpentry and joinery, Isaac Wills, 18 March 1733/4.

31 TCD MUN P/2/65/2, 'Proposalls of James Morris Bricklayer of Brick and Stone Work to be Done at the New Printing House'; TCD MS MUN P/2/65/4, 'Proposals made by John Plummer Bricklayer for Building a Printing House'; TCD MS MUN P/2/65/1, 'Proposals made by Moses Darley Stone Cutter for Building a Printing house', n.d., c.1733–4. No other bids for stonecutting survive.

32 Yeomans, 'Managing eighteenth-century building', 11. See also Campbell, *Building Saint Paul's*.

33 Hayes, 'Retrieving craft practice on the early eighteenth-century building site', 177–8.

34 Registry of Deeds (RD), 100/454/78632, 15 March 1743.

35 See TCD MS MUN P/2/68/5–12, orders of payment to John Connell, carpenter, for work done on the Printing House, 1734–7; no detailed bills survive for the structural carpentry at the Printing House, nor does a proposal from John Connell, with which we might compare proposed costs; Isaac Wills does not appear to have worked at the Printing House, though he had worked extensively on the Library at Trinity (and elsewhere with Thomas Burgh) and carried out other carpentry works at the college up until 1736.

36 TCD MS MUN P/2/65/5, 'An Estimate of the Expence of the Printing House Intended to be Built in Dublin College'.

37 TCD MS MUN P/2/76, 'An Estimate for Building a Steeple'; Nathan Hall, Head Porter was responsible for coordinating general labour at the Library, from the removal of 'rubbish from the stone-cutters sheds' (TCD MS MUN P/2/27/29), carriage of stone from the quarry and the supply of tools such as hand barrows and riddles 'for ye stone-cutters' (TCD MS MUN P/2/23/ 43 and 44), to sawyers work in 'oak and firr timber' (TCD MS MUN P/2/27/27 and 28).

38 Stephenson, *Contracts and Pay*, 99.

39 Petworth House Archive (PHA) 6290, Articles of agreement between the Duke of Somerset and Thomas Larkin, St Martins in the Fields, Joyner, 23 December 1686.

40 Stephenson, *Contracts and Pay*, 84, citing a letter from Sir Christopher Wren to John Fell, Bishop of Oxford, when he was undertaking the erection of Tom Tower at Christchurch College, Oxford, in 1681.

41 Somerville, *Early Residential Buildings*, 36, 124. Numerous examples of such building agreements or contracts survive for English universities and publics works, while an illustrative Irish example is preserved at the National Library of Ireland (NLI) MS 10,770 (2), articles of agreement and accompanying plans for the Court House at Roscommon, by George Ensor in 1762.

42 Gibney, *The Building Site*, 46; Morris, *Defence of Ancient Architecture*, 102.

43 Stephenson, *Contracts and Pay*, 80.

44 TCD MS MUN P/2/79, Letter from Richard Castle to the Provost and Co. concerning his plan for a hall, n.d.

45 TCD MS MUN P/2/84/14, 'Stone Cutters work Done in the New Hall in Trinity College', David Sheehan, n.d.

46 TCD MS MUN P/2/78, 'An Estimate of the Charge for building a Hall in Trinity College'; TCD MUN P/2/84/4, 'Carpenters Work Done in New Hall in Trinity College', John Connell, 1743–5; TCD MUN P/2/84/20, Bill for 'plastering in the bill cellar under the great hall', Isabella Wall, 1744.

47 Yeomans, 'Managing eighteenth-century building', 6.

48 For such disputes in the Office of Works see Yeomans, 'Managing eighteenth-century building', 12.

49 TCD MS MUN P/2/80, Estimate of the cost of carpentry work in the New Hall, Steeple, House, Library and Printing House. n.d.

50 TCD MS MUN P/2/89, Memorandum signed Mich. Wills, 20 April 1745.

51 McParland, 'Trinity College, Dublin II', 1244.

52 Somerville, *Early Residential Buildings*, 168.

53 See McParland, 'The Papers of Bryan Bolger, Measurer', 120.

54 Gibney, *The Building Site*, 40; Nisbet, *A Proper Price*, 25–6 notes that several of the measurers received considerable remuneration for their services, while others occupied 'positions of some influence'.

55 PHA 6290, Mr Barton's articles of building work, 1688.

56 Nisbet, *A Proper Price*, 26, argues that the level of arithmetic and geometry understood by those who wrote books on measurement was not the same as those who undertook measurement. See Ayres, *Building the Georgian City*, 35–7, Appendix II on publications on measurement and wage rates.

57 Hawney, *The Compleat Measurer*, 219, 225.

58 Casey, 'A Dublin pirate at the Huntington', 98.

59 National Archives of Ireland (NAI) 1A/58/129, The papers of Bryan Bolger, measurer. Cited in Casey, 'A Dublin pirate at the Huntington', 98.

60 Nisbet, *A Proper Price*, 30, notes the measure and value system was used in the Military Barracks Office in 1806, but was soon replaced by another, the general contractor. See Port, 'Office of Work and building contracts', 105, for late eighteenth-century testimony reading issues with the measure and value system.

61 Coventry Records Office, PA811/6/1, Articles of Agreement, 17 March 1721, notes that Job Ensor of Coventry, carpenter, was to erect a new building on the western side of West Orchard. George, John Ensor's half-brother was born in 1724 in Coventry.

62 John Ensor first appears in the muniments in 1738 (TCD MS MUN P/2/68/4), receiving payment on Castle's behalf. He is first recorded acting as measurer on Moses Darley's bill for stonecutter's work in April 1739 (TCD MS MUN P/2/73/6). Prior to this the college employed measurers on their own behalf, including William Halfpenny and Simon Ribton, who measured slater's work on the Printing House in 1734 (TCD MS MUN P/2/68/1).

63 Sadleir, 'Richard Castle, architect', 244; TCD MS MUN P/4/49/37 and 43, Bursar's vouchers for stationery ordered/received by John Kane (overseer of labourers) including two memorandum books for Kane's use suggests he may also have made use of 'Mr Castle's Office'.

64 TCD MS MUN P/2/81/46, William Wall, bill for plastering and painting work done at Trinity College, 1741. Measured by John Ensor, 26 October 1741.

65 TCD MS 1743, Clements correspondence, letter 68, n.d., Susannah Este to Nathaniel Clements.

66 Irish Architectural Archive (IAA), Guinness Collection, Acc. 96/68/3/1/2–5, plans and an elevation in Richard Castle's hand, unsigned, n.d.; IAA, Guinness Collection, Acc. 96/68/3/1/7 'Plan of the Principal Floor by Mr Castle', in Castle's hand; IAA, Guinness Collection, Acc. 96/68/3/1/8–9, plan showing the first floor, 'Plan of the Attic Floor', both in Richard Castle's hand; IAA, Guinness Collection, Acc. 96/68/3/1/10, plan and elevation. The drawing style is less resolved than the other plans and may be in Ensor's hand.

67 NLI MS 25, 386, Headfort Papers, folios 46–54, ledger payments to Richard Castle, 1736–40. I am very grateful to Professor Christine Casey for bringing this discovery to my attention. Griffin, 'Design for Headfort, Co. Meath', 269, notes that Castle was responsible for Taylor's Dublin house, Bective House, Smithfield, built 1738–9, though the above payments, which total almost £3,000 would seem too great for this work alone.

68 RD 133/259/90865, Lease for 'new dwelling house in the south side of Ann Street near Dawson St', 11 April 1749; RD 140/434/995819, Lease for a new dwelling house on the neighbouring plot, 7 August 1750; RD 145/515/99725, Lease for a house on Coote Street, 24 July 1751.

69 IAA, Guinness Collection, Acc. 96/68/4/1–3, unsigned and undated street elevation and floor plans, attributed to Richard Castle; IAA, Guinness Collection, Acc. 96/68/4/4–5,

unsigned ground-floor plans of the house as executed, probably by John Ensor. See Griffin, 'Designs for Doneraile House'.

70 NLI MS 34,165, Building accounts for Doneraile House, Kildare Street. John Ensor issued his bill for £13 13s. on 25 March 1748 but did not receive payment until 25 June 1753.

71 See Stephenson, *Contracts and Pay*, 80, for discussion of this term.

72 Webb, 'Letters and drawings of Nicholas Hawksmoor', 147, Letter from Hawksmoor to Lord Carlisle, recommending a 'man' who 'serv'd at Greenwch Hospital' to act as overseer. See McParland, *Public Architecture*, 84, 146 and Gibney, *The Building Site*, 34, on the team of craftsmen employed by Burgh throughout his works in Dublin.

73 Stephenson, *Contracts and Pay*, 80, 89.

74 NLI MS 41,588/2, Smythe of Barbavilla MSS, Michael Ledwidge to William Smyth, n.d., c.1738.

75 For more on such links between building craftsmen and the College Bursar, see Somerville, *Early Residential Buildings*, 152–7.

76 See McParland, 'The geometry of rustication', 226, 229 and McParland *Public Architecture*, 159 for critique of Darley's skill and performance at Trinity.

77 TCD MS MUN P/2/68/17, 'The Measure of Portland stone wanting to the Printing House' refers to Thomas Gilbert; see McParland, 'The geometry of rustication', 229 for the potential involvement of Thomas Gilbert at the Printing House.

78 Hayes, 'Retrieving craft practice on the early eighteenth-century building site', 171.

79 Hayes, 'Retrieving craft practice on the early eighteenth-century building site', 171.

80 Anon., 'History of the Fine Arts in Ireland', 242.

81 McParland, *Public Architecture*, 159.

82 McParland, 'Trinity College, Dublin II', 1243.

83 Somerville, *Early Residential Buildings*, 170.

84 TCD MS MUN P/2/94/49, 'Stonecutters work Done at the Steeple in Trinity College per David Sheehan'.

85 For example see TCD MS MUN P/2/23/48, Nathan Hall, Head Porter, bill for securing delivery of 'walling stones from Palmerstone' for the new Library, 1713, or 'Oak Timber sawed for ye stares' in 1721 (TCD MS MUN P/2/42/31); Somerville, *Early Residential Buildings*, 96–7.

86 Morris, *Defence of Ancient Architecture*, 106.

87 TCD MS MUN P/2/86/28, Payment from the Bursar of Trinity College Dublin to John Tigh, received 3 November 1744.

88 TCD MS MUN P/2/68/28 and 30; TCD MS MUN P/2/85/6, 8–9; TCD MUN P/2/94/33, Payment to William Lovely, 'Stones Quaryed for Trinity College'; see also TCD MUN P2/82/2, 'Account of work done at tennis court examined July ye 29 1741 by Rich.d Castle', refers to 'Stone's Quarry'd for ye tennis courts by William Lovely stone for walls and shore'; TCD MUN P/2/83/25, 'Stones quarried for the use of Trinity College by William Lovely 1742, measured by Ensor R Castle, order for payment'.

89 TCD MS MUN P/2/94/1, Payment to Henry Armstrong, 17 February 1743, 'To carrying 4 Blocks of Portland Stone from Marlborough Street to the College containing 6 ¾ Tun at 4s. per Tun for the use of the Steeple'; TCD MS MUN P/2/94/17, Payment to Henry Darley, 'To 106 ¾ feet Sollid of Portland stone in 4 blocks delivered for the Upper Part of the ye Steeple at 2s. 4d. per ft., £12 9s.1d.'.

90 TCD MS MUN P/2/81/14, 'Portland stone delivered to Mr Moses Darley for use of Trinity College per Catherine Clarke. Measured by Simon Ribton', 22 April 1741.

91 TCD MS MUN P/2/94/50, Payment to 'Mess.ors James and Isaac Simon by order Richard Castle Esq. & for account of the College'; TCD MS MUN P/2/94/51, Bill for 70 ½ 'tuns of Portland Stones Imported by order Richard Castle Esq. & for account of Trinity College Dublin'.

92 Public Record Office of Northern Ireland (PRONI) D719/37; D719/64; D719/71; T1073/6, Black Correspondence; T3019/1443, Request for relief for two Protestant churches in Dublin founded by French refugees, signed by Theophilus Desbrisay, Lewis Marcell, James Simon, Daniel Gervais, and Joseph Meissonier, November 1749; Vicars, *Index to the Prerogative Wills of Ireland*, 426, '1774, Simon, Isaac, Dublin, a native of France'; *The monthly chronologer for Ireland*, 279.

93 Bodleian MS DON. c. 113, Tucker papers; see Campbell, 'Supply of stone', 33–5 for Gilbert's family interest in stone quarrying at Portland, Dorset.

94 TCD MS MUN P/2/94/27, Payment to John K/Cane, 30 July 1740.
95 TCD MS MUN P/2/74/18, 'Rec.d for the Carpenter that was Makeing the Shade', Henry Darley, 5 August 1740; Lincolnshire Archives, THOR VI/III/I, Carpentry and joinery, work done at Syston Park, John Langwith, 1775.
96 TCD MS MUN P/2/74/6, Carpentry bill, John Connell, 30 March 1740.
97 TCD MS MUN P/2/74/6, Carpentry bill, John Connell, 7 April 1740.
98 Stephenson, *Contracts and Pay*, 34, 51, 100, 102–3; Campbell, 'The finances of the carpenter in England 1660–1710'; Stephenson, '"Real" wages?'; Colvin, 'The Townesends of Oxford', 53–4; see also Nisbet, *A Proper Price*, 29–30, on contractors' margins of 15 per cent; Allen, 'Real wages once more', 745–7, who argues against the theory that contractors charged higher day rates for labour than was paid to workers, proposes a 5–15 per cent differential between rates charged for journeymen (those of a master craftsman) and those paid. He also concedes that a surcharge of 15–20 per cent on materials and labour was standard in contractors' bills. The day rates charged at TCD tally with those given by D'Arcy, 'Wages of skilled workers in the Dublin building industry, 1667–1918', 21–3, for skilled and unskilled labour in this period. For differentials between day rates in London and elsewhere, and seasonal variants see Ayres, *Building the Georgian City*, 37–8.
99 TCD MS MUN P/2/84/1, 'Boards Poles and Puttlocks Delivered for the Use of the New Hall in Trinity College', John Connell, 1743; Wilson, *Dublin Directory*, 9.
100 RD 110/497/78975, Deed of Lease, 9 May 1744, John Connell, carpenter to Thomas Kingsbury Esq., refers to an earlier lease to Connell; RD 189/292/125485, Deed of Mortgage, 22 August 1757, between Henry Volquartz of the City of Dublin Merchant, John Connell, Merchant, and Oliver Grace, carpenter, refers to ground and two new dwelling houses at Earle Street; RD 607/175/415482, Will of 1808, refers to an earlier lease of a plot of ground on Merrion Square to John Connell, deal merchant, 27 August 1759; RD 216/120/142036, refers to John Connell of Merrion Street, Dublin; RD 272/435/175664, 10 May 1769, John Connell sold two houses on the east side of Merrion Street to Lord Fitzwilliam.
101 RD 313/311/208646, refers to John Connell of College Street, Dublin, deceased, timber merchant (testator) and Mary Connell, his widow (beneficiary).
102 TCD MS MUN P/2/94/91, Payment to John Connell by order of R. Castle, £40.
103 TCD MS MUN P/2/34, 'Admeasurement of painting done by George Spike at the Provost's House', measured by J. Connell, 12 September 1717; TCD MS MUN P/2/41/29, Isaac Wills, carpenter, work at the 'New Kitchen measured by J. Connell and allowed by Thomas Burgh', 1720.
104 See *Wilson's Dublin Directory* for the years 1769–86; Dublin City Libraries and Archive, Ancient Freemen of Dublin, Midsummer 1766, Richard Connell, carpenter, 'by service with John Connell'.

References

Allen, Robert C. 'Real wages once more: A response to Judy Stephenson', *Economic History Review*, 72:2 (2019): 738–54.

Anon., 'History of the fine arts in Ireland: Richard Castles', *Anthologia Hibernica* (October 1793): 242–3.

Ayres, James. *Building the Georgian City*. New Haven, CT and London: Yale University Press for the Paul Mellon Centre for Studies in British Art, 1998.

Campbell, James W. P. 'Nicholas Hawksmoor's building notebook', *Construction History*, 20 (2004): 21–44.

Campbell, James W. P. 'The finances of the carpenter in England 1660–1710: A case study on the implications of the change from craft to designer-based construction'. In *L'Edilizia Prima della Rivoluzione Industriale. Secc. XIII–XVIII*, edited by Simonetta Cavaciocchi, 313–46. Prato: Instituto Internazionale di Storia Economica F. Datini, 2005.

Campbell, James W. P. *Building Saint Paul's*. London: Thames and Hudson, 2007.

Campbell, James W. P. 'The supply of stone for the rebuilding of Saint Paul's Cathedral 1675–1710', *Construction History*, 28:2 (2013): 23–49. Accessed 8 January 2024. https://www.jstor.org/stable/43856562.

Campbell, James W. P. and Andrew Saint. 'Bibliography of works on brick published in England before 1750', *Construction History*, 17 (2001): 17–30.

Casey, Christine. 'A Dublin pirate at the Huntington', *Huntington Library Quarterly*, 61:1 (1998): 93–99. Accessed 8 January 2024. https://doi.org/10.2307/3817624.

Colvin, Howard. 'The Townesends of Oxford: A firm of Georgian master-masons and its accounts', *The Georgian Group Journal*, 10 (2000): 43–60.

D'Arcy, Fergus A. 'Wages of skilled workers in the Dublin building industry, 1667–1918', *Saothar*, 15 (1990): 21–37.

Downes, Kerry. *Hawksmoor*. London: Thames and Hudson, 1969.

Gibney, Arthur. *The Building Site in Eighteenth-Century Ireland*, edited by L. Hurley and E. McParland. Dublin: Four Courts Press, 2017.

Griffin, David J. 'Richard Castle's designs for Doneraile House, Kildare Street, Dublin', *Martello Arts Review* (Spring 1990): 1–6.

Griffin, David J. 'A Richard Castle design for Headfort, Co. Meath'. In *Dublin and Beyond the Pale: Studies in honour of Patrick Healy*, edited by Conleth Manning, 269–72. Bray, County Wicklow: Wordwell in association with Rathmichael Historical Society, 1998.

Hanson, Brian. *Architects and the Building World from Chambers to Ruskin: Constructing authority*. Cambridge: Cambridge University Press, 2003.

Hawney, William. *The Compleat Measurer: Or, the whole art of measuring*. London: D. Browne, 1717.

Hayes, Melanie. 'Retrieving craft practice on the early eighteenth-century building site'. In *Enriching Architecture: Craft and its conservation in Anglo-Irish building production, 1660–1760*, edited by Christine Casey and Melanie Hayes, 160–96. London: UCL Press, 2023.

Klausmeier, Axel. 'Houghton, Raynham and Wolterton Halls on Thomas Ripley's major works in Norfolk: Architectural success amidst political tensions', *Norfolk Archaeology*, 43:4 (2001): 607–29.

The London Magazine, and Monthly Chronologer: The monthly chronologer for Ireland (May 1751): 279.

McParland, Edward. 'The papers of Bryan Bolger, measurer', *Dublin Historical Record*, 25:4 (September 1972): 120–31.

McParland, Edward. 'Trinity College, Dublin II', *Country Life*, 159:4115 (13 May 1976): 1242–5.

McParland, Edward. 'The office of the Surveyor General in Ireland in the eighteenth century', *Architectural History*, 38 (1995): 91–101.

McParland, Edward. *Public Architecture in Ireland 1680–1760*. New Haven, CT and London: Yale University Press, 2001.

McParland, Edward. 'The geometry of rustication: An eighteenth-century case-study'. In *Enriching Architecture: Craft and its conservation in Anglo-Irish building production, 1660–1760*, edited by Christine Casey and Melanie Hayes, 219–33. London: UCL Press, 2023.

Morris, Robert. *An Essay in Defence of Ancient Architecture*. London: D. Browne, 1728.

Nisbet, James. *A Proper Price: Quantity surveying in London 1650–1940*. London: Stoke Publications, 1997.

Port, M. H. 'The Office of Works and building contracts in early nineteenth-century England', *Economic History Review*, New Series 20:1 (April 1967): 94–110.

Price, Francis. *Builder's Guide or The Carpenter's Plain and Exact Rule*. Dublin: Printed by James Hoey, 1738.

Sadleir, Thomas U. 'Richard Castle, architect', *Journal of the Royal Society of Antiquaries of Ireland*, Sixth Series 1:3 (30 September 1911): 241–5.

Somerville, R. A. *The Early Residential Buildings of Trinity College Dublin: Architecture, financing, people*. Dublin: Four Courts Press, 2021.

Stephenson, Judy Z. '"Real" wages? Contractors, workers, and pay in London building trades, 1650–1800', *Economic History Review*, 71:1 (2018): 106–32.

Stephenson, Judy Z. *Contracts and Pay: Work in London construction 1660–1785*. London: Palgrave, 2020.

Stubbs, John William. *The History of the University of Dublin: From its foundation to the eighteenth century*. Dublin: Hodges, Figgus & Co., 1889.

Vicars, Arthur Edward. *Index to the Prerogative Wills of Ireland, 1536–1810*. Dublin: E. Ponsonby, 1897.

Webb, Geoffrey. 'The letters and drawings of Nicholas Hawksmoor relating to the building of the Mausoleum at Castle Howard', *The Volume of the Walpole Society*, 19 (1930–1): 111–64.

Wilson, Peter. *The Dublin Directory, for the Year 1751: Containing an alphabetical list of names and places of abode of the merchants and traders of the city of Dublin.* Dublin: P. Wilson, 1751.

Yeomans, David. 'Managing eighteenth-century building', *Construction History*, 4 (1988): 3–19.

5
Artisans and architecture in eighteenth-century Saxony

Nele Lüttmann

Richard Castle (c.1691–1751), 'Ireland's most prolific Palladian architect',[1] is in many ways still an enigma, despite decades of research.[2] In particular, much remains unexplained about his background and career prior to his arrival in Ireland and the training which enabled him to establish such a successful architectural practice. We know from Castle's own writings that he travelled from the port of Hamburg through continental Europe in the early 1720s, arriving in London sometime around 1725 and from there made his way to Ireland, about 1728.[3] We learn of his interest in hydraulic engineering and inland navigation, including bridge construction and fortifications, suggesting a background in civil or military engineering, though there is little or no mention of his architectural training. Recent research has added to this picture, not only in relation to the wider context in which Castle emerged in Britain but also, significantly, with regard to his family's connection to Dresden in Saxony.[4] This chapter will consider this wider Dresden context, in particular the organisation of the Electoral Saxon *Oberbauamt*, in an attempt to reconstruct various possible settings for Castle's training, based on his later career and achievements.

The Electoral Saxon *Oberbauamt*, the supreme building department, equivalent to the Office of Works in Britain, was the leading organisation for the training and continuing education of building specialists and architects, besides a crafts training or an academic education.[5] Academies were still in their early stages of development in the German realms, and training there only became increasingly important for architectural education in the course of the eighteenth century. The *Oberbauamt* was one of the main employers for building professionals, working to satisfy the enormous demand for representative and efficient architecture on the part of the Saxon rulers. Thus, the *Oberbauamt* gave rise to many eminent artisans and architects, among them Matthäus Daniel Pöppelmann (1662–1736), who is considered the first major architect in 'Germany' to emerge from a building authority as a state building official.[6] Although distinctly bureaucratic in its organisational structure (which likely derived from the Royal Building Administration in France) there was a practical craft-oriented approach to training at the *Oberbauamt* that can be compared with the Office of Works in England. In drawing out these points of continuity, this chapter not only sheds light on the wider arena of artisanal training in Europe, but also on one potential context in which Richard Castle might have received his architectural training.

Richard Castle, recent investigations

Addressing the Commissioners for Tillage, sometime around 1730, Richard Castle remarked on his newly arrived status in Ireland: 'I lye under the disadvantage of being a Stranger in this Kingdom, and destitute of any other recommendation, to your Honours, than what hath arisen from the indulgence of those Gentlemen for whom I have conducted some considerable works sinc[e] my coming'.[7] Long thought to have been of Huguenot origins, research by Loreto Calderón and Konrad Dechant reveals that Castle's family lived in Dresden (Saxony's capital, Fig. 5.1) at the beginning of the eighteenth century, where they mixed with the upper echelons of the Saxon court.[8] According to their research, Castle, who was in fact born David Richardo (later modified to David de Richardi), was one of four sons of an English-born and English-speaking Jew, Joseph Israel Richardo (or Richardi) and Rachel Elizabeth de Bourges (or Burges) from Bombay.[9] Castle's father was employed by the Elector of Saxony as Director of Munitions, Provisions and Mines, overseeing 'supplies, purchases and manufacture to and from foreign places ... of all sorts of munitions ... metals and materials'; he also spent time as a merchant in the Netherlands, which is where he and his wife's family lived.[10] Indeed, possible connections of Joseph Richardo to the Electorate of Hanover have emerged from my own research: several letters from Electress Sophia of Hanover to her circle, in 1703, speak of a 'joly offisié du Roy de Pologne ... un Anglois nommé Richart' (a handsome officer of the King of Poland ... an Englishman named Richart) and 'Monsr de Richard Anglois ... Colonnel Artillerie du Roy de Pologne' (Mister de Richard Englishman ... Colonel of Artillery for the King of Poland).[11]

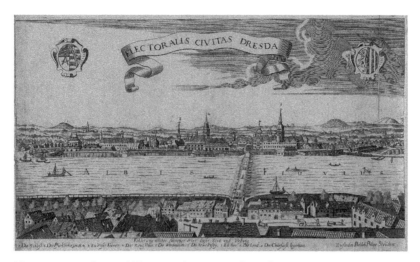

Figure 5.1: Johann Philipp Steudner, *View of Dresden*, copper engraving, circa 1700, Sächsische Landesbibliothek – Staats- und Universitätsbibliothek Dresden (SLUB), Kartensammlung (SLUB/KS B8026).

SLUB / Deutsche Fotothek, Public Domain.

In 1708 Joseph Israel Richardo purchased a house in Dresden from the jurist and later mayor of Dresden, Georg Friedrich Steffigen (in office 1715–36).[12] My own research in the Saxon archives confirms that the Richardo family was well established in more respectable circles in Dresden.[13] The house was located in the Meißnische Gasse, a busy trade road near the market square. At the northern end of the street, the Holländisches Palais was built, 1715–17, and acquired by Augustus the Strong in 1717. He commissioned the most renowned architects in Dresden, Matthäus Daniel Pöppelmann, Jean de Bodt, Zacharias Longuelune and Johann Christoph Knöffel, to convert the building into the Japanisches Palais. Both Joseph and Rachel Richardo were buried at the old Christian cemetery of the Drei-Königs-Kirchgemeinde in Dresden, which suggests a change of religion.[14] Indeed, it has recently been proposed that Rachel may have not been Jewish herself.[15] Documentation of 1730–1 records Castle as a royal lieutenant in England, while his brothers, Captain Johann Samuel de Richardi, Captain and Chevalier Garde Daniel de Richardi, and Captain and Royal Squire Benjamin de Richardi, were also of a military background.[16] Daniel von Richardi, a colonel in the Saxon Chevalier Guard, the household guard of the Saxon sovereign, later lodged in a house in Dresden Neustadt, another prime location next to the Royal Palace and Palais Brühl in Dresden.[17]

Beyond Castle's own account of works (in water supply and navigation) he encountered in Gloucestershire and London, there is little documentary evidence of his time in Britain.[18] Research by Melanie Hayes explores the wider context in which Castle emerged in Britain, in particular the interwoven network of Irish peers in eighteenth-century Hanoverian Britain.[19] Sir Gustavus Hume, Castle's first patron and commissioner in Ireland, and his connections to the British court, are particularly important. Commonly credited for having invited Castle to Ireland,[20] Hayes points out that as Groom of the Royal Bedchamber, Hume was not only directly acquainted with King George I (whom he accompanied to Hanover and Aachen on more than one occasion), but also with the inner court circle which predominately consisted of Germans.[21] Hayes concludes that it was 'in the burgeoning architectural culture of London's West End that Richard Castle first came in contact' with Hume.[22] While Castle's British connections still remain largely elusive, what is clear from this and related research into the House of Hanover by Barbara Arciszewska, is the importance of German influence in the wider court culture of Hanoverian Britain.[23]

Eighteenth-century Saxony

Before considering the Saxon building office in more detail, a brief introduction to eighteenth-century Saxony may be useful. During the Thirty Years' War, which raged largely within the Holy Roman Empire, many German lands were destroyed. However, after the Peace of Westphalia in 1648, Saxony recovered relatively quickly and during the reign of Augustus II (1670–1733), from 1694 onwards, the electorate flourished. Also known as Augustus the Strong, he led the country to economic, infrastructural, and especially cultural prosperity. In 1697 he was crowned King of Poland, giving him command of the Electorate of Saxony as well as the Kingdom of Poland and the Grand Duchy of Lithuania (Fig. 5.2). As an enthusiast of the arts, Augustus the Strong was keen to impose his rule on these territories through cultural means (Fig. 5.3). By promoting art and architecture, Dresden was transformed into a grand Baroque city during his reign. His son inherited the crown in 1733 and succeeded him not only politically, but also as patron of the arts (Fig. 5.4). While Augustus III's main concern was the curation of his art collection, his reign saw the execution of several elaborate building projects throughout the realm. In their architectural endeavours, the two Saxon rulers and their court relied on the Saxon *Oberbauamt*, which, in

Figure 5.2: Map of Europe circa 1740, from Alfred Baldamus et al., *F. W. Putzgers Historischer Schul-Atlas zur Alten, Mittleren und Neuen Geschichte*. Bielefeld: Velhagen & Klasing, 1918. Marked in red is the territory of the Polish-Saxon Union in the eighteenth century.

Public Domain via GEI-Digital.

its capacity as the exemplary early modern court building administration of the Holy Roman Empire, assembled and administered the most respected building professionals.[24]

Bureaucracy and administration in the Saxon *Oberbauamt*

While the court building offices of the seventeenth century had initially been craft-oriented, over time there was an increasing move towards bureaucratisation. However, this bureaucratisation took different forms in the various German states. Given the turmoil of war, territorial shifts and post-war rebuilding in Brandenburg and Prussia, for example, many building officials appear in the records, but a systematic administration was lacking.[25] The professionalisation of the Saxon *Oberbauamt*, by contrast, seems to have been constantly enhanced because of the more favourable conditions there. Quite probably, the Royal Building

Figure 5.3: Louis de Silvestre the Younger, *August II the Strong, 1670–1733, Elector of Saxony, King of Poland*, oil on canvas, 145 × 111 cm, Nationalmuseum Stockholm (NMGrh 1280).

Public Domain.

Figure 5.4: After Louis de Silvestre the Younger, *Fredrik August II / August III (1696–1763), Elector of Saxony, King of Poland, g.m. Maria Josefa, ärkehertiginna av Österrike*, oil on canvas, 148 × 112 cm, Nationalmuseum Stockholm (NMGrh 1286).

Public Domain.

Administration in France, with its delegation of the responsibilities of business administration, drawing, planning, site supervision and engineering, influenced the structuring within the *Oberbauamt*, as was also the case with the Office of Works in Britain.[26] As with all royal building offices of German rulers, however, the Electoral Saxon *Oberbauamt* never equalled the staff numbers of the French precedent: in 1706 the Inspector General or *Surintendant des Bâtiments* was responsible for 145 people, more than double the numbers of their Saxon counterpart.[27] Responsibility of the *Oberbauamt* included the maintenance and new construction of all electoral buildings ranging from outlying estates, bridges and roads, to palaces and, until 1744–5, fortifications.[28] From that point onwards, civil and military construction were separate offices, given that the scope of construction activity had increased to such an extent that there was no longer sufficient capacity to handle all matters in one office.[29] The head of the department was the so-called *General-Intendant der Civil und Militär-Gebäude* – general administrator of civil and military buildings – a position similar to the Inspector General of the French Royal Building Administration, who was in a sense a business administrator.[30] The British counterpart in the Office of Works would have been the Surveyor-General. From 1696 until 1728 this position was held by General Field Marshal August Christoph Graf von Wackerbarth (1662–1734). Having previously been employed at the court of Charles Louis (1617–1680), Elector Palatine in Heidelberg, Wackerbarth influenced the style of working and success of the *Oberbauamt*, with his brisk organisational activities and his skills in maths, architecture and engineering.[31] Following the election of Augustus the Strong as King of Poland, Wackerbarth also managed building activity in Poland.[32] The militarily-trained architect and engineer Jean de Bodt (1670–1745) succeeded him in office in 1728 and held the post of general administrator until 1744.[33] Intriguingly, De Bodt had started his career in the British army as 'Engineer of the Tower' and submitted proposals for Whitehall Palace and the Royal Hospital in Greenwich, in 1698.[34] He later worked as an architect for the Prussian king, but his relations with England did not cease during his time in Berlin. In 1708–9 he prepared drawings for Wentworth Castle, the country house of the English ambassador in Berlin, Thomas Wentworth, 3rd Baron Raby, which 'remains as a remarkable and almost unique example of Franco-Prussian architecture in Georgian England' (Fig. 5.5).[35] The general administrator had under his control the architects of the *Oberbauamt* with the respective administrative staff

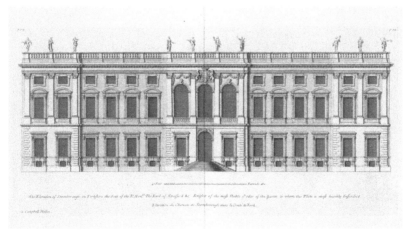

Figure 5.5: 'The Elevation of Stainborough in Yorkshire' (Wentworth Castle), in Colen Campbell, *Vitruvius Britannicus, or The British Architect* (London: Printed by the author, 1715), 93–4.

Internet Archive. Getty Research Institute.

as well as the artists and craftsmen of the court. The Electoral Saxon state directory, *Königlich-Polnischer und Churfürstlich Sächsischer Hoff- und Staats-Calender* – Royal Polish and Electoral Saxon Court and State Calendar – which was published for the first time in 1728, registered 59 people working at the building authority in that year (Fig. 5.6).[36] This included, besides the *General-Intendant der Civil und Militär-Gebäude*, five assessors, amongst whom were *Oberlandbaumeister* (chief state master builders) and architects, a secretary, officers and servants, one *Landbaumeister* (state master builder) and three *Conducteure* (conductors) two building clerks, one scribe, three gardeners, three master shipwrights, three artists, five painters, five sculptors, various craftsmen such as stone carvers, master masons, master carpenters, joiners, metal workers, as well as several commissioners, one factor and one agent.[37] Given Augustus the Strong's interest in architecture (both as an instrument of power and in drafting his own designs), as well as his willingness to mobilise funds for building projects, the availability of an efficient building authority was essential. With the help of a streamlined organisation and capable employees, the Saxon *Oberbauamt* became a major 'think tank' in terms of design and construction issues.

In other territories of the Holy Roman Empire the situation was quite different. Until the second half of the eighteenth century, there

Figure 5.6: Index of people working at the Saxon building department ('Bau-Ambt') in 1728. In *Königlich-Polnischer und Churfürstlich Sächsischer Hoff- und Staats-Calender auf das Jahr 1728*, 97–8. Leipzig: n.p., 1728.

Public Domain via Klassik Stiftung Weimar.

was no comparably effective building authority, and building officials did not have a good reputation. Prussia's king, Frederick the Great (1712–1786), for example, stated once that 'all ... master builders are idiots or deceivers'.[38] Instead of them being employed in the construction of several farm buildings and stables, he requested honest master masons or carpenters to be responsible, given that a mason could do this just as well as a Palladio.[39] The Ludwigsburg building office in the historical territory Württemberg, as well as the building offices in Salzburg and Ansbach, were likewise organised in a less bureaucratic but more practical, crafts-based manner. The position of *Conducteur* did not exist here, instead there were *Adjunkte* (assistants), who worked for the master builder and master craftsmen.[40]

On the other side of the Channel, in Britain, the Office of Works was an equally important and prestigious organisation, comparable to the Saxon *Oberbauamt*. Although there were at times structural problems, 'frauds and abuses',[41] and accusations of inefficiency and corruption in the management of the works, after a restructuring in 1715 the office embarked on gathering the largest and most renowned architectural expertise in the country: 'Between 1718 and 1782 almost every English architect of importance held a post in the Royal Works'.[42] As in Saxony, this office was responsible for maintaining the crown's existing buildings and undertaking new developments commissioned by the king or his ministers. At the top of the office was the Surveyor-General of Works, who from 1715 received an annual income of £500, which was raised to £900 in 1726.[43] In addition, there were further principal officers, consisting of Paymaster, Surveyor of the King's Private Roads and the Surveyor of Gardens and Waters. However, the appointment to these positions was often based less on actual expertise and competence but rather on political nepotism.[44] Other employees of the office included the Comptroller, Deputy Surveyor, several clerks, a purveyor, and craftspeople such as master mason, master carpenter, master bricklayer, master joiner, and so on. While this hierarchical staff structure was similar to that in the Saxon *Oberbauamt*, there was a board that administrated the activities of the office. It was composed of the Surveyor and the Comptroller as well as the Master Mason and the Master Carpenter and was completed by a secretary and a clerk.[45] Although initially the leading officials of the Saxon *Oberbauamt* discussed building projects in weekly plenary meetings chaired by the general administrator, craftsmen and artists do not seem to have participated. In contrast, the board meetings of the Office of Works were attended by master craftsmen. In the course of the eighteenth century, the management at the *Oberbauamt* became increasingly monocratic, resulting in the gradual hierarchical downgrading of building professionals and artisans and ultimately in their replacement by administrative staff.[46] The Saxon building authority thus appears to have been administered in a more centralised and autocratic manner than its British counterpart. The latter seems to have followed a more collaborative modus operandi which is among others reflected in the relatively diverse Office of Works or the division of responsibilities according to different building projects and sites. Nevertheless, there too was a 'pecking order'. When John Vanbrugh (1664–1726) learned that Thomas Ripley (1682–1758), a craftsman, had been appointed Master Carpenter instead of Nicholas Hawksmoor (1661–1736) in 1721, he wrote: 'such a Laugh came upon me, I had like to Beshit my self'.[47]

A set of regulations from 7 February 1718 lay out the internal organisation of the Saxon building department.[48] It not only mentions the rules for the schedule and account of charges, but also defines the competences of the leading officials.[49] The regulations specify that after the royal decision for a building project had been made, the general administrator had to ensure that the required drafts and proposals were prepared. These were to be examined by the general administrator to determine the costs and time required. The reviewed and approved drawings, which were to include plan, elevation, and section, as well as cost estimate and other documents, were then to be submitted to the king. If the king approved the proposal, the most competent and capable craftsmen and artists received the drawings according to which they were to work. It is further noted by whom the work was to be diligently inspected and who was responsible for ensuring that everything was done in accordance with the drawings, in a proper and lasting manner. These comprise *Oberlandbaumeister, Landbaumeister, Architecte, Conducteurs, Hof-Mäurer* and *Zimmermeister* – chief state master builder, state master builder, architect, conductors, courtly master masons and master carpenters.[50] The regulations include further instructions, as well as the naming of the personnel of the upper ranks of the *Oberbauamt*. *Oberlandbaumeister* – chief state master builder – Johann Friedrich Karcher (1650–1726), for example, was to manage the horticultural section, *Oberlandbaumeister* Matthäus Daniel Pöppelmann was to attend to palace buildings, and *Architecte* Raymond Leplat (1664–1742) was to look after the interior fittings of the royal apartments and palaces.[51] In this case, *Architecte* seems to relate to the actual profession. In terms of the duties, these were comparable to the administrative position of the *Oberlandbaumeister*.[52] The reason why Leplat is described as an architect might be due to his responsibility for the interior design. In contrast to this, the term *Baumeister* (master builder) was almost always used to denote administrative roles and positions, rather than specific occupations. For example, despite holding the title of *Landbaumeister* (state master builder), Johann Adam Hamm's profession was that of a master stonemason. Therefore, *Baumeister* was not simply an occupational title, but an official title.[53] How then, did one become a state building official in the Saxon *Oberbauamt*?

Conducteure

From 1696 onwards, so-called *Conducteure* – from the French, supervisors or conductors – were permanently employed by the *Oberbauamt*.[54] In 1641, this office had already been introduced in the Munich *Hofbauamt* (court building office), the first German territory to do so.[55] The closest English equivalent to this role might be the Clerk of Works, who among others was responsible for stores, building materials, and measuring workmanship.[56] In France this might be the position of the Inspector, who 'did drafting, drew up specifications, and directed the masons on the actual building sites'.[57] The Saxon *Conducteure* were specially trained as officials for the service of the building department and appear at the very bottom of the listings of building officials in the payrolls. In a salary list from 1764, for example, their annual wages are quoted between 50 and 200 *Reichsthaler* which roughly corresponded to the salaries of court craftsmen, although the latter were hierarchically below them. In the upper ranks of the building department, other salaries were paid at that time. An *Oberlandbaumeister*, for example, received an annual salary of 1900 *Reichsthaler*, while a *Landbaumeister* earned 500 *Reichsthaler* annually. However, especially at the beginning of their employment, *Conducteure* often did not receive any payment at all, or only very little. Yet, they were by no means employees without previous knowledge. They were to a large extent fully trained or had already completed a technical basic training, for example a craft apprenticeship as mason or carpenter, given that some kind of professional training was a requirement for the placement as conductor.[58] In a letter of recommendation for the position of *Conducteur* from 1756, for example, it was noted that Dresden architect Johann Daniel Schade (1730–1798) had studied mathematics and already worked in the field of architecture.[59] Further conclusions on the existing level of knowledge of the *Conducteure* can be drawn from a document from 1735, by general administrator Jean de Bodt, regarding a qualifying test for conductors at the military building department.[60] He required testing the applicants in the disciplines of arithmetic, geometry, trigonometry, planimetry, surveying, mechanics, perspective, fortification, and drawing, among others. Article 10 of the memorandum notes, for example, that engineering candidates were required to prepare various plans of fortifications, including elevations, as well as plans and sections of all such structures for fortifying ground.[61] Point 11 details that in the assessment of prepared drawings, not only their accuracy, decorative value and good taste were to be judged, but also whether the draughtsman could suitably depict all specifics, terrains and plains, including mountains, rocks, woods, mires, ploughed and cultivated fields, pastures, lakes, rivers, and suchlike.[62]

The tasks of the *Conducteure* were demanding and required both technical and organisational skills. Their field of duties can be reconstructed by looking at respective appointments and instructions preserved in the Hauptstaatsarchiv Dresden, which date largely from the later eighteenth century.[63] One example, for Christian Heinrich Schütze, dated 28 June 1754,[64] first mentions his position as *Conducteur* within the hierarchy of officials, which was below the *Oberlandbaumeister* and *Landbaumeister*, and above certain craftsmen like masons, carpenters and handymen. It also sets out his administrative tasks and duties, which included finances, management of workers, and control of working hours. Schütze further had to survey construction and purchase of building materials. Paragraph six of his instruction reads as follows: 'Should he be sent to purchase building materials, or otherwise be used for this purpose, he may not sign any agreement without the approval of master builder Schüze [sic] and deputy Müldner'.[65] It continues: 'He shall pay due attention to the materials supplied for construction, so that they are used for the purpose for which they are intended, and that nothing is unnecessarily cut or even carried off and stolen'.[66] In the last paragraph, Schütze is instructed that any remaining materials such as stones, lime, bricks, old timber, boards and rods, are to be handed over to the deputy for safekeeping.[67] Given the *Conducteur*'s position within the organisational hierarchy, such skills must have been acquired prior to entering the building department.

The responsibilities of a clerk in the Office of Works in Britain were likewise more or less equally divided between administrative and organisational tasks and the preparation of reports.[68] The royal instructions provide insight into the manifold duties assigned to them. They were, for instance, required to be 'well skilled in all kinds of admeasurements, in drawing, making planns of the palaces, taking elevations, and competently versed in all parts of architecture'.[69] Regular attendance at board meetings also formed part of their role, in addition to the afore-mentioned responsibility for measuring 'all work that can be measured'.[70] They further had to submit weekly written estimates of necessary works to be approved by the board. Besides, they were required to keep accurate records of their expenses, to calculate and purchase materials and to prevent theft.[71] This diverse range of responsibilities of clerks is reflected in that of the Saxon *Conducteure* and is similarly reminiscent of the measurers working in Ireland at the time.[72]

In the archive in Dresden a template of an instruction for *Conducteure* (from 1746–73) offers further insights into the requirements of the role at the Saxon building department.[73] Besides loyalty and zeal for Electoral Saxony, it required an accurate and timely production of drawings: 'He has to perform all tasks, that are assigned to him when recording the sites, preparing the drawings and constructing the buildings, in a timely manner with all accuracy, diligence and zeal, but shall not make known anything about the projects assigned to him prematurely'.[74] Although no specific details are given as to what type of drawings were to be produced, it can be assumed, in view of the fact that different types of drawings were required at different stages of construction, such as pres-entation drawings for approval by the king, working drawings for the craftsmen, and so on, that *Conducteure* were capable of producing any of these, depending on the commands or order.

Certain regulations in the instruction template show fascinating parallels to Richard Castle's skillset and way of working. For example, a conductor was to supervise the work of artists and craftsmen, requiring competent knowledge in painting, sculpture and plastering.[75] Castle's technical expertise across a range of craft skills, which is discussed in Melanie Hayes's chapter in this volume, may suggest an interaction with a bureaucratic office like the Saxon *Oberbauamt*. Another regulation required that poorly executed or inefficient work was to be destroyed by the *Conducteur*: 'His attention shall be directed to the work of the artists and craftsmen, and that which is found faulty or inefficient shall be rejected outright, and by no means tolerated'.[76] This calls to mind Castle's reported action on a building site: 'When the effect of his works was not such as he liked, he frequently pulled them down'.[77] This rigorous approach is another point of correlation between the Saxon building authority and Castle's later workshop practice in Ireland.

In the template it was furthermore determined that alongside the day-to-day business, a conductor must continue his studies in architecture and related sciences, like drawing, arithmetic, geometry, perspective, mechanics and hydraulics. Such knowledge could be applied to palaces, churches, steeples, bridges, gardens, grottos and fountains, requiring stability and endurance.[78] A *Conducteur* further had to acquire knowledge about the building of infrastructure: 'He will also acquaint himself with the construction of dykes, embankments and roads, and seek to explore them in detail'.[79] After all, such knowledge had to be applied in the senior positions in the *Oberbauamt*. For example, as *Oberlandbaumeister*, Pöppelmann designed and built dykes and embankments for the Elbe and Mulde rivers and was responsible for the design and construction of several new bridges.[80] In addition, he served as an inspector for bridge maintenance and was in charge of the site management of roads and hydraulic engineering.[81] Cascades, grottos and fountains were similarly incorporated into Pöppelmann's designs for the extension and redevelopment of the Royal Palace in Dresden from about 1715–18 (Fig. 5.7).[82] Although most of these designs were not executed, the preparation of such required a certain knowledge in this field, which Pöppelmann may have acquired in his position as *Conducteur*. It further demonstrates the technical and engineering expertise of Pöppelmann and the general engineering objectives of the *Oberbauamt*. Castle, too, had knowledge of hydraulic engineering. His manuscript, 'Essay on artificial navigation', is a 'statement on canal construction' featuring six colour-washed views of various locks

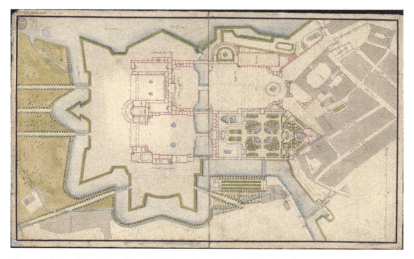

Figure 5.7: Matthäus Daniel Pöppelmann, *Site plan for the construction of a new residential palace in the area of the Zwinger and the Marstall (so-called Große Schlossplanung)*, pen and ink with polychrome washes, circa 1716/18.

SächsStA-D, 11345 Ingenieurkorps, B. III Dresden, Nr. 35e.

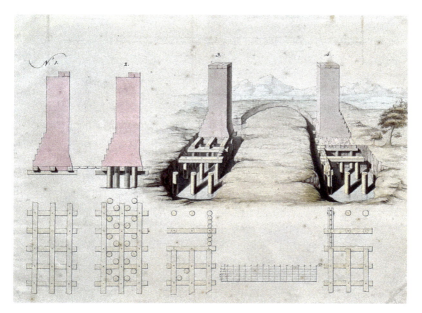

Figure 5.8: Richard Castle, 'An illustrated essay on artificial navigation', written in connection with the construction of the Newry Canal, Figure 15, circa 1733–6, NLI MS 273.

Courtesy of the National Library of Ireland.

and lock systems, bridge piers and piles, as well as pile constructions, that showcase his draughtsmanship in engineering (Fig. 5.8).[83] With this series of polychrome drawings, with which Castle applied for the Newry Canal works, he approximated the drawing conventions employed in the wider European military and engineering sectors and appealed to the visual understanding of the commissioners that resulted from these conventions. In doing so, however, Castle was less reliant on the strict colour system established by French military engineer Sébastien Le Prestre de Vauban (1633–1707), which made use of conventional colours to achieve uniformity in drawings (for example, red for completed works and yellow for planned structures).[84] Instead, he seems to have applied a more imitative colour system in his Newry Canal drawings, adjusting the colours according to the materials (red primarily represents masonry walls, grey the paved banks, timber and beam structures appear in a yellowish wash). Castle furthermore designed sophisticated waterworks and cascades for his commissions in Ireland, for example for the terraced gardens at Powerscourt House, County Wicklow, in 1739.

How *Conducteure* acquired the required expertise in the various fields as prescribed in the regulations is difficult to determine. Officials in the building department had to self-finance their studies, and this was certainly also the case for the *Conducteure*.[85] Their training, which might have been similar to a sort of apprenticeship, was likely guided by the building officials employed by the sovereign.[86] The quality of such training within the building department can be difficult to establish and always depended on the interest and engagement of the teacher. In a letter of recommendation dating from 1730,[87] master mason Andreas Adam (1699–1746) is stated to have worked for six years as *Conducteur* for Matthäus Daniel Pöppelmann and his son, and always showed good manners.[88] Several attached drawings by Adam (now lost) were to demonstrate his skills in draughting, especially in the field of civil architecture. Training by imitation was clearly important, and in some cases the trainee was allowed to measure from a building designed by the teacher and draw up a plan accordingly.[89] It appears that employees of the Office of Works similarly received their training there. Henry Joynes (c.1684–1754), who became Clerk of the Works at Kensington Palace in 1715, was probably trained there by Nicholas Hawksmoor after joining the Office of Works in 1700.[90] Hawksmoor in turn had served his 'apprenticeship' under Christopher Wren. Hawksmoor and Joynes worked together on various projects, including for Vanbrugh, who had been commissioned with the building of Blenheim Palace, in Oxfordshire. As more of a gentleman architect, Vanbrugh was dependent on skilled professionals. Correspondence between Hawksmoor and Joynes reveals their independent collaboration and work-sharing regarding the production of drawings for Blenheim. In a letter dated 26 July 1705, Hawksmoor instructs Joynes to make three copies, namely of 'the great plan of ye house on a scale of 10f in one Inch'.[91] Hawksmoor specified exactly how the drawings were to look: two of the plans were to be executed 'in black lead only', given that Hawksmoor intended to settle the 'plann of ye cellar and Attick Storys' himself on site.[92] On the third plan, Joynes was to insert in pencil 'My Laydy Duchess's appartment lying next ye East'.[93] From this evidence it appears that Joynes was following Hawksmoor's instructions and that some of the construction related matters were only decided on site.

Landbaumeister and *Oberlandbaumeister*

From the assistant post of *Conducteur* in the Saxon *Oberbauamt*, it was possible to gain promotion to *Landbaumeister*, entailing a higher degree of professional responsibility. This could be achieved through self-taught study, satisfactory completion of administrative duties, and a proven track record in all disciplines of architecture, including bridge, road, and hydraulic engineering.[94] A *Landbaumeister* was primarily responsible for the supervision of the rural building industry, which included the state outworks, bridges, mills, forestry, and raft buildings. In doing so, steady communication with the *Oberlandbaumeister* had to be maintained. Oversight of the building scribes and craftsmen likewise formed part of the duties of a *Landbaumeister*, as did the review of estimates and the monitoring of prices, disciplinary supervision and auditing of accounts. Unlike a *Conducteur*, he was furthermore entitled to prepare his own designs and to execute them, after approval by the *Oberlandbaumeister*.[95] The latter in turn had supreme superintendence over the buildings of the court and of the technical condition of river, dyke, and defence structures. His function was primarily to approve and instruct: he specified the designs, attested drawings, supervised the execution, and monitored the progress of construction and the accounting.[96]

Often, conductors were promoted to *Oberlandbaumeister* or comparable jobs within the hierarchy of officials even before a post became available through the decease of the current officeholder. In contrast to their colleagues, who were not previously employed as *Conducteure*, they received directorships or similar positions more often.[97] Pöppelmann, for example, worked as conductor at the *Oberbauamt* from about 1691 to 1704, after having obtained an unspecified permanent position there in 1686, and probably some kind of architectural or craft training.[98] He then became *Landbaumeister* from 1705 to 1718. It was during this time that Pöppelmann travelled from Prague and Vienna to Rome and designed the Dresden Zwinger, the construction of which began in 1710. In the course of this, a large number of drawings was prepared, which is considered to be Pöppelmann's main architectonic work and partly reflects the influence of Carlo Fontana (1638–1714), whom Pöppelmann met in Rome (Fig. 5.9).[99] From 1718 until 1736, Pöppelmann held the post of *Oberlandbaumeister*.[100] Johann Christoph Knöffel (1686–1752) trained as a mason and entered the *Oberbauamt* around 1708. Here he met architects such as Pöppelmann and Zacharias Longuelune (1669–1748), who exerted a considerable influence on his development.[101] Two years later Knöffel was employed as conductor and in 1722 was promoted to *Landbaumeister*, his patron being the general administrator of the *Oberbauamt*, Wackerbarth. In 1728 he rose to *Oberlandbaumeister*, alongside Pöppelmann.[102] While in this position, Knöffel requested that anyone entering the *Oberbauamt* as a *Conducteur* must be trained as a mason.[103] This suggests that he considered such

Figure 5.9: Matthäus Daniel Pöppelmann and an anonymous draughtsman, *Design for the rampart pavilion (Wallpavillon) of the Dresden Zwinger*, pen, graphite and brush with grey, blue and opaque white washes, circa 1713–14, SLUB, Handschriftensammlung (SLUB/HS Mscr.Dresd.L.4).

SLUB / Deutsche Fotothek / DDZ, Public Domain.

craft training fundamental and essential for advancement in the building industry. Knöffel himself demonstrated that a masonry apprenticeship provided the springboard to a successful career, for he became the architect of choice for Augustus III and worked for the most important political figures in Saxony. In this context it is of note that Wren's draughtsman and assistant surveyor at the building office of St Paul's, Edward Woodroffe (c.1622–1675), was a mason by trade.[104] While most of the buildings designed by Knöffel have not survived, a large body of drawings has been preserved (Fig. 5.10).[105] Knöffel's drawings are characterised by the exclusive use of a brush, even for the finest lines, shading in the form of grey wash and a delicacy in the polychrome washes. It is likely that Knöffel acquired his drawing skills in the course of his masonry apprenticeship and continued refining them thereafter. Samuel Locke (1710–1793), who like Knöffel first undertook a masonry apprenticeship, worked under French architect Longuelune, in Dresden, from whom he acquired his excellent drawing skills.[106] From 1734 until 1745 Locke was employed by Knöffel, for whom he produced a large number of drawings. The drawing of an elevation of Grochwitz

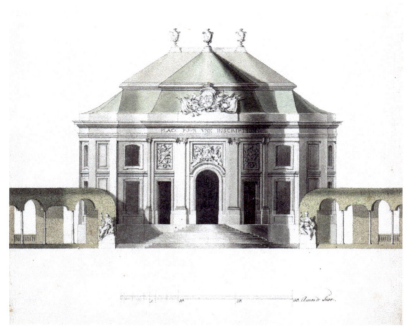

Figure 5.10: Johann Christoph Knöffel, *Design for the Belvedere in Brühlscher Garten, Dresden*, pen, brush, ink with grey and green washes, 1748–55 (Landesamt für Denkmalpflege Sachsen, Plansammlung, inv. no. M 76.233 / 97107).

Dresden, Landesamt für Denkmalpflege Sachsen.

Palace, in present-day Brandenburg, dated to 1736 and signed by Locke, corresponds to Knöffel's drawing conventions and reveals the latter's influence on Locke (Fig. 5.11). In 1739, Locke received the salaried position of a *Cammer-Conducteur*, a post he surely owed to Knöffel, who had financed him previously. The post was external to the building department, yet it enabled Locke to continue working as master mason and provided him with further opportunities to earn money.[107] From 1751 onwards, Locke is finally recorded as conductor in the *Oberbauamt* and one year later he gained promotion to *Akzisebaudirektor* (excise building director).[108]

Such advancements within the Saxon *Oberbauamt* were often tied to examinations, as was the hiring process in the building department in general. These were not subject to fixed rules. In 1730, for example, Pöppelmann tested three competing candidates that had applied for the post of *Landbauschreiber* (state building scribe).[109] A building scribe administered the *Baucasse* (building funds). He was mainly responsible

Figure 5.11: Samuel Locke, *Grochwitz, Palace Design, Elevation of the Façade*, pencil, pen and ink with coloured washes on paper, 45.6 × 61.8 cm, 1736, SLUB, Kartensammlung (SLUB/KS B1711).

SLUB / Deutsche Fotothek / DDZ, Public Domain.

for the accounting, but also for the supervision of the building work on site, as well as the complete and accurate documentation of the work.[110] Pöppelmann required the three applicants to submit a 'building cost estimate, and a drawing for testing' as well as a 'most humble report'.[111] The one possessing 'both intuition of buildings on land and water' was to be given the post as building scribe.[112] This is reminiscent of Castle's own practice in Ireland which, although not documented for recruitment tests in his office, obtained competitive quotes from various craftsmen for the Printing House at Trinity College Dublin, which is discussed by Melanie Hayes in Chapter 4.[113] Arthur Gibney compares this to Wren and his efforts to control prices in London.[114] From the mid-eighteenth century onwards, officials in the entire Holy Roman Empire had to testify their qualifications in state entrance examinations to join the civil service. This included the building officials. These tests required not only expertise in the subject matter but also strong character traits, which are not evident from the archival material today.[115] In Prussia, for example, there is evidence from the *Oberbaudepartment* in Berlin, founded in 1770, that all senior building officials had to take a uniform examination in which their knowledge of technical mechanics, arithmetic, geometry, fortification, hydrostatics, as well as masonry and carpentry were tested. Drawings and estimates for major land and water structures were also required, along with an oral examination.[116]

Several developments in the second half of the eighteenth century eventually led to the downsizing and reorganisation of the *Oberbauamt* in Saxony, and to its increasingly diminished influence. It was now mainly local professionals who worked there, and the appointment of internationally experienced and therefore expensive architects was avoided. The cost cutting within the building authority enormously limited career opportunities; Johann Daniel Schade, for example, remained *Conducteur* for a lifetime, even though he was one of the most active architects in Saxony. The Dresden Academy of Arts, founded in 1764 following the Parisian example, now largely provided the new generation of architects; an academic training was henceforth an important criterion for the appointment of architects – a training within the building authority became a thing of the past.

Castle and his management

Castle's technical knowledge of craft skills, his control over and collaboration with his craftsmen, his assurance of the quality of materials and workmanship, and his involvement in structural building innovations have been highlighted previously.[117] His practice is, for example, linked to the introduction of new carpentry techniques in Ireland, particularly regarding the change from framed floor structures to long joists.[118] Furthermore, his directorship on the Newry Canal and his application for the Dublin pipe-water scheme show his broader involvement in engineering practice.[119] On the other hand, his meticulous workshop practice and building organisation, with the employment of various measurers, the minute control of materials, the certification of costs and the involvement in the assessment of bills, might indicate that he was familiar with bureaucratic structures, too. The fact that John Ensor, one of Castle's measurers, was responsible for providing estimates at the youthful age of 18, is another testament to the expert organisation of hierarchies and the division of tasks in his office.

The parallels between Castle's modus operandi and the Saxon *Oberbauamt* suggest his knowledge of the structures of that office. His wide-ranging knowledge in the various disciplines that, for example, a conductor had to dispose at the *Oberbauamt* might likewise be an indication of Castle's training there. No direct evidence of this has been found so far. However, in addition to the posts already mentioned, there was a large number of other employees within the *Oberbauamt*, some of whom are not recorded in the personnel records of the Saxon archives and are therefore not easy to identify. This includes craftsmen engaged on a contract basis, but also the draughtsmen of the architects working in the building office.[120] These drawing assistants or architectural students were privately paid until the end of the eighteenth century, which is why no documents on salaries, appointments or similar can be found. Nevertheless, their contribution to the design process, in terms of draughtsmanship and productivity, should not be underestimated, as recent research has shown.[121]

To conclude, the Saxon *Oberbauamt* presents a potentially important context for the instructional background of one of Ireland's premier early eighteenth-century architects. As the principal and exemplary organisational form of a grand building authority within the entire Holy Roman Empire, from its beginnings in the late fifteenth century until the reorganisation of the building industry in Prussia in 1770, it was the major force in the pedagogic and administrative culture of eighteenth-century architecture in Saxony (Fig. 5.12). Surviving source material, like appointments, instructions, or letters of recommendation, enable us to track the scope of activities of the officials. For the *Conducteure*, it is difficult to determine the exact procedure and content of the training itself, which can be understood more as an

Figure 5.12: Canaletto (Bernardo Bellotto), *Dresden from the Right Bank of the Elbe, below the Augustus Bridge*, oil on canvas, 133 × 237 cm, 1748, Staatliche Kunstsammlungen Dresden (Gal.-Nr. 606).

© Gemäldegalerie Alte Meister.

advanced training. What is clear, however, is that a previous training, whatever it looked like, was a precondition for this varied position of responsibility within the building authority.[122] In general, it can be observed that many of the employees who joined the *Oberbauamt* had already been trained as craftsmen. They brought with them their respective knowledge and individual experience and skills, and were taught a bureaucratic approach to building-management in the office. This combination of craft background and hierarchical administrative structure is not only found in the building office in Saxony, but also, around the same time, in the Office of Works in England, and was likely modelled on the Royal Building Administration in France. 'Craftsmen-architects' or 'artisan-architects' such as Pöppelmann, Knöffel and Locke in the Saxon *Oberbauamt* had their counterparts in England, including Ripley, Henry Flitcroft (1697–1769) and Isaac Ware (1704–1766), all of whom had received a craft training before joining the Office of Works, with the support of powerful contacts.[123] Each of them rose to influence and held various positions in the respective offices. The skills acquired through a craft training and their relevance for a career in the building profession must therefore not be underestimated. In this context, the possibility that Castle received a craft training prior to some kind of involvement in the structures of a building office, whether the Saxon *Oberbauamt* or the British Office of Works, gains more plausibility.

Acknowledgements

My sincere gratitude to my colleagues Melanie Hayes and Andrew Tierney for their editorial advice, which has contributed greatly to this paper.

Notes

1 Griffin, 'Richard Castle's Egyptian Hall', 119; see also Sharkey, 'Belvedere House', 249.
2 For scholarship on Richard Castle see Sadleir, 'Richard Castle, architect', 241–5; The Knight of Glin, 'Richard Castle', 31–8; Laffan and Mulligan, 'His name is Castle', 41–9; Hayes, 'Anglo-Irish architectural exchange', 56–67. For most recent research on Richard Castle's office practice in Ireland, see Hayes, 'Retrieving craft practice on the early eighteenth-century building site', 160–96.
3 National Library of Ireland, MS 2737, 'An essay on artificial navigation by Richard Castle written in connection with the construction of the Newry canal', illustrated, c.1730.
4 Hayes, 'Anglo-Irish architectural exchange'; Calderón and Dechant, 'New light on Hugh Montgomerie', 174–96.
5 For an overview of the various training opportunities in the field of eighteenth-century architecture, see Schmidt, 'Open to all: Architectural education', 5–32.

6 Heckmann, *Matthäus Daniel Pöppelmann*, 132; Jahn, 'Matthäus Daniel Pöppelmann', 217. In the interest of convenience, I shall use the term 'Germany' or 'German territories' here, which is representative of the territory under the rule of the Holy Roman Emperors from the late Middle Ages until 1806.

7 NLI MS 2737, 'An essay on artificial navigation'.

8 Calderón and Dechant, 'New light on Hugh Montgomerie', 174–96.

9 Calderón and Dechant, 'New light on Hugh Montgomerie', 187–90. In the late 1990s, German art historian Jacqueline Eick likewise investigated Castle's background and suspected a Saxon origin. Her studies, however, remain unpublished.

10 Calderón and Dechant, 'New light on Hugh Montgomerie', 195–6. For the original archival document see Sächsisches Staatsarchiv, Hauptstaatsarchiv Dresden (SächsStA-D), 10026 Geheimes Kabinett, Nr. Loc. 03540/01. A prenuptial agreement for the marriage of Joseph Israel Richardo and Rachel Elizabeth de Bourges from April 4, 1968, in the Utrecht Archives, locates Joseph in Weesp near Amsterdam and Rachel's family in Maarsen nearby Utrecht. cf. Het Utrechts Archiv, 34–4 Notarissen in de stad Utrecht 1560–1905, 927 Protokol, 1681–92,145 (U117a001). Accessed 5 January 2024. https://hetutrechtsarchief.nl/collect ie/609C5BB6214D4642E0534701000A17FD. I am indebted to Brendan Glass for providing transcript and translation.

11 Leibniz-Forschungsstelle Hannover der Akademie der Wissenschaften zu Göttingen, *Gottfried Wilhelm Leibniz*, 120 f.

12 Calderón and Dechant, 'New light on Hugh Montgomerie', 190.

13 This research was undertaken as part of CRAFTVALUE, a four-year research project funded by the Irish Research Council and led by my supervisor Professor Christine Casey at Trinity College Dublin.

14 For Joseph Israel Richardo's death in December 1713, see Stadtarchiv Dresden (StAD), 2.1.3-C.XXI.20.9, p. 284 verso; for his burial, see StAD, 2.1.3-C.XXI.20.9, p. 292 recto; for Rachel Richardo's burial in January 1730, see StAD, 2.1.3.C.XXI.20.20, p. 19 recto.

15 Freitag, 'The troubled life of Richard Castle'. This raises the question of interfaith marriage, which is forbidden in Judaism. Marital liaisons between Jews and non-Jews were limited in the early modern period. See Judith Bleich, 'Intermarriage in the early modern period', 136.

16 Calderon and Dechant, 'New light on Hugh Montgomerie', 187, 192–4. Note that documents pertaining to this family in the Saxon archives refer to Captain Johann Samuel de Richardi, who owned the *Vorwerk Neugarden* in the mining town of Altenberg in Saxony. Daniel von Richardi is described in 1763 as 'Lieutenant Major and Chevalier Garde, of Golmicau', while documents appertaining to the sale of the family home in 1731 refer to Benjamin de Richardi as a Captain in the service of the Landgrave of Hesse-Cassel.

17 Anon., *Das ietztlebende Königliche Dresden in Meißen*, 74. Accessed 5 January 2024. https:// digital.slub-dresden.de/werkansicht/dlf/9278/91.

18 Castle, 'An essay on artificial navigation'; Castle, 'An essay toward supplying the city of Dublin with water'.

19 Hayes, 'Anglo-Irish architectural exchange'; Hayes, 'Sir Gustavus Hume'; Hayes, 'An Irish Palladian in England'.

20 Anon., 'History of the fine arts in Ireland: Richard Castles', 242.

21 Hayes, 'Anglo-Irish architectural exchange', 51.

22 Hayes, 'Anglo-Irish architectural exchange', 53.

23 See Arciszewska, 'A villa fit for a king', 41–58; Arciszewska, *The Hanoverian Court*.

24 Bognár, 'Das Sächsische Oberbauamt vom Ende des Dreißigjährigen Krieges bis zum Tod Augusts des Starken', 1. I am highly indebted to Dr Anna-Victoria Bognár for providing her unpublished paper and knowledge on the Saxon *Oberbauamt*.

25 Bognár, 'Stellen und hierarchische Strukturen in Hofbauämtern des Alten Reichs', 64.

26 For a detailed discussion of the Office of Works see Colvin, *The History of the King's Works*. For an overview of the history of the Royal Building Administration in France see Rosenfeld, 'The royal building administration in France from Charles V to Louis XIV', 161–79.

27 Haupt, 'Fürsten, Hofkünstler und Baubeamte: Architekten am sächsischen Oberbauamt im 18. Jahrhundert', 214.

28 Mertens, 'Das kursächsische Oberbauamt und Matthäus Daniel Pöppelmann', 30.

29 Reeckmann, *Anfänge der Barockarchitektur in Sachsen*, 14.

30 Rosenfeld, 'The royal building administration in France from Charles V to Louis XIV', 161.

31 Zedler, 'Wackerbarth' in *Grosses vollständiges Universal-Lexicon aller Wissenschaften und Künste*.
32 Scholze, 'Oberlandbaumeister Christoph Beyer', 45.
33 Meinert, 'Zur Geschichte des kursächsischen Oberbauamtes im 18. Jahrhundert', 289; Kuke, 'Kurven und Geschosse', 222.
34 Kuke, *Jean de Bodt 1670–1745: Architekt und Ingenieur im Zeitalter des Barock*, 23, 27.
35 Colvin, *A Biographical Dictionary of British Architects,* 121.
36 Haupt, 'Fürsten, Hofkünstler und Baubeamte: Architekten am sächsischen Oberbauamt im 18. Jahrhundert', 214.
37 Anon., *Königlich-Polnischer und Churfürstlich Sächsischer Hoff- und Staats-Calender auf das Jahr 1728*, 97–8.
38 Königliche Akademie der Wissenschaften, *Die Behördenorganisation und die allgemeine Staatsverwaltung,* 565: 'Alle unßere landtbauMeisters sindt Idiohten oder betriger, also erneüere ich die orders Ehrliche Mauer oder Zimermeisters zu solchen bau zu Employiren. Paleste seindt nicht zu bauen, Sondern Schaf Ställe und Wirtschaftsgebeüde, das kann ein Mauerer So guht als paladio' – All of our state master builders are idiots or deceivers, so I am renewing the order to employ honest masons or master carpenters for building such structures. Palaces are not to be built, but sheepfolds and farm buildings, which a mason can do just as well as Palladio. See also Strecke, *Anfänge und Innovation der preußischen Bauverwaltung,* 59.
39 However, Frederick made no effort to provide the master builders with a profound and organised training. Their only opportunity to obtain a training was as assistants to the building directors, under whom they practised their skills in surveying, drawing, preparing cost estimates, and structural matters relating to bridge, lock, and industrial construction. See Krüger, 'Das Bauwesen in Brandenburg-Preußen im 18. Jahrhundert', 50.
40 Bognár, 'Stellen und hierarchische Strukturen in Hofbauämtern des Alten Reichs', 69.
41 Thomas Archer cited in Colvin, *The History of the King's Works*, 48.
42 Colvin, *The History of the King's Works*, ix.
43 Colvin, 'Lord Burlington and the Office of Works', 97.
44 Colvin, *The History of the King's Works*, 70–1.
45 Colvin, 'Lord Burlington and the Office of Works', 98.
46 Meinert, 'Zur Geschichte des kursächsischen Oberbauamtes im 18. Jahrhundert', 300.
47 Cited after Colvin, *The History of the King's Works*, 88.
48 A transcript of the regulations can be found in Sponsel, *Der Zwinger, die Hoffeste und die Schlossbaupläne zu Dresden*, 125–9.
49 Haupt, 'Fürsten, Hofkünstler und Baubeamte', 214.
50 Cited after Sponsel, *Der Zwinger*, 126–8.
51 Sponsel, *Der Zwinger*, 128.
52 Bognár, 'Das Sächsische Oberbauamt', 8.
53 Bognár, *Der Architekt in der Frühen Neuzeit*, 47. Such distinctions between professional and official titles also existed in England. John Oliver, a surveyor by profession and a glazier by trade, succeeded Woodroffe in the City church and St Paul's offices in 1675. See Geraghty, 'The drawings: technique and purpose'.
54 Bognár, 'Stellen und hierarchische Strukturen in Hofbauämtern des Alten Reichs', 66, 68.
55 Bognár, 'Stellen und hierarchische Strukturen in Hofbauämtern des Alten Reichs', 66.
56 Colvin, *The History of the King's Works*, 68.
57 Rosenfeld, 'The royal building administration in France', 173.
58 Bognár, 'Das Sächsische Oberbauamt', 5. cf. also Bognár, *Der Architekt in der Frühen Neuzeit*, 120; Haupt, 'Fürsten, Hofkünstler und Baubeamte', 215; Heckmann, *Baumeister des Barock und Rokoko in Sachsen*, 7.
59 Bognár, *Der Architekt in der Frühen Neuzeit*, 109.
60 Bognár, *Der Architekt in der Frühen Neuzeit*, 109.
61 Cited after Bognár, *Der Architekt in der Frühen Neuzeit*, 110. SächsStA-D, 10026 Geheimes Kabinett, Nr. Loc. 01080/02, 166v.
62 Cited after Bognár, *Der Architekt in der Frühen Neuzeit*, 110.
63 Almost no such records survive for the early eighteenth century as they may have been lost. However, it could be that the later instructions or appointments that have survived were similar, given that it was common practice for these to be used over a longer period of time for

specifying the post. See Bognár, 'Das Sächsische Oberbauamt vom Ende des Dreißigjährigen Krieges bis zum Tod Augusts des Starken', 2.

64 SächsStA-D, 10036 Finanzarchiv, Nr. Loc. 32799, Rep. 52, Gen. Nr. 1072, 219r–221r. Transcribed in Bognár, *Der Architekt in der Frühen Neuzeit*, 468–70, app. 5.1.26.

65 Translated after Bognár, *Der Architekt in der Frühen Neuzeit*, 469, app. 5.1.26: 'Daferne er zur Einkauffung Bau Mate-/ rialien verschicket, oder sonst dazu ge= / brauchet werden sollte, so darf derselbe / kein Accord ohne Genehmhaltung des / Baumeister Schüzens und Amts-Verwalter / Müldners schließen'. *Conducteur* Schütze is not the same person as master builder Schütze, but it seems likely that both are members of the same family of building officials. cf. Bognár, *Der Architekt in der Frühen Neuzeit*, 113.

66 Translated after Bognár, *Der Architekt in der Frühen Neuzeit*, 470, app. 5.1.26: 'Hat er auf die zum Baue gelieferten / Materialien wohl Achtung zugeben, / daß solche zu dem, wozu sie bestimmet, / verbrauchet, daran nichts unnöthiger / Weise zerschnitten, oder gar verschleppet / und entwendet werde'.

67 Bognár, *Der Architekt in der Frühen Neuzeit*, 470, app. 5.1.26.

68 Klausmeier, *Thomas Ripley*, 32.

69 Cited after Klausmeier, *Thomas Ripley*, 32, note 71.

70 Cited after Colvin, *The History of the King's Works*, 68, note 10.

71 Klausmeier, *Thomas Ripley*, 33.

72 For more information on the responsibilities of measurers see Melanie Hayes's chapter in this volume.

73 SächsStA-D, 10036 Finanzarchiv, Nr. Loc. 32799, Rep. 52, Gen. Nr. 1074, 1r–6r. Transcribed in Bognár, *Der Architekt in der Frühen Neuzeit*, 466–8, app. 5.1.25. Even though the document dates to the second half of the eighteenth century, Anna-Victoria Bognár remarks that the lack of cited informatory literature indicates a long usage of the template. See Bognár, *Der Architekt in der Frühen Neuzeit*, 117. It is therefore not unlikely that the same or similar guidelines were used in the first half of the eighteenth century, for appointing and instructing *Conducteure*.

74 Translated after Bognár, *Der Architekt in der Frühen Neuzeit*, 466, app. 5.1.25: 'Hat er diejenigen / Dienste, welche bey / Aufnehmung der / Pläze, Verferti= / gung der Riße, / und Aufführung / derer Gebäude ihm / aufgetragen werden, zu rechter Zeit mit / aller accuratesse, / Fleiß und Eyfer / zu verrichten, jeden= / noch was denen / aufgegebenen Pro= / jecten wor der Zeit / nichts bekannt zu / machen'.

75 Bognár, *Der Architekt in der Frühen Neuzeit*, 116.

76 Translated after Bognár, *Der Architekt in der Frühen Neuzeit*, 467, app. 5.1.25: 'Wird sein Augen= / merck auf die / übrige Arbeit derer / Künstler und Hand= / wercker gerichtet, / und dasjenige, was / mangelhafft oder / unthüchtig zu finden / ist, schlechterdings / verworffen, und / keinesweges ge= / duldet'.

77 Anon., 'History of the fine arts in Ireland: Richard Castles', 243.

78 Bognár, *Der Architekt in der Frühen Neuzeit*, 116, 468.

79 Translated after Bognár, *Der Architekt in der Frühen Neuzeit*, 468, app. 5.1.25: 'Wird er sich auch die Bäue derer / Dämme, Ufer und / Straßen bekannt / machen, und genau / zu erforschen su= / chen'.

80 Heckmann, 'Arbeitsumfang und Bauweise eines Baubeamten', 252.

81 Böhner, 'Die Ingenieurleistungen', 421, 423.

82 Goode, 'Pöppelmann, Matthäus Daniel'.

83 Farrington, 'Richard Castle's "Essay on artificial navigation"', 67.

84 For the use of the different colour systems in European architectural drawings of the early modern period see Baudez, *Inessential Colors*.

85 Bognár, *Der Architekt in der Frühen Neuzeit*, 118.

86 Bognár, *Der Architekt in der Frühen Neuzeit*, 103, 120.

87 SächsStA-D, 10036 Finanzarchiv, Nr. Loc. 33084, Rep. 52, Spec. Nr. 0874, Nr. 4. Extracts printed in Bognár, *Der Architekt in der Frühen Neuzeit*, 118 and Heckmann, *Baumeister des Barock und Rokoko in Sachsen*, 300.

88 Heckmann, *Baumeister des Barock und Rokoko in Sachsen*, 300.

89 Bognár, *Der Architekt in der Frühen Neuzeit*, 118.

90 Downes, *Sir John Vanbrugh*, 297.

91 Downes, *Sir John Vanbrugh*, 297. For the original letter see British Library (BL), Add MS 19607, Correspondence of Henry Joynes with Nicholas Hawksmoor, Assistant Surveyor of the works at Blenheim, 1705–15. A transcript of the letter can be found in Downes, *Hawksmoor*, 235–6.
92 Downes, *Sir John Vanbrugh*, 297.
93 Downes, *Sir John Vanbrugh*, 297.
94 Böhner, 'Die Ingenieurleistungen', 420.
95 Meinert, 'Zur Geschichte des kursächsischen Oberbauamtes im 18. Jahrhundert', 290.
96 Meinert, 'Zur Geschichte des kursächsischen Oberbauamtes im 18. Jahrhundert', 289.
97 Bognár, *Der Architekt in der Frühen Neuzeit*, 112.
98 Jahn, 'Matthäus Daniel Pöppelmann', 217.
99 Tiller and Lieber, *Pöppelmann 3D: Bücher – Pläne – Raumwelten*, 9.
100 Heckmann, *Baumeister des Barock und Rokoko in Sachsen*, 11f; Bognár, 'Das Sächsische Oberbauamt vom Ende des Dreißigjährigen Krieges bis zum Tod Augusts des Starken', 6.
101 Schuster, 'Johann Christoph Knöffel', 325.
102 Heckmann, *Baumeister des Barock und Rokoko in Sachsen*, 231–5.
103 Schuster, 'Johann Christoph Knöffel', 325.
104 Geraghty, 'The drawings: technique and purpose'.
105 Hentschel and May, *Johann Christoph Knöffel*, 47.
106 Heckmann, *Baumeister des Barock und Rokoko in Sachsen*, 345.
107 Hentschel and May, *Johann Christoph Knöffel*, 56.
108 Heckmann, *Baumeister des Barock und Rokoko in Sachsen*, 346.
109 Bognár, *Der Architekt in der Frühen Neuzeit*, 119.
110 Bognár, *Der Architekt in der Frühen Neuzeit*, 213.
111 Translated from SächsStA-D, 10036 Finanzarchiv, Nr. Loc. 33084, Rep. 52 Spec. Nr. 087, Nr. 5: 'einen Bau Anschlag, und Riß zur Probe anfertigen laßen, als denn solche nebst unterthänigsten Bericht einsenden'.
112 Translated from SächsStA-D, 10036 Finanzarchiv, Nr. Loc. 33084, Rep. 52 Spec. Nr. 087, Nr. 5: 'und wer unter diesen dreyen sowhol intuitu der Land- als Wassergebäude der geschickteste zu der vacanten Landbauschreiber Dienst seyn möchte'.
113 Gibney, *The Building Site*, 34. The relevant documents are cited by Gibney (note 46) and are in Trinity College Dublin (TCD), MS MUN P/2/65/1–4.
114 Gibney, *The Building Site*, 34.
115 Bognár, *Der Architekt in der Frühen Neuzeit*, 119.
116 Krüger, *Das Bauwesen in Brandenburg-Preußen im 18. Jahrhundert*, 158.
117 Most recently, for example, Gibney, *The Building Site*, 68, 80–1; Casey, 'Ornament and craftsmanship in the architecture of James Gibbs', 36; Casey, 'Silent partner', 137; Hayes, 'Retrieving craft practice', 174, 189. See also Melanie Hayes's chapter in this volume.
118 Gibney, *The Building Site*, 80.
119 For a more detailed discussion on Castle's Irish engineering ventures see Casey 'Books and builders', 190–219.
120 Bognár, *Der Architekt in der Frühen Neuzeit*, 304.
121 Bognár, *Der Architekt in der Frühen Neuzeit*, 304. Bognár refers to the research project: 'Matthäus Daniel Pöppelmann (1662–1736): The palace and Zwinger designs for Dresden by Peter Heinrich Jahn', which is based at the Technische Universität Dresden.
122 Bognár, *Der Architekt in der Frühen Neuzeit*, 116.
123 For the classification of the different groups of architects in the early eighteenth century, see Jenkins, *Architect and Patron*, 46–66.

References

Anon., *Königlich-Polnischer und Churfürstlich Sächsischer Hoff – und Staats- Calender auf das Jahr 1728*. Leipzig: n.p., 1728. Accessed 5 January 2024. https://haab-digital.klassik-stiftung.de/viewer/resolver?urn=urn:nbn:de:gbv:32-1-10000558626.
Anon., *Das ietztlebende Königliche Dresden in Meißen*. Dresden: Robring, 1738. Accessed 5 January 2024. https://digital.slub-dresden.de/werkansicht/dlf/9278/1.

Anon., 'History of the fine arts in Ireland: Richard Castles', *Anthologia Hibernica* (October 1793): 242–3.

Arciszewska, Barbara. 'A villa fit for a King: The role of Palladian architecture in the ascendancy of the House of Hanover under George I', *Revue d'art canadienne / Canadian Art Review*, 19:1/2 (1992): 41–58.

Arciszewska, Barbara. *The Hanoverian Court and the Triumph of Palladio: The Palladian revival in Hanover and England, c.1700*. Warsaw: DiG, 2002.

Baudez, Basile. *Inessential Colors: Architecture on paper in Early Modern Europe*. Princeton, NJ: Princeton University Press, 2021.

Bleich, Judith. 'Intermarriage in the early modern period'. In *Defenders of the Faith: Studies in nineteenth- and twentieth-century orthodoxy and reform*, 136–73. Boston: Academic Studies Press, 2020. https://doi.org/10.1515/9781644691458-007.

Bognár, Anna-Victoria. 'Stellen und hierarchische Strukturen in Hofbauämtern des Alten Reichs'. In *Hofkünstler und Hofhandwerker in deutschsprachigen Residenzstädten der Vormoderne*, edited by Andreas Tacke, Jens Fachbach and Matthias Müller, 58–74. Petersberg, Hesse: Michael Imhof Verlag, 2017.

Bognár, Anna-Victoria. *Der Architekt in der Frühen Neuzeit: Ausbildung – Karriereweg – Berufsfelder*. Heidelberg: Heidelberg University Publishing, 2018. Accessed 5 January 2024. https://doi.org/10.17885/heiup.580.

Bognár, Anna-Victoria. 'Das Sächsische Oberbauamt vom Ende des Dreißigjährigen Krieges bis zum Tod Augusts des Starken: Stellenprofile der Amtsträger zwischen Planung, Bauausführung und Bauadministration'. In *Zwinger & Schloss: Die Dresdner Residenz Augusts des Starken im europäischen Kontext (1694–1733)*, edited by Henrik Karge and Peter H. Jahn. Heidelberg: Heidelberg University Publishing, forthcoming.

Böhner, Winfried. 'Die Ingenieurleistungen'. In *Matthäus Daniel Pöppelmann 1662–1736 und die Architektur Augusts des Starken*, edited by Kurt Milde, Klaus Mertens and Gudrun Stenke, 418–34. Dresden: Verlag der Kunst, 1990.

Calderón, Loreto and Konrad Dechant. 'New light on Hugh Montgomerie, Richard Castle and number 85 Saint Stephen's Green'. In *The Eighteenth-Century Dublin Town House: Form, function and finance*, edited by Christine Casey, 174–96. Dublin: Four Courts Press, 2010.

Campbell, Colen., *Vitruvius Britannicus*. 3 vols. London: Printed and sold by the author, 1715–25.

Casey, Christine. 'Books and builders: A biographical approach to Irish eighteenth-century architecture'. PhD dissertation, Trinity College Dublin, 1991.

Casey, Christine. 'Ornament and craftsmanship in the architecture of James Gibbs', *The Georgian Group Journal*, 27 (2019): 27–42.

Casey, Christine. 'Silent partner: Design and making in the Early Modern architecture of Britain', *R.A.: Revista de Arquitectura* (2021):132–45.

Castle, Richard. 'An essay on artificial navigation'. Dublin: n.p., 1733.

Castle, Richard. 'An essay toward supplying the city of Dublin with water'. Dublin: n.p., 1735.

Colvin, Howard. *The History of the King's Works*, vol. 5: *1660–1782*. London: Her Majesty's Stationery Office, 1976.

Colvin, Howard. *A Biographical Dictionary of British Architects, 1600–1840*. London: J. Murray, 1978.

Colvin, Howard. 'Lord Burlington and the Office of Works'. In *Lord Burlington and His Circle: Papers given at a Georgian Group symposium at the Victoria and Albert Museum on the 22nd May 1982*, 97–101. London: Georgian Group, 1982.

Downes, Kerry. *Hawksmoor*. London: Zwemmer, 1959.

Downes, Kerry. *Sir John Vanbrugh: A biography*. New York: St. Martin's Press, 1987.

Farrington, John H. 'Richard Castle's "Essay on artificial navigation", 1730', *Transport History*, 5:1 (March 1972): 67–89.

Freitag, Barbara. 'The troubled life of Richard Castle'. Lecture, 'Richard Castle, architect', Symposium, Russborough House, 4 November 2022.

Geraghty, Anthony. 'The drawings: Technique and purpose'. Accessed 5 January 2024. https://library.asc.ox.ac.uk/wren/Technique_purpose.html.

Gibney, Arthur. *The Building Site in Eighteenth-Century Ireland*, edited by L. Hurley and E. McParland. Dublin: Four Courts Press, 2017.

Goode, Patrick, ed. 'Pöppelmann, Matthäus Daniel'. In *The Oxford Companion to Architecture*. Oxford: Oxford University Press, 2009. Accessed 5 January 2024. https://www.oxfordreference.com/display/10.1093/acref/9780198605683.001.0001/acref-9780198605683-e-10 19?rskey=AGN1CK&result=1.

Griffin, David. 'Richard Castle's Egyptian Hall at Powerscourt, Co. Wicklow', *The Georgian Group Journal*, 5 (1995): 119–24.

Haupt, Isabel. 'Fürsten, Hofkünstler und Baubeamte: Architekten am sächsischen Oberbauamt im 18. Jahrhundert'. In *Architekt und/versus Baumeister: Die Frage nach dem Metier*, edited by Werner Oechslin, 212–20. Zürich: Gta-Verlag, 2009.

Hayes, Melanie. 'Anglo-Irish architectural exchange in the early eighteenth century: Patrons, practitioners and pieds-à-terre'. PhD dissertation, Trinity College Dublin, 2015.

Hayes, Melanie. 'Sir Gustavus Hume (1677–1731): Courtly connections and architectural connoisseurship in the early eighteenth century', *Irish Architectural and Decorative Studies*, 19 (2017): 36–53.

Hayes, Melanie. 'An Irish Palladian in England: The case of Sir Edward Lovett Pearce', *The Georgian Group Journal*, 29 (2021): 41–66.

Hayes, Melanie. 'Retrieving craft practice on the early eighteenth-century building site'. In *Enriching Architecture: Craft and its conservation in Anglo-Irish building production, 1660–1760*, edited by Christine Casey and Melanie Hayes, 160–96. London: UCL Press, 2023.

Heckmann, Hermann. 'Arbeitsumfang und Bauwesen eines Baubeamten im 18. Jahrhundert. Zum 300. Geburtstag des Zwingererbauers M. D. Pöppelmann', *Die Bauverwaltung*, 5 (1962): 252–4.

Heckmann, Hermann. *Matthäus Daniel Pöppelmann: Leben und werk*. Berlin: Deutscher Kunstverlag, 1972.

Heckmann, Hermann. *Baumeister des Barock und Rokoko in Sachsen*. Berlin: Verlag für Bauwesen, 1996.

Hentschel, Walter and Walter May. *Johann Christoph Knöffel: Der architekt des sächsischen Rokokos*. Berlin: Akademie Verlag, 1973.

Jahn, Peter Heinrich. 'Matthäus Daniel Pöppelmann (1662–1736): "Premier Architecte de Sa Majesté". Sein Wirken und künstlerisches Selbstverständnis als Dresdner Hofbaumeister unter August dem Starken'. In *Hofkünstler und Hofhandwerker in deutschsprachigen Residenzstädten der Vormoderne*, edited by Andreas Tacke, Jens Fachbach and Matthias Müller, 216–54. Petersberg, Hesse: Michael Imhof Verlag, 2017.

Jenkins, Frank. *Architect and Patron: A survey of professional relations and practice in England from the sixteenth century to the present day*. London: Oxford University Press, 1961.

Klausmeier, Axel. *Thomas Ripley, Architekt: Fallstudie einer karriere im Royal Office of the King's Works im zeitalter des Neopalladianismus*. Frankfurt am Main: Lang, 2000.

The Knight of Glin. 'Richard Castle, architect, his biography and works', *Quarterly Bulletin of the Irish Georgian Society*, 6:1 (January–March 1964): 31–8.

Königliche Akademie der Wissenschaften, ed. *Die Behördenorganisation und die allgemeine Staatsverwaltung Preußens im 18. Jahrhundert, 7 Akten vom 2 Januar 1746 bis 20. Mai 1748*. Berlin: Parey, 1904.

Krüger, Rolf-Herbert. 'Das Bauwesen in Brandenburg-Preußen im 18. Jahrhundert', *Jahrbuch für brandenburgische Landesgeschichte*, 64 (2013): 37–58.

Krüger, Rolf-Herbert. *Das Bauwesen in Brandenburg-Preußen im 18. Jahrhundert*. Berlin: Berliner Wissenschafts-Verlag GmbH, 2020.

Kuke, Hans-Joachim. *Jean de Bodt 1670–1745: Architekt und ingenieur im zeitalter des Barock*. Worms: Werner, 2002.

Kuke, Hans-Joachim. 'Kurven und Geschosse: Barockarchitekten in Deutschland und ihr verhältnis zum militär'. In *Mars und die Musen: Das wechselspiel von militär, krieg und kunst in der frühen neuzeit*, edited by Jutta Nowosadtko, 213–27. Berlin/Münster: LIT, 2008.

Laffan, William and Kevin V. Mulligan. 'His name is Castle'. In *Russborough: A great Irish house, its families and collections*, edited by William Laffan and Kevin V. Mulligan, 41–9. Russborough: Alfred Beit Foundation, 2014.

Leibniz-Forschungsstelle Hannover der Akademie der Wissenschaften zu Göttingen, ed. *Gottfried Wilhelm Leibniz: Sämtliche schiften und briefe*, vol. 1: *Allgemeiner politischer und historischer briefwechsel. Zweiundzwanzigster band Januar–Dezember 1703*. Berlin: Akademie Verlag, 2011. Accessed 5 January 2024. https://doi.org/10.26015/adwdocs-138.

Meinert, Günther. 'Zur Geschichte des kursächsischen Oberbauamtes im 18. Jahrhundert'. In *Forschungen aus Mitteldeutschen Archiven: Zum 60. Geburtstag von Hellmut Kretzschmar*, edited by Staatliche Archivverwaltung im Staatssekretariat für Innere Angelegenheiten, 285–303. Berlin: Ruetten & Loening, 1953.

Mertens, Klaus. 'Das kursächsische Oberbauamt und Matthäus Daniel Pöppelmann'. In *Matthäus Daniel Pöppelmann 1662–1736 und die Architektur Augusts des Starken*, edited by Kurt Milde, Klaus Mertens and Gudrun Stenke, 28–39. Dresden: Verlag der Kunst, 1990.

Reeckmann, Kathrin. *Anfänge der Barockarchitektur in Sachsen: Johann Georg Starcke und seine zeit*. Cologne: Böhlau Verlag, 2000.

Rosenfeld, Myra Nan. 'The Royal Building Administration in France from Charles V to Louis XIV'. In *The Architect: Chapters in the history of the profession*, edited by Spiro Kostof, 161–79. New York: Oxford University Press, 1977.

Sadleir, Thomas U. 'Richard Castle, architect', *Journal of the Royal Society of Antiquaries of Ireland*, 1:3 (September 1911): 241–5.

Schmidt, Freek. 'Open to all: Architectural education'. In *Companions to the History of Architecture*, vol. 2: *Eighteenth-century architecture*, edited by Caroline van Eck and Sigrid de Jong, 5–32. Chichester: Wiley Blackwell, 2017.

Scholze, Hans-Eberhard. 'Oberlandbaumeister Christoph Beyer: Ein beitrag zur geschichte des kurfürstlich-sächsischen Oberbauamtes', *Wissenschaftliche Zeitschrift der Technischen Hochschule Dresden*, 6:1 (1956–7): 39–49.

Schuster, Martin. 'Johann Christoph Knöffel (1686–1752)'. In *Heinrich Graf von Brühl (1700–1763): Bauherr und Mäzen*, edited by Landesamt für Denkmalpflege Sachsen, 324–7. Dresden: Neue Druckhaus Dresden GmbH, 2020.

Sharkey, Olive. 'Belvedere House, gem of the Irish Midlands', *The GPA Irish Arts Review Yearbook* (1989): 248–53.

Sponsel, Jean Louis. *Der Zwinger, die Hoffeste und die Schlossbaupläne zu Dresden*. Dresden: Kunstanstalt Stengel & Co., 1924.

Strecke, Reinhart. *Anfänge und Innovation der preußischen Bauverwaltung: Von David Gilly zu Karl Friedrich Schinkel*. Cologne: Böhlau, 2002.

Tiller, Elisabeth and Maria Lieber, eds. *Pöppelmann 3D: Bücher – pläne – raumwelten. Online-katalog zur ausstellung im Buchmuseum der Sächsischen Landesbibliothek – Staats- und Universitätsbibliothek Dresden (SLUB) vom 17 Mai bis 01 September 2013*. Accessed 5 January 2024. https://nbn-resolving.org/urn:nbn:de:bsz:14-qucosa-118312.

Zedler, Johann Heinrich. 'Wackerbarth'. In *Grosses vollständiges Universal-Lexicon aller Wissenschaften und Künste*. Leipzig: Zedler, 1732–54.

6

Between concept and construction: conservation insights into the building of Damer House

Máirtín D'Alton and Flora O'Mahony

In April 2023, the Office of Public Works (OPW) completed a three-year programme of repair to Damer House, an early eighteenth-century pre-Palladian house sited within the walls of a thirteenth-century castle, in the centre of the town of Roscrea, County Tipperary. It has tall narrow windows in nine bays, and three full storeys over a half-raised basement (Fig. 6.1). Although the castle had been declared a national monument in 1908, the house was threatened with demolition in the 1970s and twice saved by the Irish Georgian Society, and Old Roscrea Society, who restored and opened it to the public in 1977. The house and castle precinct in which it is sited came into state ownership in 1986, since which time the OPW has carried out extensive conservation and restoration works. Damer House bears many similarities to the eighteenth-century houses attributed to the Rothery family of artisans and tradesmen (principally architect John, who died in 1736, his son Isaac and brother James), whose work is documented at Mount Ievers, County Clare (c.1733–7).[1] Other attributions to the family include Shannongrove (c.1723) and Riddlestown (c.1730), both in County Limerick.[2] Somewhat *retardataire*, they are sometimes described as 'Dutch Style' or 'Queen Anne', although they are much later than Queen Anne herself, who died in 1714. It has been argued that the design for Mount Ievers (Fig. 6.2) was inspired by that of Chevening in Kent, a house attributed to Inigo Jones in vol. 2 of *Vitruvius Britannicus*.[3] In the absence of documentary sources, close examination of the building fabric, particularly during interventions for its conservation and repair, can offer a way into exploring this uncharted early history. Detailing the process of decay, repair and renewal at Damer House, this chapter reveals hitherto unseen insights into the material performance of the building and the craft practices

Figure 6.1: Damer House, Roscrea, County Tipperary.
Photograph by Andrew Tierney.

Figure 6.2: Mount Ievers Court, County Clare.
Photograph by Andrew Tierney, reproduced by kind permission of Norman and Karen Ievers.

employed in its original construction. In so doing it will consider the various roles and responsibilities of those involved in its building and speculate on the rationale behind the material finishes employed.

Family background and occupancy

The exact dates of the commencement and completion of Damer House are unknown. It is believed that the house succeeded an earlier dwelling inhabited in 1631 by Sir George Hamilton, who was married to Mary Butler, daughter of the 11th Earl of Ormond – the latter having been owners of the Roscrea estate until 1703.[4] Maurice Craig claimed that the house was begun in the second quarter of the eighteenth century and took 20 or 30 years to build, so that it looks older than it is.[5] The history of the family provides some guide both to its construction and its subsequent decay. Joseph Damer (1630–1720) established himself as a banker and moneylender in Ireland in the aftermath of the Cromwellian conquest. Not having a direct heir, he left his Irish estates to his nephew John Damer (c.1673–1768) of Shronell, County Tipperary, who purchased Roscrea in 1722. His English estates were left to his other nephew, Joseph Damer (1676–1737), MP for Dorchester 1722–7, and subsequently, MP for Tipperary, 1735–7. It seems most likely that Joseph Damer built Damer House as his Irish seat.[6] In his will, dated 1 January 1736, he left his Tipperary estates to his son Joseph (created Baron Milton (1753 Ireland, 1762 Great Britain) and Earl of Dorchester in 1792), except for 'the Manor and Lordship of Roscrea', which he left to his son John.[7] The latter married the sculptor Anne Seymour Conway, and they lived extravagantly before separating without issue. Having got into huge debt, in 1776, at the age of 34, John shot himself, in London.[8] The property passed to Lionel, third son of the earl, who also died without issue.[9] All Lionel's siblings died without children, and the male line and title became extinct with the death of his elder brother, the 2nd earl, in 1808.[10]

Historical tradition claimed that the house was never used as a family residence,[11] or if it was, only for a short period, and repeated changes in occupancy likely hastened its decay.[12] During the eighteenth-century the house was leased to a succession of tenants, including the Church of Ireland Bishop of Killaloe, Nicholas Synge (1746–1771),[13] a local merchant, Patten Smith, in the 1790s (for £200 a year), and the Barracks Board in 1798, who purchased the entire complex outright in 1858. In 1906 Damer House became 'Mr French's Academy', a preparatory school for boys, before returning to military use during the Irish Civil War, when four men found in possession of arms were executed in the small courtyard on the morning of 15 January 1923. In 1924 the house became a sanatorium, and in 1932 it reverted to being a school, until 1956.[14]

Fabric and conservation

By 2019 the sash boxes of the windows in Damer House were beginning to rot, and a programme of repair was required. The walls are constructed of coursed rubble, in this case locally sourced sandstone, over a stone plinth, with a stone cornice under the eaves of a hipped roof with a centre valley. There does not appear to be any evidence of brick in the construction of the main walls of the house, only some individual bricks and half bricks were found in the window reveals during the course of these works. There are no quoins, string courses, or lugged surrounds, the details which enliven the elevations of Mount Ievers. The windows have simple sandstone architraves but incorporate an acanthus leaf in the keystones (Fig. 6.3).[15] The architraves feature a concave profile with a triple recessed architrave, with a slight chamfer of 1 mm difference towards the inside of the profile, a very unusual detail, not seen by any of the OPW masons previously (Fig. 6.4). Lacking the heavier 1730s glazing bars found at Mount Ievers, the existing windows were installed in the latter half of the eighteenth century but retain a good deal of

Figure 6.3: North façade, Damer House. Structural failure to window 1, with sagging of random rubble stone masonry.

Photograph by Máirtín D'Alton, courtesy of the OPW.

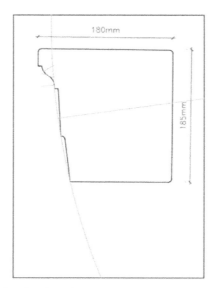

Figure 6.4: Window lintel profile, Damer House.
Drawing by Máirtín D'Alton, courtesy of the OPW.

crown glass (presumably of that date).[16] Inspection revealed that the water ingress was due to deterioration of the window fabric, and also to the stone window surrounds.[17] There were large gaps between the stone window jambs and the timber sash boxes, and the joints at each individual window jamb had deteriorated, with large parts of the stone having eroded, compromising the external envelope (Figs 6.5a and b). This necessitated a much larger programme of repairs, not only to the windows, but also to the stone jambs, sills, keystones and lintels, in order to make the building weather tight.

The entire façade was scaffolded, to closely inspect the fabric of the walls and windows before any work was undertaken. Though expertly carved, the window surrounds were sometimes worked on the wrong face and subsequently incorrectly placed in the building. Varying lengths of stone were apparent in the jambs and sills; while not uncommon, this is not as aesthetically pleasing from a consistency point of view, nor as technically satisfactory. Sedimentary rocks, like sandstone, are laid down in beds. Defects can arise if a stone piece is incorrectly placed in a building, relative to its bedding plane. When placed in a wall, a stone should lie in its bedding position. This means the layers should run horizontally in the manner that the stone was originally formed. The stone is much stronger in this position. If the stone is face bedded, then

Figure 6.5: (a) Decayed joint between window jambs reinforced with stainless-steel helical bars, Damer House; (b) Erosion had produced significant gaps between the window jambs and the window sash boxes, Damer House.

Photographs by Máirtín D'Alton, courtesy of the OPW.

the layers are vertical. This leaves the stone more vulnerable to decay, due to spalling (loss of the surface face), delamination and surface granulation, than would otherwise be the case if it were properly placed. This was presumably because of insufficient natural height of the quarry bed. Over the years, it had led to the serious deterioration of the stone, from weathering. Not all the stone was bedded in this manner, but for those that were, some faces had delaminated, resulting in the complete loss of the surface and carved detailing (see Fig. 6.3). In some cases, the stone had degraded into fine sand and disintegrated. While a lack of adequate material may account for these failures, some responsibility must lie with the masons for failing to lay the stone correctly, and, perhaps, a lack of oversight by the executant architect or clerk of works. This in turn raises questions over the varying skill levels, and quality control involved. It is worth noting the contrastingly crisp preservation of the limestone used on contemporary buildings, such as Castletown and Mount Ievers. Craig, commenting on nearby Ballyfin

House, states: 'The fractured volutes of the Ionic capitals illustrate the folly of executing such work in sandstone'.[18]

The window openings consist of a three-element pseudo flat arch (see Fig. 6.3). Due to the absence of a relieving arch, eccentric loading was placed upon the elements of the lintels, meaning that there was greater stress on the lintels, as only the central element functioned as a keystone/voussoir. This meant that many of the windows had fractured at the corners and failed, and some were on the point of collapse. In some cases the walls were only prevented from collapse by the sash boxes alone (Fig. 6.6).

The inspection revealed further details. The OPW masons saw evidence of five separate hands in the working of the decorated stonework of the windows. The quality of carving was very good, the work precise, the keystones the same size with evidence of a numbering and assembly system in the lintels and jambs (observed on their removal). However, our masons concluded that the use of inappropriate poor-quality stone was an unfortunate economy, forced on the original craftsmen. Almost every window was found to have slightly different widths. The two-part sills (Fig. 6.7) led to a 10 mm variation in the average width of the openings for the jambs, due to the joint, further exacerbated by the inconsistent joints in the rubble walling. While the window heads were consistently carved of two lintels and a keystone, the pieces in the jambs were of random height. Larger blocks would appear to have been scarce, forcing the original masons to carve whatever was to hand. The front steps are

Figure 6.6: Timber lintels above window boxes, Damer House.
Photograph by Máirtín D'Alton, courtesy of the OPW.

Figure 6.7: Window sill, Damer House.
Photograph by Andrew Tierney.

similarly made of many pieces rather than single blocks. This suggested money saving measures in the sourcing of materials. At the same time, as noted above, this may also suggest a lack of on-site supervision and control of materials.

Observing that the stones were not levelled and some pinnings protruded, our masons concluded that the eighteenth-century builders intended the random rubble stonework of the walls to be rendered, which would have covered up the uneven quality of the surface. The render would also have provided a material and texture contrast to the decorated sandstone of the window architraves and front door. It would further explain why the window profiles project so far out from the walls; some 40 to 70 mm, to leave space for the render. Rendering would also have made the interior of the house waterproof. Currently, in periods of rain, the walls retain a great deal of water. It was difficult to find evidence of surviving render, however this does not mean that it was not there originally.[19]

The masonry repair revealed at least two distinct construction periods for the main house. The basement and ground floor appeared to represent one construction phase, following the extensive excavation and preparation of the foundations and basement area. When the damaged stonework was removed from the ground floor level, it was found that some keystones had been narrowed, behind the face, to allow the lintels to fit in behind. This indicated that the openings were not constructed wide enough to take the two lintels and the keystone (see Fig. 6.3). The mason could not cut the keystone because it would be clearly visible to the eye if one of the keystones was narrower. This was evidence for the cut stone having been carved and finished prior to the construction of the tripartite walls,[20] and the first phase of builders having to improvise in the instance of trouble with the opening sizes during construction.

On the two higher levels, some of the keystones sagged substantially, and timber wedges were found to have been left in situ in the joints of the keystones. This would indicate that the openings on the upper levels were constructed slightly too wide, and after the sills and jambs were fitted, the individual lintels and keystones ended up being too narrow to fit the opening. The solution found was to put wedges in the joints between keystones and lintels. The wedges were resting on the timber frame of the windows, supporting the lintels and keystones. That could have only been done if carpenters and masons worked in unison during construction. The majority of the broken lintels were on the first floor (Fig. 6.8), which may mean that the build was rushed. This could be evidence of work stopping at ground floor level for a period, or a new crew of masons arriving to work on the rest of the build, or both. All timber wedges (Fig. 6.9) were removed during

Figure 6.8: First-floor windows, Damer House.
Photograph by Andrew Tierney.

Figure 6.9: Master mason Gunther Wolters displays construction wedges used to support a timber lintel from the first-floor windows. Damer House.

Photograph by Máirtín D'Alton, courtesy of the OPW.

the OPW recent conservation work and the sagged keystones put into the correct position during the repair.

Was the house finished?

The protracted building period, traditionally claimed, but for which evidence has now been found, may mean that the house was never properly finished.[21] Certainly, the plan (Fig. 6.10) is curious, despite the great size of the house, there are few magnificent chambers within. The great anticipation of the elaborate carved staircase (Fig. 6.11) is unresolved; the space peters out in a landing, without leading to any great room in particular. The main stair at Mount Ievers similarly terminates at the first-floor landing; however, Mount Ievers at least has a long gallery on the top floor, something for which there is no evidence now at Damer House, if it ever existed.

    The entire front hall may have originally been panelled in pine, like the staircase, or possibly in oak. It is likely as well that at least some of the reception rooms were similarly panelled, as at Mount Ievers and other contemporary houses. This would have greatly added to the internal comfort. That this has not survived may be on account of the walls not being rendered or lined internally with brick, and thus often being damp, which could have caused the wooden panelling to rot. This, however, would not explain why it did not survive on the internal partition walls. Taken together, the above evidence suggests compromises were made

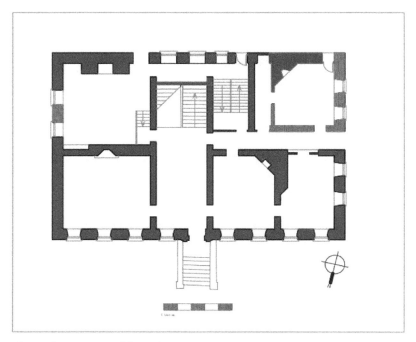

Figure 6.10: Ground floor plan, Damer House.
Drawing by Máirtín D'Alton, courtesy of the OPW.

in the construction of Damer House. Perhaps the creative impetus ceased with the death of Joseph Damer in 1737. The ennoblement of the family and the construction of larger houses at Shronell in south County Tipperary and Milton Abbey in Dorset in the mid eighteenth century directed financial resources away from Damer House, which by this point, situated as it was in the centre of a small town, rather than a large country estate, was decidedly out of fashion and less desirable.

The magnificent front doorcase in the façade of the house (Fig. 6.12), squeezed in under the central first-floor window, which it slightly obscures, seems like an afterthought, or was perhaps made off-site. Similar to the door formerly at No. 10 Mill Street, Dublin (long disappeared), it lends a note of magnificence to an otherwise plain façade. There was once more to it. An early photo of Damer House shows a sculptural bust of a lady, contained within the broken scroll, also paralleled at Mill Street, which shows a pedestal for something similar (Figs 6.13 and 6.14).[22] Recently, the many layers of paint that have been applied to the doorcase have been removed, revealing the

Figure 6.11: Pine staircase, Damer House.
Photograph by Andrew Tierney.

Figure 6.12: Doorcase, Damer House.
Photograph by Andrew Tierney.

Figure 6.13: Old photo of doorcase, Damer House.

Courtesy of the National Library of Ireland.

Figure 6.14: No. 10 Mill Street Dublin, built circa 1720. Photograph taken prior to 1891.

Patrick Healy Collection, South Dublin Libraries. CC-BY-NC.

crisp sandstone detail for the first time in many years, preserved under its multiple layers of military-grade paint (Fig. 6.15). The process also revealed damage and crude repairs over time. Other doorcases in the vicinity suggest that they may be 'one-off' pieces from the atelier that produced the decorated stone to Damer House.[23]

Repairing the stonework

Only stone which was damaged beyond repair was replaced with new stone. All damaged stone up to 150 × 150 mm was repaired with lime-based restoration mortar to match the colour of the existing stone (Fig. 6.16). Damaged stone above this size was replaced with indents. Broken jambs, lintels and keystones that could not be salvaged were replaced with new stone (Figs 6.17a and b). It was fortunate that a local quarry was able to supply the appropriate replacement stone. This is a Silurian Upper Old Red Sandstone, a cross bedded stone, from Kinsella's quarry above Roscomroe in the Slieve Blooms.[24] In order to

Figure 6.15: Sample cleaning portion of doorcase with decorated floral scroll, Damer House. The scrolls are enriched with *cyma recta* consoles, forming a deep reveal enriched with dentils. The frieze is supported on fluted pilasters with lively Corinthian capitals and plain bases. A *cyma recta* curve is also a feature of the window surrounds.

Photograph by Máirtín D'Alton, courtesy of the OPW.

Figure 6.16: Repaired joint with lime repair mortar and simulated silica sand joint, Damer House. The repair mortar will harden and darken on exposure to the environment.

Photograph by Máirtín D'Alton, courtesy of the OPW.

expose the natural colour of the existing stone, to correctly match it with appropriate new stone and repair mortar, it was necessary to remove an algae-lichen composite biofilm which made the stone appear redder than it was.

Figure 6.17: Window 11, Damer House, prior to repair (a); following repair (b). This was one of the more badly decayed windows.

Photograph courtesy of the OPW.

In total less than eight per cent of the original stone was replaced, with the rest being repaired with reinforced repair mortar, and stone consolidation measures. The stone was pointed with lime mortar and resin injection was utilised to keep water out of grikes and cracks. The keystones were very decayed on the ground and first-floor level, but had survived in better condition on the second floor. Using a profile comb on the best remaining keystones, a profile was drawn and a clay model of the keystone made by master mason Gunther Wolters (Fig. 6.18). From the model, a master copy was carved in sandstone by Wolters. The local stone was used to carve the first keystone. Stonemasons generally were unfamiliar with this material due to it being commonly used in wall building and for landscaping. Initially the masons and stonecutters did not like it much, because it was hard on the chisel, and on the mason. The material 'stood well to the chisel' as stonemasons say, and it turned out to

Figure 6.18: Gunther Wolters with removed keystone and clay model of acanthus keystone.

Photograph by Andrew Tierney.

Figure 6.19: New carved keystones on display for 30 August 2021 Heritage Week event at Damer House.

Photograph by Máirtín D'Alton, courtesy of the OPW.

be carvable. After the master copy was carved, the four additional OPW stonemason apprentices (see below) carved the keystones that needed replacing and left their individual masons' mark in the stones they carved (Figs 6.19 and 6.20). Traditionally, masons' marks are banker

Figure 6.20: Different stages of carved keystones on display for 30 August 2021 Heritage Week event at Damer House.

Photograph by Andrew Tierney.

marks used to identify the mason for payment per piece. Historically, master masons would get an elaborate mason's mark from the cathedral or workshop where they trained. These marks were based on either a square, triangle or circle, as a template. The mark would be drawn in the template and when the mason looked for work somewhere else, he was given a square, a compass and a ruler to construct the template and then insert his sign into the template, to prove his qualifications.[25] No original masons' marks were identified on any of the removed stones.[26]

The recent conservation work not only allowed the team to repair Damer House (Fig. 6.21) but opened a window on the hitherto uncharted early history of its construction. A great deal has been learned simply by the process of repair: the long-term performance of the local sandstone; the limitations of its extraction from narrow beds; the failure of the masons to lay the stone correctly, and resultant spalling; the mechanics of the wall construction; the temporal sequence of stone cutting and rubble construction and related problems; evidence for an intended plaster finish. Certainly, the design of the house as constructed may not represent the original intentions of either architect or patron. The high-quality front door and the magnificent staircase within hint at a grand architectural conception that was only partially realised, while the poor quality of the wall construction suggests a project lacking in sustained supervision by a single architect or clerk of works. Given the relative wealth of the Damer family, one would expect their mansion to be larger and better finished than Mount Ievers – but the quality of

Figure 6.21: North façade, Damer House, following completion of repair work in April 2023.

Photograph by Máirtín D'Alton, courtesy of the OPW.

stonework in the latter far exceeds it. Nevertheless, the greater width of Damer House, with its two extra windows on each floor, indicates the scale of Joseph Damer's ambition, but the historical evidence presented here suggests his successors lacked the funds or inclination to complete it, as their interests pivoted to other architectural projects elsewhere in Britain and Ireland.

OPW team

Tobias Burke	Carpenter, OPW
Brian Clancy	Carpenter, OPW
Mason Clifford	Carpenter, OPW
Máirtín D'Alton	Architect, OPW
Robbie Donnelly	Stone Mason, OPW
Kevin Lyons	Chargehand Roscrea, OPW
Tadhg McCarthy	Stone Mason, OPW
Conor O'Brien	Stone Mason, OPW
Des O'Connell	Carpenter, OPW
Flora O'Mahony	Senior Architect Kilkenny District, OPW
Stephen Quinn	Stone Mason, OPW
Eamonn Rafter	District Manager Kilkenny, OPW
Gunther Wolters	Master Stone Mason, OPW

Notes

1 *Georgian Society Records*, 24–9.
2 Bence-Jones, *Burke's Guide to Country Houses*, 242, 258; Craig, *Classic Irish Houses of the Middle Size*, 74.
3 Girouard, 'Mount Ievers, County Clare'; Craig, *The Architecture of Ireland*, 178. For a discussion of Jones's involvement in the design of Chevening, see Worsley, *Inigo Jones and the European Classicist Tradition*, 78–9.
4 Manning, *Excavations at Roscrea Castle*, 32; Dúchas, *Roscrea Visitors' Guide*.
5 Craig, *The Architecture of Ireland*, 181. Timber wedges, of a timber as yet unidentified, salvaged from the lintels and above the lintels of the upper windows during the course of the recent repair work, may in the future reveal the completion date of the house. Many wedges were found in the windows of the first- and second-floor windows of Damer House between the keystones and lintel stones, and on top of the window box under the original timber lintels. These have been retained at the OPW depot along with the replaced decorative stone, for further dating.
6 See Bergin, 'Damer, Joseph'; Bence-Jones, *Burke's Guide to the Country Houses of Ireland*, 99, claims it was this Joseph, 'father of the earl of Dorchester' who built Damer House.
7 Fraser, 'Joseph Damer', 50.
8 Noble, *Anne Seymour Damer*, 47, 57, 60.
9 Wilson, *Post-Chaise Companion*, 158. In 1793 it was recorded as the property of the Right Hon. Lord Milton, along with the rest of the town, see Anon., *Anthologia Hibernica*, 1: 81.
10 Burke, *A Genealogical and Heraldic Dictionary of the Peerages of England, Ireland and Scotland*, 156.
11 This tradition may have been conflated with accounts of Damer Court (Shronell) west of Tipperary town: 'Upon this property, about a century ago, the Damer family erected a most extensive mansion, which they intended for a place of permanent residence in Ireland. Lady Caroline Sackville, however … who was married to a Damer, refused, upon being brought to Tipperary, to take up her residence in this country. The consequence was that the house was never finished, and in 1776 was almost wholly taken down, and the Damers for two generations became absentees. Nothing now remains of Damer Court, but a shell of the building, and the ruins of the walls which were intended to surround the grounds.' W. T. H. *Encumbered Estates of Ireland*, 36.
12 O'Byrne, 'Bon anniversaire'.
13 Manning, *Excavations at Roscrea Castle*, 8.
14 Manning, *Excavations at Roscrea Castle*, 8; O'Byrne, *The Irish Georgian Society: A celebration*, 112–18.
15 The closest parallel is the treatment of the sandstone window architraves at Gloster, 8 km northwest.
16 Surviving building accounts for Mount Ievers show the house was commenced in 1733 and completed in 1737. See *The Georgian Society Records*, vol. 5, 25–6.
17 For sandstone decay, see Kissane et al., 'Characterisation of Irish sandstones used for building', 155–60. See also Pavía and Bolton, *Stone, Brick and Mortar: Historical use, decay and conservation of building materials in Ireland*. For Roscrea sandstone specifically see the references in Wilkinson, *Practical Geology and Ancient Architecture in Ireland* and Kinahan, 'Economic geology of Ireland'.
18 Craig, *The Architecture of Ireland*, 204. The original upper storeys of the Old Library, Trinity College Dublin, as noted by Casey, was 'pale sandstone from the Darley quarries of Scrabo in County Down which failed within decades and was replaced with granite in the C19'. Casey, *Dublin*, 402. See also Wyse Jackson and Caulfield's chapter in *Enriching Architecture*, 242–3. Accessed 15 January 2024. https://www.uclpress.co.uk/products/209667.
19 Heritage plasterer Paul Griffin stated that many historic buildings were stripped of their render (pers. comm.).
20 Tripartite wall construction has been described as 'identical in most respects to medieval walling … built as two separate masonry membranes forming the exterior and interior faces of the wall, and the space between them filled with a core of mortar imbedded with loose unbonded rubble stones'. Gibney, *The Building Site*, 124–5. The use of this constructional

system at Damer House may be further evidence of the economisation found elsewhere by the masons.

21　Craig, *The Architecture of Ireland*, 180.

22　The sculpture shares certain stylistic features with the *oeuvre* of Anne Seymour Conway (1748–1828), who married John Damer in 1767, but separated from him in 1774, with Damer dying two years later. She died in 1828. Known for her bust portraits, she exhibited her works at the Royal Academy. See Noble, *Anne Seymour Damer: A woman of art and fashion*. Anecdotal evidence, imparted by the masons from a local (undocumented) source, suggests that the sculpture survives safe somewhere nearby.

23　Such as Ballymachreese, Ballyneety, County Limerick, and Lisduff, Blackfort, County Tipperary.

24　Feehan, *The Geology of Laois and Offaly*, 56.

25　As documented by Gunther Wolters, master mason.

26　It has been stated that whereas most architects and building contractors get to leave a visual physical legacy of their work right across our cities, towns and rural landscapes, when conservation architects, craftsmen and conservation contractors have completed their work, there is often little evidence of the fruits of their labour. It was with this in mind that OPW organised some open-day events during heritage week in 2021 and 2022 to showcase and explain the repair work that had been carried out by the stonemasons and the conservation team at Damer House.

References

Anon., *Anthologia Hibernica: Or monthly collections of science, belles-lettres and history*, vol. 1: January to June. Dublin: n.p., 1793.

Bence-Jones, Mark. *Burke's Guide to Country Houses*, vol. 1: *Ireland*. London: Pergamon, 1978.

Bergin, John. 'Damer, Joseph', *Dictionary of Irish Biography*, edited by Eoin Kinsella. Royal Irish Academy, 2009. Accessed 15 January 2024. https://doi.org/10.3318/dib.002390.v1.

Burke, John Bernard. *A Genealogical and Heraldic Dictionary of the Peerages of England, Ireland and Scotland: Extinct, dormant and in abeyance*. London: Henry Colburn, 1846.

Casey, Christine. *The Buildings of Ireland: Dublin*. New Haven, CT and London: Yale University Press, 2005.

Craig, Maurice. *Classic Irish Houses of the Middle Size*. London: Architectural Press, 1976.

Craig, Maurice. *The Architecture of Ireland from the Earliest Times to 1880*. London: Batsford, 1982.

Dúchas. *Roscrea Visitors' Guide*. Dublin: Dúchas, The Heritage Service, n.d.

Feehan, John. *The Geology of Laois and Offaly*. Roscrea: Offaly County Council / The Geological Survey of Ireland, 2013.

Fraser, M. 'Joseph Damer: A banker of old Dublin', *Dublin Historical Record*, 3:3 (March–May 1941): 41–53.

Georgian Society. *Georgian Society Records of Eighteenth-Century Domestic Architecture and Decoration in Dublin*, vol. 5. Shannon: Irish University Press, 1969.

Gibney, Arthur. *The Building Site in Eighteenth-Century Ireland*, edited by L. Hurley and E. McParland. Dublin: Four Courts Press, 2017.

Girouard, Mark. 'Mount Ievers, County Clare', *Country Life*, 133 (8 March 1962): 1152–5.

Jackson, Patrick N. Wyse and Louise Caulfield. 'The rough and the smooth: Stone use in Dublin 1720–60'. In *Enriching Architecture: Craft and its conservation in Anglo-Irish building production*, edited by Christine Casey and Melanie Hayes, 234–61. London: UCL Press, 2023.

Kinahan, George Henry. 'Economic geology of Ireland', *Journal of the Royal Geological Society of Ireland*, 18 (1885–9): 1–14.

Kissane, Paul, Sara Pavía and Oliver Kinnane. 'Characterisation of Irish sandstones used for building'. In *Civil Engineering Research in Ireland*, edited by Sreejith Nanukuttan and Jamie Goggins, 155–60. Belfast: CERAI, 2014.

Manning, Conleth, ed. *Excavations at Roscrea Castle*. Dublin: Wordwell, 2003.

Noble, Percy. *Anne Seymour Damer: A woman of art and fashion, 1748–1828*. London: Kegan Paul, Trench, Trübner & Co., 1908.

O'Byrne, Robert. *The Irish Georgian Society: A celebration*. Dublin: Irish Georgian Society, 2008.

O'Bryne, Robert. 'Bon anniversaire', *The Irish Aesthete* (23 September 2013). Accessed 15 January 2024. https://theirishaesthete.com/tag/damer-house/.

Pavía, Sara and Jason Bolton. *Stone, Brick and Mortar: Historical use, decay and conservation of building materials in Ireland.* Dublin: Wordwell, 2000.

Wilkinson, George. *Practical Geology and Ancient Architecture in Ireland.* London: John Murray, 1845.

Wilson, William. *Post-Chaise Companion.* Dublin: Printed for the author, 1786.

Worsley, Giles. *Inigo Jones and the European Classicist Tradition.* New Haven, CT and London: Yale University Press, 2008.

W. T. H. *Encumbered Estates of Ireland.* London: Bradbury and Evans, 1850.

Part 2
Representation

7
Architects and craftsmen: a theme with variations

Alistair Rowan

In the creation of great architecture, a fixed sequence of process is always present: there is first the intellectual concept of how the work is to be formed and how it will appear; there is then the input of the client, or patron – or whoever commissions the building – dependent on which, a second process of detailed design will follow, specifically to align the initial concept with the particular requirements of the client. In large undertakings, the process of detailed design can often be protracted, extending over many years, yet it remains clear that it is only after the first essential sequence of processes has run its course, or reached a point of common agreement, that the real business of constructing a work of architecture can begin. A predilection in contemporary architectural history, based perhaps on an egalitarian concept of equality of esteem, tends to emphasise the contribution of craftsmen, tradesmen and labourers, who have previously been ignored, and to showcase the processes of 'building construction' at the expense of 'architectural design'. Thus Joseph Sharples, in an article which 'offers a fresh decentred view of a familiar monument', studies with scrupulous detail the identity of the workers who built the first phase of George Gilbert Scott's University of Glasgow,[1] and in a similar vein James Campbell takes the view that throughout the course of construction of a great fabric, such as St Paul's Cathedral in London or equally, perhaps, at Stanstead airport in Essex, the role of the architect, here Sir Christopher Wren or Lord Norman Foster, is significantly moderated by the craftsmen working on the job.[2] The argument is that the building process, complicated by the nature and range of the materials employed and evolving through time, is a matter of such breadth and complexity that the notion that one single person should be identified as responsible for the entire structure is patently false. The statement seems clear and sensible. It has a ring of truth about it and yet, it may be countered that it is nonetheless not quite correct or, rather, that it misses the point. Consider the frequent, yet normally unrecorded, site visits paid in the past by an architect to any building in the course of its construction and the opportunity provided by these site visits for aspects of a design to be altered and for such problems as are thrown up in the course of the building process to be resolved by discussions on site.[3]

A second, more subtle, analysis of the true role that has been played by architects at different times, questions the recurrent preference of historians to develop a narrative which is based, almost exclusively, on biographical material. Political, social and cultural history in Europe – and certainly within Britain and Ireland – has tended to be conceived in terms of the great figures in any movement or discipline. The British *Dictionary of National Biography*, published between 1883 and 1901, set the pattern in this regard, followed for English architecture by the four editions of Sir Howard Colvin's *Biographical Dictionary of British Architects*, first published in 1954. As an historian, Colvin's primary purpose was to establish a secure, documentary basis – free from attribution or guesswork – for the history of buildings in Britain between 1600 and 1840. His example has been followed in Ireland and extended, for the Victorian, Edwardian and modern periods in Britain, so that, almost by default, architectural history has tended to be formed by a biographical approach. In military history, the foot soldiers are left out; and the same, it can be argued, has occurred within building history.[4] That said, it is still the case that throughout history, and also to a large extent even today, the architect or the architectural practice retains control and Wren or Foster may surely – and securely – be credited as the agents of their own designs.

It is the interface between the first conception of a building and its ultimate delivery as a solid habitable form, occupying and enclosing space, that presents the architectural historian with the real challenge. How is the building to be read? How did it come about? Who made it and for whom? What was its real purpose and finally – crucial to the assessment of the contribution of the craftsmen involved – who deserves the credit for its final appearance: the workmen or the architect? Here a distinction has to be drawn between the history of construction (with all the minutiae of practice within different trades, however interesting) and the generative concept of a building as a solid structure established first in drawn plans, elevations, sections and details, each part originating in the mind of its creator or, with complex modern building, conceived collectively by a design team. Architects and architectural firms call architecture into being: the artisans necessary for the execution of their designs are their collaborators. That said, the quality of the participation of craftsmen is crucial to a building's success since they have the power, as individuals, to make or to mar the outcome of any work.

The history of the building trades in Britain from the seventeenth to the early nineteenth century reflects a sustained, if gradual, rise in the status of the artisan: this may be illustrated neatly by contrasting the treatment meted out, around 1595, to 'the rude mechanicals' assembled by Shakespeare in *A Midsummer Night's Dream* – a carpenter, a joiner, a weaver, a bellows maker and a tinker, of whom Bottom the weaver was 'simply the best wit of any handicraft man in Athens' – who become the collective butt of patronising comments at a ducal court, while by 1779, Elizabeth Montagu, one of the most celebrated society hostesses in Georgian London, allowed herself to be detained for an entire morning by 'a regiment of artificers' – a bricklayer, a stonemason, a carpenter and a decorative painter – at her house in Portman Square. There is, no doubt, a witty irony in Mrs Montagu's reference to these tradesmen as 'important people' yet, two centuries after Shakespeare, her architect thought it proper for her to meet the craftsmen who were to carry out improvements for her, nor did she demur at meeting them.[5]

The change in status is characteristic of the Age of Reason, where it is evident that master craftsmen – masons, bricklayers, carpenters, joiners and plasterers – could and often did rise to positions of affluence and even to social standing, as a consequence of the conduct of their trade.[6] In civilised societies dexterity of execution, whether in music or the arts, has always been valued and no doubt Mrs Montagu was well aware of the claims of the virtuoso when she chose to meet the men who were to improve her house.

The practice of architecture has regularly encountered a fashionable patronage, at least since the Renaissance, where educated clients have wanted to master or, at least, to understand the concepts and criteria that come into play within a building project. In considering John Shute's *First and Chief Groundes of Architecture*, published in London in 1563 and the earliest book on architecture to be written in English, Lawrence Weaver comments on the cultured classes, 'agog to gather up any crumbs of the new learning and the new taste that were so firmly establishing themselves'.[7] Shute – a painter/stainer and, perhaps only theoretically, an architect – had read widely and took pains to point out the full range of knowledge and, thereby, the superior education to be expected of anyone claiming the distinction of being an architect.[8]

He travelled in Italy shortly before 1550 and clearly enjoyed examining and explaining not only the basis of the proportional systems of classicism but also the new vocabulary and terminology required to describe the elements of 'ancient and famous monuments'; thus, in the plates he consistently labels the different parts that make up a structural member or a moulding, as '*Plinthus, Astragalus, Echinus*' and so on (Fig. 7.1). In this way, and almost inevitably, the architectural terms, set out for the benefit of Shute's contemporaries, were picked up generally within the building world of Britain and Ireland, to be employed alike by patrons, architects and artisans for more than three hundred years.[9]

If the esteem for classical architecture was widely shared throughout the seventeenth and eighteenth centuries, the focus of interest among the different classes varied. The aristocracy and great landowners wished, as Weaver comments, to be au fait with classical norms; professional architects needed to understand the 'grammar' and intellectual principles behind the new visual language, while artisans – principally masons, joiners and plasterers – had to master the details to be able to reproduce them convincingly. European architectural publications mirror the requirements of the different types of purchasers closely: large folio volumes, well-illustrated with finely engraved plates, came into being principally to adorn the shelves of noblemen's, landowners' or connoisseurs' libraries; larger quarto volumes, either on architectural theory or containing designs for buildings, were produced by and for the profession, while a wide range of smaller volumes, usually octavo or of a lesser size, provided rudimentary guides to the orders with additional practical information for builders and other tradesmen. Within the last category, two Italian publications, Vignola's *Regola delli Cinque Ordini di Architettura* (*The Five Orders of Architecture* – short and concise, first published in 1562) and Scamozzi's *L'Idea della Architettura Universale* (*The Idea of Universal Architecture* – a sprawling compendium in six books, published in 1615, during the last year of the architect's life) gave rise to a large number of translated and condensed texts, aimed at the working man. In Britain, the spate of building in the aftermath of the Fire of London created a constant need for reliable manuals on architecture, largely met through the publications of Robert Pricke, who between 1669 and 1679 issued at least thirteen titles on drawing, architecture and ornament.[10] In addition, Joachim Schuym's *The Mirror of Architecture: Or the ground rules of the art of building, exactly laid down by Vincent Scamozzi, master builder of Venice,* first appeared in 1669 in an English translation by William Fisher, amplified with 'The description and use of an ordinary joint rule' by John Brown, and in 1700

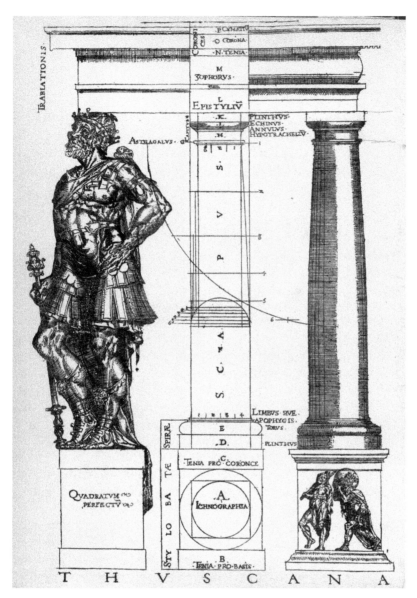

Figure 7.1: 'The Tuscann Order' in John Shute, *The First and Chief Groundes of Architecture*, London, 1563 (1912 reprint). Shute's volume, of which only four copies survive, is the first book to be published explaining Classical architecture for an English-speaking audience.

Getty Research Institute. Internet Archive.

by William Leybourne's 'Architectionice, or a compendium of the art of building', running to a total of eight editions by 1752 (Fig. 7.2).[11] Both additions make an important point in relation to the literature produced for tradesmen, which is that the artisan was required to master a range of quite different and at times precise skills that were of no concern to the patron and not always of direct interest to architects, since, even though they had entered their profession through one of the building trades, they had no need to master the technical details of the others.

While patrons and architects subscribed to the great assembly of the best of British architecture in the three volumes of Colen Campbell's *Vitruvius Britannicus*, of 1715, 1717 and 1725, and to James Gibbs's *Book of Architecture* of 1728, the many productions of Batty Langley and his brother Thomas, issuing from Meard's Court, Dean Street, in London where the brothers ran an evening school for builders, were produced for the trade. *The Builder's Chest-book* of 1727 is described as 'a necessary companion for gentlemen, as well as Masons, Carpenters, Joyners, Bricklayers, Plasterers, Painters and all others concerned in the several parts of Building in General'; *The Builder's Jewel or Youth's instructor* of 1741 offers 'short and easy rules made familiar to the meanest capacity', while *The City and Country Builder's and Workman's Treasury of Designs* of 1740, a handsome volume with 'upwards of four hundred grand designs, finely engraved on 186 large quarto plates', includes a subscription list of no less than 306 bricklayers, carpenters, carvers, cabinetmakers, figure makers, joiners, masons, painters, plasterers and surveyors, all characterised by Dr Eileen Harris as 'the forgotten men who did the daily work of building'.[12]

It should be emphasised that the skills which the craftsmen acquired were different, and in a sense also more practical, from those which an architect, as the designer of a building, necessarily possessed. Merely to list the names of the different irons used by a working mason in the eighteenth century may illustrate this point: masons used a 'pitcher', which was a rough cleaning tool; a 'bolster' or 'quick', which was a broad finishing tool; a 'punch' or 'spike', and a 'claw', the last two also known as a 'broach' and a 'drove'. In deciding the profile for an element of classical architecture – a cornice, architrave or other moulding – the architect had at his disposal a wide range of examples whose relative proportions were set down. It was his job to select the pattern of the moulding. The mason had to make it.

Today, though the work of individual masons is largely undocumented and must therefore remain anonymous, the results of their activity – the skill they possessed and their careful selection of different

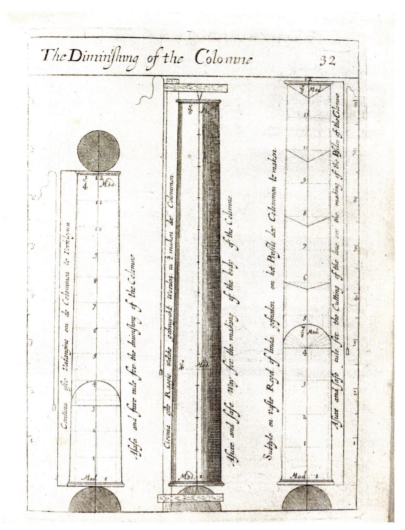

Figure 7.2: 'The Diminishing of the Colomne', from *The Mirror of Architecture: Or the ground-rules of the art of building, exactly laid down by Vincent Scamozzi, master-builder of Venice.* London, 1721, 6th edition. Plate 32.

Learning Resources, Glasgow School of Art. Internet Archive. CC-SA 3.0.

irons for the dressing of each piece of stone – may be detected clearly in the finished surface of many buildings. The stonework of William, 'Speaker' Connolly's great house at Castletown, County Kildare in Ireland, building from 1722, provides numerous examples of masons at work and of the independent character that is implicit in the mason's craft. Two details of stonework on the garden front may illustrate this point (Figs 7.3 and 7.4): the block of a lugged architrave from one of the ground-floor windows and the moulding of a window sill. For the lugged architrave the mason has dressed the flat surfaces with a horizontal tooling, while the curved sections of the architrave – a semicircular roll and a cyma moulding – are dressed with a finer chisel which follows the run of the moulding, that is they are vertical where the moulding is vertical and horizontal where it turns at 90 degrees. It should be noted that the outermost edge of the architrave has been tooled horizontally and with a finer chisel, which adds precision to the stonework.[13] Beyond the architrave the blocks of stone, used in building the wall of the house, have been finished vertically with a serrated chisel or 'drove' which gives a slightly ribbed effect to the face of the stone. For the window sill the mason has consistently applied the principle that the curved surfaces are tooled horizontally, in line with the lie of the stone, while the flat surfaces are tooled vertically. The droved finish used on the blocks of stone in the wall is clear in Figs 7.3 and 7.4.

Evidence of the specialist knowledge of craftsmen who worked in timber, the carpenters who provided the beams and joists for floors and ceilings and the wall-plates, trusses, purlins and rafters for a roof, or the joiners, who supplied the finished woodwork, is harder to detect. The carpenters, though their contribution was indispensable, are the invisible agents on a building site since all of their work was made to be covered up: they trimmed the joists round fireplaces to accommodate stone hearths, framed masonry openings to provide fixings for doors and windows and, when required, it was they who assembled and dismantled whatever scaffolding was needed. Traces of the activity of an individual are sometimes evident in the practice of numbering the trusses and rafters of a roof – a job that was perhaps given to an apprentice or journeyman – where the numbers are always formed in Roman numerals, I, II, III, IV, V, VI, and so on, since these were easy to cut with a chisel, while the curves of Arabic numerals were not. In a finished building the work of the joiners, making doors and their surrounds, window sashes, shutters, stairs and panelling, was evident and continually on view, while the additional trades of smith, glazier, plumber, slater, hardly engaged attention on the part of patrons. In many contracts, the smiths performed the vital auxiliary function of sharpening the masons' tools, as well as the pickaxes that were used to dig foundations.[14]

While it is easy to understand the desire of historians to reinstate these unknown operatives, it is rare, without access to the details of a particular building account, to find documentary reference to the tradesmen routinely involved in construction, beyond the employment

Figure 7.3: Details of the dressing of the stonework on the garden front of Castletown House, County Kildare, showing the base of the lugged architrave.

Photograph by Alistair Rowan.

Figure 7.4: Details of the dressing of the stonework on the garden front of Castletown House, County Kildare, showing a window sill.

Photograph by Alistair Rowan.

of those specialists – joiners, plasterers or workers in parquetry or stone inlay – who enjoyed such a reputation for excellence in their lifetime as to be employed by name with an individual contract. These men, the most recognised craftsmen of architectural history – Grinling Gibbons, Nicholas Rose, Robert West – may have identifiable careers whose history is well known yet, in general, the men 'who did the daily work of building', remain anonymous.[15] This is the reality of most building history, though it can also occasionally happen that the character of an individual, unnamed craftsman stands out as exceptional for the extraordinariness or excessive invention of his performance. Such a man might be called 'a rogue craftsman', a type of tradesman whose technical capacities and enthusiasm for the practice of his craft – aided no doubt by an understandable desire to increase the amount of work he secured – overtook any proper judgement. An excessive performance which they intended as an embellishment in reality disfigures the building. Elsewhere, a rogue craftsman, overconfident though lacking any basic understanding of architectural principles, may produce what is simply an ignorant piece of work.

The Preface to James Gibbs's *Book of Architecture* of 1728 confronts these problems directly, setting out both the architect's intentions in producing the book, as an aid to those building 'in the remote parts of the country', and warning proprietors against putting their trust in uninformed workmen:

> Persons of great distinction were of the opinion that such a Work as this would be of use to such Gentlemen as might be concerned in building, especially in the remote parts of the country, where little or no assistance for Designs can be procured. Such may be here furnished with draughts of useful and convenient buildings and proper ornaments; which may be executed by any workman who understands lines either as here designed or with some alteration, which may be easily made by a person of Judgement. I mention this to caution gentlemen from suffering any material change to be made in their designs, by the forwardness of unskilful workmen, or the caprice of ignorant, assuming Pretenders. Some from want of better helps, have unfortunately put into the hands of common workmen the management of buildings of considerable expense; which when finished they have had the mortification to find condemned by persons of Taste to that degree that sometimes they have been pulled down, [or] at least altered at a greater charge

than would have procured better advice from an able Artist; or if they have stood they have remained lasting monuments of Ignorance or Parsimoniousness of the owners [or] of wrong judged Profuseness.[16]

Examples of the category of building which Gibbs describes, clumsy in design or overexuberant in ornament, crop up continually within the provincial architecture of Europe. Here, the example of one Irish country house, Florence Court, near Enniskillen in County Fermanagh, may stand for many (Fig. 7.5). The house, as it exists today, was built for John Cole, Lord Mount Florence, between 1758 and 1764. Its architecture is endearing rather than fine, with a showy façade which degenerates into a very plain rendered block at the sides and back. Though the names of the craftsmen employed at Florence Court have not been recorded, it is clear that each of the principal tradesmen – stonemason, joiner and

Figure 7.5: Entrance front of Florence Court, County Fermanagh, building from 1758. T. U. Sadleir and P. L. Dickinson. *Georgian Mansions in Ireland*, Plate LIII.
Dublin University Press, 1915.

plasterer – though technically competent in their craft, worked independently with little concept of the building as a whole, so that the final appearance of the house, lacking the input of an architect or other 'person of judgement', such as Gibbs advised, is much less satisfactory than it might otherwise have been.[17] In detail the front is quite crazy: anyone who stands opposite the front door and looks at the façade will soon detect the vaingloriousness of a provincial hand.

> Rustication, keystones, and lugged surrounds run riot. The window surrounds are not the same on any two floor levels, and those on the ground and first floors are of a curious Gibbs type gone wrong, with the rusticated blocks moved sideways, set beyond the edge of the architrave surround and not laid over it … The centre, projecting slightly, is a welter of jumbled scales. The main door, flanked by side lights and surmounted by a big Doric pediment is supported on illiterate rusticated pilasters that shrink to a thin line between the rusticated blocks. Above, a rusticated Venetian window with blind balustrading almost sits on the point of the pediment and is flanked by two niches in aedicules different in scale from anything else on the façade. A third, fatter niche, flanked by paired rusticated pilasters, is squashed in between two burly attic windows on the top floor.[18]

It is as if the mason had simply selected the various elements of the façade from different pattern books and assembled them at random.[19]

Similar confusions occur in the interior (Figs 7.6 and 7.7). In the entrance hall, the decision to make all the doors of the same height as the front door, left the joiner with the problem of an unusually high and narrow opening. The solution to take a standard five-panel door – a pattern often found on the bedroom-floor of Irish houses – and heighten it by the addition of two panels is distinctly awkward and there is also an uncomfortable shift in scale between the pattern of these seven-panel doors, set neatly within lugged architraves, yet surmounted by rectangular moulded panels filled with large and clumsy drapery swags above them. In the hall the room cornice is Doric, yet the scale adopted by the plasterer robs the order of all authority, reducing it to a diminutive decorative pattern, where a meaningless egg-and-dart moulding separates the triglyphs from the mutules. Where the wall steps forward over a gargantuan arched niche, the triglyphs are reduced in an illiterate way to two upstands. No ruling hand controlled the work in the hall, where the joiners and plasterers were left to muddle along as best they could.

Figure 7.6: One side of the entrance hall at Florence Court, County Fermanagh.

Hugh Doran Collection, Irish Architectural Archive.

While the space of the stair hall is undeniably handsome, the work of the plasterer is literally 'all over the place' and, though technically accomplished, is marred by the juxtaposition of decorations set within fixed rectangular panels and a freely-worked bracketed cornice, lavishly formed of alternating ogee and cusped arches which, as they are too deep for the space available for them, collide with the arches at the bottom and the top of the stairs. Here the exuberant work of the artisan displays all the dangers of 'a wrong-judged profuseness' (as Gibbs would say), encouraged perhaps by imprudent patronage and uncontrolled by the input of any architect.[20]

James Gibbs's advice that 'a person of Judgement' should be consulted in selecting or making any alteration to an architectural

Figure 7.7: The staircase at Florence Court, County Fermanagh. T. U. Sadleir and P. L. Dickinson, *Georgian Mansions in Ireland*, Plate LV.

Dublin University Press, 1915.

design, raises important questions as to what is meant by 'judgement', who possesses it, and – by inference – what ought to be the relationship between an architect and an artisan? The antithesis, set up in Gibbs's text, contrasts gentlemen, who are by definition educated, with common workmen who, as they are not, may therefore be described as unskilful, ignorant or presumptuous. Those who design buildings form part of an elite professional class, jealous of its own expertise, as was Gibbs himself, and determined to retain and to exercise control over those who built their buildings. It is here that the kernel of the excellence of much Baroque and eighteenth-century architecture lies. The professionals understood the norms and rules of architecture: they had a vested interest in seeing that they were respected and that, for the most part, the rules of architecture were applied. There was, however, a paradox, since 'a person of judgement' might concede that rules, on occasion, could be broken, so long as that was done 'with taste'. The accepted forms of British neo-Palladianism offer a clear example of the problem: while they were evidently reliable, they ran the risk of becoming a straitjacket that might stifle originality. So, the question of how to retain an overall control, while at the same time respecting and even fostering originality, was crucial to a positive relationship between an architect and an artisan. The crux of the problem is set out, with considerable brio, in four well-known lines from Alexander Pope's 'An Essay on Criticism' (1711):

> Great wits sometimes may gloriously offend,
> And rise to faults true critics dare not mend.
> From vulgar bonds with brave disorder part
> And snatch a grace beyond the reach of art.

A rogue craftsman, with such a mantra, might claim exemption from criticism, yet an excellent performance remains the essential criteria and such an outcome could hardly be claimed for the ill-assorted elements brought together on the façade and in the hall and staircase of Florence Court.

A more complicated situation arises, where a team of expert, international craftsmen, left to its own devices, produces an assemblage of decorative elements that is somehow unconvincing. Was their uncontrolled activity intended to nurture fresh originality – 'a grace beyond the reach of art' – or is it simply the case that the specialist craftsman, working without constraint, runs the risk of making work that is ill conceived? Consideration of the stuccowork executed by the Artari workshop from 1707, in the nave of Fulda Cathedral, raises precisely these problems (Fig. 7.8).[21] Both the Bishop, who provided the theological programme, and the architect, Johann Dientzenhofer, who negotiated the Artari contract, must, in some measure, have approved the work, even so there is a disconcerting clumsiness in the finished interior, where different scales are employed in the figurative work on the nave arcade. First, in the size of the large standing figures of saints, in niches; second, in the realistically modelled female heads, atop a cartouche in the centre of each arch; and third, in the much smaller, allegorical figures of virtues, lodged uncomfortably and almost seeming to slip down the curving architrave of each arch. Here, while the quality of the craftsmanship

Figure 7.8: The nave of Fulda Cathedral, Hesse, Germany. Detail of the Artari workshop stucco decorations of about 1710.

Photograph by Christine Casey.

is beyond reproach, there remains an unexpected carelessness in the finished result. Who is to blame here, the craftsman or the architect? If the Artari work in the nave of Fulda Cathedral is, to use Gibbs's language, 'ill judged', the decorative plasterwork, of unknown authorship, in the staircase of Russborough House, in County Wicklow, Ireland, is surely an instance of a craftsman hired on his own terms and determined to give such a display of his abilities that could be matched by no-one else. In musical terms the Russborough staircase is like the clumsy cadenza added to a concerto, where the artist is determined to show off his technical capacities irrespective of their effect: the plasterwork of the staircase at Russborough certainly makes a lot of noise (Fig. 7.9).[22]

In reviewing the general relationship between architects and craftsmen, it may be helpful to look closely at a particular example and to consider the situation of the Adam family in eighteenth-century Scotland.

Figure 7.9: The stair hall at Russborough, County Wicklow.
Photograph by Andrew Tierney.

Though the family descended from the fifteenth-century proprietors of a small landed estate at Fanno in Angus, John Adam, the grandfather of John and Robert Adam, the celebrated architects in London, had moved sometime in the early 1680s to Kirkcaldy in Fife, where he earned his living as a master mason and builder. His only surviving son, William Adam, born in 1689, was trained, like his father, as a mason but, in the course of his career, took to designing buildings and in time became the leading Scottish architect of his day. Each of William Adam's four sons, John, Robert, James and William, were to describe themselves as architects, so that in the course of three generations the Adams moved from being masons and builders, to mason-architects and ultimately to professional men.[23] The pattern is widely represented in many British architectural families – Brettingham, Deane, Hayward, Mylne, Wyatt – yet a particular quality, existing within each of the Adam generations, is their direct familiarity with building construction, their understanding of the particular skills required in different trades, and the value they placed on good craftsmanship. The Adams as architects knew the quality of the artisans with whom they worked.

The career path that William Adam followed, shifting from that of builder to designing the buildings that he built, and becoming effectively their architect, was aided, in the first place, by the close friendships he formed with members of the Scottish nobility, well-educated men, who were in a position to critique his plans;[24] second, by the magnificent library of European architectural volumes which he assembled in the course of his practice, which offered exemplars for his own work;[25] and thirdly, by his ambitious and proudly nationalist proposal to publish a survey of Scottish architecture, in the manner of Colen Campbell's *Vitruvius Britannicus*, to be entitled *Vitruvius Scoticus*.[26] If the volume pays lip service to the origins of classical architecture in Scotland, including the work of John Mylne, Sir William Bruce, Alexander McGill and James Smith, most of its 160 plates record Adam's own buildings, both those where he had been employed as a builder and had subsequently collaborated with a patron in their design and those where he worked as an architect from the start.

William Adam took a robust approach to architecture. Though some of his buildings are in a straightforward Scottish vernacular style, such as any mason in the period might employ, the more ambitious draw both their form and their detail from European Renaissance or Baroque models, and are distinctly different from the ordered neo-Palladianism of England, held in such repute in the reigns of George I and George II. Two houses in Midlothian, Mavisbank, designed with Sir John Clerk of Penicuik, which Adam built for his client from 1723, and Arniston, designed by Adam and built for the Solicitor General, Robert Dundas from 1726, amply demonstrate both the ambition and the freshness of his style as an architect (Figs 7.10 and 7.11). On occasion, façades by

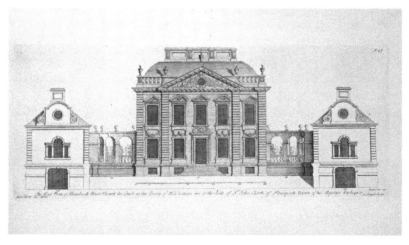

Figure 7.10: William Adam, entrance front of Mavisbank, Midlothian, Scotland, built from 1723 for Sir John Clerk of Penicuik. In William Adam, *Vitruvius Scoticus*, Plate 47.

Internet Archive. Getty Research Institute.

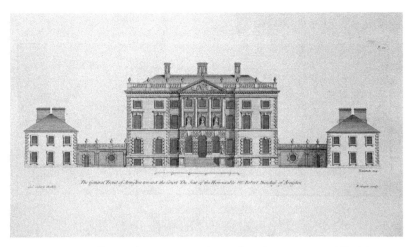

Figure 7.11: William Adam, entrance front of Arniston House, Midlothian, Scotland, built from 1726 for Robert Dundas, Lord Advocate of Scotland. In William Adam, *Vitruvius Scoticus*, Plate 42.

Internet Archive. Getty Research Institute.

William Adam can perhaps display a little too much business, with a tendency to overload subsidiary areas of a front, or to switch the scale between one part and another, yet their architecture always carries conviction, is strongly formed and is far removed from the solecisms of the tradesmen who created Florence Court.

Hopetoun House, in West Lothian, one of William Adam's grandest building projects, offers a unique opportunity to examine the relationship existing between the eldest of William Adam's sons, John, and the tradesmen whom he employed during the completion of the house. Hopetoun was one of the grandest and certainly the longest lasting of William Adam's country-house commissions, with members of his family employed there from 1721 until well into the later 1750s. The job undertaken by William Adam involved the enlargement of the house designed by Sir William Bruce in 1699, completed in 1703 and then partially enlarged between 1706 and about 1710.[27] Adam's patron, the 1st Earl of Hopetoun, wanted a house that would have a grander effect than the compact classical block which had been built for him by his mother, Lady Margaret Hope. Accordingly, William Adam was commissioned, both as an architect, in which capacity he worked jointly with his patron, and as a building contractor, to create an heroic new façade to replace the modest entrance front that Bruce had designed (Fig. 7.12).[28] When completed, the new

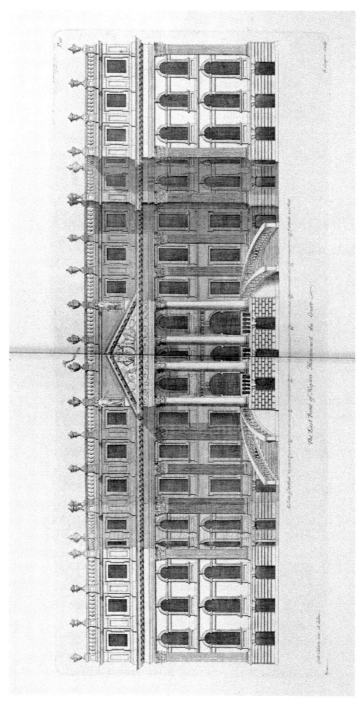

Figure 7.12: William Adam, entrance front of Hopetoun House, West Lothian, Scotland, built from 1721 to 1731 for John Hope, 2nd Earl of Hopetoun. In William Adam, *Vitruvius Scoticus*, Plate 16.

Internet Archive. Getty Research Institute.

front at Hopetoun stood four storeys high, with an elevated basement supporting a parade of giant order Corinthian pilasters, and a tall attic storey, topped by a balustrade and fringed with urns. Under Adam, the new front – nineteen windows wide – was further extended by quadrant colonnades linked to a pair of single-storey pavilions, each of which had a cupola-topped tower rising at the centre (Fig. 7.13). The full length of William Adam's façade, which with the quadrants and wings enclosed a broad forecourt, extended to a width of 500 feet. To give focus to this sprawling composition, a Corinthian portico of four columns, approached by a pair of curving steps, was proposed for the centre of the main block.

In contrast to his younger brothers, Robert and James, who both studied at the University of Edinburgh, John Adam became an assistant to his father immediately on leaving school. He was trained first as a mason, then turned to architecture and, on the death of William Adam in 1748, took over all his father's operations. By that time, the completion of Hopetoun was largely concerned with the construction of William Adam's portico and the creation of a suite of state rooms behind the northern end of the façade. John's first decision, taken perhaps on structural as much as on economic or aesthetic grounds, was to eliminate the portico.[29] The broad flight of straight steps which took its place and the sober succession of Corinthian pilasters at the centre of the façade are each characteristic of the architect's careful approach to design (Figs 7.14 and 7.15). By that time there could be no doubt that John Adam was familiar with and possessed a mastery of every masonry technique as used in Scotland. That this was so is demonstrated by a very precise memorandum which he prepared, on 27 August 1751, as a specification for cutting and laying the sixteen steps of the external stair. The functional elegance of John's design appears clearly in the first 'wedge step', built in such a way as to be level at its centre with the carriageway paving and to fall gently by six inches to the outer edges. To make the masonry firm, even in its exposed position, John adopted the unusual technique of cutting two steps out of one block of stone, so that the mass of the individual stones is greatly increased, while the number of horizontal joints in the stair is reduced by half. With the exception of the outermost sides of the stair, the stones of the steps are laid 'edgeways', another technical novelty, which, as it sets the bed of the stone in a vertical line, effectively prevents any damage to the surface of the treads by flaking, which is a problem that often disfigures sandstone buildings. Each tread of 1½ ft has a fall, or in John Adam's terminology, 'a washing' of ⅛ in. to throw off the rain, while the tread and risers are dressed, with practical good sense, not as ashlar but 'broached or striped

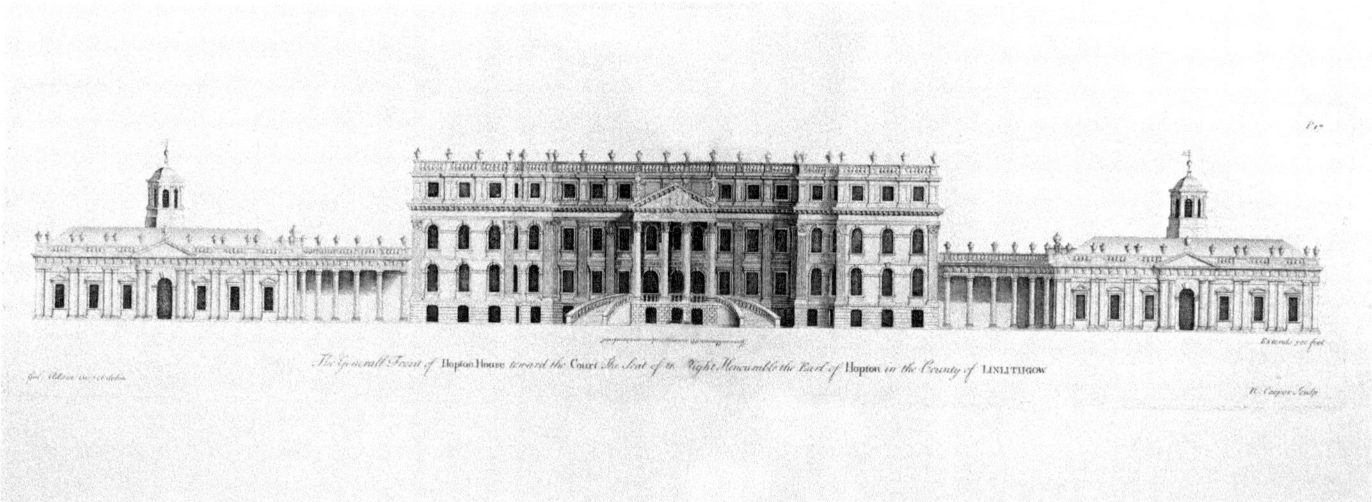

Figure 7.13: William Adam, entrance front of Hopetoun House, showing the pavilions and colonnades. In William Adam, *Vitruvius Scoticus*, Plate 17.

Internet Archive. Getty Research Institute.

Figure 7.14: William and John Adam, entrance front of Hopetoun House, as completed in 1754.

Photograph by Alistair Rowan.

Figure 7.15: Masonry of the front steps of Hopetoun House, built in accordance with John Adam's specification of 27 August 1751.

Photograph by Alistair Rowan.

to conceal the joints' and 'not diagonally or longwise' but down the tread, with the stratifications of the stone, so that 'the rainwater will run cleverly off, as though through so many channels'. Such precise and intelligent specification has meant that, more than 270 years later, the front steps at Hopetoun survive in perfect condition.

The State Apartments at Hopetoun, planned by William Adam and fitted out by his son, from 1752 to October 1757, are the grandest rooms in the house. It is typical of William Adam's inspired planning that the State Dining Room, which opens directly off the hall, should have a view in one direction overlooking the eastern approaches to the house, while the State Drawing Room, which is aligned on the identical access as the door into the dining room, enjoys views in the opposite direction, commanding a wide prospect, from five tall windows, across the gardens to the parkland on the west. Beyond the drawing room, and always on the same access, was the State Bedroom with a dressing room and closet. The architectural style, which John Adam employed in fitting out these rooms is one of opulent refinement (Figs 7.16 and 7.17). He avoids using the orders or any type of complicated door surround, such as his father might have employed, and relies instead on carefully detailed joinery and plasterwork in each room. At Hopetoun two expert craftsmen executed his designs: John Paterson, a joiner who had worked at the house since 1743, and John Dawson, an experienced plasterer and

Figure 7.16: The State Drawing Room at Hopetoun House.
Photograph by Alistair Rowan.

Figure 7.17: The ceiling of the State Drawing Room at Hopetoun House.
Photograph by Alistair Rowan.

woodcarver whom the Adams had encouraged to return to Scotland in 1751. Paterson laid the floors in the new wing and supplied and fitted the skirting boards, chair rails, doors, windows and shutters for all the new rooms. The work was carried out in two phases between 1752 and October 1757. Lord Hopetoun's factor, Alexander Williamson, was inclined to dispute the joiner's charges for both phases of the work, yet on each occasion John Adam fully supported the artisan: 'there is no doubt the prices seem high', he wrote in April 1756, 'and would really be so for any other work, but as it is the best of kinds that ever I saw, there is no doing a thing in an extraordinary manner without a price adequate to the pains'. A detail of the junction between the chair-rail with the side of a doorway in the drawing room may illustrate the precision and fineness of Paterson's work (Fig. 7.18).

With John Dawson, Adam secured the services of a well-trained Scottish tradesman, who had been apprenticed to the Anglo-Danish stucco worker, Charles Stanley, in Westminster, London, in 1738. Dawson first appears in the Hopetoun accounts, when he is paid two guineas 'for the head and foliage done upon the keystones of the Venetian window' lighting the Library in the south pavilion, a small but lively piece of stone carving which may demonstrate the versatility of many eighteenth-century craftsmen. Though he was to work principally as a plasterer in Scotland, Dawson is also recorded as a woodcarver as

Figure 7.18: The State Drawing Room at Hopetoun House. A detail of the chair-rail decoration and door panels.

Photograph by Alistair Rowan.

well as a man who could sculpt in stone. Examples of his work survive at Hopetoun in the plain coved ceiling of the dining room, decorated solely with Rococo medallions at the corners and in the more elaborate coved ceiling of the drawing room (see Fig. 7.16), where the central oval panel, extending into square ends, is typical of John Adam's selection of a neo-Palladian pattern. The Venetian window motif converted to represent a thatched primitive hut at either end of the room is Dawson's own invention!

Besides the entries in the Hopetoun papers, additional notes on craftsmen are found in a pocket book – more properly a commonplace book – which John Adam kept for much of his career.[30] Today, it is salutary to realise the extent to which prices were stable throughout the eighteenth century so that a great many of the entries were to provide references to the costs of various kinds of work: the 'Expense of Working Marble at Leith in 1729'; a 'Computation of the expense of Burning Tyles & Bricks at Links' in July 1745', and the 'Prices of Deals given to Mr. Skinner by Mr. Small, Timber Merchant at Southwark, London, compared with the prices from Leith in 1756'. Scrupulous in the conduct of his business, both as an architect and as a government contractor,[31] it was essential to John Adam to have accurate information for his clients. That no doubt explains one of the most interesting sections of the notebook, 'Questions put to Mr. Morris [the surveyor, Robert Morris] about the methods of measuring & the prices of different kinds of work in London with his answers thereto'.[32] The record of these discussions, neatly written out and illustrated by Adam's own diagrams, accounts for fourteen pages of text.

Inevitably much of the book is taken up with notes of the prices paid to different tradesmen in different locations during the years when John Adam ran the business. The names of more than twenty artisans may be extracted from these entries and occasionally, where the same name crops up at different sites, a suggestion of the career of a particular person may begin to emerge.[33] Nevertheless, a list of names is dull reading and it is only rarely that something of the character of a workman jumps out from a page. One instance occurs under the heading 'Prices settled for John Paterson for Wright work in the Great Apartment at Hopetoun house 1756'. Here the authentic voice of the tradesman seems almost to bubble through what the architect writes:

> John says there is not one of the doors but cost him 24 shillings & at the above prices amounting to £13 4sh, being 11 in number, whereas of account they only amount for both rooms to £10. 12. 21/2. The floor in the dining room cost him in laying for time, dowels and nails somewhat above £10 & the whole account thereof is only £10 16. 6 so that he has next to nothing for working the deals. He says there is 4,500 nails and dowels in the Dining room floor.[34]

No doubt it was the burden of this discussion and the joiner's urgent argument that gave John Adam the determination to see that Paterson's bill when it was submitted properly represented the work that he had done and that it was paid in full. At Hopetoun it is clearly the case that John Adam and the artisans work purposefully and effectively together and yet a question remains: a well-laid floor is a well-laid floor, and a neat keystone is a nice piece of carving, but neither the floor nor the keystone is integral to the meaning of the house as a work of art or architecture. Even John Dawson's ceiling for the state drawing room, a splendid piece of exuberant Rococo workmanship, is contained within a deep cove and a framework of oval and rectangular beams, made popular by Isaac Ware whom John Adam followed here.[35] Who then, in the final analysis, should be given the credit for the whole: the architect or the craftsman?

As a final consideration in evaluating what might be just and fair in the balance of reputation between the architect and the artisan, it may be helpful to examine how similar issues arise within the sister art of music, and to consider how the differing roles of responsibility are treated within a musical context. An awareness of the kinship which music and architecture share is as old at least as Vitruvius. Each art, while essentially practical in its objectives, is defined by an abstract code of beauty experienced through space – either physically or in time – and understood in terms of measure, interval, rhythm and the pleasurable expectation of repetition as perceived by the eye or the ear. This is the undeniable compatibility encapsulated in Goethe's brilliant description of architecture as frozen music.

Composers cannot create music beyond the scale of the resources available to them and are dependent on the level of technical dexterity of the musicians who play for them, just as architects are constrained by the competence of the craftsmen with whom they have to work to create their buildings. In this analogy, the players within an orchestra perform a role equivalent to that of the craftsmen. There are of course, as the notes to many a concert programme will point out, numerous well-documented occasions in history, where an individual performer may be credited with a direct personal contribution to the creation of a piece of music. In writing his concerto for the then recently invented basset clarinet, Mozart undoubtedly took advantage of the advice and professional knowhow of Anton Stadler, a close friend and fellow Freemason in Vienna who was among the first to play the instrument. The soaring leaps found in the writing of the solo soprano parts in Schubert's Latin masses, where the voice rises to astonishing heights, depends on the unique ability of Therese Grop, a member of the choir of Lichtental parish church, for which the masses were first written. Equally, Brahms, when composing his violin concerto, benefitted from a close friendship with the violinist, Joseph Joachim, who helped the composer with the writing for strings and even marked up the parts. Does this mean that Stadler, Grop and Joachim ought therefore to be credited in some way with the creation of these compositions? In writing an orchestral work it is the composer who creates the score, not an individual performer, however able or engaged.[36] Even so the composer, just as the architect, depends on the coordination of a multiplicity of talents and abilities to bring his creation to life. Here the parallel must be with the conductor, who controls and draws the best playing from the different members of an orchestra into an agreed whole, just as the clerk of works on a building site will supervise and oversee the physical realisation of an architect's design. Since we cannot single out the performance of an individual player in an orchestra, it seems misdirected to focus undue attention on the diffuse talents of the different craftsmen who help to make a piece of architecture a physical reality. Just as Mozart, Schubert and Brahms deserve the unique credit for the music that they wrote, or as Bach, Beethoven and Bruckner are recognised as composers whose auditory imagination creates vast aural structures within their work, so too Sir Christopher Wren and Norman Foster – perhaps also John Adam – merit proper recognition for their unique achievement as architects. The role of the craftsman corresponds closely to that of an individual performer in an orchestra – no more and no less.

Notes

1   Sharples, 'The workers who built the University of Glasgow'.
2   In *Building Saint Paul's*, Campbell sustains that the famous inscription to Sir Christopher Wren – *Lector, si monumentum requiris, circumspice* – reader, if you seek a monument, look around – 'could be applied not just to Wren but to all those involved in the construction', 41.
3   A point raised by Edward McParland at the conference, 'Artisans and Architects', Trinity College Dublin, 7–8 April 2022.
4   Saint, 'The conundrum of "by"'.
5   The text of Mrs Montagu's celebrated letter is quoted in Bristol, '22 Portman Square, Mrs Montagu and her Palais de la Vieillesse'. It has often been stated that the architect mentioned in the letter was Robert Adam, however Kerry Bristol shows convincingly that Mrs Montagu was writing about James 'Athenian' Stuart. The relevant part of her letter, written to the Duchess of Portland in July 1779, is as follows:

> I was greatly mortified that it was not in my power to wait on Mrs. Delaney one morning when she told me she would be at home, but I was detained at my new house by my architect with whom I had before made an appointment. He came at the head of a regiment of artificers an hour after the time he had promised. The bricklayer talked about the alterations to be made in a wall: the stone mason was eloquent about the coping of the same wall: the carpenter thought the internal fitting up of the house not less important: then came the painter who is painting my ceilings in various colours according to the present fashion. The morning and my spirits were quite exhausted before these important persons had the goodness to release me. I did not get back to my dinner till near 5 o'clock.

I am obliged to Colin Thom for providing this up-to-date information.
6   An essential overview of the history and evolving role of the building trades in Britain may be found in each of the four editions of Sir Howard Colvin's *Biographical Dictionary of British Architects*, 1954 to 2008.
7   Shute, *First and Chief Groundes of Architecture*.
8   'Architecture (by the common consent of many notable men) as Cesarius sayth, is of all arts, the most noble and excellent, containing in it sundry sciences and knowledge wherewith it is furnished and adorned, as full well Vitruvius doth affirm and declare by his writing. For saith he, an Architect must be sharp of understanding and both quick and apt … so that plainly and briefly he may discuss and open demonstrations of that which shall be done or mete to those persons [the tradesmen] that shall be the founders of any noble work'. See the heading: 'What the Office and Duetie is of him that wyll be a Perfecte Architecte or Mayster of buyldings', unpaginated, [4].
9   An instance of the enduring use of such terms by tradesmen well into the twentieth century may be recorded in the almost universal use of 'astragal' by Edinburgh joiners as meaning a glazing bar, whereas an astragal was only one of several mouldings that were commonly in

use on glazing bars throughout nineteenth-century Scotland. At the time that The Edinburgh New Town Conservation Committee was set up in 1969, grants were made available for the replacement of Victorian plate-glass windows by Georgian six-pane sashes when the fitting of new 'astragals' was widely encouraged in conservation circles.

10 For an invaluable and meticulously detailed guide to architectural publications in Britain, see Harris and Savage, *British Architectural Books*. For Pricke's titles, see 379–80.

11 Harris and Savage, *British Architectural Books*, 409–11.

12 Harris and Savage, *British Architectural Books*, 268.

13 As a testimony of the mason's skill, it should be noted that no less than seven lengths of stone are used in building each side of the window architraves at Castletown. The profile of the moulding at the junction of one block of stone with the other has to be accurate to within a tolerance of perhaps not more than a millimetre and, since there are 38 windows on each front of the house, the masons must have set out and cut this exact profile for the face of the architrave 456 times on either front.

14 National Archives of Scotland (NAS), Ailsa MSS, GD/25, The accounts of Hugh Cairncross, Master of Works at Culzean Castle, Ayrshire, record a payment of £29 11s. 4d. made in 1780 to the local smith, John Niven, for sharpening 28,831 masons' irons and 3,112 picks.

15 Harris and Savage, *British Architectural Books*, 263.

16 Gibbs, *Book of Architecture*, i–iii.

17 For two extensive accounts of Florence Court see McParland, 'Florence Court' and Rowan, *North West Ulster*, 298.

18 Rowan, *North West Ulster*, 300.

19 McParland, 'Florence Court', 1242–5. In discussing the possible contribution of Davis Ducart to the design of Florence Court, McParland writes 'all that can be said is that the sophistication by plan is worthy of him, even if the detail of execution – at least in the central block – shows that the Florence Court masons were untroubled by any rigorous supervision by "the last Palladian in Ireland"'.

20 It is sometimes suggested that Florence Court might be the work of an amateur architect, possibly by John Cole the proprietor of the estate. However if this were the case, there should be other buildings in the area that might be attributed to the same hand and there are none. It seems more likely that Cole contrived the design, directly in discussion with the mason, timber wright and plasterer and without the advice of any architect, until the advent of Ducat who very probably added the lateral arcades and terminal blocks.

It should be emphasised that the Florence Court blunders are far from exceptional within eighteenth-century architecture in Ireland. The masonry of Drewstown, at County Meath, an ambitious mid-century house with a seven-bay three-storey front, is equally clumsy while, in its interior, the joinery is bulky and much too large for the space it occupies. The vagaries of the sequence – tripartite door, Venetian window and Diocletian attic – on the frontage of innumerable small houses in Ireland are beyond dispute. In truth, Gibbs's complaint can only reflect the architect's experience and ham-fisted classicism in a provincial setting is widely encountered throughout Europe.

21 Casey, *Making Magnificence*, 110–14.

22 Casey, *Making Magnificence*, 257–8 and Plate 246. The comparison of the decoration of the Russborough staircase with the musical convention of a cadenza is elaborated in footnote 35.

23 The education which the different generations of the family received underscores their rising social status: William Adam went to the Borough School in Kirkcaldy; his eldest son, John, was sent to Dalkeith Academy and the younger boys went to the Royal High School in Edinburgh; John Adam's second son, John, was sent to Eton.

24 Key figures in Adam's formation as an architect are: Sir John Clerk of Penicuik, with whom he built the villa of Mavisbank, the Marquis of Annandale and the 1st Earl of Hopetoun at Hopetoun House, and the 2nd Earl of Stair, with whom he worked at Newliston House and who was a particular patron of the architect. He also knew and was in touch with the exiled 'amateur architect' the Earl of Mar, and James Gibbs.

25 William Adam's library contained over 140 titles of architectural volumes from Italy, France, Germany, the Netherlands and Britain. Far from being a mere provincial collection, the library was the creation of a cosmopolitan connoisseur. See Rowan, 'William Adam's library'.

26 As a book and vehicle of self-publicity, *Vitruvius Scoticus* failed, since it was not completed within William Adam's lifetime. Subsequently it was taken up by John Adam who added a

number of plates of recent Adam works in Scotland, yet the collection remained unpublished, and it was left to John's son, William Adam, to secure its publication in about 1812. An edition of 400 copies was published in facsimile by Paul Harris Publishing, Edinburgh in 1980, with an extensive introduction and excellent notes on the plates by James Simpson.

27   There are two versions of the Bruce house at Hopetoun: the first is the building described in the mason's contract, from the end of 1698, which was completed by 1702; the second, which envisaged a grander entrance front, with convex colonnades and flanking stable offices, is published in *Vitruvius Britannicus,* vol. 2, in 1717. It is not clear that this second house, on which work began on the east wing in 1706, was ever completed. Compare Rowan, 'The building of Hopetoun' and Macaulay, 'Sir William Bruce's Hopetoun House'.

28   Lord Hopetoun's motives in embarking on an enlarged version of Bruce's first plan only to jettison the design in favour of a physically much larger scheme by William Adam, starting in January 1721, which was less than fourteen years after the Bruce enlargement had been begun, are worth analysis. As a patron and amateur architect, the 1st Earl seems to have enjoyed a form of intense creative collaboration with the men who worked up the designs for his house. Sir William Bruce died in 1710 and, though his scheme for enlargement was certainly begun, the death of its architect removed the opportunity of any further collaboration for the Earl, while offering, in the same moment, a convenient break in which to review the design that was then in hand. It seems highly unlikely that Lord Hopetoun would have paid for the completion of the entire house that was shown in *Vitruvius Britannicus* in 1717, only to knock it all down four years later. Adam's bill of £96 in the autumn of 1721 'to taking down of old house and S stairs' suggests a much more modest demolition.

29   It seems probable that the deeply projecting Corinthian portico and double ramps of quadrant steps proposed by William Adam, and of a distinctly Baroque character, did not accord with his son's more restrained views on architecture in the 1750s. Lord Hopetoun was seventeen years older than John Adam and may well have hesitated to follow the suggestion of his first architect's son, even though to scrap the portico saved a huge expense. The existence among the Hopetoun papers of a list of eleven examples of houses with straight stairs, taken from *Vitruvius Britannicus, Desgodetz, Gibbs and Ware's Designs of Inigo Jones,* illustrates both the use to which such architectural volumes could be put and the means whereby John Adam sought to assuage his client's doubts.

In addition, there may well have been insuperable structural problems in the construction of a portico to the scale proposed in William Adam's scheme. The intercolumniation of the Corinthian giant order, shown in the elevation, is twelve feet; the portico was to project fifteen feet in front of the return column at the side and the height of the column shafts – including the bases and capitals – was thirty feet. These dimensions, and particularly the architrave beams of the entablature, would have been well nigh impossible using the Craigleith sandstone with which Hopetoun was built.

30   The pocket book is kept among the Adam family papers at Blair Adam. It is quite large, measuring 18.5 × 11.5 cm, and appears to have been ready made and sold as a pocket book, since it is contained between marbled boards and has a flap which can be folded across the ends of the open pages and inserted into a slot on the face of the cover, to keep the book closed. This, and its size, make it exactly suitable to be carried in an eighteenth-century greatcoat pocket. There are 220 pages in the book with an index added as an additional signature. Commonplace books were much used in Adam's lifetime and generally range widely over the interests of the compiler. Adam's book has much of this character though he does not write down any jokes: the well-known commonplace books kept by the second Viscount Palmerston, 1739–1802 (Connell, *Portrait of a Whig Peer* and John G. Murray, *A Gentleman Publisher's Commonplace Book),* both do.

31   In 1748 John Adam had inherited his father's position as Master Mason of the Crown in Scotland and, as such, was responsible for the construction of Fort George on the Moray Firth and all the routine work of the Board of Ordinance.

32   Robert Morris (1703–1754), the most important British writer on architectural theory in the first half of the eighteenth century and a surveyor whose volume *The Qualifications and Duty of a Surveyor* of 1752 will have been of particular interest to John Adam.

33   Tradesmen mentioned by name are, masons: David Gordon, Walter Fiddes, William Cowan and William Farquhar, working at Leith; William Christie, working at Fort George and at Dumfries House; David Frew, working at 'Mr. Hope's offices'; wrights: Charles Freebairn,

who prepared an estimate for Alva, John Paterson and James Buchan working at Hopetoun; Mr Chessels 'wright to the Duke of Hamilton', Charles Burt, working at Southall; Alex Gowan at Dumfries House; plasterers: Thomas Clayton at Hamilton Palace, John Dawson at Hopetoun and Arniston; Philip Robertson at Hopetoun and Dumfries House; Andrew Cowie and John Loro at Edinburgh Castle.

34 Murray, *Commonplace Book*, 134–5.

35 It may be noted that over the years the use of the State Apartments changed. A grand procession for the tenantry to view each addition to the Hope line – beginning in the front hall and passing through the dining room, drawing room and into the State Bedroom (to encounter Lady Hopetoun with her latest child) and then exit by the north colonnade – went out of fashion by the early nineteenth century. At that time the State Dining Room became the Yellow Drawing Room, the State Drawing Room became the Red Drawing Room and the State Bedroom and Dressing Room were thrown together to create a new State Dining Room designed by James Gillespie Graham.

36 Within the conventions which govern the creation of an eighteenth- or nineteenth-century concerto, it should be noted that composers would regularly create a moment, within the score, where the soloist is given free rein to launch into an improvised 'cadenza', based on themes from the movement but with the explicit scope of impressing the audience by the dexterity and complexity of the player's mastery of their instrument. The prime role of the cadenza is not therefore to amplify the musical content of the concerto but to allow a soloist to show off his or her skill – as the rogue plasterer did at Russborough – and, since neither the conductor nor the individual members of an orchestra have any prior knowledge of how or when this egocentric performance is to end, convention also dictates that a cadenza should terminate on a sustained trilled supertonic note indicating, to the orchestra and to the audience, that it is time to return to the composer's score.

References

Adam, William. *Vitruvius Scoticus*. Edinburgh: Printed for Adam Black and J. & J. Robertson, 1810.

Adam, William. *Vitruvius Scoticus*. Edinburgh: Paul Harris Publishing, 1980.

Bristol, Kerry. '22 Portman Square, Mrs Montagu and her Palais de la Vieillesse', *British Art Journal*, 2:3 (2001): 72–85.

Campbell, Colen. *Vitruvius Britannicus or The British Architect: The plans, elevations, and sections of the regular buildings, both publick and private in Great Britain*. 3 vols. London: n.p., 1715–25.

Campbell, James. *Building Saint Paul's*. London: Thames & Hudson, 2007.

Casey, Christine. *Making Magnificence: Architects, stuccatori and the eighteenth-century interior*. New Haven, CT and London: Yale University Press, 2017.

Colvin, Howard. *Biographical Dictionary of British Architects, 1954–1840*. New Haven, CT and London: Yale University Press, 2008.

Connell, Brian. *Portrait of a Whig Peer*. London: Andre Deutsch, 1957.

Desgodetz, Antoine. *Les Edifices Antiques de Rome Dessinés et Mesurés Très Exactement par Antoine Desgodetz*. Paris: Jean Baptiste Coignard, 1682.

Gibbs, James. *A Book of Architecture: Containing designs of buildings and ornaments*. London: n.p., 1728.

Harris, Eileen and Nicholas Savage. *British Architectural Books and Writers, 1556–1785*. Cambridge: Cambridge University Press, 1990.

Langley, Batty. *The Builder's Chest-Book: Or a complete key to the five orders of columns in architecture*. London: Printed for J. Wilcox, 1727.

Langley, Batty. *The City and Country Builder's and Workman's Treasury of Designs*. London: T. Langley, 1740.

Langley, Batty and Thomas Langley. *The Builder's Jewel or Youth's Instructor*. London: Printed for R. Ware, 1741.

Macaulay, James. 'Sir William Bruce's Hopetoun House', *Architectural Heritage*, 20:1 (2009): 1–14.

McParland, Edward. 'Florence Court', *Country Life*, 169 (May 7 and 14, 1981): 1242–5.

Murray, John G. *A Gentleman Publisher's Commonplace Book*, London: John Murray, 1996.

Rowan, Alistair. *North West Ulster: The buildings of Ireland.* Harmondsworth: Penguin Books, 1979.

Rowan, Alistair. 'The building of Hopetoun', *Architectural History*, 27 (1984): 183–209.

Rowan, Alistair. 'William Adam's library', *Architectural Heritage*, 1:1 (1990): 8–33.

Saint, Andrew. 'The conundrum of "by"'. In *Architectural History After Colvin*, edited by Malcolm Airs and William Whyte, 58–70. Donington: Shaun Tyas, 2013.

Scamozzi, Vincenzo. *L'Idea della Architettura Universale.* Venice: published by the author, 1615.

Schuym, Joachim, ed. *The Mirror of Architecture: Or, the ground-rules of the art of building*, 6th edition. London: Printed for B. Sprint, 1721.

Sharples, Joseph. 'The workers who built the University of Glasgow', *Architectural History*, 65 (2022): 261–92.

Shute, John. *First and Chief Groundes of Architecture.* A facsimile of the first edition with an introduction by Lawrence Weaver. London: Country Life, 1912.

Vignola, Giacomo da. *Regola delli Cinque Ordini di Architettura.* Rome: n.p., 1562.

Ware, Isaac. *Designs of Inigo Jones and others.* London: n.p., 1731.

8
Classical profiles: the 'alphabet of architecture'?
Edward McParland

For John Harris

In the study of Antique architecture, mouldings, profiles and their enrichments are, as shown by Lucy Shoe in works such as *Profiles of Western Greek Mouldings* (1952), and *Etruscan and Republican Roman Mouldings* (1965), important areas of research. Their importance also for the study of medieval architecture is well understood. They are less well recognised as a distinct area of study in post-medieval classicism, though an exhibition in 2021 in Zurich, *The Hidden Horizontal*, was devoted to cornices in art and architecture. Looking at a great classical building such as Sir William Chambers's (1723–1796) Casino at Marino (Fig. 8.1) one can appreciate that mouldings and profiles are integral to quality. Of course the density of invention in the Casino, its complexity of geometry (and of how this is worked out in three dimensions), its evocation of the Franco-Roman world of the eighteenth century, the relationship of its interior to the exterior, and its original setting, are all essential components of this quality. But it is thrilling to see how these features are worked out in impeccable and learned detail, with a finesse no doubt derived from the supervision by the sculptor Simon Vierpyl (c.1725–1810) of the stone carving. A remarkable pleasure of the façade of Michelangelo Buonarroti's (1475–1564) Palazzo dei Conservatori derives from its fastidious profiles and their relationship, one to the other. And while Francesco Borromini's (1599–1667) interior of San Giovanni in Laterano is superb, its quality is unforgettably reinforced by the inventive profiles of the bases of his pilasters and aedicules (Fig. 8.2).

Encouragement to consider the importance of mouldings and profiles is to hand from John Soane (1753–1837): 'The art of profiling

Figure 8.1: William Chambers, Casino at Marino, Dublin, begun 1758, detail. The sculptor Simon Vierpyl supervised the stonework.

Photograph by Roger Stalley.

and enriching the different assemblages of mouldings', he wrote, 'although now much neglected, is of the highest importance to the perfection of architecture. Perhaps the mind of a great artist is never more visible to the judicious observer than in the practice of this part of his profession'.[1] For Stephen Riou (1720–1780) in *The Grecian Orders of Architecture* (1768), mouldings were the 'alphabet of architecture … without a perfect knowledge of their several distributions and combinations, it is impossible to acquire any proficiency'.[2] Charles François Roland le Virloys's *Dictionnaire d'Architecture* of 1771 claims that the principal beauties of architecture derive from a just proportion and elegance of profiles. In illustrating these points many of the examples in this chapter are drawn from buildings in Dublin. In these, an increasing theoretical correctness of profiles in the work of the near-monopolistic Darley shop of stone masons is surely due to the instruction and example of architects. But such a connection between the worlds of design and of craft are not merely local: general conclusions, it is hoped, can emerge from the unlikely conjunction below of Borromini and the Irish architect Thomas Cooley (1740–1784).

Rules for mouldings and profiles proliferate. Enriched mouldings should alternate with plain, and curved with flat; enrichment on convex

Figure 8.2: Francesco Borromini, San Giovanni in Laterano, Rome, 1646–9, bases in the nave.

Photograph by Edward McParland.

mouldings should be incised, while on concave ones it should be in relief; mouldings of coloured marble should not be enriched.[3] Notwithstanding many counter examples from Antiquity, in the case of heavily enriched entablatures some theorists insist on the vertical alignment of elements such as individual modillions, dentils, ovolos (as in the Temple of Castor and Pollux in the Roman Forum). And, as Quinlan Terry emphasises in his recent book, *The Layman's Guide to Classical Architecture* (2022), the geometry of dentils and modillions is exacting, particularly at corners. This, for instance (Fig. 8.3), is how modillions *should* accommodate a salient entablature, with a square coffer at the outside corner, and the outer tips of modillions just meeting at an inner one. But this projection of the façade of the Royal Exchange in Dublin (Fig. 8.4) was too shallow to obviate a collision of modillions. When we remember that the depth of this projection had been determined at the level of the foundations,

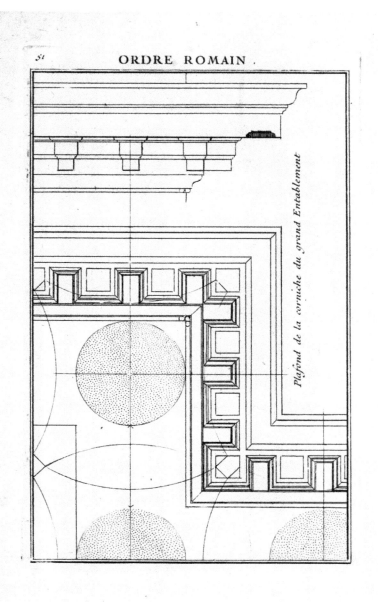

Figure 8.3: Sébastien Le Clerc, modillion cornice from *Traité d'Architecture*, Paris, 1714.

Internet Archive. Getty Research Institute.

Figure 8.4: Thomas Cooley, Royal Exchange, Dublin (now the City Hall), 1769–79, detail of cornice with merged modillions.

Photograph by Edward McParland.

it becomes clear that cornice and foundation are implacably linked in the discipline of classicism. At least Thomas Cooley's Royal Exchange avoided the gaucheries of Carlo Rainaldi's (1611–1691) Santa Maria in Campitelli in Rome (Fig. 8.5).

Figure 8.3 and its statement of the rules of how to arrange modillions at a corner can be used to illustrate the difference between theory and practice, which often calls for imagination in the reconciliation of conflicting demands. Consider the related case of James Gandon's (1743–1823) mutular cornice in his Custom House (Fig. 8.6). Mutules 'should be' equidistant from each other; they 'should be' placed centrally over the columns below them; the end ones 'should be' withdrawn from the end of the cornice to align with the angle of the building. These rules, or conventions, or traditions are mutually irreconcilable in Gandon's design; he chose to flout the first of them. Part of the skill of a classical architect is in making the 'correct' mistake.

Rules, of course, derive from the custom of Antiquity. But at the heart of architectural classicism is the unruly variety of Antiquity itself. How could 'rules' be derived from what Giacomo da Vignola (1507–1573) referred to as the 'quasi infinite varietà' of Antique

Figure 8.5: Carlo Rainaldi, Santa Maria in Campitelli, Rome, 1658–74, detail of entrance door.

Photograph by Edward McParland.

architecture? Were the ancients any good as guides if, as Soane claimed, they 'have not in any two edifices used the same orders with the same proportions, forms and ornaments'?[4] Jacques-François Blondel (1705–1774) admitted that the ancients 'ont leurs caprices aussi bien que les Modernes'– have their whims as well as the Moderns.[5] Notwithstanding this 'almost infinite' variety, it was a variety played out on remarkably few basic profiles and canonical enrichments. Chambers enumerated only eight 'regular' mouldings: ovolo, talon, cyma, cavetto, torus, astragal, scotia and fillet. As for enrichments, egg, dart, anthemion, Greek fret, Vitruvian scroll and their like are timeless and universal.

The question of the reliability of Antiquity as precedent was raised by Augustin-Charles Daviler (1653–1701) in his *Cours d'Architecture* of 1691 when, having said that excellence of profiles is an essential part of architecture, he observed that in this respect Antiquity was more *hardie* (daring or rash) than correct, as, he added, was Michelangelo.[6] Stephen Riou in 1768 parrots this opinion. Daviler's criticism extended to the mouldings of the Temple of Fortuna Virilis which – to him – were disproportionate. Sebastiano Serlio (1475–1555) says of the enrichments

Figure 8.6: James Gandon, Custom House, Dublin, 1781–91. The intervals between the mutules in the cornice vary in width.

Photograph by Edward McParland.

of the profiles of the Arco degli Argentari in Rome (third century AD) 'things of this sort ought never to be built'.[7] To Blondel, Vitruvius's (c.80BC–c.AD15) Ionic base was *estropiee* (imperfect and crippled).[8] And one doesn't go to the Pantheon for lessons in the management of mouldings (Fig. 8.7).

Antiquity, in other words, was of limited use as a source of rules. How right Alberti was to say that even Vitruvius seemed to speak Greek to the Latins, while to the Greeks he seemed to 'babble' Latin! What was one to think of the triglyph and metope frieze of the fourth century BC Ionic colonnade in Labraunda? Did these arise from error, or deliberation, or mannerism? So, what was to stop Giacomo Quarenghi (1744–1817) giving his Ionic colonnade a Doric entablature on the canal front to the Anichkov Palace in St Petersburg (Fig. 8.8)? Perhaps this was not academically correct, but Quarenghi cited Antique examples of mixed orders and asserted that no architect of talent should follow rules pedantically. The way was thus open for critics and theorists to cherry-pick which Antique models appealed to them, and which did not. They then invented academic rules for modern work which reflected personal taste as much as Antique

Figure 8.7: Pantheon, Rome, early second century, the discontinuity between portico and body of the temple is believed to be due to a change of intention during erection.

Photograph by Edward McParland.

'rules'. The result not surprisingly was debate, not consensus, as to what was 'correct': Blondel criticised some of Vignola's profiles, Chambers some of Andrea Palladio's (1508–1580), and Daviler some of Serlio's.

Mouldings and their enrichments also raise questions about the transmission and reception of ideas, and about decisions shared between designer, supervising builder, craftsman and client, all of which are central to the concerns of this volume. In drawing a door surround, James Gibbs (1682–1754) sometimes showed, in summary fashion, the enrichment of a moulding on only part of the

Figure 8.8: Giacomo Quarenghi, Anichkov Palace, St Petersburg. A range of shops along the Fontanka, commissioned 1803. The Doric frieze over Ionic columns is unconventional.

Photograph by Edward McParland.

Figure 8.9: Christopher Wren, Sheldonian Theatre, Oxford, 1664–9, detail.

Photograph by Edward McParland.

architrave. The joiner could be expected to know his eggs and his darts, and that the enrichment was to be continued for the full length of the moulding. More surprising is the discontinuity of enrichment on executed mouldings on Wren's Sheldonian Theatre in Oxford (Fig. 8.9). Sometimes the client was as demanding as Thomas Cooley thought Archbishop Richard Robinson was being when in the 1770s he offered the archbishop a choice of impost mouldings for the windows of his library in Armagh (Fig. 8.10). When these beaded blocks were

Figure 8.10: Thomas Cooley, Public Library, Armagh (now Armagh Robinson Library), established in 1771, with alternative proposals for a window drawn in 1770.

Image reproduced by kind permission of the Governors and Guardians of Armagh Robinson Library.

Figure 8.11: Thomas Burgh, Old Library, Trinity College Dublin, 1712–32. Detail of architrave.

Photograph by Edward McParland.

inserted in the architrave of the Old Library in Trinity College Dublin, about 1720 (Fig. 8.11), were they trial pieces used as models to be followed in all neighbouring blocks, did the architect notice them, was the client trying to save money by recycling, was the mason joking? To whom would this have mattered?

In the case of the façade of Gian Lorenzo Bernini's (1598–1680) church of Santa Maria di Galloro, near Ariccia (Fig. 8.12), it's possible by close attention to the mouldings to answer the questions of the historian who asks if the use of a Tuscan capital is a 'draftsman's mistake, or a foreman's incompetence', or one of the kind of errors 'that we have come to expect from Bernini himself'.[9] The fact is that there is no Tuscan order here. What Joseph Connors saw as capital is in fact a salience of the Ionic architrave; what is seen as the shaft of a Tuscan pilaster is in fact the lower part of a framing band encompassing both storeys. Carolina Mangone's recent discussion of this façade, while acknowledging the debt to the Capitoline palaces, again confuses architrave profile for capital, insisting on a '*triple* superimposition' (author's italic)

Figure 8.12: Gian Lorenzo Bernini, Santa Maria di Galloro, near Ariccia, 1624. Façade.

Photograph by Edward McParland.

of orders, which Connors had called 'the main architectural issue' at Ariccia.[10] But it all comes, profile by profile, from the Corinthian and Ionic of Michelangelo's Capitoline palaces (Fig. 8.13), where impeccable management of mouldings found no place for the Tuscan.

Examples concerning enrichments of mouldings, as in the case of Gibbs, imply some discretion being left to the carver, who could easily find details of familiar enrichments in pattern books. But the outline of the profiles themselves were of more importance than the enrichments, as Johann Baptist Izzo (1721–1793) makes clear in his *Elemens de l'Architecture Civile* of 1772, when he says that profiles must be determined by the architect and never left to the craftsmen. He's talking here of important buildings: on the other hand, the flawless cornices of many eighteenth-century houses in Dublin and

Figure 8.13: Michelangelo, Palazzo dei Conservatori, Rome, begun 1563.
Photograph by Edward McParland.

elsewhere, designed by craftsmen-builders, were free of any architect's supervision. And independence of expertise on the part of artisans is suggested by Daviler's list of workmen's own terms for profiles, different to those of architects – *baguette* for *astragale*, *boudin* for *petit tore*, and so on.[11]

The trouble with horizontal mouldings is that they are likely to interrupt vertical elements of the wall – engaged columns, pilasters, door surrounds – or they meet other mouldings generated from different origins. On exteriors, Blondel suggested that cornices of windows, if extended across the façade, might be reduced to 'demi-corniches' or platbands, so that they would not project beyond the face of pilasters.[12] Chair rails may collide with the order rising from the floor unless, as sometimes happens, the chair rail is interrupted and returned just before the meeting (Fig. 8.14). Cooley offered a different solution in the Royal Exchange in Dublin (Fig. 8.15). But Robert Adam (1728–1792) in Syon and Home House, and James Wyatt (1746–1813) in Heveningham and Castle Coole, were unconcerned that their orders were colliding with chair rails and hence were rising *through* the pedestal zone. The understanding of the dado as pedestal zone, of which the chair rail is cornice, is commonplace. Isaac Ware (1704–1766) insisted on the agreement of entablature and virtual order, objecting to the 'idle transgression' of having a Corinthian cornice above an Ionic dado: 'Let it all be of a piece' he demands.[13]

The meeting of different horizontal mouldings can vary from the cavalier to the fastidious. So prominent is the discordant

Figure 8.14: Castletown House, County Kildare, entrance hall, detail.
Photograph by Andrew Tierney.

Figure 8.15: Thomas Cooley, Royal Exchange, Dublin (now the City Hall), 1769–79, detail.

Photograph by Edward McParland.

junction at Louis Le Vau's (1612–1670) Collège des Quatre-Nations (Fig. 8.16), that he must have condoned it. But another extreme is seen in Borromini's bases of pilasters in San Giovanni in Laterano (see Fig. 8.2). These are superlative abstract developments of the Antique Attic base, in an extraordinary conversation with his adjacent aedicules. Thomas Cooley never saw a building of Borromini's and would probably have hated it if he had. But in the meeting of his mouldings of bases in the Royal Exchange in Dublin (Fig. 8.17) the continuities and variations are part of a familiar classical discipline which is independent of style.

In many cases mouldings are among the principal vehicles of decoration on a building. The enrichment of mouldings must have delighted

Figure 8.16: Louis Le Vau, Collège des Quatre-Nations, Paris (Institut de France), begun 1662.

Photograph by Edward McParland.

ostentatious clients like Nicolas Fouquet in Vaux-le-Vicomte. An elaborate theory was enunciated in France in the late eighteenth century on the extent to which cornices and their enrichment determined the 'character' of interiors, by being in step with the developing formality of rooms through which one passed. In Nicolas Le Camus de Mézières's (1721–1793) *Genie de l'Architecture* of 1780, the vestibule with its waiting servants may be without a cornice, but if there is one it should have very few mouldings. In the third antechamber (where certain people of distinction await entry to saloon or cabinet) the cornice may be carved but decoration should be moderate so as not to compete with that of the subsequent rooms. In the master's bedroom profiles should be more severe than in his wife's and appropriate to his station: if he is a soldier, there should be plenty of squared-off profiles with nothing 'mannered' in them.

Figure 8.17:   Thomas Cooley, Royal Exchange, Dublin (now the City Hall), 1769–79. Detail of bases in the rotunda.

Photograph by Charles Duggan.

A less elaborate but nonetheless specific gradation of mouldings, which develops as one moves through the house, can be clearly traced in James Wyatt's Castle Coole and in the Provost's House in Dublin, where the enrichment of profiles – from skirting boards, chair rails, door surrounds to cornices – follows and articulates the hierarchy of the interiors and the uses of the rooms. The richness of the mouldings of the Provost's Dining Room, for example – unseen in other rooms except the Saloon – together with its commissioning Provost's known appetites and hospitality, is a guide to how the house was used.

Enriched mouldings are, of course, more expensive than plain, and no doubt it was often economy that reduced the amount of enrichment. But its absence could be a deliberate aesthetic choice. Discretion was called for: it was to be sparing on cornices, 'comme le sel pour les ragoûts' – like salt in a stew, according to Le Camus de Mézières's *Le Génie de l'Architecture*,[14] which went so far as to recommend that enriched mouldings be confined to interiors, since exterior ornament could compromise scale, or corrode, or stain with age. This was asking too much: some theorists, Daviler among them, asked only that ornament on internal mouldings be in lower relief than on external ones. Such discretion lies behind much of the power of Edward Lovett Pearce's (c.1699–1733) façade of the Parliament House in Dublin. This is almost contemporary with Thomas Burgh's (1670–1730) Old Library in Trinity College. One is grateful that the austerity of Burgh's façades is relieved by the richness of an entablature (Fig. 8.18). Economy is an unlikely explanation of Pearce's austerity (Fig. 8.19): I see it as a reaction against elaboration such as Burgh's, and as an eloquent and conscious expression of the New Junta's Hellenism.[15]

For another example of the power of unenriched profiles consider James Gandon's Custom House and its extraordinary entablature (see Fig. 8.6). In this building, with its rich programme of sculptural decoration, the entablature on the four pavilions is plain. And not just plain, but aggressively so, with fused architrave and frieze. This simplified profile recurs on all four corner pavilions. Few things contribute more to

Figure 8.18: Thomas Burgh, Old Library, Trinity College Dublin, 1712–32. Detail of architrave.

Photograph by Edward McParland.

258   BETWEEN DESIGN AND MAKING

Figure 8.19: Edward Lovett Pearce, Parliament House, Dublin (now the Bank of Ireland), begun 1729. Entablature.

Photograph by Edward McParland.

the compositional unity of the Custom House than the plain entablature with its insistent mutular cornice.[16]

Is the language of architectural classicism – with its basic components of Attic, Tuscan, Doric, Ionic, Corinthian, Composite – amenable to laws as strict as those of grammar and syntax? Serlio's simplified canon (shirking the difficulties of Attic and Tuscan) implies as much. But was this language in its Antique form not infinitely varied (Vignola), capricious (Blondel), more daring than correct (Daviler)? Was not Serlio's canon largely his own invention (Summerson)? Was not this language 'bien peu systématique' – unsystematic?[17] (Similar questions could be raised in the revival of Antique imperial capital lettering.) It was, of course, variety, and caprice, and invention that ensured the vitality of post-medieval classicism, and its capacity for self-renewal.

And while new rules proliferated in the academies, there were Michelangelo's 'hardie' (in Daviler's words) profiles, and Borromini's in San Giovanni in Laterano, and Soane's incised profiles on the gate at Tyringham Hall, to show students that getting it 'right' wasn't enough.

Acknowledgements

I am grateful to Charles Duggan, Peter Fox, Melanie Hayes, Eileen Punch, and Andrew Tierney for assistance in preparing this chapter.

Notes

1   Watkin, *Sir John Soane*, 47.
2   Riou, *Grecian Orders*, 17.
3   Lemonnier, *Procès-verbaux de l'Académie Royale d'Architecture*, 32.
4   Watkin, *Sir John Soane*, 85.
5   Blondel, *Cours d'Architecture*, 88.
6   Daviler, *Cours d'Architecture*, iv.
7   Serlio, *l'Architecture*, Book 3.
8   Blondel, *Cours d'Architecture*, 35.
9   Connors, 'Bernini's S. Andrea al Quirinale', 15–37.
10 Mangone, *Bernini's Michelangelo*.
11 Daviler, *Cours d'Architecture*, iii.
12 Blondel, *Cours d'Architecture*, 467–8.
13 Ware, *A Complete Body of Architecture*, 473.
14 Le Camus de Mézieres, *Le Génie de l'Architecture*, 52.
15 See McParland, *Public Architecture in Ireland*.
16 See McParland, *James Gandon*.
17 Lemerle, 'L'ionique: Un ordre en quête de base', 11.

References

Blondel, Francois. *Cours d'Architecture, Enseigné dans l'Academie Royale d'Architecture*. 2 vols. 2nd edition. Paris: L'Auteur/Le Cointe, 1698.
Connors, Joseph. 'Bernini's S. Andrea al Quirinale: Payments and planning', *Journal of the Society of Architectural Historians*, 41 (1982): 15–37.
Daviler, Augustin-Charles. *Cours d'Architecture qui Comprend les Ordres de Vignole*. 1st edition. Paris: Chez Jean Mariette, 1691.
Izzo, Johann Baptist., *Elemens de l'architecture civile, à l'usage des cavaliers du College Roïal Thérésien*. Vienna: Joseph Kurzböch, 1772.
Le Camus de Mezieres, Nicolas. *Le Génie de l'Architecture*. Paris: Auteur, 1780.
Le Clerc, Sébastien. *Traité D'Architecture*. Paris: Pierre Giffart, 1714.
Lemerle, Frederique and Yves Pauwels. 'L'ionique: Un ordre en quête de base', *Annali de Architettura*, 3 (1991): 7–13.
Lemonnier, M. H. *Proces-verbaux de l'Academie Royale d'Architecture, 1671–1793*, vol. 2: *1682–1696*. Paris: Jean Schemit, 1912.
Mangone, Carolina. *Bernini's Michelangelo*. New Haven, CT and London: Yale University Press, 2020.

260   BETWEEN DESIGN AND MAKING

McParland, Edward. *James Gandon: Vitruvius Hibernicus*. London: Zwemmer, 1985.

McParland, Edward. *Public Architecture in Ireland 1680–1760*. New Haven, CT and London: Yale University Press, 2001.

Roland le Virloys, Charles François. *Dictionnaire D'Architecture, Civile, Militaire Et Navale, Antique, Ancienne Et Moderne, Et De Tous Les Arts Et Métiers Qui En Dépendent*. Paris: Libraires Associés, 1771.

Riou, Stephen. *The Grecian Orders*. London: J. Dixwell, 1768.

Serlio, Sebastiano. *L'Architettura*, Book 3: *Delle antichità*. Venice: Francesco Marcolini, 1540.

Shoe, Lucy. *Profiles of Western Greek Mouldings*. Rome: American Academy in Rome, 1952.

Shoe, Lucy. *Etruscan and Republican Roman Mouldings*. Rome: American Academy in Rome, 1965.

Terry, Quinlan. *The Layman's Guide to Classical Architecture*. Stockholm: Bokförlaget Stolpe, 2022.

Ware, Isaac. *A Complete Body of Architecture*. London: T. Osborne, J. Shipton and others, 1767.

Watkin, David, ed. *Sir John Soane: The Royal Academy lectures*. Cambridge: Cambridge University Press, 2000.

9
Allegorising the space between architecture and craft: mural painting 1630–1730
Lydia Hamlett

The interiors of elite houses in the long seventeenth century entertained many ways of viewing, and the vital contribution of the intermedial partnership of architecture and craft via architect and artisan is explored throughout the current volume.[1] In Baroque interiors, there is another medium through which architecture and craft can be understood – that of mural painting, which adorned the literal space between them.[2] Murals were an integral part of a house's walls and ceilings, whilst they also interacted with real crafted architectural elements and media including other types of painting and decorative arts. It is within mural painting in fact where these different media and the roles of their creators are celebrated and brought together, extending our vision from real space to an imagined dimension. This chapter will explore how muralled surfaces, whilst classed neither as architecture nor craft, could nonetheless serve as allegorical loci where the very idea of artistic creation – concepts such as *techne* and *poesis* – could be brought to life. Illuminating this intermedial space between architecture and craft, it will bring to light cases where muralists, alongside architects and craftsmen, were employed by patrons to give meaning to, and make sense of, their own family seats following a time of profound crisis.

Craft and paint in the Baroque interior

The Baroque mural flourished in the British Isles in particular from around 1630 to 1730. The influence of Peter Paul Rubens's (1577–1640) canvases for the Banqueting House at Whitehall (1630s) provided huge inspiration in the earlier half of this period, whilst the genre was given a boost after the Restoration of Charles II and the ambitious cycle he instigated at Windsor Castle (1670s on).[3] Under William III, it became de rigueur for newly-built aristocratic houses and, increasingly, those of professional gentlemen alike, to have murals in at least one location. The genre flourished like never before under Queen Anne, but was falling out of fashion by the 1730s. British mural cycles revolved largely around pagan themes, rather than biblical ones. They celebrated the dynastic lineage of patrons, whilst also communicating their personal virtues and beliefs. Particularly after the Glorious Revolution, patrons exercised their freedoms in this aspect of the visual culture of their houses, putting themselves at the centre of their mural cycles and frequently employing satirical messages within.[4]

It seems obvious to state that real crafted elements and mural painting coexist in interiors, with murals being viewed in situ alongside actual crafted elements, wrought ironwork staircases, carved overmantels, wainscots and stucco frames. Nonetheless, the intention behind these intermedial collaborations – executed in parallel or in close succession by artisans and artists – is significant. The vital synergies of mural painting and craft have recently been highlighted at Chatsworth House, where the mural painter Antonio Verrio (c.1639–1707) included natural forms and motifs in painted ceilings that woodworkers soon afterwards rendered on the walls below. Laurel Peterson's doctoral thesis examines intermediality at work in the country house. Her work on the Chatsworth archives has revealed that, in the Great Hall, Verrio finished his ceiling painting just before the limewood carvers Joel Lobb, William Davis and Samuel Watson undertook their work. Both were paid for by William Cavendish, 1st Duke of Devonshire (1640–1707), with the woodworkers being renumerated £50 less than Verrio and his team for painting.[5] Both woodwork and mural deal in the business of material metamorphosis and illusion, conjuring up the appearance of natural forms such as fruit, fish or flowers (Fig. 9.1).[6] The Great Stairs and Chapel at Chatsworth contain some of the greatest examples of craft and painting, two- and three-dimensional elements working together to make sense of interiors, coming closest to what we think of as the Baroque *bel composto* in Britain (Fig. 9.2).[7] The staircase was designed by William Talman (1650–1719) in 1689–90, and contains statues and doorcases by Danish-born sculptor, Caius Gabriel Cibber (1630–1700), an ironwork balustrade by Jean Tijou (fl. 1689–1712) and mural paintings by Verrio. The ceiling shows Cybele, Mother Earth, in a lion-led chariot, with Ceres, goddess of the harvest, and Bacchus, god of wine, and figurations of the continents (Fig. 9.3). The illusionistic

Figure 9.1: The Great Chamber, Chatsworth House, detail showing painted ceiling by Antonio Verrio and limewood carving by Joel Lobb, William Davis and Samuel Watson.

Photograph by Daderot. Public Domain, Creative Commons CC0 1.0 Universal Public Domain Dedication.

Figure 9.2: The Great Stairs, Chatsworth House, detail showing statues by Caius Gabriel Cibber.

Photograph by Daderot. Public Domain, Creative Commons CC0 1.0 Universal Public Domain Dedication.

stone garland that frames the main narrative scene is echoed in the real carved swags above the doorcases and sculptural niches, which are filled with real sculptural busts that interact with painted figures on the walls. Illusionistic bas reliefs with triumphs of Cybele, Ceres and Bacchus, and Hercules and the Sphinx, and sculptures in niches, fill the stairwell.[8] The whole staircase is a playful vortex of activity generated from above, the energy drifting in and out of the real and fictive spaces.

The liturgical east end of the chapel contains a similar interaction of real and painted elements, with the sculptural stone figures of the altar frame extended into painted representations beyond, in the muralled wall, by Louis Laguerre (1663–1721) (Fig. 9.4). The painted sculptural figures engage with the painted figures within the narrative.[9] It is unlikely that any one person was responsible for conceiving the overall design of interiors. It is clear from preparatory drawings that Laguerre and other mural painters took into consideration the illusionistic craft and architectural framing of their narratives (even though these were often developed in the final product), and that, as mentioned above, Verrio likely finished his ceilings before the woodcarvers did their work. It would be sensible to assume, from the close working proximity both in time and across locations of painters and artisans, and the close personal

Figure 9.3: The Great Stairs, Chatsworth House, showing painted ceiling by Antonio Verrio.

Photograph by Daderot. Public Domain, Creative Commons CC0 1.0 Universal Public Domain Dedication.

Figure 9.4: The Chapel, Chatsworth House, detail showing mural by Louis Laguerre.

Photograph by Daderot. Public Domain, Creative Commons CC0 1.0 Universal Public Domain Dedication.

links between many of them (for example, Laguerre was the son-in-law of Tijou), that there was a sense of collaboration and mutual inspiration from both sides.

At Chatsworth, in both the staircase and Chapel as well as its vast *enfilade* of state rooms, and in many other elite houses, the imagined landscapes depicted in mural painting were anchored to the physical reality of the building by referencing empirical details relating to its material culture. Through murals' depictions of illusionistic architecture and craft, they were able to wittily explore the effects and affects of different media, surprising and capturing the attention of the viewer. The representation of such crafted items is rife in mural painting. These could be interior features such as illusionistic frames, stone, wood or metalwork, stuccoes, medallions, rosettes, decorative swags and coffering. These are often so naturalistically painted that it presents a challenge to tell what is real and what is not, even with our well-worn, twenty-first-century vision. In Celia Fiennes's contemporaneous diary, which does not generally prioritise a concern for artistic affect, the artistic details that capture her imagination are those that are rendered most naturalistically from across various media – sculpture, carving and wall painting – described by her as 'curious', or 'real'. They include the large painted curtain on the King's Staircase at Hampton Court Palace (Fig. 9.5), also by Verrio, about 1700, that frames the scene of Julian the Apostate at his writing desk, 'drawn soe bold as if real wth gold ffringe'.[10] Here, once again, we see the collaborative enterprises of Verrio and his kinsman Jean Tijou, who executed the fine wrought-iron balustrade with panels of scrolling acanthus-leaf ornament, about 1699.[11] As well as Chatsworth and the state rooms at Burghley House, Lincolnshire, the Queen's Drawing Room at Hampton Court Palace, 1705 (Fig. 9.6), is perhaps the apogee of intermedial illusionism, where it is almost impossible to distinguish from sight whether surfaces were paint or craft, including mosaics and textiles. As Cécile Brett has noted, although we have no records of precisely who was working for Verrio at Hampton Court, besides the gilder Peter Cousin, it is likely they included a number of those artist-craftsmen he employed at Burghley: Alexandre Souville, René Fouillet, Demouille and Francis Ricard, an architectural painter who had come to England with Laguerre.[12] Both Peter and René Cousin, unlike many of the others, did not rely on Verrio directly for their payments and instead submitted their bills via another route (in the latter's case, the 5th Earl's steward, Culpepper Tanner).[13]

Fictive architectural elements could also serve to enhance the reality of an interior, revelling in the freedoms of a world beyond financial or

Figure 9.5: The King's Staircase, Hampton Court Palace, mural by Antonio Verrio depicting Julian the Apostate, detail.

© Historic Royal Palaces 2023.

material constraints. At Petworth House, West Sussex, the idiosyncratic architectural language of Laguerre's Great Stairs (Fig. 9.7), executed about 1720 following a fire in 1714,[14] endows it with a luxury that would have been impossible to achieve in three dimensions, and which stands in stark contrast not only to the measured French classicism of the house's exterior (built about 1686) but also to elements of the stair hall itself. The staircase (parts of which may have been altered later) was rebuilt sometime after 1722, seemingly by the London joiner John Simmons, who submitted costs to the Duke of Somerset (1662–1748) in July 1722

Figure 9.6: The Queen's Drawing Room, Hampton Court Palace, showing mural by Antonio Verrio and gilding by Peter Cousin.
© Historic Royal Palaces 2023.

for 'Stairs of right wainscot [oak] ... with two bannisters on each step (as before)'.[15] Simmons appears to have been constrained in replicating the earlier scheme, though economy may also have been a factor. Scale aside, relatively cheap deal (fir or pine softwood) timber was specified, alongside oak, for parts of the raised and fielded panelling and doors. The architectural ornament too seems relatively restrained, consisting of 'Rt Wainscot bolechon work as before' and a 'Modillion Cornish Running round the staircase and upper landing', perhaps intended as a foil for the more elaborate fictive setting. A drawing by Laguerre of the south wall of the staircase shows his concern with the architectural setting of the painting.[16] Here the richly decorated columns and deeply bracketed frieze serve to elevate the subject of the main wall: the Duchess of Somerset (1667–1722) riding towards her house in a triumphal carriage. The painted architecture references an unusual Antique idiom informed by both western and eastern influences, its intricately carved columns and pilasters uniting the Duchess and her mythological parallel Pandora in a shared space.[17]

Certain recurring types of painted craft elements could set the scene for mural narratives, chronologically and iconographically. Monochrome illusionistic stone bas-reliefs, frequently found in the subsidiary areas of muralled interiors, provided a kind of contextual stage-setting for the

Figure 9.7: The Grand Staircase, Petworth House, showing ceiling painting of Pandora and the Gods by Louis Laguerre.

Public domain. Creative Commons Attribution 2.0 Generic license. Photograph by tpholland.

main narratives within. At the Painted Hall of the Royal Naval Hospital in Greenwich, James Thornhill's (1675–1734) painted bas-reliefs on the walls of the upper hall served to provide context for the west wall's central scene, with George I and his family, allegory mixed with contemporary detail. On the north wall is an allegory of William III arriving at Torbay, whilst the mirroring south wall shows William riding towards

Christopher Wren's east front of Hampton Court Palace, Cibber's relief of Hercules triumphing over Envy just visible in its pediment. Another common trope is the animated statue breaking the boundaries of the architectural niche, serving to draw the viewers' attention to the central narrative and pre-empt or mimic our reactions to them. They, as we, become witnesses to the unfolding of contemporary histories as well as mythological and allegorical ones. We are forced not only to check whether the crafted architectural surfaces are real or not, but also whether we agree with the versions of history they convey. The onus is on the viewer to check, through experience, what they believe, and to test it out.

Crafted object as allegory

Murals' contribution to the visual culture of the city- and country-house-building renaissance that occurred in the late seventeenth century was to offer a space through which histories could be experienced anew.[18] In mural schemes, mythological themes could be represented in art on a grand physical scale, through which families keen to establish their lineage and power through building could animate the interiors of their houses. The painted interior offered a fully immersive allegorical way of viewing, a Benjaminian encounter with a series of narrative allegories opening and folding within an architectural space, an *enfilade* of rooms or the wall and ceiling surfaces of a grand staircase.[19] But they are also integral to an intermedial whole, wherein the parts cannot be seen in isolation.[20] In this way murals are akin to other experiential allegorical art forms of the time, including masques, later plays and operas, that relied for their effects on other arts, including dance, music and costume, and indeed they shared many of their intertextual iconographies.[21] The most popular source for mural subjects, Ovid's *Metamorphoses*, an epic poem powered by allegory, was similarly mined by muralists to reflect political and world views of the patrons. As well as the patrons themselves being immortalised via portraits in their murals, the representation of real crafted elements from the household also extended the idea of a metamorphosis from real to imagined form, whilst at the same time transforming interiors into spaces of memory and imagination. The crafted object was central to mural painting, often used to punctuate its unfolding allegorical narratives, and represented not once but multiple times.

At Petworth House, the seat of the Duke and Duchess of Somerset, the mural scheme revolves around the jar, or *pithos*, given to Pandora, which

Figure 9.8: The Grand Staircase, Petworth House, showing mural by Louis Laguerre.

Photograph by Josep Renalias. Creative commons attribution-sharealike 3.0 unported license.

is shown at least three times in the mural paintings, understairs, on the first floor and on the ceiling (Fig. 9.8). The whole scheme revolves around stories of creation, of the first man, made from clay by the Titan Prometheus, and a painting of the first woman, Pandora, fashioned by Vulcan (Hephaestus) to bring about the Titan's downfall. The impact of these creations on humankind is notorious, in that all the evils of the world were released from 'the box' (or jar); although in this staircase the protagonist is Pandora and the blame is laid squarely on Epimetheus for opening it.[22] The jar is not only represented in paint but would also have been referenced in displays of the Duchess's china collections, around the house and perhaps in the stairwell itself. The creation myth of Pandora thus provided an allegorical, mythological link to the role of women, and more specifically the Duchess, in the creation of these spaces, the crafted object woven into the very architecture of her house via its muralled interior.[23] An interesting contemporaneous German parallel can be seen at the Schloss Favorite Rastatt, where the patroness's porcelain collection was shown off in the mural painting and where putti are depicted throwing her pots from the illusionistic realm, as if to land on the real ground below.

Other crafted objects, key to mural narratives that combined ancient history and modern history, are the armour of Achilles or Aeneas, created at the behest of Thetis or Venus respectively. At Hanbury Hall, Achilles's armour is key to the main narrative scenes painted by James Thornhill in around 1710. In the first scene encountered on the stairwell, a helmet, breastplate, sword and spear are shown being created by the Cyclopes in Vulcan's workshop, under the watchful gaze of Achilles's mother, Thetis. We, the viewer, then follow the items' journey throughout the narrative: first, revealing the real person of Achilles in the court of Lycomedes, and then, following the hero's demise, at the centre of the famous debate between Odysseus and Ajax, on the virtues of brute strength versus rhetoric. This narrative unfolds, scene by scene, as the viewer ascends the stairs. The climax of the scheme is presented within the staircase ceiling, which includes a painted version of a contemporary print portraying Dr Henry Sacheverell (1674–1724), who was accused by the Whigs (including Hanbury's owner, Thomas Vernon MP (1654–1721) of using rhetoric to ill effect. The armour appears in the ceiling, too, the spear now elevated in the hands of Athene (a likeness of Queen Anne) instead of being wielded by Achilles in the court of Lycomedes (Achilles is, in fact, a portrait of the Duchess of Marlborough (1660–1744). In effect, the armour provides continuity of meaning to the visual narrative. There is some interesting precedent for the inclusion of armour and weaponry on staircases in British Baroque interiors – the real armour arranged by Prince Rupert on the stair to the keep at Windsor (as described by John Evelyn in 1670), the carved weaponry on the staircase at Ham House of 1638–40, which includes cannon and had a painted finish by Matthew Goodricke (1588–1645), and the painted weaponry at Marlborough House, executed by Laguerre for the Duchess of Marlborough, about 1712.[24]

Vulcan's skill at crafting is explored elsewhere through the story of Venus, Vulcan and Mars, an episode frequently depicted in British Baroque murals. In the narrative first told by Homer, and retold by others, including Ovid, the metal mesh of Vulcan's net is so finely crafted it is barely visible, and this quality enables him to catch his wife with her lover, revealing the truth of their liaison: 'See how our slow moving Hephaestus (i.e. Vulcan) has caught Ares (i.e. Mars), though no god on Olympus can run as fast. Hephaestus may be lame, but his craft has won the day'.[25] The myth is used as political allegory in the largest state room at Burghley, for example, where it has been argued that it communicates the politics of its owner, the 5th Earl of Exeter (1648–1700), with humour, referencing a contemporaneous play by Peter Motteux (1663–1718) that sang the praises of William III and generally signalled allegiance, but with a humorous edge that demonstrated the renewed

Figure 9.9: The Heaven Room, Burghley House, paintings by Antonio Verrio.
Reproduced by kind permission of Burghley House.

freedoms of members of the aristocracy (Fig. 9.9). The craft of metalwork is hammered home (quite literally!) on the other side of the room, where Vulcan and the Cyclopes that work for him are shown in his forge. It is noteworthy that this Baroque interest in finely crafted wrought iron is echoed in Jean Tijou's entrance gates to the remodelled Burghley House.

It was less common for crafted objects to be included in murals, to bring biblical stories to life. The murals in the chapel of Wimpole Hall, Cambridgeshire, painted in the 1720s by Thornhill, encapsulate this idea of the mural surface as a locus for the play between reality and unreality, projected through the representation of craft, in this case the painted surface of enormous illusionistic urns, themselves adorned with gilt reliefs of biblical narratives. With such plastic and lively carved figures, one feels as though one could close one's eyes and decipher the narrative by touch alone; except, of course, it is only the plane of a flat surface you would feel if you tried. These elements of visual *ekphrasis* remind us of objects from ancient literature such as the shields of Achilles or Aeneas, or the temple friezes crafted for affect, intended to evoke pathos in the viewer.[26] This is also reflected in the architectural background to the *Adoration of the Magi*, on the main altar wall of the Wimpole chapel. Preparatory drawings show that this was always intended by its artist, James Thornhill, to be a mix of the rustic-built structure (recalling the stable), and the Antique temple.[27] The final version as executed, though, foregrounds the wooden frame that lies beneath, showing the lintel above the Madonna and Child in the form of a Union flag with the remnants of blue and red colouring – a nod, perhaps, to exquisite British craftsmanship.[28]

Murals afforded the opportunity for elite families not only to weave political allegories around specific crafted objects but also to celebrate the poetic origins of entire building projects. The story of Philemon and Baucis was originally planned by Verrio for the Heaven Room at Burghley, presumably as a metaphor for the refashioning of the house itself, architectural improvement as a result of its owners' virtue. One extant example that celebrates the *poesis* behind building projects is the mural scheme at Powis Castle, Powys, re-established as the seat of the Herbert family after they returned from exile under William, on the accession of Queen Anne. The Grand Staircase at Powis was a key part of a series of murals that used portraits of the family members in allegorical scenes, and the staircase itself was at its heart.[29] The walls were painted in around 1705 by Gerard Lanscroon (c.1655–1737), fresh from his experience at Hampton Court. The main scenes are sea triumphs, suggestive of the family's return from overseas, and on the first wall the viewer sees the marriage of Neptune and Amphitrite, surrounded by nymphs. One nymph is delivered to the rocky foreground, which morphs into a platform with stairs leading to it, with curved treads that mirror those at the entrance to the main house. A group of figures personifying the Arts, with Apollo playing his lyre, are seen to the far right, with Architecture holding up a sketch of Amphion, whose heavenly music prompted the walls of Thebes to effortlessly construct themselves.

The analogy of poetry and architecture given by Horace became a popular trope associated with new building projects in contemporary poetry, but is given extra meaning at Powis via the figurations of painting and poetry.[30] Furthermore, details such as the musical score provide both an emblematic nod to the Herberts' musical patronage and also is no doubt taken from a real composition. The seamless mix of the allegorical and the real serves as anchorage for the Herberts after years of instability and exile, marking for them a triumphant return in the visual culture of their country house, allegory providing the providential context required for such a project. There is a parallel to be made here between the country house poem and the mural painting typologies. Judith Dundas has argued that the country house poem as a genre reflects the inner mind or imagination, using *ekphrasis* as a way to recall and describe the physical details of the house and gardens and to lead the reader around it.[31] This function is taken on by the interiors themselves, in the way in which they capture the viewer's imagination through their physical,

Figure 9.10: The Double Cube Room, Wilton House. Painted ceiling by Emmanuel De Critz and Edward Pearce (detail) and stuccoed frames.

Reproduced with permission of the Earl and Countess of Pembroke and Trustees of Wilton House Trust.

material contexts, and lead them to an allegorical fantasy realm.[32] In this pursuit, the mural as allegorical locus between architecture and craft is vital. Within the intermedial context of the painted interior, the very idea of *poesis*, craftsmanship and building were made immanent to the architecture, together demonstrating the hope of transformation through their forms.

Techne's downsides

Just as painted craft in murals could be used as a metaphor for celebrating poetic agency, it could also be used to demonstrate the terrible things that can happen when humans square up to the *techne* of the gods.[33] Such tragedies abound in classical literature and many of them accordingly took the centre stage in Baroque murals. The family seat represented the fortunes and families of the elite, whilst the inclusion of such allegories warned them not to overreach themselves, and often presented an exercise of exploring fallibility in the secular sphere. The earliest mythological British Baroque mural scheme, in the Single Cube room at Wilton House (1636, rebuilt c.1648–51 following a fire), Wiltshire, centres on the story of Daedalus and Icarus, when the wings the craftsman makes for his son fail, as the wax meshing their feathers melts and Icarus falls to his death.[34] The myth mirrored themes in identifiable contemporary masques and spoke of the political instability that marked the career of their patron, the 4th Earl of Pembroke (1584–1650). In the next room, the Double Cube room, Perseus is presented as the antidote to failure, a bringer of harmony paralleled with the earl himself (Fig. 9.10). Here, the ingenuity of the craftsmen sits alongside that of the painter, with the stuccoed fruits and flowers framing the triumphant scenes of Perseus, in the ceiling, whilst the wainscotting below framed many other family portraits, carefully positioned to communicate with the ceiling above.[35]

Another ancient story of hubris as a result of overreaching ambition and the failure of *techne* – this time, of the gods – is enacted within the interior of the dome at Castle Howard, North Yorkshire, some sixty years after Wilton (Fig. 9.11).[36] The mural painting was executed by Giovanni Antonio Pellegrini (1675–1741) in 1709–12, and according to Anthony Geraghty, 'responds to the architecture of the house with a complexity and sophistication that is without parallel in the history of decorative painting in England'.[37] High up in the soffit of the dome, the chariot driven by Phaeton, son of the sun god Helios, crashes to earth.[38] In the hall below, the god Vulcan, who made the chariot but who could not have imagined it being used in such a way, sits bent over in sorrow, shielding his eyes from the disaster unfolding above (Fig. 9.12). The ornate overmantel, the work of Luganese *stuccatore* Giovanni Bagutti (1681–1753) and a 'Signor Plura', in 1709–10,[39] in which Vulcan is represented, serves not only to link him with the roaring fire below but also marks him out as a figure of significance, framing him as would an altarpiece in a Baroque church. Elsewhere, painted garlands of musical instruments articulate the planar surfaces of wall piers and spandrels of the arches. This cohesion between mural painting and stucco frame, between real architectural elements and the fictive embellishments which adorn the architectural features, clearly demonstrates the collaborative achievement of artists and artisans in the creation of such a monumental interior. There are similar mural-sculpture ensembles in the chapel at Chatsworth.[40] Once again, art and craft work together to endow the very fabric of the building with meaning. The centre staging of hubris works at Castle Howard for the patron as it did earlier at Wilton, as the Earl of Carlisle (1679–1738) rebuilt his family seat around this time, on leaving the courtly sphere, which he judged to be corrupted by power and money. His aim was to focus on the virtue afforded by the country house.[41] It was also a myth used as a metaphor for temperate political leadership, and in this context as an allegory for the

Figure 9.11: The Great Hall, Castle Howard. Dome interior with Fall of Phaeton, originally by Giovanni Antonio Pellegrini, repainted by Scott Medd in the 1960s, following a fire in 1940.

Reproduced by kind permission of Castle Howard.

Figure 9.12: The Great Hall, Castle Howard, painting of Vulcan by Giovanni Antonio Pellegrini, overmantel by Giovanni Bagutti and 'Signor Plura'.

Reproduced by kind permission of Castle Howard.

dangers of absolutism, and was frequently cited in contemporary visual culture, including other mural schemes.

These subjects were not solely a male preserve, as mythological women who squared up to the artistry of the gods, and were punished as a result, also took centre stage in murals. The story of Arachne, who took part in a weaving competition with Minerva, goddess of wisdom and craft, was popular. Minerva was so enraged by Arachne's skill that the mortal was driven to hang herself and transformed into a spider. The subject is depicted in large paintings by Pellegrini and Marco Ricci (1676–1730) painted from around 1709–11, once integral to the architecture of Burlington House, probably commissioned by the 3rd Earl of Burlington's mother, Juliana Dowager Countess of Burlington (née Noel, 1672–1750).[42] It was also a subject referenced in both literary and scientific works of the time.[43] Soon after, Pellegrini drew on the same myth as inspiration for his murals in the High Saloon at Castle Howard. Minerva's other craft-related roles are also explored in this room, showing her role of patroness of woodworking in the ship, built to her orders, that brought Helen from Troy. In the ceiling above, Minerva is shown orchestrating the whole. The joinery and carved frieze in this suite of rooms was carried out by William Thornton (1670–1721) of York. As Geraghty notes, Nicholas Hawksmoor's correspondence suggest that the precise detailing of the joinery in the earl's apartments was left to the craftsmen.[44]

Craft collaborations

As much as the process of making a Baroque interior was a collaborative effort, the same principle applied within each of the media represented. Although named mural painters were singled out for their part in the overall design, and certain individuals highly rewarded, they worked with vast teams of assistants who each had specialties in painting different types of object, including flowers, portraits or architecture, each responsible for adding their own contribution, from their own creative imagination, to the overall scene. Verrio, Louis Chéron, Laguerre and Thornhill all included self-portraits in their most major mural commissions, at Burghley, Boughton Hall, Northamptonshire, Blenheim Palace, Oxfordshire, and the Painted Hall at Greenwich, respectively, that showed them in the centre of medial melees. Verrio is shown sketching the Cyclopes, metal-working in Vulcan's forge, next to a fictive bronze shield with the head of the Medusa. Chéron placed a portrait of himself in a triumph of Bacchus, wherein the god of wine was his patron Ralph Montagu and he himself was a satyr. Francois Marandet has pointed out that the scene was intended as an allegory of the old craft of making and repairing wooden wheels, from which his name derived.[45] A bricklayer was sent from Ditton Park to Boughton, to sit for Chéron, and Tessa Murdoch has suggested that he also may have been the model for the muscular figure of Hercules in the great Hall.[46] Laguerre places himself within a fictive colonnade, his signature chiselled in the (painted) stone ledge below (Fig. 9.13). Thornhill has laid down his palette in order to gesture to the royal family of George I, as a director would a cast on the stage. In the distance behind him is his other great mural commission of around the same time, Wren's dome of St Paul's, for which he had recently completed the lives of the eponymous saint, in grisaille (Fig. 9.14).

In each of these examples artists are choosing to represent not their own individual genius but their art as being part of something greater than themselves. This idea of artistic collaboration had literary parallels, at a time when the first collaborative translations of classical texts, for example, were being published, of which John Dryden's edited translation of Ovid's *Heroides* (1680) was the first. Neither was the idea of cross-chronological copying from Antique or later sources viewed as

Figure 9.13: The Saloon, Blenheim Palace. Detail showing mural by Louis Laguerre.

Reproduced by kind permission of His Grace the Duke of Marlborough.

a thing of lesser artistic import. Although the seventeenth century saw a hierarchical system of the arts being codified in French courtly circles, which had a great effect on the arts as viewed in the eighteenth century in Europe, the visual culture of Baroque Britain still revelled, as literature and music, in collaboration.[47] The story is well known, of how history painting and craft were separated out, with craft coming low down in the hierarchy of media, from the late seventeenth century, as visual media was increasingly divided into distinct categories.[48] But the Baroque interior flourished until as late as the 1730s, when histories began increasingly to be wrested from the wall to canvas.

The intermedial interiors of the British Baroque were a celebration of creative collaboration – architects, muralists, craftsmen as well as playwrights and poets – rather than individual invention or genius, and this moreover reflected on their patrons. Mural painting complicated the glorious architecture it animated through schemes that sought to explore the biases of our vision, to ward against human fallibility as much as to glorify individual subjects.[49] The private, elite interiors of the town and country house, apparently influenced by continental religious and political absolutism, may seem reactionary in terms of the more public art forms being developed at the time, including prints and pamphlets. But in fact they were dynamic sites that were concerned with exploring issues

Figure 9.14: The Painted Hall, Old Royal Naval College, Greenwich. West wall by James Thornhill.

Public domain.

of identity, societal structure and dynastic virtues, following a time of profound crises that characterised the seventeenth century. Architecture of the time has long been acknowledged as a sign of rebuilding power after the Restoration, but mural painters contributed to this by offering the opportunity of transformation and hope, combining Antique themes with contemporary issues. The work of artisans was similarly pivotal to this relationship, with craft sitting at the boundary of art (the histories) and architecture (the physical boundaries), an intercessory link between time and space. This literal crafting of identities within mural painting restates an argument made throughout this volume, that craft was equally as important as the other visual media, of architecture and paint, in terms of bestowing meaning on the elite house.

Conclusions

Mural painting placed the individual within a wider conceptual exploration of the impetuses behind art and architectural projects. It is as much the processes of building, crafting and the crafted object and their allegorical importance to contemporary life – historical, political, social – that is their real subject. Whereas the work of mural painters does not fit comfortably into either category of craft or architecture, they can illuminate the space between them. Calling them murals, rather than decorative painting, can help us get a more accurate sense of their original functions which was inherent to the physical boundaries of things. Most importantly within the purview of this volume, the refusal of mural painting to adhere to the distinct categories that grew up within the visual arts over the eighteenth century, shines a light on the blurred boundaries between all categories of visual-arts media in the long seventeenth, which included equal importance being placed on painted walls and ceilings, craft and architecture. It is not only mural painting that has been mislabelled and misunderstood, due to the subsequent hierarchies and historiographies of the genres, but the integral relationship of all media in the British Baroque, and their refusal to elevate the individual genius, the individual patron, the symbol or what Adamson would term the 'unitary sign'.[50] Mural paintings brought together in one allegorical locus painted architecture, painted craft and craft as allegory, providing a place to explore the transition of the real to the fantastical through narrative and *ekphrasis*. Here ideas of material metamorphosis, of *poesis* and the creative impulse, and of *techne*, could be explored and brought to life. In this sense, painted interiors take us beyond iconography to experience.

Notes

1   On the variety of ways of viewing in the historic house, see Dimmock, Hadfield and Healy, *Intellectual Culture*; Barber, *British Baroque*.
2   On mural painting in the British Baroque, see Hamlett, *Mural Painting in Britain*; and Strunck, *Britain and the Continent*.
3   A useful recent summary of the building works and murals is provided by Thurley, 'The Baroque castle, 1660–1685', 216–39.
4   See Hamlett, *Mural Painting in Britain*, 60–83.
5   See Peterson, *Making Spaces*, 63.
6   On woodcarving, see De Wit, *Grinling Gibbons*.
7   On the staircase, see Peterson, 'A new golden age'.
8   Croft-Murray, *Decorative Painting*, vol. 1, 237.
9   The Chatsworth chapel is explored in Ricketts, *English Country House*, 191–5.
10 Fiennes, *Through England on a Side Saddle*.
11 Gardner, *English Ironwork*, 104.
12 Brett, 'The apotheosis of Queen Anne', 25–6.
13 Eric Till, 'Verrio's decade at Burghley'.
14 For dates and documentary sources on Laguerre's work at Petworth, see Hamlett, 'Pandora at Petworth House', 950.
15 West Sussex Records Office, Petworth House Archive (PHA) 6293, 'Prices of work [joinery] for his Grace the Duke of Somerset', John Simmons, 1722. I am grateful to Melanie Hayes for highlighting this source.
16 British Museum, 1971, 0724.3, Louis Laguerre, *Design for the decoration of the staircase at Petworth*.

17 Hamlett, 'Pandora at Petworth House'.
18 Hamlett, 'Painted interiors', in Barber, *British Baroque*.
19 See, for example, Benjamin, *The Origin of German Tragic Drama*, 175–7.
20 This is discussed at length in Adamson, 'Craft and the allegorical impulse'.
21 Hamlett, *Mural Painting in Britain*, 17–19.
22 Hamlett, 'Pandora at Petworth House', 951.
23 See Hamlett, 'Pandora at Petworth House', 952–4 for discussion of this depiction of female virtue and the Duchess's potential involvement in commissioning the murals in the Great Staircase at Petworth.
24 See Hamlett, 'Pandora at Petworth House', 952; Hamlet, 'Rupture through realism', 195–216.
25 Homer, *Odyssey* 8, 329–32 (after the 1946 translation by E. V. Rieu in the *Penguin Classics* series), quoted in Enenkel and de Jong, *Re-inventing Ovid's Metamorphoses*, 124, n.19.
26 Hamlett, *Mural Painting in Britain*, 98.
27 There are two preparatory drawings at the Tate, for the altar wall of the chapel, T08522 and T08521, and neither includes this compositional element.
28 As communicated to me in situ by Dr Amy Lim.
29 On Powis, see Hamlett, *Mural Painting in Britain*, 51–6, 84–8.
30 See Horace, *Ars Poetica*, lines 394–6, in Horace, *Satires, Epistles*, 483. On Amphion and architectural metaphor in the seventeenth century, see Van Eck, 'Figuring the sublime in English church architecture', 233–5.
31 Dundas, 'A pattern of the mind', 22–47.
32 Adamson, 'The real in the Rococo', in Hills, *Rethinking the Baroque*, 143–57.
33 On *techne*, see Shiner, *Invention of Art*, 19–21.
34 On Wilton, see Hamlett, *Mural Painting in Britain*, 20–34.
35 As explored in Higgott and Grimstone, 'Drawings by Edward Pearce senior'.
36 On Castle Howard, see Hamlett, *Mural Painting in Britain*, 91–102, and Geraghty, 'Castle Howard'.
37 Geraghty, 'Castle Howard'.
38 The dome interior was repainted according to the original composition by Scott Medd in the 1960s, following the fire of 1940.
39 Casey, *Making Magnificence,* 182–3.
40 Ricketts, *English Country House*, 191–5.
41 Hamlett, *Mural Painting in Britain*, 92–8.
42 All the paintings in this series are now at Narford Hall. Knox, 'Antonio Pellegrini and Marco Ricci'.
43 For example, by John Gay and Henry Power.
44 Geraghty, 'Castle Howard'.
45 Marandet, 'Louis Chéron', 5.
46 Murdoch, *Boughton House*, 71.
47 On creativity and copying in seventeenth-century England, see Herissone and Howard, *Concepts of Creativity*; on France, see Duro, 'Imitation and authority'.
48 Kristeller, 'The modern system of the arts', especially 196–204.
49 Hamlett, *Mural Painting in Britain*, 7–8.
50 Adamson, 'Craft and the allegorical impulse', 94–5.

References

Adamson, Glenn. 'Craft and the allegorical impulse'. In *Material Perceptions*, edited by Knut Astrup Bull and Andrè Gali, 93–114. Stuttgart: Arnoldsche, 2018.
Barber, Tabitha, ed. *British Baroque: Power and illusion*. London: Tate, 2020.
Benjamin, Walter. *The Origin of German Tragic Drama*, translated by John Osborne. New York: Verso, 1998.
Brett, Cécile. 'The apotheosis of Queen Anne', *British Art Journal*, 20:3 (Winter 2020): 22–7.
Casey, Christine. *Making Magnificence: Architects, stuccatori and the eighteenth-century interior*. New Haven, CT and London: Yale University Press, 2017.

Croft-Murray, Edward. *Decorative Painting in England 1537–1837*. 2 vols. London: Country Life, 1960–2.

De Wit, Ada. *Grinling Gibbons and His Contemporaries (1650–1700): The golden age of woodcarving in the Netherlands and Britain*. Turnhout: Brepols, 2022.

Dimmock, Matthew. *The Intellectual Culture of the English Country House, 1500–1700*, edited by Andrew Hadfield and Margaret Healy. Manchester: Manchester University Press, 2018.

Dundas, Judith. 'A pattern of the mind: The country house poem revisited', *Connotations*, 8:1 (1998–9): 22–47.

Duro, Paul. 'Imitation and authority: The creation of the academic canon in French art, 1648–1870'. In *Partisan Canons*, edited by Anna Brzyski, 95–113. Durham, NC: Duke University Press, 2007.

Enenkel, Karl A. E. and Jan L. de Jong, eds. *Re-inventing Ovid's Metamorphoses: Pictorial and literary transformations in various media, 1400–1800*. Leiden: Brill, 2021.

Fiennes, Celia. *Through England on a Side Saddle in the Time of William and Mary: Being the diary of Celia Fiennes*, edited by Emily Wingfield Griffiths. London: The Leadenhall Press, 1888.

Gardner, J. Starkie. *English Ironwork of the XVIIth and XVIIIth Centuries: An historical and analytical account of the development of exterior smithcraft*. London: B. T. Batsford, 1911.

Geraghty, Anthony. 'Castle Howard: The architecture of the interior', *Art and the Country House*. Accessed 17 January 2024. https://doi.org/10.17658/ACH/CHE523.

Hamlett, Lydia. 'Pandora at Petworth House: New light on the work and patronage of Louis Laguerre', *The Burlington Magazine*, 158:1365 (December 2016): 950–5.

Hamlett, Lydia. 'Rupture through realism: Sarah Churchill and Louis Laguerre's murals at Marlborough House'. In *Court, Country, City: British art and architecture, 1660–1735*, edited by M. Hallett, N. Llewellyn and M. Myrone, 195–216. New Haven, CT and London: Yale University Press, 2016.

Hamlett, Lydia. *Mural Painting in Britain 1630–1730: Experiencing histories*. 2nd edition. New York and Oxford: Routledge, 2022.

Herissone, Rebecca and Alan Howard, eds. *Concepts of Creativity in Seventeenth-Century England*. New York and Martlesham: Boydell & Brewer, 2013.

Higgott, Gordon and A. V. Grimstone. 'Drawings by Edward Pearce senior (fl. c. 1630–c.1658): Painter, decorator and interior designer', *The Volume of the Walpole Society*, 82 (2020): 1–114.

Hills, Helen, ed. *Rethinking the Baroque*. London and New York: Routledge, 2011.

Horace. *Satires. Epistles. The Art of Poetry*, translated by H. Rushton Fairclough. Loeb Classical Library 194. Cambridge, MA: Harvard University Press, 1926.

Knox, George. 'Antonio Pellegrini and Marco Ricci at Burlington House and Narford Hall', *The Burlington Magazine*, 130:1028 (November 1988): 846–53.

Kristeller, Paul Oskar. 'The modern system of the arts'. In *Renaissance Thought and the Arts*, 163–227. Princeton, NJ: Princeton University Press, 1980.

Marandet, François. 'Louis Chéron (1660–1725) at Boughton House: New reflections on the genesis and the interpretation of the murals of "Mister Charron"', translated by Cecile Brett, *British Art Journal*, 18:1 (December 2018): 48–56.

Murdoch, Tessa. *Boughton House: The English Versailles*. London: Faber and Faber, 1992.

Peterson, Laurel O. 'Making spaces: Art and politics in the Whig country house interior, 1688–1745'. PhD thesis: Yale University, 2018.

Peterson, Laurel O. 'A new golden age: Politics and mural painting at Chatsworth', *Journal 18*, 9 (Spring 2020). Accessed 17 January 2024. https://www.journal18.org/4775.

Ricketts, Annabel. *The English Country House Chapel: Building a Protestant tradition*. Reading: Spire Books, 2007.

Shiner, Larry. *The Invention of Art*. Chicago: University of Chicago Press, 2001.

Strunck, Christina. *Britain and the Continent 1660–1727*. Berlin: De Gruyter, 2021.

Thurley, Simon. 'The Baroque castle, 1660–1685'. In *Windsor Castle: A thousand years of a royal palace*, edited by Steven Brindle, 216–39. London: Royal Collection Trust, 2018.

Till, Eric. 'Verrio's decade at Burghley, 1686–1697: An account of his decorative paintings derived from the Exeter MSS'. Unpublished notes.

Van Eck, Caroline. 'Figuring the sublime in English church architecture 1640–1730'. In *Translations of the Sublime: The early modern reception and dissemination of Longinus' Peri Hupsous in rhetoric, the visual arts, architecture and the theatre*, edited by Caroline van Eck, 221–45. Leiden: Brill, 2012.

10

Material, curiosity and performance: the reception of workmanship in early modern Britain and Ireland

Andrew Tierney

Until recently the question of what was seen, registered and recorded by visitors to buildings, has been more the purview of literary and social historians than architectural historians. While the idea that language, narrative, space and materiality are mutually dependent is commonplace within literary studies, the implications of that are little understood for formalist appraisals of early modern architecture. That the eighteenth century was a transformative period in visualising the built environment is clear from the work of Cynthia Wall and others, albeit largely understood through the lens of the novel, with its attendant interest in concepts of home and societal articulations of public and private space.[1] How the creative agency of architects and artisans (and the technical literature they produced) may have contributed to such shifts is less well understood.[2] Stead and Freeman, in their 2013 edited volume on architectural reception, ask the critical question: 'By whom is architecture received, and when? Are other architects the principal, intended addressees and, if so, what agency is granted to the much larger audience, public, and community to actively receive and interpret architectural ideas and buildings?'[3] These same questions might be asked of workmanship, though inevitably entangled, and sometimes in contest, with the wider reception of architecture. The following analysis of the reception of workmanship rests on a range of texts from the sixteenth century to the late eighteenth century, from topographical writing, to diary entries and technical treatises.

While it is unwise to define too narrowly the genres operating within early modern literature, particularly where such texts were not intended for publication, there is nevertheless a fair degree of intertextuality, whereby writers echo one another, or simply copy ideas and modes of expression. The dominance of voices in print media could reverberate over centuries. Caroline Lybbe Powys, writing in 1757, for example, cites William Camden's *Britannia* (first published in 1586) as her reason for wanting to see inside the church at Axminster.[4] She may just as easily have cited John Leland, born almost fifty years earlier, whom Camden himself drew upon. The work of both writers continued to be reprinted throughout the eighteenth century and cited in the itineraries of later writers and, as will be seen below, had a cultural perspective on materials and workmanship that reflected the values of their own times.[5] Deference to authoritative voices was perhaps inevitable where arcane knowledge or opaque manual skill was under review. Even in the absence of published authorities, received opinion – presumably transmitted by word of mouth and private correspondence – might be relied upon.

Sumptuous materials

David Pye has commented that it is not in the specification of the designer that we find the use of 'good materials', but in the ability of the craftsman to work it into something of quality.[6] Roger North had said something similar in his seventeenth-century tract on building, remarking that 'The very materialls … are the product of men's labour'.[7] Recent research in this area has shown that materials, and a practical experience of their qualities,[8] were central to medieval and early modern understandings and appraisals of buildings; so in seeking early responses to workmanship, we must look outside writing that is explicitly architectural in a Renaissance sense. A good place to start is John Leland's itinerary of the 1530s, which was the first text to take stock of England's major buildings. Published in six volumes by Oxford antiquary Thomas Hearne in 1710–12 (and subsequent editions thereafter), and thus well-positioned to influence eighteenth-century conceptions of national identity, it evoked the appearance of buildings largely through materials, principally stone, brick and timber, or a combination of these. Implicit here is an acknowledgement of both labour and craft. Leland frequently identified quarries, sometimes even quarry beds, occasionally assessing a stone's hardness, its colour and whether it was hewn, or 'well-squared', and its variegated character.[9] The parish church at Scrooby in Nottinghamshire, for example, he described as 'not bigge, but very well buildid *ex lapide polite quadrato*' – from a polished square stone – a phrase also used to describe a 'praty house' in the suburbs of Northampton; or the timber hall of the manor house of the Bishop of York, which he noted has a brick front and 'wich *ascenditur per gradus lapideos'* – ascended by stone steps.[10] Or the altar stone in the collegiate parish church of Darlington in Yorkshire, 'an exceeding long and fair altare stone *de vario marmore, hoc est, nigro albis maculis distincto'* – of variegated marble, that is, black distinguished by white spots.[11] At Coventry he appraised the 'grite and colour' of the stone 'a darkeshe depe redde, as it were ferragineus colour'.[12] At Nottingham Castle, he singled out 'a right sumptuous pece of stone work' in one of the towers, and in the town of Wells commended the market cross with the same phrase.[13] In this case, the sumptuousness resides somewhere between the material and the labour employed to shape it. Sumptuary laws for apparel regulated the types, qualities and colours of materials that could be worn by different classes,[14] and 'marble' can be found among the colours listed for cloth during the Tudor period.[15]

This medieval eye for materials lingers long into the seventeenth century. Anne Hultzsch has commented on the limited vocabulary of seventeenth-century English travel writers, in describing towns and cities. John Bargrave's account of Siena Cathedral, she notes, pays most attention to the building's surfaces. While this may, as Hultzsch argues, have served 'to fix the objects of interest thus ordering and interpreting them', it also reflects the lack of any other verbal equipment for descriptive analysis.[16] Questions of style and composition were not yet subjects of scrutiny, so writers focused on size, material and colour. Even John Evelyn's eye, one of the best travelled and most architecturally informed of the century, was constantly drawn to that which he found 'sumptuous' and the result of 'exquisite' or 'incomparable' workmanship. In his account of his European tour of the 1640s he rarely missed an opportunity to appraise surfaces and textures.[17] The font and pulpit of the duomo in Pisa were, he remarked, of 'inestimable value' for 'the preciousness of the materials' but he had nothing to say about their form.[18] He commented on the use of coloured marble at St Peter's, Rome, St Mark's in Venice, and the duomo at Siena 'showing so beautiful after a shower has fallen',[19] and most of all at Florence. When listing the most famous Florentine masters of art, he led with craftsmen who specialised in *pietra-commessa* (Florentine mosaic) or *pietre dure* (hard stones) from one of whom he commissioned a cabinet with some nineteen different stones, now in the Victoria and Albert Museum in London. The finest sculptor in the city he reckoned to be a 'Vincentio Brocchi', whom he praised principally for his ability to make plaster and pasteboard resemble copper. His description of the famous

Tribuna of the Uffizi leads, not with an account of its paintings, but of its materials – pearl, ebony, lapis lazuli and jasper.[20] The choir of the Jesuit church in Antwerp, which he visited in 1641, was 'a glorious piece of architecture', due to its inlaid and polished marbles, gemstones, carvings and paintings.[21] In his architectural tract of 1664, he lavished praise on the 30 separate stones and minerals in the Borghese Chapel in Santa Maria Maggiore, in Rome (Fig. 10.1).[22] Fascinated by the material

Figure 10.1: Altar of Borghese Chapel.
Photograph by Carlo Raso. Flickr. Public Domain.

qualities of porphyry, in Florence he noted a statue: 'the first which had been carved out of that hard material, and brought to perfection, after the art had been utterly lost; they say this was done by hardening the tools in the juice of certain herbs'.[23] Only at the Louvre does this priority of material and craft over design falter: 'We went through the long gallery, paved with white and black marble, richly fretted and painted à fresco. The front looking to the river, though of rare work for the carving, yet wants of that magnificence which a plainer and truer design would have contributed to it'.[24] What a 'truer design' might have comprised of, he did not specify.

Porphyry was of particular interest to seventeenth-century writers.[25] So large and hard were the columns of porphyry at Palmyra that William Halifax, who visited the site in the 1690s, assumed it was some kind of artificial stone, writing of their 'mixture and composition', 'the Art of making which, I think is quite lost'.[26] This idea was quickly rejected by Edmund Halley, who cited Pliny's references to the great size of Porphyry blocks raised in Egyptian quarries, marvelling at the distance across land that they must have travelled.[27] Likewise, Evelyn had earlier written of 'the pillars' at Salisbury Cathedral, 'reputed to be cast', which he argued 'are of stone manifestly cut out of the quarry'.[28] William Camden had proposed the same idea to explain the massive stones at Stonehenge, basing his theory on Pliny's description of Roman concrete, in his *Naturalis Historia*, an idea rejected by Joshua Childrey, in 1662, in favour of natural stone.[29]

More than mere economy, artisans' ability to imitate such stones in other materials invited response merely by challenge of identification from the learned eye. What Evelyn called the 'agreeable cheat' of quadratura painting, depended on the painter's mastery in rendering stone.[30] In Wren's St Mary-le-Bow, Edward Hatton, in his proto-Pevsnerian *New View of London* of 1708, identified '2 spacious beautiful Columns, painted in imitation of *Lapis Lazuli*; and their Entablature ... painted like Prophiry', a practice of imitating stone that first appeared in the late sixteenth century but which would go into decline with the rise of Palladianism.[31] Stone itself might be transformed into another kind of stone. Evelyn recorded Christopher Wren presenting him with 'a piece of white marble, which he had stained with a lively red, very deep, as beautiful as if it had been natural'.[32]

The interest in richly coloured stones lingered into the following century. Jocelyn Anderson recently commented on the enduring appeal of precious stones in English country-house collections during the eighteenth century, remarking that 'at Stourhead, a single *pietre dure* cabinet dominated accounts of the interior of the house'.[33] But in architecture itself, as the Baroque style gave way to the Palladian, an excessive use of rich materials began to attract negative attention. Cannons, built by the Duke of Chandos in the early 1700s, became a byword for poor taste, due to the immense amounts of marble and mahogany employed, in an effort to impress. By the 1740s, Horace Walpole could dismiss it as 'the great standard of bad taste'.[34] A similar sentiment led him to condemn Vanbrugh, whom he said (paraphrasing Pope) 'composed heaps of littleness' and 'hollowed quarries rather than ... built houses.'[35]

Fragmented appraisals

Embedded in early modern aesthetic evaluation is some sense of the object as one that is made or fabricated by labour. Leland does not refer to 'a building' or 'architecture', but generally to 'a piece of work', most often in reference to a part of a building. The lack of a single contractor and the common method of paying for buildings through piecework did not support architectural appraisal of a whole building unless the building was itself conceived metaphorically as a 'piece of work'. St Mary's Church, Lichfield, for example, he described as 'a right bewtyfull pece of worke'.[36] This falls in with the more fragmented understanding of buildings, as entities that are not necessarily yet the sum of their parts. Labour itself then, divided into a series of parts under the control of master craftsmen (who may themselves pay their workers by the day), became a key component of qualitative aesthetic evaluation in the late medieval period.[37] Hints of this can be seen in other terms of appraisal. One of Leland's is 'praty'. The word evolved its modern aesthetic sense of 'pretty' from its older meaning of 'cunning, crafty', which came to mean 'clever, skilful, able', and may explain its common applicability to buildings during the Tudor period (though it had by then also become more widely applied).[38] By the eighteenth century the term had become debased. John Scattergood, in commenting on the nobility of Chatsworth in the 1720s, stated: 'I saw nothing mean about the house; or that would admit of so low an epithete as pretty'.[39]

John Shute, in his rather garbled reading of Vitruvius, valued the orders not so much for their intrinsic form but rather as a framework for the assemblage of materials and embellishments. He praised the 'order ... calleth picnostylos', which piller is sembled or to be compared unto Composita having in it the full beawtie of al the forsaid measures and garnishments, for al excellent artificers, beawtifully to set furth whether it be in golde or silver or other riche stone or fine woodes in marketrey or imbosinge or carving as shalbe thought pleasant & necessary for noble prices [princes?] or for divers other estates lovers of excellency or coninge.[40]

This fits well with his understanding of columns as 'garnish' for princely palaces, a term he uses repeatedly, and captures his sense of architecture as essentially a form of artisanal enrichment. Shute likewise uses the term 'sumptuous' to describe what he imagined was the appearance of the earliest works of antiquity, and thus intricate workmanship was implicit in the Tudor understanding of architecture.

Leland had paid much less attention to interior enrichments, particularly of churches, possibly because their 'cult value', to use Walter Benjamin's phrase,[41] was still dominant. Such value registers clearly in writings of the Catholic historian Tadhg O'Cianán, from Fermanagh, who visited churches across Europe in the years following the Flight of the Earls in 1607, itemising relics and recounting their associated miracles.[42] This stands in contrast to the anatomisation and dissection of church interiors by seventeenth-century English Protestant antiquaries, a century after the Reformation, when the relative merit of the workmanship was starting to yield to comparative analysis, and their 'exhibition value', again to use Benjamin's phrase, was supplanting their ritualistic purpose. However, it is worth noting that the tension between cult and exhibition value remained strong enough for Horace Walpole's *Aedes Walpolianae*, cataloguing the Old Master collection at Houghton, to conclude with a sermon attacking the superstitious intentions of Romish art, but which notably declared the act of painting itself 'innocent'. 'No Art, no Science can be criminal; 'tis the Misapplication that must constitute the Sin'.[43] In this context, discourses on 'workmanship' in the seventeenth and eighteenth centuries were largely confined to religious texts, promoting the generative powers of God, and man as his greatest work. Explanations for human creativity deferred to biblical passages concerning the building of Solomon's temple, such as that given from the pulpit of Mary-le-Bow, as part of the Boyle lectures in the period 1711–12, by theologian and Royal Society member, Rev. William Derham:

But not only Skill in superior Arts and Sciences, but even in the more inferiour mechanick Arts, is called by the same Names, and ascrib'd unto GOD: Thus for the Workmanship of the Tabernacle, Exod. 31. 2. to 6. v. 'See, I have called by Name Bezaleel. And I have filled him with the Spirit of God, in Wisdom, and in Understanding, and in knowledge, and in all Manner of Workmanship. To devise cunning Works, to work in Gold, Silver, and Brass; and in cutting of Stones, to set them, and in carving of Timber, to work in all Manner of Workmanship.[44]

This argument also formed a refutation of atheism at St Mary-le-Bow, that the world is 'the Product and Workmanship, not of blind Mechanism or blinder Chance; but of an Intelligent and Benign Agent'.[45] In such an account, design and workmanship are closely aligned phenomena, both requiring skill and wisdom.

The tension between the sacred and the secular was nowhere more hotly contested than in Ireland. As early as 1654, Sir James Ware, in his *De Hibernia et Antiquitatibus eius Disquisitiones*, written immediately after Cromwell's harrowing excursions across the country, singled out specific examples of high-quality workmanship in medieval churches, such as the construction and glazing of the east window in St Canice's Cathedral, Kilkenny, which he dated from archival sources to the fourteenth century, and which he remarked 'was of such excellent work, that it exceeded all other in Ireland'.[46] Likewise the east window of the thirteenth-century chapel of the Friars Minor, in Dundalk, which he said was 'for the Excellency of the Work … much admired in Ireland'.[47]

A much more microscopic lens was thrust upon late medieval workmanship two years later by William Dugdale in *The Antiquities of Warwickshire* (1656), which used archival research to find the names of the craftsmen who built the late medieval Beauchamp Chapel in the Collegiate Church of St Mary, in Warwick (Fig. 10.2). He published the contract for the work between the patron and craftsmen, listing the names of marbler, iron founder, coppersmith, goldsmith, glazier, painter and carpenter. This source material, replete with costs, stressed the monetary value of good workmanship and materials. The marbler, John Bourde, of Corfe Castle in Dorset, was to use 'good and fine Marble, as well coloured as may be had in England', while the glazier was to source his glass on the continent.[48] Dugdale, to give his readers a better sense of its value, translated the costs of the chapel into the relative costs of oxen between the fifteenth century and his own time. While Rosemary Sweet's contention that 'prior to Gough, almost all scholarly interest in

Figure 10.2: The Beauchamp Chapel at the Collegiate Church of St Mary, Warwick.

Photograph by Vauxford. CC BY-NC 4.0.

tombs had focused upon the individuals being commemorated rather than the tombs themselves as works of monumental art' is broadly true, Dugdale's scrutiny of makers' names and associated costs shows an emergent scholarly interest in both art and workmanship as early as the mid seventeenth century.[49]

It is hard not to see in this enthusiasm for enriched late medieval surfaces some parallel in the mid- to late-seventeenth century taste for complex schemes of enrichment in a Baroque idiom, such as the staircases associated with Edward Pearce and his circle. Forde Abbey, remodelled in the 1650s, is an example of the fluid movement between late medieval tracery and Baroque open-work carving. Celia Fiennes, one of the most celebrated witnesses to late seventeenth-century architecture, who declared the late-medieval cross at Coventry to be the finest building in England (Fig. 10.3), glided between an appreciation of the workmanship of both periods without much comment as to shifts in style, or in some cases even technique.[50] In every instance she encountered elaborately wrought ironwork in the manner of Jean Tijou, at Burghley, Newby Hall, Windsor and Hampton Court, she described it as 'carved', rather than wrought, perhaps a natural response for a person brought up in an age of high-quality woodwork and learned treatises on gardens

MATERIAL, CURIOSITY AND PERFORMANCE   297

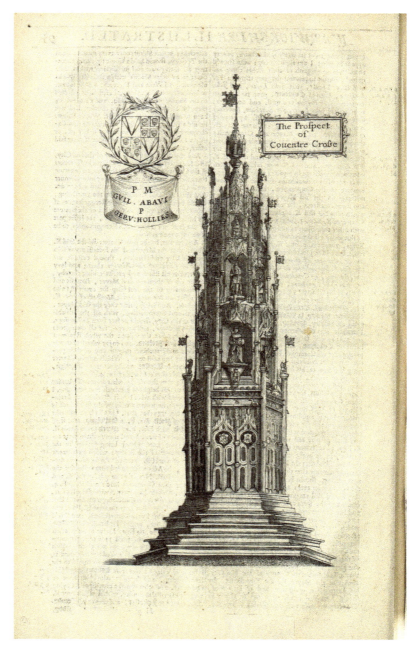

Figure 10.3: The late medieval cross at Coventry, from William Dugdale's *The Antiquities of Warwickshire Illustrated*. London: Printed by Thomas Warren, 1656.

Getty Research Institute. Internet Archive.

and forestry. She was able to view interiors with an almost taxonomic eye as to the use of timber, most famously in her oft-cited description of Chippenham Park in Cambridgeshire, built in 1669 and remodelled in the 1690s:[51] 'the hall ... very noble ... wanscoated with Wallnut tree the panels and rims round with Mulbery tree that is a lemon coullour and the moldings beyond it round ... of a sweete outlandish wood not much differing from Cedar but of a finer graine, the chaires ... all the same'.[52] John Evelyn, perhaps the most learned exponent of woodworking of that period, preferred the wainscot in unpainted Spanish oak to the fir wainscot that had been painted at the new seat of the Earl of Arlington, and commented on the rich pargeting of wainscot in cedar, yew and cypress at the new palace of the Duke of Norfolk, at Weybridge.[53] Evelyn's appreciation of timber, of course, was extensive enough for him to produce *Sylva* in 1664, in which he discoursed on the superiority of different kinds of timber for various artisanal purposes. He regarded English oak as 'infinitely preferrable to the French', for its spring and toughness, but thought French joiners and cabinet makers made much better use of walnut for 'the best grain'd and colour'd' wainscotting and inlay. The lightest sands, he thought, produced the most fine-grained oak, which is 'of all other the most useful to the Joyner'.[54]

It is worth considering the degree to which Evelyn's presentation of the practical use of timber is framed by a classical epistemology that includes writers such as Pliny the Elder, Varro, and Columella. In this context, craftsmanship was not merely the means of making but a means of harnessing the medium to the classical subject it was normally called upon to bear. The tacit knowledge of the craftsman is thus mediated through the lens of antiquity, and a model of imperial patronage of mechanical arts that was derived from the Augustan age.[55] Evelyn acknowledged that much had already been achieved by 'the late reformation and improvement' in various trades, which he reckoned made English joiners the best to be found anywhere. It is perhaps unsurprising then that Evelyn made the plea that workmen (including everyone from quarrymen to sculptors) be admitted to university 'and not thrust out as purely Mechanical, inter opifices, a conversation hitherto only admitted them' and suggested that there should be 'Lectures and Schools endow'd and furnish'd with Books, Instruments, Plots, Types and Modells'.[56] Reviewing a range of his writings, Paddy Bullard has argued for Evelyn as 'one of the earliest British writers to envision a new role for technical and manual expertise in the intellectual lives of highly educated members of the governing classes'.[57] Certainly some artisans did succeed in breaking through established boundaries between gentility and trade.

The joiner William Cleere, who constructed the great model of St Paul's, in 1676 produced a design for Stowe House, for Sir Richard Temple. In the contract for the latter, he was referred to as both 'surveyor' and 'gent', though he continued to act solely as joiner on other projects after this.[58] The master joiner Charles Hopson, who worked on St Paul's and other London churches for Christopher Wren, became Sheriff of London and was knighted.[59] Nevertheless, Evelyn distinguished what he ironically referred to as 'Gentlemen-Mechanicks' at home from those who 'have meritoriously attained to the Titles of Military Dignity' on the continent, with whom he identified several Renaissance and Baroque masters.[60]

Curiosity

If there was an emerging consensus around the value of the Gothic workmanship of the past, such consensus also rapidly formed around newer work. In 1690 William Winde, architect of a new wing at Combe Abbey, praised plasterer Edward Goudge as 'now looked on as the beste master in England in his profession', citing his work on three previous projects as evidence.[61] At more famous buildings, such as Windsor, Celia Fiennes was able to cite received opinion on the quality of Grinling Gibbons's carvings and Antonio Verrio's paintings, where elsewhere she relied on her own judgement. Verrio's frescos in St George's Hall, Windsor, she wrote, were 'the Standard for Curiosity in all places you see painting'.[62] 'Curious', in its various iterations, was the term most employed to describe good craftsmanship either side of 1700. As a term with multifaceted meanings in the early modern period it has received increasing amounts of attention from scholars, but its particular association with workmanship requires further elaboration.[63] This use is attested in English as early as the fourteenth century, meaning 'Made with care or art; skilfully, elaborately or beautifully wrought', a meaning now obsolete.[64] It is in a similar sense that it appears in the early sixteenth-century indenture for the glazing for King's College Chapel, Cambridge, in which the workmen were charged with setting up the glass in a manner that was workmanly, substantial, curious, and sufficient.[65] Stow, in his survey of London, used the term some 15 times, as an adverb, entirely in the sense of workmanship. Celia Fiennes employed it some 64 times in her diary, most often to describe intricate carving.

Some crafts were understood to have greater degrees of 'curiosity' than others. Joseph Moxon, writing in 1677, some twelve years before

Jean Tijou's elaborate ironwork productions, defended his decision not to introduce his *Mechanick Exercises* with 'a more curious, and less Vulgar Art, than that of Smithing' on the grounds that all the other trades depended on it.[66] Joiners, he noted, 'work more curiously, and observe the Rules more exactly than Carpenters need do'.[67] The source of curiosity was the subtle work of the hand and he counted it 'a piece of good Workmanship in a *Joyner*, to have the Craft of bearing his Hand so curiously even, the whole length of a long Board; and yet it is but a sleight to those, Practice hath inur'ed the Hand to'.[68] Batty Langley, in his *A Sure Guide to Builders* of 1729, used the term more expansively, describing his designs for doors, windows, chimneypieces and ceilings as 'useful and curious'.[69] His curious designs were also, we are told, 'curiously selected', 'curiously engraven', and 'well worth the notice of the most Curious'.[70]

During the mid-to-late eighteenth century 'curious' was used less commonly to describe workmanship. Walter Harris's account of public buildings in Dublin, published in 1766, used the term only for older work at the chapel and hall of the Royal Hospital at Kilmainham, which were 'curiously decorated', the 'stucco and carving of the chapel … masterly'.[71] By the mid-century, references to 'curious workmanship' had become increasingly accompanied by, and sometimes qualified by, 'taste', as in the descriptions of new discoveries at Herculaneum in 1755, which complimented both the architecture and the furnishings within a newly discovered house as being of 'curious workmanship' and 'in a most elegant taste'.[72] Elizabeth Berkeley, wife of the 4th Duke of Beaufort, in those extracts from her *Observations on Places* (1750–62) published by John Harris, does not use the term at all, describing the elaborately carved staircase at Sudbury as merely 'handsome', an adjective she uses six times in a quite generic way, for everything from doorcases to whole rooms.[73] Isaac Ware in his *Complete Body of Architecture* of 1756 used 'curious' to describe the discerning observer rather than the skill of the artisan, while Horace Walpole, in his letters, largely uses it in its modern sense, to mean things that are rare, strange or interesting, such as old books and medals.

The 1759 *New Oxford Guide*, in discussing Blenheim, wished for 'uniformity of design, rather than multiplicity of ornament', reflecting a pivot away from the particular elements of a building in favour of a holistic appraisal.[74] In the same volume's commentary on Ditchley Park, references to 'curious workmanship' are reserved for furnishings, while the hall is described as 'finely proportioned, and elegantly decorated', privileging the conception and design over the challenge of execution.[75] However, Philip Luckombe's *Beauties of England*, of 1757, aimed at a popular audience, and reissued in several editions in the following decades up to the 1790s, is full of references to 'curious workmanship', with comparatively few references to 'taste'. By the time of Brewer's *Beauties of England and Wales*, of 1818, this association with workmanship had been eradicated, and Walpole's intellectual use of the term predominates.

The shift away from the 'curiosity' of workmanship towards a more abstract appraisal of design is in evidence in the stylistic shift towards Neoclassicism. Further research will be required to understand the socio-cultural reasons for this shift, but it seems likely that it follows the rising authority of the architect and diminishment of artisan autonomy in the second half of the eighteenth century. Robert Wood, in his 1753 account of the antiquities at Palmyra, made no use of the term, despite the extent of richly carved ornament.[76] The coffering and modillions of Plate VII he described as 'finished in the highest manner', while the workmanship of a door at Baalbek (1757) was 'finished with great delicacy', two of the few direct appraisals of carved ornament in these volumes.[77] In contrast, William Halifax's 1695 description of Palmyra had been effusive about 'the exquisiteness of the workmanship', praising 'the most curious and exquisite Carvings in Stone which perhaps the World could ever boast of'.[78] The new interest in 'finish' possibly migrated to architecture from critical treatises on painting where the treatment of the planar surface was an obvious concern. A late eighteenth-century description of Blenheim praised the 'highly finished' marble columns of the Library and Rysbrack's 'highly finished' statue of Queen Anne, while the Saloon, with its marble wainscotting, was 'a highly finished room'. The great columns in the hall were described as 'in elegance and dimensions almost unrivalled', but nothing is said of the richly carved capitals by Grinling Gibbons.[79] The focus on 'finish' appears closely related to Edmund Burke's idea of elegance. In 1757, the same year Wood published his volume on Baalbek, Burke had attempted to define 'elegant' as 'any body ... composed of parts smooth and polished ... affecting some regular shape', which he thought particularly apt for buildings and furniture, as they 'imitate no determinate object in nature'.[80] The deeply undercut carving at Palmyra and Baalbek is reduced to refined planar surface in the orthographic drawings of Wood's tidy volumes (Fig. 10.4). Although elegance was an occasional term of appreciation by the late seventeenth century – usually in the form 'elegancy' – by the time of Thomas Pennant's travel writing in the 1760s–90s, terms such as 'elegant', 'beautiful' and 'handsome' dominate descriptions of architecture, and are applied to Gothic and modern buildings alike.[81]

Figure 10.4: Plate VII from Robert Wood et al., *The Ruins of Palmyra, Otherwise Tedmor, in the Desart.* London: Robert Wood, 1753.

Courtesy of Professor Lynda Mulvin.

So too workmanship, which becomes 'beautiful workmanship' or 'elegant workmanship'. Fine chimneypieces are those that might be produced 'by the most elegant chisel'.[82] In his description of Lichfield Cathedral alone, Pennant uses some variation of 'elegant' eight times.

Such shifts in language did not necessarily imply a rejection of earlier modes of craftsmanship, but rather a reframing of them. Writing in the 1760s, Horace Walpole had a high appreciation of the work of Grinling Gibbons, at a time when elaborate carving was going out of fashion; his father's house at Houghton included several carvings by Gibbons, a portrait of the artist, and several works of art that had been in Gibbons's own collection.[83] However, it is notable that the terms of this appreciation – in volume 3 of his *Anecdotes of Painting in England* (1763) – are quite different to those used by Gibbons's contemporaries. While the naturalism of his work retained its value, Walpole reframes its formal characteristics to better reflect contemporary ideals. Firstly, the 'noble profusion' of this kind of carving by Gibbons and his contemporaries in 'picture-frames, chimney-pieces, and door-cases' is described as a result of a taste for collecting 'ornaments by the most eminent living masters'. This raises architectural carving into the same league as painting, alongside which it is invited to appear. It also foregrounds the eye of the collector as pre-eminent in its production. Taste itself is posited as a driving force. We are told that Charles II employed Gibbons 'on the ornaments of most taste in his palaces'.[84] This recalls William Aglionby, who in his *Painting Illustrated* (1685) had praised his patron's understanding of painting: 'in the knowledge of which, you show as much skill as the artists themselves do in execution'.[85] To some extent, Walpole used Gibbons's work as a counterpoint to Verrio, whose work, uncontrolled by cabinet or frame, he hated. At Petworth, which he called 'the most superb monument of his skill', he noted that Gibbons carved 'an antique vase with a baserelief, of the purest taste, and worth the Grecian age of Cameos'. His assistant, Seldon, he added, lost his life attempting to save this particular carving from a fire.

Perhaps most noteworthy in Walpole's account is his attempt to highlight the names and contributions of Gibbons's assistants, singling out Seldon at Petworth, Watson at Chatsworth, and Dievot of Brussels, and Laurens of Mechlin as his 'principle journeymen' – though he mistook much of Watson's work at Chatsworth for that of Gibbons.[86] Caroline Lybbe Powys, writing in 1757, also appreciated his work, visiting Trinity College Oxford 'on account of the peculiar elegance of its chapel', where there are 'many festoons so finely executed that 'tis unnecessary to inform any that has seen his performances that they were done by Grindeline [sic] Gibbons'. Perhaps most reflective of a distinctive encounter with workmanship in wood, she comments: 'the screen, rails and altar-piece is cedar inlaid (the fine scent of which on entering is very agreeable)'.[87] Gibbons's supposed work at Chatsworth also featured prominently in Thomas Martyn's *The English Connoisseur*, published in 1766, which otherwise (in terms of paintings) 'has very little in it that can attract the eye of the connoisseur'.[88]

The shift in the terms used to describe workmanship reflects a shift from an appraisal of process to an appraisal of effect. Something that is 'curiously carved' is not the same as 'elegantly carved'. In the latter, the phrasing does not reflect the method, but rather the outcome. The former contains some appreciation of the action of the hand. In tandem with this, the performative component of workmanship was something more often expressed in the early eighteenth century than later, as shall be seen in the next section.

On performance

For John Stow, whose *Survey of London* was published in 1603, the manual arts were purely an urban phenomenon, which nowhere else would be either 'maintained or amended'.[89] Nicholas Barbon, writing in 1678, expanded on this theme, describing how urban dwellers – in particular craftsmen – lived by their brains more than their bodies, for which work they were better paid. Upon this account they were better housed and warmer: 'By this means there [sic] Bodies are not so much exposed to the inconveniences of weather, for too much heat or cold, do either too much exhaust or chill the Protisick Spirit'.[90] This was why, he argued, wild animals procreated in the spring when the weather was more temperate. It speaks to the embodied part of workmanship, contained in the parallel use of the term 'performance' for execution. Even masonry might be described as 'performed', in the early eighteenth century, rather than simply executed, as Colen Campbell described the stonework of St Paul's, when commending the work of the Strongs: 'The whole Fabricke is performed in Stone, by those excellent and judicious Artists, Mr. Edward Strong, Senior and Junior, whose consummate Knowledge in their Profession, has greatly contributed to adorn the Kingdom'.[91]

Vanbrugh, in arguing for the retention of the Holbein Gate, described it as 'so well perform'd that although now above 200 Yrs Old, is as entire as the first day'.[92] Lawrence Braddon in 1721 described carvers as 'Men, whose good Works, necessarily require them to be, very Intense upon their Performances' – with the threat of the debtor's prison hanging over every stroke.[93] This is exactly what David Pye later defined as craftsmanship of risk, as opposed to the craftsmanship of certainty, and was so eloquently described by David Esterly in his memoir on carving in the manner of Grinling Gibbons.[94]

For Evelyn the purpose of the rich materials and workmanship of Paul V's chapel in Santa Maria Maggiore was to 'dazzle and confound the beholders'; the vault of the hall of Gregory XIII in the Vatican, likewise, 'exceeds description' in that 'it is almost impossible for the skillfullest eyes to discern whether it be the work of the pencil upon a flat, or of a tool cut deep in stone'.[95] In this sense, the knowledge and skill of the beholder is brought into play, and challenged. The costliness of material and workmanship is mirrored in the costliness of the leisure and learning required to appreciate it.[96] As the amateur musician might bring some technical knowledge to bear upon their appreciation of a great composer or performer, so too Evelyn brings a baseline of understanding to which the professional workman can perform. The amateur seventeenth-century virtuoso provided the discursive space for skill to flourish, and himself bore the 'ornaments' of his education.[97]

Where an architect acted more as conductor than composer, it served his purpose to highlight the quality of execution or 'performance' of the craftsmen he had supervised. Matthew Brettingham described the colonnade in the entrance hall at Holkham as 'well executed by the late Mr. Pickford, who also performed the greatest part of the inlay, or incrusted work of the basement' (Fig. 10.5).[98] For Brettingham, an executant architect tasked with adapting the designs of others, Holkham was most important for its exemplary execution: 'the characteristic merit of Holkham', he wrote, 'is most discernible in the accurate performance of its workmanship'.[99]

Medieval workmanship in the eighteenth century

An appreciation of 'curious' workmanship explains, at least in part, the enduring popular appeal of Gothic architecture at a time when critics condemned it as barbarous in Vitruvian terms. *A New Guide to London* of 1726, published in English and French, was able to pass over the architecture of Inigo Jones's Banqueting House without comment (though mentioned the paintings there by Rubens), but urged readers to examine the 'exquisite workmanship' of Henry VII's chapel at Westminster.[100] In contrast, St Martin-in-the-Fields was praised for its 'excellent Taste of Architecture', without a word for the sumptuous plasterwork of Bagutti and Artari.[101] Already prior to the publication of *Vitruvius Britannicus* there was a clear, if informal, canon

Figure 10.5: View of the Marble Hall at Holkham, Norfolk.
Photograph by Andrew Tierney.

of great English buildings, in travel and antiquarian literature. The most celebrated were late Gothic – most notably Henry VII's chapel at Westminster and King's College Chapel in Cambridge. Writers tended to focus on them as examples of workmanship rather than works of architecture, and their significance was characterised in distinctly nationalistic terms. In the late sixteenth century, William Camden, citing Leland, described in print Henry VII's chapel at Westminster as 'the miracle of the world', to which his later editor Gibson (from 1695) added details on stone (from Huddleston quarry in Yorkshire) and on cost.[102] Already in the 1650s Dugdale had described the Beauchamp Chapel at Warwick as 'inferior to none in England, except that of K[ing]. H[enry]. 7 [th]. in Westminster Abby', of which Thomas Delaune wrote in 1681 that 'if we respect the admirable and artificial Work without and within … it can scarce be parallel'd in the World'.[103] John Evelyn, who was later scathing about the Gothic in purely architectural terms, thought highly of King's College Chapel, praising the stonework of the roof, 'which for flatness of its laying and carving may, I conceive, vie with any in Christendom',[104] while Thomas Baskerville, in his tour of 1677–8, called it 'the wonder of England'.[105] Appreciation was usually directed towards specific elements. The anonymous author of *British Curiosities in Nature and Art*, writing in 1713, deemed King's College Chapel 'one of the most celebrated pieces of workmanship in Europe', citing the carved stone roof, the neatly paved marble floor and the painted windows, which he called masterpieces of glass painting.[106] Daniel Defoe's much reprinted tour (first published 1724–7) described it as 'deservedly reckoned one of the finest Buildings of its Kind in the World', singling out the workmanship of the stalls as 'surpass[ing] any thing of the Kind'.[107] John McKay in 1714 called it 'the longest and largest Room, without Pillars to support its Roof … perhaps in the World'.[108] Here then is not only an assertion of the significance of workmanship to the early appraisal of British architecture, but also to the formation of a qualitative canon of buildings that were seen in distinctly nationalistic terms. The global and European context of British buildings are repeatedly asserted in the late seventeenth- and early eighteenth-century topographical writing, as travellers' experience widened to the continent.[109] The quality of workmanship was a key factor in such comparative appraisals. St Paul's was the first new building to find its way into this canon, being 'esteemed the first in all the Universe' in a *New Guide to London* of 1726, its façade praised for its 'exquisite Workmanship and Taste' and its 'mathematical Marble Stairs'. Most notably, the work of master mason 'Mr Strong' is credited alongside that of Wren.[110] For James Ralph, writing about Bethlem Hospital in 1735, it was the sculpture that gave the building its significance: 'no fabric in Europe can boast finer, either as to propriety of place, or excellency of workmanship'.[111]

The reputation of King's College Chapel remained on such terms throughout the eighteenth century, mainly on account of its well-engineered roof and intricate stonework. The influence of earlier topographical surveys in establishing this canon was crucial. William Camden's late sixteenth-century work, translated from Latin into English in 1695, and remaining in print throughout the eighteenth century, made important qualitative judgements based on workmanship. St Mary Redcliffe in Bristol, for example, he proclaimed the finest of England's parish churches: 'So large is it, and the workmanship so exquisite; the roof so artificially vaulted with stone, and the tower so high; that in my opinion it far surpasses all the Parish Churches in England, that I have yet seen'.[112] Testament to the scope of Camden's perspective on workmanship, Pevsner made a fairly similar assessment of the building's significance in 1958.[113]

In contrast, doctrinaire Vitruvian classicism prompted critics to discount elaborate workmanship as evidence for quality. Roger North, writing in the late seventeenth century, saw such work as an indulgence. Of Henry VII's Westminster chapel, he complained about 'The perpetuall breaking a surface, with carving, sett offs and small members, … carving for carving sake without such use', he argued, 'is an impertinence, like babble in company, of no profit'.[114] In this he was building on a long critical tradition of recasting variety as superfluity.[115] Where others saw handicraft, he saw craftiness and cheap sleight of hand: 'The gothick way of making wonderment at the stupendious weight borne upon thredds', he wrote, 'is one of the worst of faults. Magick and trick will not serve in building, where lives depend; those are fitter for theatre, and puppet-show, where men come to be cheated a few hours with a vain shewe of what is not'.[116] Addison, who had a conception of the sublime in buildings predicated on scale, rejected its application to the Gothic, comparing the 'Greatness of the Manner in the one [Roman architecture], and the Meanness in the Other'.[117]

Nevertheless, the persistent tendency to see buildings as a series of crafted parts rather than an architectural whole can be found in the response to classical buildings too. Edward Hatton's *New View of London*, of 1708, is the most sustained example, with its endless litany of doorcases, pediments, columns and carvings. The anonymous author of *British Curiosities in Nature and Art*, of 1713, presented St Paul's Cathedral in this way too, praising the quality of its workmanship in a strangely ad hoc list of eighteen parts that included the dome, the sculpture of the west pediment, the west marble doorcase, the iron doors, the ironwork around the dome, the stonework of the outer doorcases, porticos and pediments, the wood carvings of the choir … and so on.[118] Even more narrowly, Celia Fiennes limited her assessment of St Paul's to the rich carvings of the choir and the Archbishop's seat, leaving the architecture undescribed, while Thomas Salmon, in 1732, attempted a synthesis of the choir carvings alone, writing: 'the Galleries, the Bishop's Throne, Lord Mayor's Seat, with the Stalls, all which being contiguous, compose one vast Body of curious carv'd Work of the finest Wainscot, constituting three sides of a Quadrangle'.[119] In such writings, St Paul's rarely emerged as the sum of its parts, but rather was rendered in discrete episodes. This mirrors the representation of buildings in novels, then emerging as an art form.[120]

There was some pushback against such fragmented descriptions. Wenceslaus Hollar's views of the interior of old St Paul's (1658) and David Loggan's precocious view of the interior of King's College Chapel (1690) (Fig. 10.6) were among the first to synthesise the achievements of Gothic workmanship by repackaging them into a single centralised viewpoint.[121] James Ralph, in his anonymous preface to *The Builder's Dictionary* of 1734, argued that 'The Eye is best satisfy'd with seeing the Whole at once, not in travelling from Object to Object; for then the Whole is comprehended with Pain and Difficulty, the Attention is broken, and we forget one Moment what we had observed another'.[122] Lord Kames, in his *Elements of Criticism* of 1762 described this restlessness as a 'vibration of the mind', as the eye shifted back and forth between a building and its ornamental details. He theorised that the impact of this shifting eye was not fully understood and bewailed the lack of knowledge of:

> … the precise impression made by every single part and ornament [of a building], cupolas, spires, columns, carvings, statues, vases, &c. For in vain will an artist attempt rules for employing these, either singly or in combination, until the different emotions or feelings they produce be distinctly explained.[123]

In this view, the composition of the whole within a harmonic and proportional system under the control of the architect is subject to the affective power of the individual parts.[124] However, Kames also rejected the idea that architecture, through its proportions, could produce a sense of harmony akin to music. As Tim Gough, in his essay on architectural reception, has observed: 'A literary text is rather an event – the event of reading that occurs in the interplay between the subject (the reader) and the object (the text)',[125] and this same reality only slowly dawned upon architectural commentators. Anne Hultzsch has discussed

BETWEEN DESIGN AND MAKING

Figure 10.6: View of the interior of King's College Chapel, Cambridge, from David Loggan, *Cantabrigia Illustrata*, 1690.

Getty Research Institute. Internet Archive.

this phenomenon in relation to Locke's *Essay Concerning Human Understanding*, and the problem of processing sensations produced by architectural ornament and detail into a conceptual understanding of the whole – what she describes as 'a moment of crisis in architectural perception'.[126] This can be related not just to the roving eye, but the moving body and the shifting sense of proportion and scale through space. 'Every step I take', remarked Lord Kames of his own writing room, 'varies to me, in appearance, the proportion of the length and breadth.

At that rate, I should not be happy but in one precise spot, where the proportion appears agreeable'.[127] This problem was still of concern to theorists when Wittkower proposed Albertian proportions as symbolic.[128] Gordon Higgott has since explored Inigo Jones's theory of 'varying with reason', which depended on 'Jones's alertness to the role of detail in the overall effect of a building', and his 'early understanding of Vitruvius's concept of optical correction', which depended more on the architect's wits than adherence to rules.[129] The insistence on seeing buildings as a whole to which the parts must be subservient had important ramifications for the conservation of Gothic buildings in the late eighteenth century, at which time spaces were reconfigured or decluttered to allow greater range to the eye.[130]

What is lacking in Kames's analysis is the visual effect of crafted surfaces – most notably the play of light on materials; the mediating and constantly shifting element between the eye and the object, which remained underdeveloped in eighteenth-century writing – both architectural and literary. Horace Walpole's novel, *The Castle of Otranto*, for example, fails entirely to evoke in words the architectural setting which inspired it. Not that evocative architectural writing was without precedent. Procopius, in his sixth-century description of Hagia Sophia, writes of it 'surging' and 'soaring', of the terror produced by the high floating domes, of the sun's rays reflecting off the marble, producing a radiance from within the fabric.[131] Encountering the coloured marble was, he wrote, like coming upon 'a meadow with its flowers in full bloom'. He also addressed the problem of how the eye reconciles collective impressions and the draw of detail in the dome:[132]

All these details, fitted together with incredible skill in mid air and floating off from each other and resting only on the parts next to them, produce a single and most extraordinary harmony in the work, and yet do not permit the spectator to linger much over the study of any one of them, but each detail attracts the eye and draws it on irresistibly to itself. So the vision constantly shifts suddenly, for the beholder is utterly unable to select which particular detail he should admire more than all the others.[133]

The absence of such simile and metaphor is notable in early eighteenth-century descriptions of buildings, which in literary texts remain largely unrendered in a visual sense. But by the time of Walter Scott, fifty years later, literature was laden with richly rendered architectural detail.

To conclude, materials form the starting point for workmanship and it makes sense that an appreciation of their colour, texture and finish should dominate early modern accounts of buildings. As late as the early eighteenth century, viewers unconsciously broke buildings down into bite-sized parts to better savour materials and workmanship, the appreciation of which did not require a thorough grounding in Vitruvius or Palladio. Unconstrained by the architectural conceit or laboured principles of proportion, the untutored eye was a relatively free, if somewhat promiscuous agent. It was certainly seduced by the naked skill of intricate workmanship, the wondrous transubstantiation of materials between designs, and the dizzying aerobatics of stone as it flies across gothic vaults. An appraisal of buildings as the sum (or indeed more than the sum) of their parts reflects a new conception of the generative capacity of the architect as creator and orchestrator, which has its roots in the more professional thinking of critics such as Roger North, John Evelyn and Colen Campbell. That sculptural enrichment might distract from, or even compete with, the formal conception of a building was recognised by all three of these writers. At the very least, to consume too rich an offering whole – as formal architectural appraisal demanded – would lead to indigestion. Palladianism did much to bring free-spirited artisan-designed ornament to heel, on the exterior of buildings at least, while the ornament-infused structural achievements of earlier artisan designers were banished out of sight. Nevertheless, the mass appeal of Gothic craftsmanship outlived the sniffy pronouncements of its eighteenth-century critics. The rise, during the eighteenth century, of taste, connoisseurship, and literacy in the theory of classical design, seems to have dampened such direct engagement with raw materials and free-wheeling artisan fancy, while curiosity, initially embedded in the hand, became increasingly the cranky and imperious domain of the eye. A preference for 'finish' speaks to an appetite for a more static expression of materiality. The turn to mass-produced ornament in the late eighteenth century, void of the roving imprint of thumb and hand, would eventually banish the tension between creative collaborators, leaving the architect's achievement supreme, if coldly aloof.

Notes

1   Wall, *The Prose of Things*; Fludernik, 'Perspective and focalization in eighteenth-century descriptions'.
2   For an interesting bottom-up approach, see Iliffe, 'Material doubts: Hooke, artisan culture and the exchange of information in 1670s London'.

3   Stead and Garduño Freeman, 'Architecture and "The act of receiving, or the fact of being received"'.
4   Climenson, *Passages from the Diaries*, 66.
5   For the various editions and reprints of Camden's *Britannia*, as well as Camden's use of Leland's notes, see Levy, 'The making of Camden's *Britannia*'. For an example of the later use of Leland, see the writings of Thomas Pennant. For a recent analysis of their work, see Cramsie, *British Travellers and the Encounter with Britain, 1450–1700*. For the enduring influence of sixteenth- and seventeenth-century antiquarian writers, see also Sweet, *Antiquaries*, 75.
6   Pye, *The Nature and Art of Workmanship*, 18.
7   Van Eck, *British Architectural Theory 1540–1750*.
8   See Binski, 'Reflections on the "Wonderful Height and Size" of Gothic great churches and the Medieval sublime', 133–4; Walker, *Architects and Intellectual Culture in Post-Restoration England*; Buchanan, 'Interpretations of Medieval architecture, c.1550–c.1750'.
9   See, for example, his description of the stone at Tickhill Castle in Smith, *The Itinerary of John Leland*, i, 35; or his description of the 'divers pillors of blak marble spikelid with white' in the great hall of the bishop of Durham's at Auckland, 69–70. On the collegiate parish church of Darlington (Yorkshire): 'There is an exceeding long and fair altare stone *de vario marmore, hoc est, nigro albis maculis distincto*, at the high altare in the collegeiate paroche chirch of Darlington', 69. On the isle of Axholm, Lincolnshire he wrote: 'The upper part of the isle hath plentiful quarres of alabaster, communely there caullid plaster: but such stones as I saw of it were of no great thiknes and sold for a *xijd.* the lode. They ly yn the ground lyke a smothe table: and be beddid one flake under another: and at the bottom of the beddes of them be roughe stones to build withal', 38.
10 Smith, *Itinerary of John Leland*, i, 7 and 34. See also his description of the house of a Mr Horton at Bradford in Wiltshire, 135.
11 Smith, *The Itinerary of John Leland*, i, 69.
12 Smith, *The Itinerary of John Leland*, ii, 106–7.
13 Smith, *The Itinerary of John Leland*, i, 95 and 146.
14 For a reassessment concerning compliance with sumptuary laws in Tudor England, see Hilary Doda, '"Saide Monstrous Hose": Compliance, transgression and English sumptuary law to 1533', 171–91.
15 Hayworth, *Rich Apparel*, see chapters 5–6, 9–10, 16.
16 Hultzsch, *Architecture, Travellers and Writers*, 74.
17 An account subject to later revision and indebted to the work of other writers. On this point, see Hultzsch, *Architecture, Travellers and Writers*, 29.
18 Bray, *The Diary of John Evelyn*, i, 88; Evelyn revised his early diary entries later in life so the date of his aesthetic judgements cannot be pinned down exactly, see Darley, *John Evelyn*, 23.
19 Aubrey de La Mottraye's assessment of San Marco in Venice published in 1723 was that 'it is more valuable for the Sumptuousness of its Materials, than for its Architecture … above 360 Columns of different sorts of Marble, Sizes and Colours, the most Part Oriental; the rich *Mosaick* of its vaulted Roof, and the curious inlaid Work of the Pavement … are ornaments that … give an entire Satisfaction to all who view them', La Mottraye, *The Voyages and Travels of A. de la Motraye*, i, 65.
20 Bray, *The Diary of John Evelyn*, i, 188 and 91. Evelyn's interest in craft and materials at Florence contrasts with those of later tourists drawn to the city for its associations with Renaissance painting and sculpture. On the latter, see Sweet, *Cities and the Grand Tour*, 65–98.
21 Bray, *The Diary of John Evelyn*, i, 30.
22 Freart (trans. Evelyn), *A Parallel of the Antient Architecture with the Modern*, 141.
23 Bray, *The Diary of John Evelyn*, i, 89–90.
24 Bray, *The Diary of John Evelyn*, i, 49.
25 See Matthew Walker's discussion of seventeenth-century interest in porphyry in *Architects and Intellectual Culture in Post-Restoration England*, 124.
26 Halifax, 'A relation of a voyage from Aleppo to Palmyra in Syria', 102.
27 Halley, 'Some account of the ancient state of the city of Palmyra', 162–3.
28 Bray, *The Diary of John Evelyn*, 290.
29 Childrey, *Britannia Baconica*, 49.

30 On Cardinal Richelieu's villa at Rueil, he wrote of the 'Citronière, which is a noble conserve of all those rarities; and at the end of it is the Arch of Constantine, painted on a wall in oil, as large as the real one at Rome, so well done, that even a man skilled in painting, may mistake it for stone and sculpture. The sky and hills, which seem to be between the arches, are so natural, that swallows and other birds, thinking to fly through, have dashed themselves against the wall. I was infinitely taken with this agreeable cheat', Bray, *The Diary of John Evelyn*, i, 52. On the papal apartments in the Vatican, he wrote: 'what exceeds description is, the *volta*, or roof itself, which is so exquisitely painted, that it is almost impossible for the skillfullest eyes to discern whether it be the work of the pencil upon a flat, or of a tool cut deep in stone', i, 136.

31 Hatton, *A New View of London*, 369; Thornton, *Seventeenth-Century Interior Decoration in England, France and Holland*, 74; Fowler and Cornforth, *English Decoration in the 18th century*, 189–93.

32 Bray, *The Diary of John Evelyn*, i, 289.

33 Anderson, *Touring and Publicizing England's Country Houses*, 144. This cabinet remains in situ to this day, see https://www.nationaltrustcollections.org.uk/object/731575. Accessed 20 January 2024.

34 Jenkins, *Portrait of a Patron*, 48 and 57.

35 Harney, *Place-making for the Imagination*, 91–2; Walpole, *Anecdotes of Painting*, 152; Tinniswood, *The Polite Tourist*, 81–4.

36 Smith, *The Itinerary of John Leland*, ii, 99.

37 For an account of early modern working processes, see Jackson, *Wadham College*, 29–42.

38 'pretty, adj., n., and int.'. OED Online. Oxford University Press. https://www.oed.com. Accessed 23 January 2024.

39 MacArthur, 'Gentlemen tourists', 101.

40 Shute, *The First and Chief Groundes of Architecture*. Unpaginated, reverse of folio 17.

41 Benjamin, 'The work of art in the age of mechanical reproduction'.

42 Walsh, *The Flight of the Earls*.

43 Walpole, *Aedes Walpolianae*, 101.

44 Derham, *Physico-theology*, 270; for Derham's scientific endeavours, see Atkinson, 'William Derham, F.R.S. (1657–1735)'.

45 Bentley, *A Confutation of Atheism*, 20.

46 For a 1705 translation of Ware's text, see Harris, *The History and Antiquities of Ireland*, 137.

47 Harris, *The History and Antiquities of Ireland*, 91.

48 Dugdale, *The Antiquities of Warwickshire*, 354–5.

49 See Sweet, 'Antiquaries and antiquities in eighteenth-century England', 187.

50 Morris, *The Journeys of Celia Fiennes*, 112; Dugdale published an illustration by Wenceslaus Hollar of the cross in 1654, which he called 'for workmanship and beauty … inferior to none in England'. See his *Antiquities of Warwickshire*, 95.

51 For the various dates of construction and remodelling, see https://www.british-history. ac.uk/vch/cambs/vol10/pp374-379#fnn38. Accessed 20 January 2024.

52 Morris, *The Journeys of Celia Fiennes*, 153.

53 Bray, *The Diary of John Evelyn*, ii, 117 and 124.

54 Evelyn, *Sylva*, 10.

55 He invokes the precedent of Francis I, Henry IV, Cosimo de Medici, the Dukes of Urbino, Cardinal Richeleau, and Vitruvius's dedication of his treatise to Augustus. See Freart (trans. Evelyn), *A Parallel of the Antient Architecture with the Modern*, 117–18.

56 Freart (trans. Evelyn), *A Parallel of the Antient Architecture with the Modern*, 117–18.

57 Bullard, 'John Evelyn as modern architect and ancient gardener', 171–88.

58 Smith, 'William Cleere, master joiner', 23.

59 Colvin, *History of the King's Works*, vol. 5, 28.

60 Freart (trans. Evelyn), *A Parallel of the Antient Architecture with the Modern*, 119–20.

61 Hill and Cornforth, *Country Houses: Caroline, 1625–85*, 37, 142–5. See also Colvin, *Biographical Dictionary*, 1133–4; Beard, *The National Trust Book of the English House Interior*, 110.

62 Morris, *The Journeys of Celia Fiennes*, 278.

63 Findlen, *Possessing Nature*; Kenny, *Curiosity in Early Modern Europe*; Marr and Evans, *Curiosity and Wonder from the Renaissance to the Enlightenment*; Hultzsch, *Architecture,*

Travellers and Writers, 54–86; Roberts, *Problems of Architectural Experience and Architectural Description in England*, 13–18.

64 'curious, adj. and adv.'. OED Online. Oxford University Press. Accessed 20 January 2024. https://www.oed.com. Strangely, Hultzsche, who also cites the OED, describes this meaning as 'newly coined in the 1600s', *Architecture, Travellers and Writers*, 57.

65 See Walpole, *Anecdotes of Painting*, unpaginated appendix, 1.

66 Moxon, *Mechanick Exercises*, vi of unpaginated preface.

67 Moxon, *Mechanick Exercises*, 118.

68 Moxon, *Mechanick Exercises*, 69.

69 Langley, *A Sure Guide to Builders*, unpaginated preface.

70 Langley, *A Sure Guide to Builders*, unpaginated frontispiece and preface, 2 and 4.

71 Harris, *The History and Antiquities of the City of Dublin*, 113 and 437.

72 Anon., 'Further discoveries in Herculaneum', 443–4.

73 Harris, 'The Duchess of Beaufort's "Observations on places"', 36–42.

74 A Gentleman of Oxford, *The New Oxford Guide*, 95.

75 A Gentleman of Oxford, *The New Oxford Guide*, 108–13.

76 Wood et al., *The Ruins of Palmyra*, 43; Wood et al., *The Ruins of Balbec*, 25.

77 Wood et al., *The Ruins of Balbec*, 25.

78 He adds that he 'never saw Vines and Clusters of Grapes cut in Stone, so Bold, so Lively and so Nature, in any place', see Halifax, 'A relation of a voyage from Aleppo to Palmyra in Syria', 88–95. Notably, Richard Pococke, writing about Baalbek in the early 1740s, did so in a vein much closer to that of Halifax, praising the execution of the carving, describing the temple at Baalbek as 'a most exquisite piece of workmanship', though he does not employ the term 'curious' here, nor in his broader writings on Britain and Ireland. See Pococke, *A Description of the East, And Some Other Countries*, vol. 2, 108–9.

79 Anon., 'Description of Blenheim House', 468–9; for Gibbons at Blenheim, see Sherwood and Pevsner, *The Buildings of England: Oxfordshire*, 470.

80 Burke, *A Philosophical Enquiry into the Origin of Our Ideas of the Sublime and Beautiful*, 107–8.

81 Pennant, *The Journey from Chester to London*, 144–6. This itinerary dates to 1780.

82 Pennant, *Some Account of London*, 42.

83 See Walpole, *Aedes Walpolianae*, 38, 44, 51, 56, 82; Martyn, *The English Connoisseur*, 81–117.

84 Walpole, *Anecdotes of Painting in England*, iii, 84.

85 Aglionby, 'The epistle dedicatory', *Painting Illustrated*, unpaginated.

86 Walpole, *Anecdotes of Painting in England*, 87; for Walpole's misattributions at Chatsworth, see Trevor Brighton, 'Samuel Watson, not Grinling Gibbons at Chatsworth', 811–18.

87 Climenson, *Passages from the Diaries of Mrs. Philip Lybbe Powys of Hardwick House, Oxon*, 37.

88 Martyn, *The English Connoisseur*, 28.

89 Stow, *The Survey of London*, 484.

90 Barbon, *A Discourse Shewing the Great Advantages That New-Buildings and the Enlarging of Towns and Cities Do bring to a Nation*, 7.

91 Campbell, *Vitruvius Britannicus*, vol. 1, 3.

92 Cited in Roberts, 'Problems of architectural experience and architectural description in England, 1688–1750', 14.

93 Braddon, *A Proposal for Relieving, Reforming and Employing all the Poor of Great Britain*, 79–80.

94 Pye, *The Nature and Art of Workmanship*, 20–4; Esterly, *The Lost Carving: A journey to the heart of making*.

95 Bray, *The Diary of John Evelyn*, i, 111 and 136.

96 For the costliness of leisure and the class consciousness of the virtuosi, see Houghton Jr., 'The English virtuoso in the seventeenth century: Part I', 63.

97 For this use of the term ornament, see Houghton Jr., 'The English virtuoso in the seventeen century: Part I', 52.

98 Brettingham, *Plans, Elevations and Sections of Holkham*, vi.

99 Brettingham, *Plans, Elevations and Sections of Holkham*, ix.

100 Anon., *A New Guide to London*.

101 Anon., *A New Guide to London*, 25.

102 Camden (trans. Gibson), *Britannia*, 384–5.

103 De Laune, *Present State of London*, 21.
104 Bray, *The Diary of John Evelyn*, i, 300.
105 Baskerville, 'Thomas Baskerville's Journeys in England, Temp. Car. II', 264.
106 Anon., *British Curiosities in Nature and Art*, 78.
107 Defoe, *A Tour Through the Whole Island of Great Britain*, vol. 1, 95–6; Baskerville, 'Thomas Baskerville's Journeys in England, Temp. Car. II', 264.
108 McKay, *A Journey through England*, i, 147–8.
109 John Evelyn, having travelled widely on the continent, was particularly well placed to make such pronouncements – for example, his view of Salisbury Cathedral as 'the most complete piece of Gothic work in Europe, taken in all its uniformity' or his assessment of the quality of ironworking in Broad Hinton as 'more exquisitely wrought and polished than in any part of Europe'. See Bray, *The Diary of John Evelyn*, i, 290–1.
110 Anon., *A New Guide to London*, 33–6.
111 Ralph, *A Critical Review of the Publick Buildings, Statues and Ornaments in and around London and Westminster*, 8.
112 Camden (trans. Gibson), *Britannia*, 95.
113 Pevsner, *North Somerset and Bristol*, 395.
114 Colvin, *Of Building: Roger North's writings on architecture*, 21.
115 See Binski, 'Reflections on the "Wonderful Height and Size" of Gothic great churches and the Medieval sublime', 135.
116 Colvin, *Of Building: Roger North's writings on architecture*, 22.
117 Van Eck, *British Architectural Theory,* 43.
118 Anon., *British Curiosities in Nature and Art*, 33.
119 Salmon, *Modern History,* vol. 18, 261.
120 Wall, *The Prose of Things*, 4.
121 Dugdale, *The History of St Paul's*; Loggan, *Cantabrigia Illustrata.*
122 Anon. [Ralph], *Builder's Dictionary*, 1734, unpaginated preface.
123 Homes, *Elements of Criticism*, iii, 299.
124 For the development of these ideas from John Locke, see Anne Hultzsch's discussion of Tobias Smollet, *Architecture, Travellers and Writers*, 109.
125 Gough, 'Reception theory of architecture: Its pre-history and afterlife', 280.
126 Hultzsch, *Architecture, Travellers and* Writers, 108–9.
127 Homes, *Elements of Criticism*, iii, 333.
128 'It is obvious that such mathematical relations between plan and section cannot be correctly perceived when one walks about in a building. Alberti knew that, of course, quite as well as we do. We must therefore conclude that the harmonic perfection of the geometrical scheme represents an absolute value, independent of our subjective and transitory perception.' Wittkower, *Architectural Principles in the Age of Humanism*, 8.
129 Higgott, 'Varying with reason', 52.
130 On this point, see Jokilehto, *History of Architectural Conservation*, section 5.1.1.
131 Dewing, *Procopius*, vol. 7, 17–19.
132 Dewing, *Procopius*, vol. 7, 27 and 55.
133 Dewing, *Procopius*, vol. 7, 21–3.

References

Aglionby, William. *Painting Illustrated in Three Diallogues: Containing some choice observations upon the art, together with the lives of the most eminent painters, from Cimabue, to the time of Raphael and Michel Angelo*. London: Printed by John Gain for the author, 1685.
Anderson, Jocelyn. *Touring and Publicizing England's Country Houses in the Long Eighteenth Century*. London: Bloomsbury, 2018.
Anon., *British Curiosities in Nature and Art: Exhibiting an account of natural and artificial rarieties, both ancient and modern, intermixt with historical and geographical passages.* London: Chr. Coningsby, 1713.
Anon., *A New Guide to London, or, Directions to Strangers, Shewing the Chief Things of Curiosity and Note in the City and Suburbs.* London: Smith, Bowles & Bowles, 1726.

Anon., *Builders Dictionary: Or, gentleman's and architect's companion*. 2 vols. London: Printed for A. Bettesworth and C. Hitch, 1734.

Anon., 'Further discoveries in Herculaneum', *Gentleman's Magazine* (September 1755): 443–4.

Anon., 'Description of Blenheim House', *The Hibernian Magazine, or, Compendium of Entertaining Knowledge*. Dublin: Printed by Thomas Walker, 1783.

Atkinson, A. D. 'William Derham, F.R.S. (1657–1735)', *Annals of Science*, 8:4 (1952): 368–92. Accessed 23 January 2024. https://doi.org/10.1080/00033795200200282.

Barbon, Nicholas. *A Discourse Shewing the Great Advantages That New-Buildings and the Enlarging of Towns and Cities Do bring to a Nation*. London: n.p., 1678.

Baskerville, Thomas. 'Thomas Baskerville's Journeys in England, Temp. Car. II'. In *Historical Manuscripts Commission*, Thirteenth Report, Appendix, Part 2, 263–314. The manuscripts of His Grace the Duke of Portland: preserved at Welbeck Abbey. London: H. M. Stationery Office, 1893.

Beard, Geoffrey. *The National Trust Book of the English House Interior*. London: Penguin, 1990.

Benjamin, Walter. 'The work of art in the age of mechanical reproduction'. In *Illuminations*, edited by Hannah Arendt, 214–18. London: Fontana, 1968.

Bentley, Richard. *A Confutation of Atheism From the Origin and Frame of the World. Part 1. A sermon preached at St. Mary-le-Bow, October the 3d 1692*. London: Printed for Henry Mortlock, 1692.

Binski, Paul. 'Reflections on the "Wonderful Height and Size" of Gothic great churches and the Medieval sublime'. In *Magnificence and the Sublime in Medieval Aesthetics: Art, architecture, literature, music*, edited by C. Stephen Jaeger, 129–56. New York: Palgrave MacMillan, 2010.

Braddon, Lawrence. *A Proposal for Relieving, Reforming and Employing all the Poor of Great Britain*. London: n.p., 1721.

Bray, William, ed. *The Diary of John Evelyn, Esq., F.R.S.* 2 vols. New York and London: M. Walter Dunne, 1901–7.

Brettingham, Matthew. *Plans, Elevations and Sections of Holkham in Norfolk, The Seat of the Late Earl of Leicester*. 2nd edition. London: Printed by J. Haberkorn, 1773.

Brewer, James. *The Beauties of England and Wales*. London: Harris, Longman & Co., 1818.

Brighton, Trevor. 'Samuel Watson, not Grinling Gibbons at Chatsworth', *The Burlington Magazine*, 140:1149 (1998): 811–18.

Buchanan, Alexandrina. 'Interpretations of Medieval architecture, c.1550–c.1750'. In *Gothic Architecture and its Meanings, 1550–1830*, edited by Michael Hall, 25–50. Reading: Spire Books, 2002.

Bullard, Paddy. 'John Evelyn as modern architect and ancient gardener: "Lessons of perpetual practice"'. In *Ancients and Moderns in Early Modern Europe: Comparative perspectives*, edited by Paddy Bullard and Alexis Tadié, 171–88. Oxford: Voltaire Foundation, 2016.

Burke, Edmund. *A Philosophical Enquiry into the Origin of Our Ideas of the Sublime and Beautiful*. London: Printed for R. and J. Dodsley, 1757.

Camden, William. *Britannia: Or a chorographical description of Great Britain and Ireland together with adjacent islands*, translated by Edmund Gibson. London: Printed by Mary Matthews for Awnsham Churchill, 1722.

Campbell, Colen. *Vitruvius Britannicus*. 3 vols. London: Printed and sold by the author, 1715–25.

Childrey, Joshua. *Britannia Baconica: or, The natural rarities of England, Scotland, & Wales. According as they are to be found in every shire*. London: Printed for the author, 1662.

Climenson, Emily, ed. *Passages from the Diaries of Mrs. Philip Lybbe Powys of Hardwick House, Oxon*. London: Longmans, Green and Co., 1899.

Colvin, Howard. *History of the King's Works*, vol. 5. London: H. M. Stationery Office, 1963.

Colvin, Howard. *A Biographical Dictionary of British Architects, 1600–1840*. New Haven, CT and London: Yale University Press, 2008.

Colvin, Howard and John Newman, eds. *Of Building: Roger North's writings on architecture*. Oxford: Clarendon Press, 1981.

Cramsie, John. *British Travellers and the Encounter with Britain, 1450–1700*. Woodbridge: Boydell Press, 2015.

Darley, Gillian. *John Evelyn: Living for ingenuity*. New Haven, CT and London: Yale University Press, 2006.

Defoe, Daniel. *A Tour Through the Whole Island of Great Britain*. 2 vols. 3rd edition. London: Printed for J. Osborn, S. Birt, D. Browne, J. Hodges, A. Millar, J. Whiston and J. Robinson, 1742.

De Laune, Thomas. *Present State of London*. London: Enoch Prosser and John How, 1681.

Derham, William. *Physico-Theology: Or, a demonstration of the being and attributes of God, from his works of creation*. London: Printed for W. Innys, 1713.

Dewing, H. B., ed. *Procopius*. 7 vols. Cambridge, MA: Harvard University Press, 1914.

Doda, Hilary. '"Saide Monstrous Hose": Compliance, transgression and English sumptuary law to 1533', *Textile History*, 45:2 (2014): 171–91.

Dugdale, William. *The Antiquities of Warwickshire Illustrated: From records, leiger-books, manuscripts, charters, evidences, tombes, and armes: beautified with maps, prospects, and portraictures*. London: Printed by Thomas Warren, 1656.

Dugdale, William. *The History of St. Paul's Cathedral in London, from its foundation untill these times*. London: Printed by Thomas Warren, 1658.

Esterly, David. *The Lost Carving: A journey to the heart of making*. London: Duckworth, 2014.

Evelyn, John. *Sylva: Or, a discourse of forest-trees, and the propagation of timber in His Majesties dominions*. London: Printed for the Royal Society by John Martyn and James Allestry, 1664.

Findlen, Paula. *Possessing Nature: Museums, collecting, and scientific culture in early modern Italy*. Berkeley: University of California Press, 1994.

Fludernik, Monika. 'Perspective and focalization in eighteenth-century descriptions'. In *Narrative Concepts in the Study of Eighteenth-Century Literature*, edited by Liisa Steinby and Aino Mäkikalli, 99–120. Amsterdam: Amsterdam University Press, 2017. Accessed 20 January 2024. https://doi.org/10.2307/j.ctt1wn0r6q.6.

Fowler, John and John Cornforth. *English Decoration in the 18th Century*. London: Barrie & Jenkins, 1974.

Freart, Roland. *A Parallel of the Antient Architecture with the Modern, In a collection of ten principal authors who have written upon the five orders*, translated by John Evelyn. London: Printed by Thomas Roycroft for John Place, 1664.

A Gentleman of Oxford. *The New Oxford Guide: Or a companion through the University ... to which is added, a tour to Blenheim, Ditchley, and Stow*. 3rd edition. Oxford: Printed for J. Fletcher, 1763.

Gough, Tim. 'Reception theory of architecture: Its pre-history and afterlife', *Architectural Theory Review*, 18:3 (2013): 279–92. Accessed 23 January 2024. https://doi.org/10.1080/132648 26.2013.889645.

Halifax, William. 'A relation of a voyage from Aleppo to Palmyra in Syria sent by the Reverend Mr. William Halifax to Dr. Edw. Bernard Late Savilian Professor Of Astronomy in Oxford, and by him communicated to Dr. Thomas Smith. Reg. Soc. S.', *Philosophical Transactions of the Royal Society*, 19 (1695): 83–110.

Halley, Edmond. 'Some account of the ancient state of the city of Palmyra, with short remarks upon the inscriptions found there', *Philosophical Transactions of the Royal Society*, 19 (1695): 160–75. Accessed 26 January 2024. https://doi.org/10.1098/rstl.1695.0023.

Harney, Marion. *Place-making for the Imagination: Horace Walpole and Strawberry Hill*. London: Routledge, 2013.

Harris, John. 'The Duchess of Beaufort's "Observations on Places"', *The Georgian Group Journal*, 10 (2000): 36–42.

Harris, Walter, ed. *The History and Antiquities of Ireland by the Right Honourable Sir James Ware*. Dublin: Printed by A. Crook for E. Dobson and M. Gunne, 1705.

Harris, Walter. *The History and Antiquities of the City of Dublin*. Dublin: Printed for Laurence Flinn and James Williams, 1766.

Hatton, Edward. *A New View of London: Or, an ample account of that city in eight sections*. 2 vols. Printed for John Nicholson and Robert Knaplock, 1708.

Hayworth, Maria. *Rich Apparel: Clothing and the law in Henry VIII's England*. London: Routledge, 2017. https://doi.org/10.4324/9781315244150.

Higgott, Gordon. '"Varying with Reason": Inigo Jones's theory of design', *Architectural History*, 35 (1992): 51–77.

Hill, Oliver and John Cornforth. *Country Houses: Caroline, 1625–85*. London: Country Life, 1966.

Homes, Henry. *Elements of Criticism*. 3 vols. Edinburgh and London: A. Millar, A. Kincaid & J. Bell, 1762.

Houghton Jr., Walter E. 'The English virtuoso in the seventeenth century: Part I', *Journal of the History of Ideas*, 3 (1942): 51–73.

Hultzsch, Anne. *Architecture, Travellers and Writers: Constructing histories of perception 1640–1950*. London: Routledge, 2014.

Iliffe, Rob. 'Material doubts: Hooke, artisan culture and the exchange of information in 1670s London', *British Journal for the History of Science*, 28:3 (1995): 285–318. Accessed 20 January 2024. https://www.jstor.org/stable/4027646.

Jackson, Thomas Graham. *Wadham College, Oxford: Its foundation, architecture and history*. Oxford: Clarendon Press, 1893.

Jenkins, Susan. *Portrait of a Patron: The patronage and collecting of James Brydges*. Aldershot: Ashgate, 2007.

Jokilehto, Jukka. *History of Architectural Conservation*. London: Routledge, 2017.

Kenny, Neil. *Curiosity in Early Modern Europe: Word histories*. Wiesbaden: Harrassowitz, 1998.

La Mottraye, Aubry de. *The Voyages and Travels of A. de la Motraye*, revised edition. 3 vols. London: Printed for E. Symon, J. Newton, J. Oswald, L. Gilliver, J. Nourse, and T. Payne, 1732.

Langley, Batty. *A Sure Guide to Builders*. London: W. Mears, 1729.

Levy, F. J. 'The making of Camden's Britannia', *Bibliothèque d'Humanisme et Renaissance*, 26:1 (1964): 70–97.

Loggan, David. *Cantabrigia illustrata, sive, Omnium celeberrimae istius universitatis*. Cambridge: Printed for the author, 1690.

Luckombe, Philip. *The Beauties of England*. London: Printed for L. Davis and C. Reymers, 1757.

MacArthur, Rosie. 'Gentlemen tourists: Hanbury and Scattergood'. In *Travel and the British Country House: Cultures, critiques and consumption in the long eighteenth century*, edited by Jon Stobart, 85–105. Manchester: Manchester University Press, 2017.

Marr, Alexander and R. J. W. Evans, eds. *Curiosity and Wonder from the Renaissance to the Enlightenment*. London: Routledge, 2016.

Martyn, Thomas. *The English Connoisseur: Containing an account of whatever is curious in painting, sculpture, &c. in the palaces and seats of the nobility and principal gentry of England both in town and country*. 2 vols. London: Printed for L. Davis and C. Reymers, 1766.

McKay, John. *A Journey through England: In familiar letters from a gentleman here, to his friend abroad*. 2 vols. 2nd edition. London: Printed for J. Hooke, 1722.

Morris, Christopher, ed. *The Journeys of Celia Fiennes*. London: The Cresset Press, 1947.

Moxon, Joseph. *Mechanick Exercises, Or, the doctrine of handy-works*. London: Printed for Daniel Midwinter and Thomas Leigh, 1703.

Oxford English Dictionary. Oxford University Press, 2022. Accessed 23 January 2024. https://oed.com.

Pennant, Thomas. *The Journey from Chester to London*. London: Printed for Wilkie and Robinson, 1811.

Pennant, Thomas. *Some Account of London*. 5th edition. London: Printed for J. Faulder, 1813.

Pevsner, Nikolaus. *North Somerset and Bristol*. London: Penguin, 1958.

Pococke, Richard. *A Description Of The East, And Some Other Countries*. 2 vols. London: Printed for the author by W. Bowyer, 1743–5.

Pye, David. *The Nature and Art of Workmanship*. London: Herbert Press, 2007.

Ralph, James. *A Critical Review of the Publick Buildings, Statues and Ornaments in and around London and Westminster*. London: Printed by C. Ackers, 1734.

Roberts, Matthew Lloyd. 'Problems of architectural experience and architectural description in England, 1688–1750'. MA Thesis. Bartlett School of Architecture, UCL, 2019.

Salmon, Thomas. *Modern History: Or, the present state of all nations*. 28 vols. Dublin: Printed for George Grierson, 1732.

Sherwood, Jennifer and Nikolaus Pevsner. *The Buildings of England: Oxfordshire*. London: Penguin, 1974.

Shute, J. *The First and Chief Groundes of Architecture by John Shute, Paynter and Archytecte: First printed in 1563*. London: Country Life, 1912.

Smith, Lucy Toulmin. *The Itinerary of John Leland in or about the Years 1535–1543*. 5 vols. London: George Bell and Sons, 1907–10.

Smith, Pete. 'William Cleere, master joiner', *Georgian Group Journal*, 18 (2010): 8–34.

Stead, Naomi and Cristina Garduño Freeman. 'Architecture and "the act of receiving, or the fact of being received": Introduction to a special issue on reception', *Architectural Theory Review*, 18:3 (2013): 267–71. Accessed 23 January 2024. https://doi.org/10.1080/13264 826.2013.902418.

Stow, John. *A Survey of London*. London and New York: J. M. Dent & Son and E. P. Dutton & Co., 1923.

Sweet, Rosemary. 'Antiquaries and antiquities in eighteenth-century England', *Eighteenth-Century Studies*, 34:2 (Winter 2001): 181–206.

Sweet, Rosemary. *Antiquaries: The discovery of the past in eighteenth-century Britain.* London: Hambledon and London, 2004.

Sweet, Rosemary. *Cities and the Grand Tour: The British in Italy c.1690–1820.* Cambridge: Cambridge University Press, 2012.

Thornton, Peter. *Seventeenth-Century Interior Decoration in England, France and Holland.* New Haven, CT and London: Yale University Press, 1978.

Tinniswood, Adrian. *The Polite Tourist: A history of country house visiting.* London: National Trust, 1998.

Van Eck, Caroline. *British Architectural Theory 1540–1750.* London: Routledge, 2019.

Walker, Matthew. *Architects and Intellectual Culture in Post-Restoration England.* Oxford: Oxford University Press, 2017.

Wall, Cynthia. *The Prose of Things.* Chicago: University of Chicago Press, 2014.

Walpole, Horace. *Aedes Walpolianae: Or, a description of the collection of pictures at Houghton-Hall in Norfolk, the seat of the Right Honourable Sir Robert Walpole, Earl of Orford.* London: Printed for the author, 1752.

Walpole, Horace. *Anecdotes of Painting in England.* 4 vols. London: Printed by Thomas Farmer at Strawberry Hill, 1763.

Walpole, Horace. *The Castle of Otranto.* London: Printed for Tho. Lownds, 1765.

Walsh, Paul, ed. *The Flight of the Earls.* Dublin: M. H. Gill, 1916.

Wittkower, Rudolf. *Architectural Principles in the Age of Humanism.* London: Warburg Institute, 1949.

Wood, Robert, Giovanni Battista Borra and Paul Fourdrinier. *The Ruins of Palmyra, Otherwise Tedmor, in the Desart.* London: Robert Wood, 1753.

Wood, Robert, Giovanni Battista Borra and Paul Fourdrinier. *The Ruins of Balbec, Otherwise Heliopolis in Cœlosyria.* London: Robert Wood, 1757.

Index

References to illustrations are in *italics* and references to notes are shown as 'n'.

Ackerman, James S. 88
Ackermann, Rudolph 69, *69*
Adam, Andreas 168
Adam family 223, 225, 236n23, 236n26
Adam, John
   commonplace book notes 232–3, 237n30
   Fort George 237n31
   Hopetoun House 227–33, *229*, 237n29
Adam, John (d. *c*.1710) 223
Adam, Robert 223, 227, 254
Adamson, Glenn 284
Adam, William
   Arniston House *225*
   Hopetoun House 225–33, *226*, *228–9*, 237n28–9
   key figures and 236n24
   library 237n25
   Mavisbank *224*, 236n24
   Newliston House 236n24
   Vitruvius Scoticus 224, 236n26
Addison, Joseph 309
administration, bureaucracy and (Saxon *Oberbauamt*) 157–63
Age of Reason 209
Aglionby, William 304
Alberti, Leon Battista 3, 18n13, 88, 247, 317n128
Aldrich, Henry 71, 72
allegorising the space between architecture and craft: mural painting 263–84
Allen, Robert C. 149n98
All Saints church, Oxford 71

All Souls College, Oxford
   fellows' rooms 73–4, *74*
   Library *74*
   new hall 74–5
   North Quadrangle 80
   Wren's drawings 87
'alphabet of architecture' (classical profile) 241–60
altarpieces 96, 108
Anderson, Jocelyn 293–4
A New Guide to London (1726) 306, 308
Anichkov Palace, St Petersburg 247, *249*
Anna of Denmark, Queen 27, 33
Anne, Queen 11, 183, 264, 276, 302
annotations, use of 102, 107–8, 110–12, 113
Antiquity 12, 30, 243, 245–8, 295, 299
appraisals, fragmented 294–300
architects
   and artificers 119–44
   craftsmen: a theme with variations 207–35
architectural families 223
architecture and craft, allegorising the space between 263–84
'*architectus*', from 'mechanick' to 72–80
Arciszewska, Barbara 156
Arco degli Argentari, Rome 247
Arlington, Earl of 299
Arniston House, Midlothian, Scotland 224, *225*, 237n33
Arnold, Dana 10
Artari, Giuseppe 7
Artari workshop 221, *222*

artificers, architects and 119–44
artisans and architecture, Saxony
153–75
Arts and Crafts Movement 5
Arundel, Lord 30
Ashworth, Richard 41–2, 60n42
'astragals' 235n9
attribution, problems of 91
Augustus II the Strong, King 156, *158*, 159, 160
Ayres, James 11

Baalbek, Lebanon 302, 316n78
Bach, Johann Sebastian 235
Bagutti, Giovanni 7, 279, *281*
Baldamus, Alfred *157*
Balliol College, Oxford 76
Ballyfin House, Co. Laois 188–9
Banqueting House, Whitehall 28,
43, 57, 306
Barbon, Nicholas 305
Bargrave, John 291
Baroque interiors 263–84
Baroque style 72, 156, 220–1, 224,
237n29, 297
Baskerville, Thomas 308
Bath Stone 68
Baudez, Basile 91, 92
Beard, Geoffrey 9
Beaufort, Elizabeth Berkeley,
Duchess of 301
Bective House, Smithfield 147n67
Beethoven, Ludwig van 235
Belcher, John 7
Belvedere, Brühlscher Garten,
Dresden *171*
Benjamin, Walter 295
Bernini, Gian Lorenzo 251, *252*
Beurdeley, Alfred 86
Biais, Émile 86
Bishopthorpe Palace, York 291
Blenheim Palace, Oxfordshire
appraisals of 301, 302
Column of Victory 78
The Library 302
on Moore 8
murals *282*
The Saloon *282*, 302

Vanbrugh and 168
Woodstock Gate 78, *79*
Blomfield, Reginald 5
Blondel, Jacques-François 246, 247,
248, 254, 259
Bodleian Library, Oxford 65, 68,
141
Bodt, Jean de 155, 159, 163–4
Bognár, Anna-Victoria 177n73
Bolger, Brian 133
Bonneau, Madame 104
Borromini, Francesco 241, 242,
243, 255, 260
Boscry, Pierre 110
Boughton Hall, Northamptonshire
282
Bourde, John 296
Bouzonnet-Stella, Antoine 108,
115n53
Bowett, Adam 10
Boyle lectures (1711–12) 295–6
Braddon, Lawrence 305
Brahms, Johannes 234, 235
Brett, David 3
Brettingham, Matthew 306
Brewer, James 302
Bristol, Kerry 235n5
Britain 1–9
British Curiosities in Nature and Art
(anon.) 308, 309
Brocchi, Vincentio 291
Brown, John 210
Bruce, Sir William 224, 225,
237n28
Bruckner, Anton 235
Brühlscher Garten, Dresden *171*
Brunelleschi, Filippo 3, 4
building management 119–44
building trades, history of 209
Bullard, Paddy 299
bureaucracy and administration
(Saxon *Oberbauamt*) 157–63
Burford Stone 68, 72, 77
Burghley House, Lincolnshire
269–70
entrance 276
Heaven Room 275, *275*, 276
'Roman Stair' 58n12

324   INDEX

Burgh, Thomas
accounts 145n3
'casual management style' 119–20
Connell and 144
Old Library, Trinity College
Dublin 133, *251*, 258, *258*
tradesmen and 121, 137, 145n11
Burke, Edmund 302
Burlington House, London 281
Burlington, Juliana Dowager
Countess of (née Noel) 281
Butter Bench, Oxford 69, *69*
Byron, Samuel *120*, *139*, *143*

Calderón, Loreto 154
Cambridge, University of
King's College Chapel 300, 307,
308, 309, 310, *311*
Camden, William 290, 293, 308, 309
Campbell, Colen, *Vitruvius
Britannicus* 6, 16, *159*, 183,
212, 224, 237n27–9, 306
Campbell, James 2, 8, 207, 235n2
Canaletto, *Dresden from the Right
Bank of the Elbe, below the
Augustus Bridge 174*
capital, relational 137–44, 147n71
Capitoline palaces, Rome 251, 252,
253
Carfax, Oxford 69, *69*
Carlisle, Lord 148n72, 279
Carpenter's Plain and Exact Rule, The
132
Carton House, Co. Kildare 137, 138
Casey, Christine xxiii–xxv, 11–12,
147n67, 201n18
on the architect as orchestrator 11
on building professionals 2
on Chambers 3
craftsman as 'silent partner' 3
*Enriching Architecture: Craft and
its conservation in Anglo-Irish
building production,
1660–1760* 2, 12
on the measuring guides 132–3
*Making Magnificence: Architects,
stuccatori and the eighteenth-
century interior* 10, 12

on marginalized workmanship 4
on plasterwork 10
Casino, Marino, Dublin 241, *242*
Castle Coole, Co. Fermanagh 254,
257
Castle family 153, 154, 155
Castle Howard, Yorkshire 278–9,
280–1, 281
Castle, Richard
Carton House 137, 138
cost control: competitive tenders
124–7
family background 154–5
Headfort House 134, *135*, *136*
and his management 173–5
measurement and inspection
132–7
Newry Canal 166–7, *167*, 173
Parliament House 133, 144
Powerscourt 126, 129, 133, 167
recent investigations 154–6
relational capital 137–44
risk management: measured
contract 127–32
Saxony link 153
skillset 165
surveying, supervision and set up
on site 120–4
Trinity College Dublin 119–44
'An illustrated essay on artificial
navigation' 166–7, *167*
Castletown House, Co. Kildare
entrance hall 254, *254*
garden front stonework 213–14,
215
limestone 188
windows 236n13
window sill 213–14, *215*
Cavendish, William, 1st Duke of
Devonshire 264
chair rails 231, *232*, 254
Chambers, Sir William 3, 146n27,
241, *242*, 246, 248
Chandos, James Brydges, 1st Duke
of 294
'character' of interiors 256
Charles I, King 36
Charles II, King 42, 264, 304

Château d'Asnières, France 98, *98–9, 101*
Château de la Tuilerie, Auteuil 92–3, *93*
Château de Rueil, France 315n30
Chatsworth House, Derbyshire 294
  ceilings *265–6*
  The Chapel 264, 269, *268*, 279
  Gibbons and 304–5, 316n86
  Great Chamber *265*
  Great Hall 264
  Great Stairs 264–5, *265–6*, 267, 269
  limewood carving *265*, 304
  murals 264, *268*
  statues *266*
Chéron, Louis 282
Chettle, George 37, 60n42
Chevening, Kent 183
Childrey, Joshua 293
Chippenham Park, Cambridgeshire 299
Christ Church Meadow 71, 72
Christ Church, Oxford 71, 72, *73*
church interiors 292, *292*, 295
Cibber, Caius Gabriel 264, *265*, 272
Cirencester Park, Gloucestershire 78
Clandon Park, Surrey 7
Clarendon Building, Oxford *75*
Clark, Catherine 141
Clarke, Charles 146n27
Clarke, George 72, 73, *74*
Classical architecture 2–3, 5, 7–8, 28, 210–12, *211*, 224
classical literature 277–82, 299
classical profiles, 'alphabet of architecture' 241–60
Cleere, William 300
Clerk of Works 133, 163, 164–5, 168, 188, 199, 234
Clerk, Sir John, of Penicuik 224, *224*, 236n24
Clipsham Stone 72
'code' (definition) 87
codes 87–102
'codification' (definition) 87
'codified' (definition) 87
Codrington, Christopher 74

Coke, Sir Edward 56
Colbert, Jean-Baptiste 103
Cole, John, Lord Mount Florence 217, 236n20
collective multiphase work 102–12
Collège des Quatre-Nations, Paris 255, *256*
Collegiate Church of St Mary, Warwick
  Beauchamp Chapel 296, *297*, 308
colours, in ornament drawing 88, 91, 92, *92*, 114n23, 167, *167*
Colvin, Howard 2, 8, 9, 208, 235n6
Combe Abbey, Coventry 300
commonplace book (J. Adam) 232–3, 237n30
competitive tenders 124–7, 146n29
composers 234–5, 238n36
Compton Beauchamp House, Oxfordshire 78, *78*
Conducteure (Oberbauamt supervisors) 163–8, 173, 174, 177n63, 177n65
Connell family 144
Connell, John 124, 126, 131, 142–4, 146n35, 149n100–1
Connell, John (snr) 144
Connell, Richard 144
Connolly, William, 'Speaker' 213
Connors, Joseph 251
conservation insights (Damer House) 183–200
'contract drawings' 103, 104
'convention' (definition) 87
Convento della Carità, Venice 32, 41
  oval stair 27, 30–1, *32–3*, 35
Convocation House, Oxford 78
Cooley, Thomas
  Borromini and 242
  Public Library, Armagh 250, *250*
  Royal Exchange, Dublin 243–5, *245*, 254, 255, *255, 257*
Cornforth, John 8
cornices xxiv, 77, 88, 93, 110, 130–1, 139, 186, 212, 218–19, 241, *244–5*, 245, *247*, 252–4, 256–7, 259
Corpus Christi College, Oxford 71, *72*

cost control: competitive tenders 124–7, 146n29
Country Life 5, 8
Court House, Roscommon 146n41
Cousin, Peter 269, *271*
Cousin, Rene 269
Coventry 291, 297, *298*
craft and paint in the baroque interior 263–72
crafted object as allegory 272–7
craftsmen, architects and: a theme with variations 207–35
Craig, Maurice 10, 185, 188–9
Cronstedt, Carl Johan 113n1
cross, late medieval (Coventry) 297, *298*
Cure the Younger, William 43
curiosity 300–5
'curious' (definition) 300
Curran, Con 9–10
Custom House, Dublin 245, *247*, 258–9

D'Alton, Máirtín 183–200
Damer, Anne Seymour (née Conway) 185, 201n22
Damer family 185
Damer House, Co. Tipperary
    conservation insights into the building of 183–200
    doorcase 193, *194*, 195, *195*, *196*
    economy-led decisions xxiv
    entrance floor plan 192, *193*
    fabric and conservation 186–92
    family background and occupancy 185–6, 201n11
    first-floor windows 191, *191*, *192*
    front hall 192
    front steps 189–90
    front view *184*
    keystones 191–2, 197, *198–9*
    North façade 186–92, *186*, 198, *200*
    pine staircase 192, *194*
    repaired windows 197, *197–8*
    repairing the stonework 195–200
    timber lintels *189*, 191–2, *192*, 201n5

tripartite walls 191, 201n20
was the house finished? 192–5
window jambs 187, *188*, 189
window lintels 187, *187*, 189
windows 186–92
window sill 189, *190*
Damer, John 185, 202n22
Damer, Joseph (1630–1720) 185
Damer, Joseph (1676–1737) 185, 193, 199
Damer, Lionel 185
D'Arcy, Fergus A. 149n98
Darley family 242
Darley, George 132, 144
Darley, Henry 137, 141
Darley, Hugh 144
Darley, Moses 125, *127*, 137–8, 141, 147n62
Darlington 291, 314n9
Daviler, Augustin-Charles 91, 246–7, 248, 253, 258, 259, 260
Davis, William 264, *265*
Dawson, John 231–2, 233
Dechant, Konrad 154
De Critz, Emmanuel *278*
Defoe, Daniel 308
De Keyser family 44
De Keyser, Hendrick 42
Delaune, Thomas 308
Derham, Rev. William 295–6
design and making, between
    content 13–17
    context 1–13
de Voyer d'Argenson, Madame 98, *98*, 109
Dickinson, William 90
Dictionary of National Biography 208
Dientzenhofer, Johann 221–2
Ditchley Park, Oxfordshire 301
Divinity School, Oxford 65
d'Ivry, Contant 91
Djabarouti, Johnathan 4, 12
Doneraile House, Dublin 134
drawing practice, as a support for collective multiphase work 102–12

drawings
approval signatures 103, 104
Christopher Wren collection 114n5
Claude III Audran collection 113n1
Le Brun collection 113n1
Pineau collection 85–113
Dresden Academy of Arts 173
Dresden, Saxony 153, 154, 155, *155*, 156, 165, *174*
archives 164, 165
Drewstown, Co. Meath 236n20
Dryden, John 282
Dublin Volunteers *140*
Ducart, Davis 236n19
Dugdale, William 296, 297, *298*, 308
Dumfries House, Ayrshire 237n33
Dundas, Judith 277
Dundas, Robert, Lord Advocate of Scotland 224, *225*
Dupuy, Marion 86
Dyer, Walter 5

Edinburgh Castle 237n33
Edinburgh New Town Conservation Committee 235n9
Edwards, Turner 98, 111, 115n53
Egypt 293
Eick, Jacqueline 176n9
ekphrasis, visual 276, 277, 284
Electoral Saxon *Oberbauamt* 153–4, 156–7, 174–5
bureaucracy and administration 157–63
Conducteure 163–8, 173, 174, 177n63, 177n65
index of people working at 160, *160*
Landbaumeister 168–9
Oberlandbaumeister 169
ellipses, visual 94–5, 101
Ely Place, Holborn 61n66
England 92
English Civil War (1642–51) 44, 47, 61n52
Enriching Architecture: Craft and its conservation in Anglo-Irish building production 1660–1760 (ed. Casey and Hayes) 2, 12

Ensor family 133
Ensor, George 146n41
Ensor, Job 133, 147n61
Ensor, John 133–4, *136*, 141, 147n62, 147n69, 173
entablatures xxiii, xxiv, 113, 139, 243, 247, 258–9, *259*, 293
Esterly, David 306
Este, Susannah 133–4
Evelyn, John 299–300
on architects 1
on armour at Windsor 275
on Château de Rueil 315n30
Florence and 314n20
on King's College Chapel 308
on the papal apartments 315n30
Paul V's chapel, Santa Maria Maggiore 306
revises diary entries 314n18
on Salisbury Cathedral 293, 317n109
on Townesend 73
travels 291
Wren and 293
Exeter College, Oxford 71
Exeter, John Cecil, Fifth Earl of 275

fabric and conservation (Damer House) 186–92
Fellows' Building, Corpus Christi College 71, *72*
Fergusson, James 6
Feuquières, marquise de 110, *110*
Fiennes, Celia 269, 297, 299, 300, 310
Fisher, William 210
Flitcroft, Henry 175
Florence 291–2, 314n20
Florence Court, Co. Fermanagh
blunders 221, 236n20
entrance front 217, *217*
entrance hall 218, *219*
façade 218, 236n19
staircase 218, *220*
stair hall 219
Fontana, Carlo 169
Fontana, Domenico 46, 61n55
Forde Abbey, Somerset 297

Fort George, Moray Firth 237n31, 237n33
Forty, Adrian 11
Foster, Norman 207, 235
Fouquet, Nicolas 256
fragmented appraisals 294–300
France 88, 92, 114n22, 157–8, 163, 256
Frederick the Great 161, 177n38–9
Fredrik August II / August III, King 156, *158*
Freeman, Cristina Garduño 289
Friars Minor, Dundalk 296
Friedman, Alice 10
Fuhring, Peter 85
Fulda Cathedral, Hesse, Germany 221–2, *222*

Gady, Bénédicte 85–113
Gandon, James 245, *247*, 258–9
Gapper, Claire 9–10
George I, King 156, 224, 272, 282
George II, King 224
Georgian interiors, American 5
Georgian Society Records 5
Geraghty, Anthony 87, 114n6, 278, 281
Gibbons, Grinling
  assistants 304
  carvings 300, 302
  Chatsworth House 304–5
  Esterly and 306
  Petworth House 304
Gibbs, James 4, 16–17, 68, 76–7, 212, 216–20, 236n20, 237n29, 248, 252
Gibney, Arthur 10, 119–20, 129, 132, 145n3
Gilbert, Thomas 137–8, 142, 148n77
Gilles, François 100, 101, *101*, 114n13, 114n29, 115n63
Girouard, Mark 11, 46, 58
Glasgow, University of 207
Godfrey, Walter 4
Goldsmiths' Hall, City of London 57
Gomme, Andor 9
Goodman, Nelson 114n7

Goodricke, Matthew 275
Gotch, J. Alfred 6, *46*
Gothic architecture 65, 74, 300, 302, 306–12
Gothic revival 4, 5–6, 7
Goudge, Edward 300
Gough, Tim 310
Goulard, Father 107–8
Graham, James Gillespie 238n35
graphic signs 86, 87–102
Great Fire of London (1666) 66, 120
Gregory XIII, Pope 306
Grochwitz Palace, Brandenburg 170–1, *172*
Grop, Therese 234
Grumbold, Robert 66
Gunnis, Rupert 9

Hagia Sophia Mosque, Istanbul 312
Halfpenny, William 147n62
Halifax, William 293, 302, 316n78
Halley, Edmund 293
Halton, Timothy 71
Ham House, Richmond 10, 275
Hamilton Palace, Scotland 237n33
Hamilton, Sir George 185
Hamlett, Lydia 263–84
Hamm, Johann Adam 163
Hampton Court Palace, Richmond upon Thames 277
  King's Staircase 269, *270*
  murals *269–70*
  Queen's Drawing Room 269, *271*
Hanbury Hall, Worcestershire 273
Hanoverian Britain 156
Hanson, Brian 2
Harris, Dr Eileen 212
Harris, John 5, 301
Harris, Walter 301
Hatton, Sir Christopher 45–7, 52, 54
Hatton, Christopher, 2nd Baron and 1st Viscount 47, 51
Hatton, Edward 293, 309
Hatton, Lady Elizabeth 55, 61n66
Hatton family 45, 55
Hatton House, London 55–7

INDEX   **329**

Hawksmoor, Nicholas
    'apprenticeship' 168
    Blenheim Palace 78
    Lord Carlisle and 148n72
    Office of Works 121
    tradesmen and 124, 137, 281
    University of Oxford designs
        73–5, 77
    on W. Adam 67
Hawney, William 132
Hayes, Melanie 119–44, 156, 165
    *Enriching Architecture: Craft and
        its conservation in Anglo-Irish
        building production,
        1660–1760* 2, 12
Hayward, William 80
Headfort House, Co. Meath 134,
    135, *136*
Headfort Papers 134, 147n67
Headington Stone 67, 68, 72, 73,
    77
Hearne, Thomas 66, 67, 290
Henrietta Maria, Queen 27, 36, 37,
    42, 43
Henry VII, King 306, 307, 308
Herbert family 276, 277
Herbert, Philip, Fourth Earl of
    Pembroke 279
Herculaneum, Italy 301
Hermitage Museum, St Petersburg
    86, 102
Heveningham Hall, Suffolk 254
Hidden Horizontal, The (2021
    exhibition) 241
Higgott, Gordon 27–57, 312
Hill, Oliver 8
Holbein Gate, Whitehall 305
Holdsworth, Edward 76
Holkham Hall, Norfolk 306, *307*
Hollar, Wenceslaus 33, 310
Holy Roman Empire 160–1, 174
Holyrood Palace, Edinburgh 42–3
Home House, London 254
Homer 275
Hope, Charles, 1st Earl of Hopetoun
    225, 237n28–9
Hope family 238n35
Hope, Lady Margaret 225

Hopetoun House, West Lothian
    225–33
    ceilings *231*
    entrance front 225, *226*, 227,
        228
    façade 237n29
    front steps 227, *229*, 230, 237n29
    interior decor *232*
    keystones 231–2
    State Apartments 230, 237n33
    State Drawing Room 230–1,
        230–2, 232
    tradesmen 233, 237n33
    two versions 237n27
Hopetoun Papers 232, 237n29
Hopkins, Gerard Manley, 'Duns
    Scotus's Oxford' 65
Hopson, Charles 300
Horace 277
hôtel Bonneau, France *95*, *106*
hôtel Boutin, Paris 108–10, *109*
hôtel de Feuquières, Paris *103*
hôtel de Mazarin, Paris 102
hôtel d'Orrouer, Paris 115n53
Houghton Hall, Norfolk 7
Huddleston quarry, Yorkshire 308
Hultzsch, Anne 291, 310–11
Hume, Sir Gustavus 156
Hussey, Christopher 5, 8–9

inspection, measurement and
    132–7
instructions, written 96–8, 100–2,
    110–11, 168
Ireland 9–13, 174
Irish Georgian Society 183
ironwork
    Chatsworth House 264
    hôtel Bonneau 104, *106*
    Kirby Hall 46
    Queen's House, Greenwich 28,
        38–41, 39–42, 60n42
    Tijou and 276, 297, 301
Italy 91, 291
Izzo, Johann Baptist 252–3

James, John *35*, 60n34
Jesuit church, Antwerp 292

Jesus College, Oxford 70, *70*
Joachim, Joseph 234
John Hope, 2nd Earl of Hopetoun *226*
Jones, Inigo xxiii–xxiv, 27–57
  annotated copy of Palladio's *I Quattro Libri dell'Architettura* 28, *29*, 30–1, *31*, *33*, 58n5, 58n8, 58–9n13–16
  annotated copy of Scamozzi's *L'Idea della Architettura Universale* 32, 36, 59n22, 59n26
  Chevening, Kent 183
  Italian open-well suspended stone stairs 28–33
  long lodging plan, Queen's House 33, *34*
  Queen's Chapel, St James's Palace 57
  South Stair, Queen's House 37–9
  Stone and 42–4
  Tulip Stair, Queen's House 27, 37, *40–1*
  'varying with reason' theory 312
Jones Neville, Arthur 124
Jones, Owen 3
Jourdain, Margaret 10
Joynes, Henry 168

Kames, Lord 310, 311–12
Kane, John 123, 142, 147n63
Karcher, Johann Friedrich 162
Kelly, John 137
Kennet and Avon Canal 68
Kensington Palace, London 168
Kent, William 78
key-letter code *99*, 100–2
Kilburn-Toppin, Jasmine 12
Kimball, Fiske 85
King's College Chapel, Cambridge 300, 307–8, 309, 310, *311*
Kinsman, Edmond 61n55
Kirby Hall, Northamptonshire 44–55
  armorial shield 52
  basement vault 50, *50*
  brickwork 51, *52*

bust of Apollo 46, 47, 52
central tower 47, *48*
consignment of goods for 45, 55
'Green Court' 45
iron window frames 46, 52–3
Library 55
north range interior brickwork *52*
north range of courtyard 46–7, *47–8*, *53*
part-plan (Gotch) *46*
pediments 46–7
south-east staircase 28, 46, 49, *49*, 52–4, *53–4*
  tower 47–8, *48*, *50*, *53*, 54, 55, *55–6*
  tower ceiling *51*
windows 47, 52, *53*
Klein, Lawrence 12
Knight of Glin, The 10
Knöffel, Johann Christoph 155, 169–71, *171*
Knowles, Thomas 80
Krakow altarpiece 96

Labraunda, Turkey 247
Laguerre, Louis
  The Chapel, Chatsworth 267, *268*
  Grand Staircase, Petworth House 270, 272, *272*, *274*
  Marlborough House 275
  The Saloon, Blenheim Palace 282, *282*
  self-portrait 282
La Mottraye, Aubrey de 314n19
Landbaumeister (*Oberbauamt* rural building supervisor) 168–9
Landbauschreiber (*Oberbauamt* scribe) 171–2
Langley, Batty and Thomas 212, 301
Lanscroon, Gerard 277
Latham, Charles 5
Laurenti, Aurora 91, 114n25
Le Brun, Charles 113n1
Le Camus de Mézières, Nicolas 256, 257–8
Le Clerc, Sebastien 243, *244*, 245

INDEX   **331**

Leith House, Aberdeenshire 232, 237n33
Leland, John 290, 294, 295, 308, 314n9
Leplat, Raymond 162–3
Le Vau, Louis 255, *256*
Leybourne, William 212
Lichfield Cathedral 303
livre-journal (logbook) 102
Lloyd, Sir Nathaniel 80
Lobb, Joel 264, *265*
Locke, John 311
Locke, Samuel 170–1, *172*
Loeber, Rolf 9
Loggan, David 70, 310, *311*
Longuelune, Zacharias 155, 169, 170
Louvre, Musée du, Paris 113n1, 293
Lovely, William 141, 147n88
Lucey, Conor 2, 10, 12
Luckomb, Philip 301–2
Lugny tabernacle 59n16, 88, *89*, 98, 105, *107*
Lüttmann, Nele 153–75

McBride, Kari Boyd 11
McCleery, Joseph 125, 126, *126*
McDonnell, Joseph 10
McGill, Alexander 224
McKay, John 308
McKellar, Elizabeth 11
McParland, Edward 10, 137, 138, 145n11, 145n27, 236n19, 241–60
Magdalen College, Oxford 65, 76
Maidenhead Bridge 80
making, between design and content 13–17
context 1–13
Mangone, Carolina 251
Mansart de Sagonne, Jacques Hardouin- 98, *99*, 108, *109*, 113, 115n55
map, European (*c.* 1740) *157*
Marandet, Francois 282
marble
Blenheim Palace 302
cannons 294
coloured 91, 243, 291, 312

Holkham Hall 306, 307, *307*
Lugny tabernacle 88, 98
marblers 296
Pineau and 107
Stone and 44, 47, 61n49
white and black 293
Mariette, Jean 114n24
Marlborough family 78
Marlborough House, London 275
Marlborough, Sarah, Duchess of 275
Marot, Jean 88
Martínez de Guereñu, Laura 1
Martyn, Thomas 305
master builder families 2
material, curiosity and performance: reception of workmanship in early modern Britain and Ireland 289–313
curiosity 300–5
fragmented appraisals 294–300
medieval workmanship in the eighteenth century 306–13
on performance 305–6
sumptuous materials 290–4
Mavisbank, Midlothian, Scotland 224, *224*, 236n24
measured contract 127–32, 146n41
measurement and inspection 132–7, 146n54
'mechanick' to '*architectus*'?, from 72–80
Medd, Scott *279*, 286n38
Merton College, Oxford Fellows' Quadrangle 66
Michelangelo Buonarroti 241, 246, *253*, 260
Middelbourg, comte de 111–12, *111*
Mill Street Dublin, No. 10 *196*
Milton Abbey, Dorset 193
mimetic representation 88, 114n7
modillions 243, *244–5*, 245
Monastery, Lugny 59n16, 88, *89*, 98, 105–8, *107*
monographs, architect 6
Montagu, Elizabeth 209, 235n5
Montagu, Ralph 282
Moore, James 8

332 INDEX

Morris, James 125
Morris, Robert 4, 121, 129–30, 232, 237n32
Morris, William 4, 6
mosaic, Florentine 291
Motteux, Peter 275
moulding and profiles 241–58
Mount Ievers Court, Co. Clare 183, *184*, 186, 188, 192, 199, 201n16
Moxon, Joseph 300–1
Mozart, Joseph 234, 235
multiphase work, Drawing as a support for collective 102–12
mural painting (1630–1730) 263–85
    craft and paint in the baroque interior 263–72
    craft collaborations 282–4
    crafted object as allegory 273–7
    techne's downsides 277–81
Murdoch, Tessa 282
Musée des Arts Décoratifs, Paris 85, 86
musicians 234–5, 238n36
mutules 218, 245, 247, 259
Myers, Christopher 144
Myers, Graham 144
Mylne, John 224

Nash, John 6
Nationalmuseum, Stockholm 113n1
Neoclassicism 302
neo-Palladianism 76, 221, 224, 232
New College, Oxford 70
Newliston House, Edinburgh 236n24
Newman, John 58n8
New Oxford Guide 301
Newport, Sir William (*later* Hatton) 56
Newry Canal, Ireland 166–7, *167*
Nisbet, James 146n56, 146n60
No. 10 Mill Street Dublin 193, 195
Norfolk Duke of 299
Northampton 291
North, Roger 290, 309
Nottingham Castle 291

Oberbauamt, Electoral Saxon 156–7, 174–5
    bureaucracy and administration 157–63
    Conducteure 163–8, 173, 174, 177n63, 177n65
    index of people working at 160, *160*
    Landbaumeister 168–9
    Oberlandbaumeister 169
    training at 154
object, crafted (as allegory) 272–7
O'Cianán, Tadhg 295
Office of Public Works (OPW) 183, 186, 189, 192, 197
    Damer House team 199, 202n26
Office of Works 161–2
    employees 36, 124, 164, 168, 175
    role of architects 121
    structure of 158
    Surveyor-General 159
    tenders 125
O'Flaherty, Christopher 4, 12
Old Roscrea Society 183
Old Royal Naval College, Greenwich West Wall, Painted Hall 282, *283*
Oliver, John 177n53
O'Mahony, Flora 183–200
open-well suspended stone staircases 27–57
Orchard, William 65
Oriel College, Oxford 68, 76
orthogonal articulation 88
Ovid 273, 275, 282
Oxford xxiv, 65–80
Oxford, University of *see* individual colleges

Palazzo dei Conservatori, Rome 241, 252, *253*
Palladianism 8, 153, 293, 294, 312, 313
Palladian movement 7
Palladio, Andrea 29–33, 58n5, 88, 248
    section and plan of oval stair 27, 28, *29*, 38, 40
Pallasmaa, Juhani 4

Palmyra, ruins of 293, 302, *303*
Pantheon, Rome 30, *31*, 247, *248*
Paris 85, 91
Parliament House, Dublin 133, 144, 258, *259*
Paterson, John 231, 233
Pauline chapel in Santa Maria Maggiore 292, *292*
Payne, Alina 2, 3, 4
Pearce, Sir Edward Lovett xxiv, 258, *259*, *278*, 297
Peill, James 10
Peisley, Bartholomew 66
Peisley the younger, Bartholomew 68–9
Pellegrini, Giovanni Antonio 279, *279–80*, 280, 281
Pembroke College, Oxford 70, 76
Pembroke House, Whitehall 39
'pencheck' riser rebate 40–1, 60n39
Pencz, Georg 96–7
Pennant, Thomas 302–3
performance (workmanship) 305–6
Peterson, Laurel 264
Peter the Great 85
Petworth House, West Sussex
    ceilings *271*
    contracts 129, 132
    Grand Staircase 270–2, *271*, 273, *274*
    mural scheme 273, *274*
    Walpole and 304
Pevsner, Nicholas 10, 309
Pineau collection 86–7, 90
Pineau, Nicolas xxiv
    codes, conventions, circulations: drawings as an instrument of collaboration in the work of 85–113
    drawing room in the hôtel of the marquise de Feuquières, 110
    Invitation card used to sketch a wrought iron banister for the hôtel Bonneau 106
    Panelling with a mirror 92
    Plan for the bedroom of Madame de Voyer d'Argenson at Château d'Asnières 98, 98

Project for a 'cabinet en bibliothèque 93, 94, 104
Project for a 'cabinet en bibliothèque', with flap 104, 105
Project for a cartouche 90, 90
Project for a pier glass for Monsieur Fournier 97, 97
Project for a porte-cochère 95, 96
Project for a wrought iron banister for the hôtel Bonneau, 104, 106
Project for the cartouche of the porte-cochère of the hôtel de Feuquières 102, 103
Project for the door of the tabernacle at the Monastery in Lugny 89
Project for the panelling of a niche at a 'cabinet d'assemblée' at château de la Tuilerie in Auteuil 92–3, 93
Project for two keystones for the hôtel Bonneau 94, 95
right-handed 115n45
Study for the arrangement of cartouches above windows on the ground and first floors of the façade of the Château d'Asnière 98–100, 99
Study for the steps leading up to the tabernacle at the Monastery in Lugny 107, 107
Study for three mirrors over fireplaces for the house of the comte de Middelbourg in Suresnes 111
workshop 91, *92*
Pisa Cathedral 291
Pliny the Elder 293
Plot, Robert 67–8
Plummer, Gilbert 123
Plummer, John 125
Pococke, Richard 316n78
poesis concept 263, 277–8, 284
Poland 156, 159
Pons, Bruno 85
Pope, Alexander 221

Pöppelmann, Mätthaus Daniel
  career 169
  Holländisches Palais 155
  Oberlandbaumeister 154, 162, 166, 168, 171–2
  Dresden Zwinger 169, *170*
  Site plan for the construction of a new residential palace in the area of the Zwinger and the Marstall 166
porphyry 293
Portland stone
  Christ Church, Oxford 72
  Kirby Hall 46, 52
  Queen's House, Greenwich 27, 36
  Trinity College Dublin 138, 139, 141, 142
post-medieval classicism 241
Powerscourt, Co. Wicklow 10, 126, 129, 133, 138, 167
Powis Castle, Powys 277
Powys, Caroline Lybbe 290, 304
Pricke, Robert 210
Prignot, Alexandre-Eugene 91, 114n25
Procopius 312
profiles, classical 241–60
Protestant churches, Dublin 148n92
Provost's House, Dublin 257
Prussia 161, 174
Public Library, Armagh 250, *250*
Pugin, Augustus W. N. 4–5, 6
Pye, David 290, 305

Quarenghi, Giacomo 247, *249*
quarries 67, 293, 308
Queen's Chapel, St James's Palace 57
Queen's College, Oxford 70, 71, *71*, 73, *74*
Queen's House, Greenwich Palace
  balustrades *38*, 39–40, 41–2
  Cabinet Room 27
  central hall 33, 35
  chamfered soffits 38, *39*
  Great Hall 37
  ground floor plan 33, *35*
  lighting 32–3
  loggia above entrance hall 37

long lodging 33, *34*
  Portland stone 27, 36
  riser rebate steps 40–1, 60n39
  soffits 31, *39–40*
  South Stair 37–9, *38–9*, 60n32, 60n34
  Tulip Stair 27, 37, 40–1, *40–1*, 53
  two suspended stone staircases 33–44
  works 41–2

Radcliffe, Dr John 75
Radcliffe Library (Radcliffe Camera), Oxford 68, 76–8, *77*, 80
Radcliffe Quadrangle, University College 75, *76*
Rainaldi, Carlo 245, *246*
Ralph, James 308, 310
relational capital 137–44, 149n98
Renaissance architecture 3–4, 91, 224, 290, 300
Ribton, Simon 137, 147n62
Ricard, Francis 270
Ricci, Marco 281
Richardi, Daniel von 155
Richardo family 154–5, 176n16
  See also Castle family
Richardo, Joseph and Rachel 154–5, 176n10, 176n15
Richardson, Albert 6
Riddlestown, Co. Limerick 183
Riou, Stephen 242, 246
Ripley, Thomas 4, 8, 121, 162, 175
risk management: the measured contract 127–32, 146n41
Robinson, Archbishop Richard 250
Rococo style 85–113, 232, 233
Rogers, J. C. 10
Roland le Virloys, Charles François 242
Roscrea, Co. Tipperary *see* Damer House, Co. Tipperary
Rothery family 183
Rousham House, Oxfordshire
  Townesend's Building 78, *79*
Rowan, Alistair 10, 207–35
Rowan, Ann Martha 9

Rowlandson, Thomas 121, *122*
Rowney, Thomas 68
Royal Building Administration, France 157–8
Royal Exchange, Dublin xxiv–xxv
  bases 255, *257*
  cornice with merged modillions 243–4, 245, *245*
  detail 254, *255*
Royal Hospital for Seamen, Greenwich xxiii, 159, 272
Royal Hospital, Kilmainham 301
Royal Naval Asylum schools 60n34
Royal Palace, Dresden 166
Rubens, Peter Paul 263, 306
Rupert, Prince 275
Ruskin, John 4, 6
Russborough House, Co. Wicklow 222, *223*
Russia 92
Rysbrack, John Michael 7, 18n35, 302

Sacheverell, Dr Henry 275
Sackville, Lady Caroline 201n11
Saint, Andrew 1, 2, 6
St Canice's Cathedral, Kilkenny 296
St George's Hall, Windsor 300
St Giles church, Oxford 66, *67*
St Giles House, Oxford 68–9
St James's Palace 57
St John's College, Oxford 66, 76
St John the Evangelist, Westminster 124
St Leger, Hon. Hayes 134
St Mark's, Venice 291, 314n19
St Martin-in-the-Fields, London 306
St Mary-le-Bow, London 293, 295–6
St Mary Redcliffe. Bristol 309
St Mary's Church, Lichfield 294
St Michael's Street, Oxford 69
St Paul's Cathedral
  appraisals of 309–10
  Campbell on 6
  competitive tenders 125
  stonework 305
  Summerson on 7–8
  Ward on 3

Woodroffe and 170
workmanship 300, 308
Wren and 7, 66, 114n5, 207, 282, 308
St Petersburg 85, 86, 247, *249*
St Mark's in Venice 291
St Peter's, Rome 291
Salisbury Cathedral 293, 317n109
Salmon, Thomas 310
sandstone 186–9, 195, 197, 199, 201n15–18
Sangallo the Younger, Antonio da 88
San Giovanni, Laterano, Rome 241, *243*, 255, 260
Santa Maria, Campitelli, Rome 245, *246*
Santa Maria di Galloro, Ariccia 251, *252*
Santa Maria Maggiore, Rome 292, *292*, 306
Saumarez Smith, Charles 10
Saunt, Jenny 10
Saxony
  artisans and architecture in eighteenth-century 153–75
  eighteenth-century 156–7
Scale, Bernard *123*
Scamozzi, Vincent 32, 36, 40, 54, 59n18, 210, *213*
Scattergood, John 294
Schade, Johann Daniel 163, 173
Schloss Favorite Rastatt, Germany 274
Schubert, Franz 234, 235
Schütze, Christian Heinrich 164
Schuym, Joachim 210, *213*
Scott, Geoffrey 6
Scott, George Gilbert 207
Scott, Katie 85, 102, 110, 115n45
Scott, Walter 312
Scrooby, Nottinghamshire 290
self-portraits (murals) 282
Semper, Gottfried 12
Semple, George 134
Semple, John 132
Serlio, Sebastiano 247, 248, 259
Shakespeare, William 209
Shannongrove, Co. Limerick 183

Sharples, Joseph 207
Sharp, Thomas 5–6
Sheehan, David 130, 137, 138, 139, 141–2
Sheldonian Theatre, Oxford *249, 250*
Shoe, Lucy 241
Shronell, Co. Tipperary 193, 201n11
Shute, John 209–10, *211*, 235n8, 294–5
Siena Cathedral 291
'Signor Plura' 280, *280*
Silvestre the Younger, Louis de *158*
Simmons, John 270–2
Simon, James and Isaac 141, 142
Sisson, John 122
Smith, James 224
Smith of Warwick, Francis 9
Smith, Patten 185
Smyth, Edward 10
Soane, John 242, 246, 260
Soane Museum, London 48
Somerset, Elizabeth Seymour, Duchess of 272, 273
Somerset House, London 42, 146n27
Southall House, Scotland 237n33
Spiers, Walter Lewis 61n49, 61n52, 61n64
Stadler, Anton 234
Stafford, Sir Humphrey 45, 50
staircases, open-well suspended stone 27–57
Stanley, Charles 231
Stansted airport, Essex 207
Stead, Naomi 289
Steeven's Hospital, Dublin 145n3, 145n11
Stephenson, Judy 127, 137
Steudner, Johann Philipp, *View of Dresden 155*
Stevenson, Christine 11
Stewart, George 132
Stone family 60n48
Stone, Henry 60n48
Stone, Nicholas 28–57
account books 45, 55, 57, 60n42, 61n49

Banqueting House, Whitehall 43
'boutell' profile 57, 61n65
burial 61n50
Goldsmiths' Hall 57
Hatton House 55–7
Holyrood Palace 42–3
Jones and xxiv, 42–4
Kirby Hall 44–55
lawsuits 61n51
Royal Hospital for Seamen xxiii
Windsor Castle 43
Stone the Younger, Nicholas 47, 61n52, 61n55
stonework
appraisals of 305, 308–9
Casino, Marino, Dublin *242*
Castletown House 213–14, *215*
Damer House 189–90
Italian staircases 39
open-well suspended staircase 27–57
repairing 195–200
staircases 28–33
Trinity College Dublin 137–8
Stourhead, Wiltshire 293–4
Stowe House, Buckinghamshire 300
Stow, John 300, 305
Streeter, Robert 60n34
Strong, Edward and Edward 305, 308
Stuart interiors, American 5
Stuart, James 235n5
Stubbs, John William *140*
Sudbury, Suffolk 301
Summerson, John 6–8, 61n58, 259
sumptuous materials 290–4
Suresnes, Paris 111–12, *111*
Surintendance des Bâtiments du Roi 103
surveying, supervision and set up on site 120–4
Surveyor-General of Works 9, 159, 161, 162
suspended stone staircases, open-well 27–57
Italian 28–33
Suthes, William 43
Sweden 92
Sweet, Rosemary 296–7

INDEX 337

Synge, Nicholas, Bishop of Killaloe
185
Syon House, London 254

Tabary brothers 10
Talman, William 264
Tannevot, Michel 91
Taylor, Sir Robert 80
Taylour, Sir Thomas 134, 147n67
techne's downsides 278–82
Temple of Fortuna Virilis, Rome
246–7
Temple, Sir Richard 300
terms, architectural 210, 235n9
Terry, Quinlan 243
Thompson, James 124
Thornhill, James
Hanbury Hall 275
Painted Hall, Greenwich 272,
282, *283*
self-portrait 282
Wimpole Hall 276
Thornton, Peter 10
Thornton, William 282
Thorpe drawings, Soane Museum
48, 61n58
Tierney, Andre 289–313
Tijou, Jean 264, 269, 276, 297, 301
Tipping, Henry Avray 5
Townesend family 65–80, 78
Townesend's Building, Rousham
House 78, *79*
Townesend, John
career 66
monument 67, 72
Oxford designs 69, 70–1, 71, 77
Townesend, John (d. 1784) 78
Townesend, John II 67, 76–7, 80
Townesend, Stephen 80
Townesend, William 66, 67, 68–72,
72–80, *74*
travel writers 291
Tribuna of the Uffizi, Florence 292
Trinity College Dublin
Anatomy House 123
architects and artificers: building
management at 119–44
Ball Court 122–3, 147n88

Bell Tower 119, 122, 124, 127,
138–9, *140*, 143
College Green *140*
College Park 141
College Park canal 123
College Quarry 144
Dining Hall 119
Kitchen 132
Library 125, 137, *138*, 146n37
maintenance and repairs 121–2
measurement and inspection 132–7
New Hall 122, 130–2, *131*, 141, 143
Old Library 201n17, 251, *251*, *258*
park gardens *123*
Physic Garden shed 132
Portland stone 138, 139, 141,
142, *142*
Printing House 119, 123–7, *125–8*,
137–8, 141, 143, 146n29,
146n35, 146n37
risk management: the measured
contract 127–32
Steeple 124, 131, 139, 141, 144,
146n37
surveying, supervision and set up
on site 120–4
Trinity College, Oxford 76, 80, 304
Tucker, John 141–2
Tuileries Palace, Paris 103
Turner, Laurence A. 3, 7
'Tuscann Order' 210, *211*
Tyack, Geoffrey 65–80
Tyringham Hall, Buckinghamshire
260
Tythrop, Oxfordshire 5

University church of St Mary,
Oxford 77
University College, Oxford 75, 76, *76*

Vanbrugh, Sir John xxiv, 162, 168,
294, 305
Van de Steen, Mrs Elizabeth 61n51
van Eck, Caroline 3
papal apartments, Vatican 315n30
Vauban, Sébastien Le Prestre de 167
Venice 103
Vernon, Thomas 275

Verrio, Antonio
  artist-craftsmen employed by 270
  Burghley House 270, 282
  Grand Staircase, Chatsworth
    House 264, *266*, 267
  Great Chamber, Chatsworth
    House *265*
  Great Hall, Chatsworth House 264
  Heaven Room, Burghley House
    276, 277
  King's Staircase, Hampton Court
    Palace 269, *270*
  Queen's Drawing Room, Hampton
    Court Palace 269, *271*
  St George's Hall, Windsor 300
  self-portrait 282
  Walpole and 304
Vertue, George 60n48
Vierpyl, Simon 10, 241, *242*
Vignola, Jacopo Barozzi da 210,
    246, 248, 259
Vitruvius 234, 247, 294, 312
Volquartz, Henry 143

Wackerbarth, Gen FM August
    Christoph Graf von 159, 169
Wadham College, Oxford 66
Walker, Peter 50
Wall, Cynthia 289
Wall, William 122, 133
Walpole, Horace 294, 295, 301,
    304, 312
Ward, W. Henry 3, 7
Ware, Isaac 4, 175, 233, 254, 301
Ware, Sir James 296
Watson, Samuel 264, *265*, 304
Weaver, Lawrence 209, 210
Wells, Somerset 291
Wentworth Castle, Yorkshire 159, *159*
Westminster Abbey, London 90
  Henry VII's chapel 306, 307, 308,
    309
Wheatley, Francis, *The Dublin
    Volunteers on College Green,
    4th November 1779 140*
White, Adam 27–57
Whitehall Palace, London 159
Wickes, Henry 36–7

William III, King 264, 272, 275, 276
Williamson, Alexander 231
Wills, Isaac 125, 146n35
Wills, Michael 131
Wilton House, Salisbury
  ceilings *278*, 280
  Double Cube Room *278*, 279
  Single Cube room 278
Wimpole Hall, Cambridgeshire 276
Winde, William 300
Windsor Castle, Berkshire 264, 275,
    300
Wittkower, Rudolf 312, 317n128
Wolters, Gunther *192*, 197, *198*
Wood, Margaret 4
Wood, Robert 302, *303*
Woodroffe, Edward 170
Worcester College, Oxford 75
workmanship, reception of 289–313
Wren, Sir Christopher
  apprentices 168
  astronomer xxiv
  Colvin on 9
  'coordinator' 121, 125
  drawings 87, 88, 114n5
  Evelyn and 293
  foreign travels 67
  Hampton Court Palace 273
  Hopson and 300
  inscription to 235n2
  on the measured contract 129
  recognition 235
  role as architect 207
  St Mary-le-Bow 293
  St Paul's Cathedral 3, 66, 114n5,
    207, 282, 308
  Sheldonian Theatre, Oxford *249*,
    250
  Stone and xxiii
  Summerson on 7–8
  tradesmen and 137
  written instructions 96–8, 100–2,
    110–11, 168
Wyatt, James 254, 257

Yeomans, David 11, 121, 131

Zwinger, Dresden 169, *170*

INDEX **339**

www.ingramcontent.com/pod-product-compliance
Lightning Source LLC
Chambersburg PA
CBHW061146060325
22966CB00032B/13